Richard Crowder is an independent writer and historian. He studied at Oxford, and at the Kennedy School of Government in Harvard University. He works as a UK diplomat, but writes in a personal capacity.

* * *

'Richard Crowder offers an account of the main events which immediately followed the Second World War. He begins with the end of the war in 1945 and carries on through the achievements of the NATO treaty four years later. In these four years, the main institutions by which we are still governed in international affairs began to take shape. We now look at these institutions with some anxiety because they are beginning to creak rather badly. Before we begin to put them right we need to understand why they took their present shape and what were the motives of the men who set them up. Richard Crowder tells the story in straightforward language and manages to bring to life statesmen such as Marshall, Acheson and Truman who have begun to fade from our memories. I recommend this book whole-heartedly to anyone involved in handling present problems; as so often we shall not succeed in handling those problems unless we understand how and why they came about.'

Lord Hurd of Westwell

'*Aftermath* is a gripping, thoroughly researched and authoritative exploration of the powers and personalities who shaped the modern post-war world. It is a timely and important book because so many of the institutions and empires that rose from the ashes of a destroyed Europe – the global dominance of the United States; the Marshall Plan and the dream of a united Europe; the United Nations; the post-colonial settlement that partitioned India and created Israel – remain the fault-lines of today's world. Crowder brings the personalities of the era's key architects from Washington, London and Moscow to vivid life, and his exploration is told with tremendous elegance and brio.'

Owen Matthews, author of *Glorious Misadventures*

'*Aftermath* is a wise and timely book. Richard Crowder movingly tells the human story behind the history of the postwar international security system. In a narrative that is at once elegantly paced and grave, *Aftermath* reveals the simultaneous strength and precariousness of the institutions created between 1941 and 1949 to keep the peace. We encounter up close the statesmen and diplomats from the US, Britain and the USSR who crafted global institutions out of the ruins of war – some hoping to be "architects of a better world", some to advance their own national interests at any cost. These complex men of power make perilous journeys to meet on warships and country estates, in embassies and opulent palaces. Together they drink, sing and negotiate tirelessly; alone, they pray and sometimes break from nervous strain. In a brilliant touch, Crowder uses as chapter epigraphs scraps of verse, such as the lines from Alfred Tennyson's "Locksley Hall" that Harry S. Truman kept in his wallet, which imagine the earth "lapt in universal law" when at last "the war drum throbbed no longer". The drama of engagement and confrontation between Moscow and the West that Crowder describes so vividly is unfolding to this day, challenging international institutions in new ways. His book reminds us of the nature of good diplomacy, and how much it matters.'

Rachel Polonsky, author of *Molotov's Magic Lantern*

'This is scholarly history written for the ordinary reader: highly accessible, filled with insight and as exciting as a thriller while based on solid research. Read it with pleasure.'

Christopher Catherwood, author of *Winston's Folly*

AFTERMATH

THE MAKERS OF
THE POSTWAR WORLD

RICHARD CROWDER

I.B.TAURIS
LONDON · NEW YORK

To my father, Norman

'In peace, sons bury their fathers. But in war fathers bury their sons.'

Herodotus

Published in 2015 by
I.B.Tauris & Co. Ltd
London • New York
www.ibtauris.com

ISBN: 978 1 78453 102 7
eISBN: 978 0 85773 843 1

A full CIP record for this book is available from the British Library
A full CIP record is available from the Library of Congress

Library of Congress Catalog Card Number: available

Typeset by JCS Publishing Services Ltd, www.jcs-publishing.co.uk
Printed and bound in Sweden by ScandBook AB

Contents

Illustrations

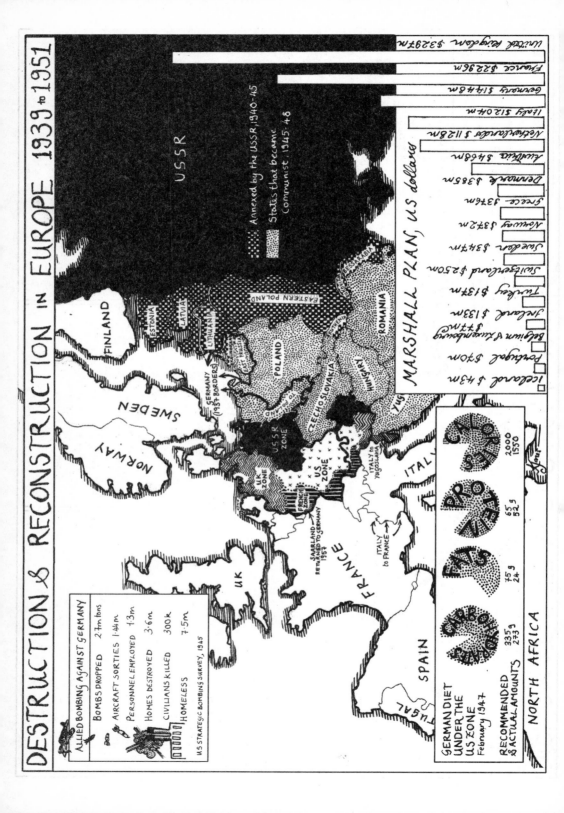

DESTRUCTION & RECONSTRUCTION IN EUROPE 1939 to 1951

MARSHALL PLAN, US dollars

- United Kingdom $3284m
- France $2296m
- Germany $1448m
- Italy $1204m
- Netherlands $1128m
- Austria $468m
- Denmark $385m
- Greece $376m
- Norway $372m
- Sweden $347m
- Switzerland $250m
- Turkey $137m
- Ireland $133m
- Belgium & Luxembourg $777m
- Portugal $70m
- Iceland $43m

Annexed by the USSR, 1940-45

Statis that became Communist, 1945-48

ALLIED BOMBING AGAINST GERMANY

BOMBS DROPPED	2.7m tons
AIRCRAFT SORTIES	1.44m
PERSONNEL EMPLOYED	1.3m
HOMES DESTROYED	3.6m
CIVILIANS KILLED	300k
HOMELESS	7.5m

US STRATEGIC BOMBING SURVEY, 1945

GERMAN DIET UNDER THE US ZONE February 1947

CALORIES — 2000 / 1550
PROTEIN — 65g / 52.9
FATS — 7.5g / 24
CARBOHYDRATES — 335g / 273g

RECOMMENDED & ACTUAL AMOUNTS

FINLAND

USSR

ESTONIA

LATVIA

LITHUANIA

EASTERN POLAND

ROMANIA

NORWAY

SWEDEN

GERMANY (1937 BORDERS)

EAST PRUSSIA

POLAND

CZECHOSLOVAKIA

HUNGARY

YUGOSLAVIA

USSR ZONE

UK ZONE

FRENCH ZONE

US ZONE

SAARLAND RETURNED TO GERMANY 1957

ITALY to YUGOSLAVIA

ITALY to FRANCE

ITALY

UK

FRANCE

SPAIN

PORTUGAL

NORTH AFRICA

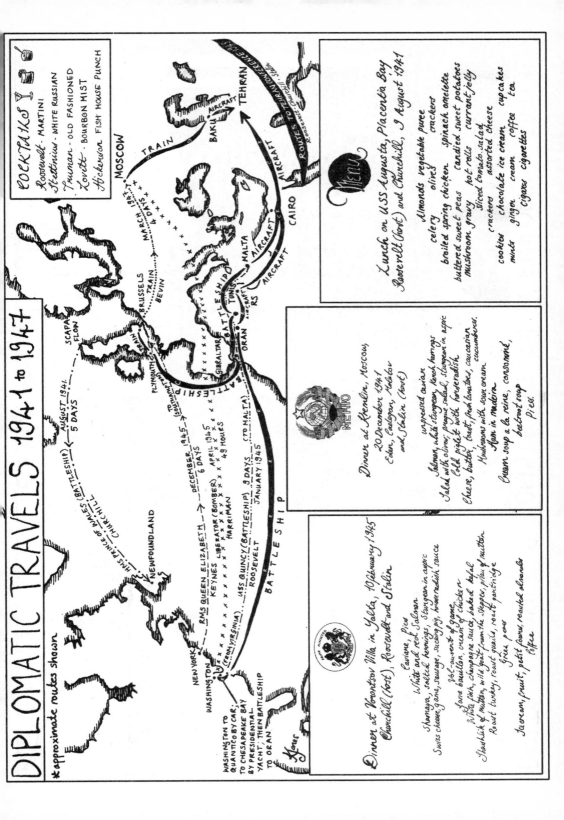

Foreword

We remember wars: in 2015, the anniversary of Waterloo; in 2014, one hundred years since the beginning of World War I. If someone asks what happened next, after the war, the answer is likely to be brief: vague memories of the Congress of Vienna, then bad memories of Woodrow Wilson's fourteen points, Versailles and the League of Nations. And after World War II, what would they say about that? That would be more difficult to pin down, even if it should be fresher in the memory.

What happens after wars is important. The meaning of a war comes not only in the fighting but also from what happens when the fighting stops. An aftermath is a beginning, not an ending.

Wars shake up national societies. They bring ruin to economies and revolutions in technology, society and sometimes politics. They shake up the international order too. Those who put the pieces together find themselves doing so in a period of great confusion. As Dean Acheson says on the first page of *Present at the Creation*:

> The period covered by this book [...] was one of great obscurity to those who lived through it. Not only was the future clouded, a common enough situation, but the present was equally clouded. [...] The significance of events was shrouded in ambiguity. We groped after interpretations of them, sometimes reversed lines of action based on earlier views, and hesitated long before grasping what now seems obvious.

At these moments in history, time speeds up. Changes that would normally take decades of debate are settled quickly – because there is no time to do otherwise. After a war, whether you have won or lost, the framework of normal life has been broken and it must be reconstructed fast, with whatever comes to hand. If politics is the art of the possible, then a postwar crisis is a moment when the realm of the possible is likely to be enlarged. The fixed points are gone, and – for a space – the solid framework of the world becomes fluid, like the chaos before the creation.

The men in charge when the war ends are probably not the same who were in charge when it began. War is a great emergency and only the best will do, not just at the top but throughout the system. Those who were not of the highest ability were discarded early on. These men will have been asking themselves how the catastrophe of war came about, and what could be done to avoid it happening again. In 1945 the men of the postwar era were thinking not just about the beginning of World War II; they had also lived through World War I. They had thought about how that began, and how it ended, and how the Allies had handled the aftermath; and then about the economic and political crises that led to World War II.

For those who are making history it is a journey without maps. One reason to study these events, therefore, is that only by knowing where we came from can we know where we are. The lessons of the past are the only guide there is to building the future.

There is another reason. As we read and re-read this history, we understand that life is a drama of which we do not know the ending. The great merit of *Aftermath* is the sense of drama it conveys – a drama played out simultaneously on different continents and in different fields. And it gives a sense too of the large cast involved. Some, like Keynes, Bevin or Marshall, would have made their mark whatever the times. But this is not a story of a few great statesmen, but of a large team, led by the unexpected president, Harry Truman, perhaps the most ordinary and the most extraordinary figure of all. Those involved, many of them people who, but for the long crisis, might have expected to live modest, hidden lives, were conscious that, for this moment, they too were playing in a world-historical drama.

That is what we have to learn; and it is what *Aftermath* teaches. If we can understand our own lives as part of a bigger story – even if it is lived in more comfortable, slow-moving times – we will leave something better behind us.

The history of the past was all that the men in this book had to go on as they made the history of the present. They invented as they went along, and changed their policies as the facts changed. The evolution of institutions, like that of plants and animals, takes place by trial and error, with this difference: that where men are making decisions they can recognise errors more quickly, and make trials of new methods as they go. But the reference point was their understanding of the recent past. That is what this book is for.

And what happened after 1989, and the end of the Cold War? We enlarged the institutions of the 1940s to bring Central Europe into Western institutions. But the real chaos of this postwar moment was inside the Soviet Union; and neither we nor they knew how to handle it. And at the end they found themselves excluded, or self-excluded from important parts of the international system. We still live today with the institutions whose beginning is described in this book. They have served us well but they belong to a different time. War or no war, it is time to think about their renewal.

Sir Robert Cooper

Preface

My mother remembers the moment that she heard about Hiroshima. A young child, she was staying with her uncle during the summer holidays in 1945. Murland Evans was a country rector, with a parish at Tittleshall, in Norfolk. He and his wife lived in a red-brick parsonage which dated back to Tudor times. My mother occupied an upstairs bedroom, painted in a duck-egg shade of light blue. On the afternoon of 7 August 1945, her aunt entered the room, whispering with her sister in serious tones. Something had happened.

Like families across the world, the Evans household doubtless spent that evening in sombre discussion. 'All the time one keeps on thinking of this bomb and what it may make the future look like,' wrote the Scottish poet Naomi Mitchison in her diary, a few days later.[1] Diplomat Oliver Harvey, who had served as chief of staff to Foreign Secretary Anthony Eden, had similar doubts. 'I don't think', he noted in his diary, 'that posterity will think it was a very creditable action.'[2]

For my mother's uncle, the reflection carried a personal edge. Murland Evans had been educated at Harrow School, in the same generation as Winston Churchill. The two young men became friends, and confided in each other their hopes of the world that lay before them. 'I see into the future,' Churchill wrote to his friend at the age of 16. 'The country will be subjected somehow to a tremendous invasion [...] but I tell you I shall be in command of the defences of London and I shall save London and the Empire from disaster.'[3] That evening, as Murland, his wife and sister-in-law talked over news of the atom bomb, the rector must have wondered about the role which his school friend had played in the path of events which had led to this moment.

Hiroshima, followed by the attack on Nagasaki a few days later, brought the end of World War II. For millions across the world, it was a chance to begin anew. My mother's cousin, John Morris, had served as an army doctor in the Far East. Once his duties were complete, he would be free to return home to his bride Estelle, whom he had married two years before in a wartime ceremony. In the meantime, he was tasked with escorting medical ships repatriating Allied soldiers liberated from horrific conditions in Japanese prisoner-of-war camps. For my father, then an 18-year-old living in Nottingham, in the midlands of England, there was opportunity of another kind. He had recently been offered a place to study at Cambridge. But, while the war continued, he remained liable to be drafted for military service. With hostilities at an end, he could embark on his university studies. Countless other families that summer shared the experience of one chapter closing, and the beginning of another.

This book is about that moment of renewal. It begins with the summer of 1941, when Churchill met with President Franklin Roosevelt at Placentia Bay, in Newfoundland. The declaration which they agreed at that meeting, called the Atlantic Charter, was intended as a beacon to mark the course towards a better world. It ends with the signing of the North Atlantic Treaty in 1949 – a moment which ensured that the transatlantic alliance would endure in peacetime, but which also symbolised the breakdown of the wartime partnership with the Soviet Union into the division of the Cold War.

The journey between these two moments was neither smooth, nor linear. Different steps happened at different times, and not always in harmony with one another. Roosevelt, and the men who supported him, believed that co-operation with Moscow might be possible after the war. They also hoped that the world economy was ready for a rapid restoration of free trade and lifting of currency controls. When, after Roosevelt's death, these assumptions were put to the test, their successors were obliged to find a different path. The Marshall Plan of economic aid to Europe, the creation of West Germany, and the North Atlantic Treaty, were all part of that different approach.

The 1940s was a time of great events. It fell to a remarkable generation to respond to them. This book is a personal story of these people: politicians like Harry Truman, Clement Attlee, Ernest Bevin, Alfred Duff Cooper, Edward Stettinius and Dean Acheson, and the public servants who supported them, men such as George Marshall, Leo Pasvolsky, John Maynard Keynes, Alan Brooke, Alec Cadogan, Charles Bohlen, George Kennan, Gladwyn Jebb and

Pierson Dixon. Posterity has remembered some of these names more clearly than others. I hope that this book can serve as a reminder of what their lives entailed, and the personal challenges which many of them faced.

It was a generation overshadowed by World War I. For Europeans, and to a lesser extent Americans, almost no family had been left untouched by the experience of that conflict. Anthony Eden, who would serve as British foreign secretary during World War II, spent his twentieth birthday in the trenches outside Ypres, at the start of the Battle of Passchendaele. A few days later, he rescued a wounded platoon sergeant from no man's land, and won the Military Cross.[4] His younger brother, Nicholas, had been killed at the naval Battle of Jutland a year before. At a personal level, the politicians, soldiers and diplomats of World War II felt a deep responsibility to avert further global conflict. 'This is the second great chance we have had,' wrote George Kennan, then the deputy US ambassador in Moscow, to his sister in 1943. 'We muffed the first. If we muff this too, can we be sure that we will be given a third?'[5]

In building a postwar order, they faced the challenge of melding two conflicting threads of history. One was national sovereignty. Since the Treaty of Westphalia in 1648, which ended the Thirty Years War, European security had been based on the principle that individual states should be independent and sovereign to decide their own affairs. Through the eighteenth and nineteenth centuries, as powerful nation states grew up in France, Germany, Britain and elsewhere, this principle was translated into a concept of the balance of power. Countries remained sovereign, but, under challenge, would ally with each other to ensure that no one state could become dominant. This approach had restored order after the Napoleonic Wars. But an entangling web of alliances had helped to drag Europe into the tragedy of World War I.

The second strand was internationalism. During the nineteenth century, many Europeans came to believe that sovereignty should be circumscribed by a higher brotherhood between nations. As economies industrialised, cross-border links increased. International bodies were established to regulate such matters as postage, telegraph traffic or even, in the early twentieth century, armaments. In the aftermath of World War I, statesmen attempted to take this further. Woodrow Wilson, president of the United States, proclaimed a manifesto of 'fourteen points', which would provide for a new

way of doing business. At his urging, the victorious powers established a
League of Nations. But this new international organisation proved incapable
of resisting expansion by fascist Germany, Japan and Italy in the 1930s.

The generation of 1945 tried to reconcile these different traditions. The
older among them, like Churchill and Roosevelt, could still remember
the world before World War I. In some ways, they sought to rebuild that
old order. But they did so with new timbers. The international system
that emerged from World War II was based on some old principles, like
sovereignty and territorial integrity, some which Wilson had introduced,
notably self-determination, and some newer ones too, such as human rights
and decolonisation. It led to co-operation between countries in hitherto
unfamiliar areas, such as the management of interest and exchange rates, or
control of nuclear energy. The aftermath of the Great War had been marked
by optimism, followed by bitterness and disillusionment. 'The old men came
out again', wrote the British adventurer and Arabist T. E. Lawrence, 'and
took our victory to re-make in their likeness of the former world they knew.'[6]
The years after 1945 had a different feel: more cautious, more realistic, more
fearful of what might go wrong.

We still live today within the house built with those timbers. For
diplomats like myself, pursuing our craft in the very different circumstances
of the twenty-first century, the same institutions remain at the heart of
international business: the United Nations, NATO, the International
Monetary Fund and the European Union. Others have been added to the
structure over the years, such as the Non-Proliferation Treaty, the World
Trade Organization, the International Criminal Court and the Organization
for Security and Co-operation in Europe. New regional groups have
emerged, in Africa and Asia. In each case, the same balance between
national sovereignty and international co-operation remains fundamental.

For our generation, the 1940s seem a different, and distant, world. The
generation which experienced these events at first hand is passing into
history. As a child, growing up in the 1970s and 1980s on the south coast
of England, in the naval city of Portsmouth, the wartime experience still
seemed close. I remember talking with the caretaker at my school, who had
directed naval gunfire on the beaches of Normandy, or a colleague of my
father, who had dug a tunnel out of a German prisoner-of-war camp, only to
be incarcerated at Colditz, the secure facility created for those most liable to

attempt escape. Such memories are now fading. But, as we pursue the same goal of peace for a new century, the need to learn from the past remains as great as ever. I hope that this book will be a modest contribution towards ensuring we do not forget what those who took part in these great events have to tell us.

In writing this book, I have enjoyed the warm support of many friends, colleagues and experts in the field. Among them, I would like to thank George Williamson, Robert Wilton, Elizabeth Gowing, Bjorn Fagerberg, Bruno Scholl, Giles Radice, Jen McNaughton, Lin Yan, Nicholas Bayne, William Kristol, Peter Hennessy, Margaret MacMillan, and William Hitchcock. Their ideas, advice and encouragement have meant a great deal. Robert Cooper has been a source of inspiration, and shown me that the qualities found among the postwar generation still live on in our own. I am grateful to my employers, in the Foreign and Commonwealth Office, for clearing publication, to the FCO Chief Historian, Patrick Salmon, for sharing his knowledge, and to Kate Jones, a talented young diplomat and artist, for drawing the maps. Staff at the Truman Presidential Library and at the Churchill Archives Centre in Cambridge were generous in their support and advice. Particular thanks are due to the team at I.B.Tauris, led by Iradj Bagherzade and Jo Godfrey, for taking my ideas and steering them through into daylight, and to Steve Williamson for arranging the text. And I am grateful to those who have given permission to use copyrighted material, including Pavel Kohout, Miles Gladwyn, the Master and Fellows of Churchill College, Warner Chappell, and Faber and Faber.

Last of all, I owe a deep debt to my wife, Hilary, our two sons Daniil and Sergei, and my mother Pauleen for their various combinations of enthusiasm, good humour and common sense. The pleasure of life shared with them, and our assorted dogs, is a daily reminder that peace is indeed worth the fight.

INTRODUCTION

Not in Enmity

Stablish our hearts, O God, in the day of battle,
And strengthen our resolve,
That we fight not in enmity against men
But against the powers of darkness enslaving the souls of men.

Prayer used in church service at Placentia Bay,
Sunday 10 August 1941

Saturday 2 August 1941 was the start of a bank holiday weekend. Great Britain had been at war for almost two years. Outside the Senate House in Bloomsbury, former home to the governing body of the University of London, blue-uniformed guards stood watch.

The art deco tower, clad in Portland stone, was the second tallest structure in London, after St Paul's Cathedral. Since the outbreak of war, it had been taken over by the Ministry of Information. This department was a new creation responsible for maintaining the morale of the British public. It had suffered a shaky start, under John Reith, the first director of the BBC, and then Alfred Duff Cooper, a diplomat and Conservative politician. Neither man had managed to turn the makeshift new organisation into an effective operation. A few weeks before, Prime Minister Winston Churchill had sacked Duff Cooper, and installed Brendan Bracken, a 40-year-old rising star in the wartime coalition government, to shake it up. The job was, he warned Bracken, 'worse than manning a bomb-disposal unit'.[1] But Bracken was determined to make it work, and had a few ideas. He had summoned Henry Vollam Morton, a journalist and travel writer, from his home in Hampshire to share one of them.

Morton was ushered past the guards and up to Bracken's office. The minister offered him a seat. He fixed Morton with his gaze, eyes smiling behind round horn-rimmed glasses and below a shock of auburn hair. An Irishman by birth, Bracken was at the height of his influence. In his twenties he ran the *Financial News*, then took a seat in Parliament for Paddington, in London. During the 1930s, he became a follower and associate of Churchill. Rumours started to circulate that he was the veteran politican's unacknowledged son. 'I looked it up,' Churchill was alleged to have told his wife, Clementine, 'but the dates don't co-incide.'[2]

'I have an extraordinary proposition to put up to you,' announced the minister. 'I want you to leave England for three weeks.'

'I regret', he added with a twinkle, 'to say that I can't tell you where you are going or what you will see when you get there.'

Morton sensed a story. Eight years older than Bracken, and better known by his initials 'H.V.', he had started his career as a correspondent for the *Daily Express*. In 1923, he was the first to break the story that Egyptologist Howard Carter had discovered King Tutankhamun's tomb. Later, he became a popular travel writer.

'Yes,' the journalist replied. 'Of course I'll go.'

Pausing before taking his leave, Morton added a question. 'Shall I pack a dinner jacket?' he asked.

'Most certainly,' responded the Irishman. 'Now goodbye, and – good luck.'

As he walked out of the Senate House, Morton wondered what was in store for him. The dinner jacket suggested a diplomatic occasion. But where, and with whom?[3]

Placentia Bay was grey and overcast. Low hills gradually appeared out of the mist, as the coast of Newfoundland loomed into view. Morton stood on the deck of the battleship *Prince of Wales*, taking in the scene. He was clad only in pyjamas and a coat. It was early morning on Saturday 9 August. Riviera, as the meeting between Prime Minister Churchill and President Franklin Delano Roosevelt had been codenamed, was about to begin.

Over the previous five days, the *Prince* had crossed the Atlantic in strict secrecy, carrying Churchill and his entourage. She was one of the newest and largest battleships in the Royal Navy. Commissioned in 1936, and built at the Cammell Laird shipyard in Birkenhead, the vessel carried ten 14-inch guns, four seaplanes, and 1,500 crew, under the command of Captain John Leach. The *Prince* had entered service in January 1941, and, four months later, played a central role in the sinking of the German battleship *Bismarck*. When Morton clambered around the ship during her crossing, he found scars from the action, including a huge sliver of twisted metal which hung over the bar in the officers' mess.

A large American flotilla awaited the British. Roosevelt was installed aboard the cruiser *Augusta*, joined by the cruiser *Tuscaloosa* and the battleship *Arkansas*, along with a flotilla of lesser destroyers. While the *Prince of Wales* was shrouded in wartime camouflage paint, the Americans were still in peacetime rig, with gleaming brass, scrubbed decks and fresh paintwork.

Roosevelt too had travelled to Placentia Bay in secrecy. On the morning of 3 August, he had slipped out of Washington abroad the presidential yacht *Potomac* and sailed up to Vineyard Sound off the coast of Massachusetts, where he transferred to the *Augusta*. While Roosevelt sped on to Newfoundland, the *Potomac* continued her leisurely cruise, as though her passenger was still aboard. One crewman was assigned to play the part of the President, and recline on deck with hat and cigarette in a holder, to fool any onlookers. 'Even at my ripe old age I feel a thrill in making a getaway, especially from the American press,' Roosevelt commented in a letter to his cousin.[4]

Once the British arrived, Placentia Bay was filled with activity. Launches ferried to and fro between the battleships. Aboard one, a tall, thin man, wearing a civilian raincoat, crossed from the *Prince of Wales* to the *Augusta*. Harry Hopkins was a former social worker from New York. During the 1930s, he had administered New Deal agencies in Washington, and then moved into the White House as a confidant to Roosevelt. In January 1941, Hopkins travelled to London as a special envoy between President and Prime Minister. He stayed for several weeks, amidst the bomb-damaged city. At a joint appearance with Churchill at the City Chambers in Glasgow, Hopkins quoted a line from the Book of Ruth: 'Whither thou goest I will go ... even to the end.' The Prime Minister was moved to tears.[5]

At Roosevelt's suggestion, Hopkins returned to Britain again in July 1941. His mission was to finalise details for the conference with Churchill, and then fly on to Moscow. There, he made contact with the Soviet leader Joseph Stalin, following the Nazi invasion of the Soviet Union the previous month. It was a hazardous journey aboard a Catalina flying boat, unpressurised and unheated. Hopkins had been diagnosed with bowel cancer two years before, and doctors had been obliged to remove three-quarters of his stomach.

Even after the operation, Hopkins remained sickly, and found it difficult to digest food. For the journey, which lasted 24 hours, he sat shivering on the machine-gunner's perch in the tail, dressed in a grey homburg hat lent by Churchill.

The route curved over the North Sea and around the Northern Cape, to Murmansk, inside the Arctic Circle, and then Archangel, on the White Sea. On the way back, the plane battled against icy headwinds. Hopkins returned just in time, exhausted and ailing. He had managed to leave his bag of stomach medicines behind in the Soviet Union, and an unpaid hotel bill at Claridge's in London, but he did bring a tin of caviar which Stalin had given him as a gift.[6] The American met Churchill and his entourage at Scapa Flow naval base off the northern coast of Scotland. On the voyage across the Atlantic, the two men played at backgammon. As the journey went on, the stakes got higher.[7]

Churchill was joined by the First Sea Lord, Sir Dudley Pound, and Field Marshal Sir John Dill, chief of the imperial general staff. From his immediate household, Lord Cherwell, the Prime Minister's scientific adviser, travelled with the party, along with Commander 'Tommy' Thompson, his personal aide. Sir Alexander Cadogan represented the Foreign Office. A Scotsman with a long face and a dry wit, Cadogan had served as permanent secretary since 1938. While a stickler for good drafting and administration, he could show a more human side. When junior officials turned to him for advice, he would often quote the words of Shakespeare's Polonius, 'To thine own self be true'.[8]

Roosevelt brought a smaller group. It was partly due to the constraints of a covert departure from peacetime Washington, and partly a reflection of his own preference for secrecy. Churchill had been obliged to inform his cabinet of his plans, and make arrangements in case news leaked while he was still out of the country. By contrast, Roosevelt kept both Cordell Hull, his secretary of state, and Henry Stimson, secretary for war, in the dark.

From the military, General George Marshall, Admiral Harold Stark and General Henry Arnold represented the different services, along with Admiral Ernest King, who commanded the Atlantic Fleet. Two of Roosevelt's sons, Elliott and Franklin D. Jr, who were serving in the navy and army respectively, were hurried to Placentia Bay to act as junior aides. On the political side, Roosevelt was joined by Sumner Welles, Hull's tall, patrician deputy at the State Department, and Averell Harriman, administrator for the Lend-Lease programme of economic assistance to Britain. Both men were cut from the same social cloth as their president: educated at Groton School, a private establishment in Massachusetts, and then at Harvard University, or, in Harriman's case, Yale. Welles had served as a page boy at the wedding of Roosevelt to his wife Eleanor in 1905. Harriman inherited his family fortune, built during America's railroad boom in the late nineteenth century. He went on to build a successful business of his own on Wall Street. In his spare time, Harriman played polo, and rose to compete for the national team.

Two hours after the *Prince of Wales* arrived, the moment had come for the first formal meeting between the two men. Along with Pound, Churchill embarked on an admiral's barge, dressed in the uniform of Warden of the Cinque Ports – one of an array of outfits in the prime ministerial wardrobe. As he climbed the gangplank of the *Augusta*, a US marine band played 'God Save the King'. The President was dressed in a light brown suit and stood to greet the Prime Minister, while leaning on Elliott for support. Twenty years before, the President had caught polio, and the disease left the muscles in his legs too weak to carry his frame unaided. Normally, the President moved around with the aid of a wheelchair. But on formal occasions such as this, in front of the cameras, he strapped his withered limbs into heavy leg braces which, concealed underneath his trousers, allowed him to stand upright.

Churchill stepped forward, and presented a letter from King George VI. As a prime minister meeting a president, credentials were required from his sovereign. 'I am sure you will agree that he is a very remarkable man,' the king had written.[9] A film crew had been lined up to capture this symbolic moment. They failed to do so on the first occasion, and both leaders were obliged to repeat it for the cameras.[10]

Roosevelt and Churchill were products of another era. The Englishman was born in 1874, and the American eight years later, in 1882. Each came from aristocratic families – the Roosevelts of Hyde Park, New York State, and the Marlboroughs of Blenheim, Oxfordshire – and enjoyed an upbringing of privilege and ease. Churchill's mother, Jennie, was American, and met his father, Randolph, during a visit to Paris. While Roosevelt attended Groton, Churchill was educated at the public school Harrow, on the outskirts of London.

Both men grew up with politics. Randolph Churchill was a Conservative politician, whose star had shone in the 1880s, when he had reached the position of chancellor of the exchequer, only to die at the age of 46, when his son was 21. Contemporaries hailed his energy, but didn't trust him. Roosevelt's cousin, Teddy, rose up through New York State politics to reach the vice-presidency. When the president, William McKinley, was assassinated in September 1901, Teddy took over the position. At 42, he was the youngest president in the history of the republic.

Roosevelt and Churchill each embarked on their political careers in the early years of the twentieth century. During World War I, they were both involved in naval affairs, Churchill as First Lord of the Admiralty, and Roosevelt as assistant secretary in the Navy Department. But thereafter their careers diverged. There was a restless quality about Churchill, which took him through a series of peaks and troughs over the next 25 years. He had started out as a Conservative, then switched to the Liberals under Prime Minister Herbert Asquith. After the war, he moved back again, to serve in his father's old post as Chancellor of the Exchequer. His name became associated with various setbacks: the failed attack on the Dardanelles in 1914–15, and then the decision to restore the pound back to the Gold Standard in 1925, which resulted in overvaluation and economic recession. Like his father, there was a streak in him which inspired suspicion in others. 'Is he more dangerous when he is for you than when he is against you?' asked Lloyd George, who succeeded Asquith as prime minister in 1916.[11]

By the 1930s, his career was all but over. Exiled to the backbenches, Churchill became a lone voice, warning of the threat from a resurgent Germany under Hitler. When war finally came in 1939, Churchill returned to his former post, at the Admiralty. Then, in May 1940, the dangerous man found his moment, and became prime minister. With the collapse of France and evacuation of British forces at Dunkirk, it was a time of unparalleled national crisis. Within days of taking office, Churchill faced daunting choices. When he had to give the order to surrender Calais, on Sunday 26 May, he told his lunch companions at Downing Street that he felt 'physically sick'.[12] A few weeks later, after France surrendered, Churchill instructed the Royal Navy to sink the French fleet, at Mers-el-Kébir in Algeria, so that it did not fall into German hands. Almost 1,300 French sailors perished.

Roosevelt carved a different path. As a young politician, he gained little of Churchill's notoriety. The turning point came when Roosevelt was struck by polio. The 38-year-old had run, unsuccessfully, as a vice-presidential candidate in 1920. The disease seemed to spell the end of his career. But Roosevelt threw himself back into politics with a new vigour. In 1928, he achieved election as governor of New York State, and then, four years later, became president, as America was sinking into the Great Depression. He launched the New Deal, a programme of massive public works and social security to stimulate the economy. By the late 1930s, the country had passed through the worst of the crisis. Roosevelt projected a jaunty, infectious optimism which seemed to symbolise the journey to recovery. And yet, in private, many found the President a difficult man to read. There was a devious side, and an inner distance from others, which could wrong-foot even his intimates.

In 1933, the same year that Roosevelt took office, Adolf Hitler was elected chancellor of Germany at the head of the National Socialist Party. He sought to reverse the territorial losses imposed at the end of World War I, under the Treaty of Versailles. In Italy, the dictator Benito Mussolini nursed similar ambitions, while in Japan a government dominated by military officers and nationalists was set on territorial expansion across East Asia.

After World War I, the victorious Allies had created a new international organisation, called the League of Nations. This was supposed to provide a forum at which states could resolve disputes. But faced by the so-called fascist powers, the League was unable to maintain the peace. In 1935, Mussolini invaded Abyssinia. Two years later, Japan attacked China. At a meeting with Hitler and Mussolini at Munich in October 1938, British Prime Minister Neville Chamberlain acquiesced in the German occupation of the Sudetenland, along the borders of Czechoslovakia, as the price of avoiding war. He hoped that it would mark the limit of Hitler's ambitions. However, the dictator continued to press his demands.

In September 1939, Germany invaded Poland. Britain and France declared war in response, but Poland was overrun within three weeks. From the east, the Soviet Union entered the conflict, attacking the Poles and annexing the eastern portion of the country under a secret pact agreed with Berlin. Ten months later, Germany turned westwards. In just six weeks of

rapid, armoured warfare, German forces knocked out France and the Low
Countries. 'Events crowd thick and fast,' wrote Harold Nicolson, a Member
of Parliament who had been a young diplomat in the British delegation
at Versailles, and served as deputy to Duff Cooper at the Ministry of
Information. 'Each one seems worse than the other.'[13] Hitler hoped to
pressure London into a peace deal, but Churchill vowed to continue the
fight. Victory by the Royal Air Force in the Battle of Britain prevented
German invasion across the English Channel, yet the British lacked the
means to carry the war back to the continent. In June 1941, the Nazi
dictator switched his attention back to the east, invading the Soviet Union
in a bid to destroy the communist regime in Moscow.

On the other side of the Atlantic, Americans watched events unfold.
Roosevelt was clear that America's interests lay with the democracies
in Europe. The fall of France came as a shockwave in Washington. That
autumn, Roosevelt ran for an unprecedented third term as president, arguing
that wartime created exceptional conditions. The following January, in his
inaugural speech, he proclaimed 'four freedoms' – of speech and religion,
and from want and fear – in a bid to align the United States with the Allied
cause. But in Congress, so-called isolationists argued that America should
remain out of the conflict. And, under the American constitution, Roosevelt
could not go to war without congressional approval.

In response, the President settled for a gradualist policy. He increased
support for Britain, and sought to shape the public mood until the right
moment came along. The Lend-Lease Act, an arrangement to provide
military equipment on a loan basis, was passed in March 1941. US naval
forces gradually, and without full public knowledge, extended a protection
zone out into the Atlantic, to defend convoys bound for Britain from
attack by German U-boat submarines. In the Pacific, Hull sought through
diplomacy to limit Japanese ambitions, which had steadily expanded since
invasion of the Chinese mainland in 1937.

This policy could only bring limited results. While America remained
out of the war, Britain was unable to land a decisive blow on Nazi Germany.
In the Mediterranean, British forces had been pushed out of Greece, where
they had intervened against German invasion, and were forced back in the
Western Desert, on the borders of Libya and Egypt. Meanwhile, in Russia,
German forces were capturing vast numbers of prisoners and swathes of

territory. In America, the public mood remained cautious. The previous September, Roosevelt and Marshall had overseen a first draft of conscripts into the military. Those men would shortly complete their twelve months' service, and return to civilian life. Sceptics argued that the whole exercise had been unnecessary.

In a wider sense, too, there was a feeling of failure. In the years before World War I, as Churchill and Roosevelt's generation reached adulthood, globalisation had begun to take root. Money, goods, people and ideas criss-crossed the globe, carried on steamers, railroads and telegraph lines. Men had begun to argue that war was unthinkable. There was even talk, at the Hague conferences, of making it impossible, through international law and disarmament.

By 1941, all that seemed a distant dream, a lost golden age. Between 1914 and 1918, Europe had torn itself apart, slaughtering a generation, and, with them, the old certainties which had underpinned the late imperial age. Hatred and violence found a new voice. 'Oh why was I born for this time?' lamented Lady Cynthia Asquith to her diary in 1915. 'Before one is thirty to know more dead than living people?'[14] When it was all over, the delegates who had signed the Treaty of Versailles hoped to prevent such barbarism from happening again. But now, 20 years later, it had all fallen apart.

The conference at Placentia Bay ran over four days, from Saturday 9 August through to Tuesday 12 August 1941. The centrepieces were the encounters between Churchill and Roosevelt, mostly conducted over the meal table. The two men ate a total of seven lunches and dinners together, split between the *Augusta* and *Prince of Wales*.

The first night was hosted by Roosevelt, with American chicken and a dessert of ice cream, cookies and cupcakes. Full mess silver was on display. Hopkins gave a summary of his visit to Moscow; this was followed by a presentation from Churchill and his senior military commanders on the course of the war. Subsequent dinners on Sunday and Monday were more intimate, with only an inner circle of favourites on either side.

The emotional high point came on Sunday morning, with a church parade on the *Prince of Wales*. Churchill had come up with the idea during his voyage across the Atlantic. When he proposed it to Roosevelt at their first meeting, the latter rose to the occasion with alacrity, seizing a hymn book and suggesting what anthems to include. The next day, the American destroyer *McDougal* drew up alongside the *Prince of Wales*, and a gangplank was strung across. Supported by Elliott, Roosevelt made the long walk to the foredeck of the British ship, and assumed his seat under the mighty 14-inch guns. The Union Jack and Stars and Stripes fluttered alongside each other in the gentle breeze.

Around the two leaders and their military commanders, some 250 British and American sailors gathered in an open square. Morton sat a few rows back, incognito. When the Americans had learned of Bracken's initiative, they had not reacted kindly. Roosevelt had deliberately come without journalists, and could not afford a clash with the Washington press corps if the British were seen to have received more favourable treatment. Morton was told to keep a low profile.

Padres from both navies took the service, while Captain Leach read the lesson. The hymns came from the heart of the Anglican tradition: 'O God Our Help In Ages Past' (which, as Churchill later recalled in a radio broadcast, had been sung by Cromwell's Ironsides as they carried John Hampden to his burial); 'Onward Christian Soldiers'; and 'Eternal Father, Strong to Save'.

The reading came from the First Book of Joshua – 'I will not fail thee, nor forsake thee. Be strong and of good courage.' There followed prayers for the President, the King, and all victims of the war, and then a prayer for the victory of right and truth: 'Stablish our hearts, O God, in the day of battle, and strengthen our resolve, that we fight not in enmity against men but against the powers of darkness enslaving the souls of men.'

As the ceremony came to a close, both President and Prime Minister had tears welling in their eyes. Even the phlegmatic Cadogan noted in his diary that it had been 'very impressive'.[15]

After the church parade, the congregation broke up into a loose melee around the two men. Sailors snapped photos while Churchill smoked a cigar and Roosevelt a cigarette, lodged in a holder. Then they retired for lunch in the wardroom, where the British served grouse, purloined before the party had left Scapa Flow six days before, and turtle soup. Back in London, Churchill had remembered a custom dating from the days when men o' war returning from guard duty with Napoleon on St Helena brought back a turtle with them, to serve up to Lords of the Admiralty. The enterprising Thompson had spotted tins of turtle soup at a grocery shop in Piccadilly, exempt from wartime rationing, and bought up the entire stock for his master's table.

After lunch, Churchill escorted the President back to *McDougal*. The two were followed by Blackie, ship's cat on the *Prince of Wales*. For a moment, the cat attempted to follow the President up the gangplank. A timely prime ministerial intervention saved him from defection to the United States. Afterwards, when the *McDougal* had pulled away, Churchill stood alone, leaning on the guard-rail, and watching the American ship withdraw to the other side of the bay.[16]

That afternoon, Churchill, Harriman, Cadogan and Thompson took a boat ashore. They clambered around a shingle bay for exercise. 'PM like a schoolboy and insisted on rolling boulders down a cliff,' noted Cadogan in his diary. Returning in the ship's boat, Churchill held a bunch of wild pink flowers, picked from the shores of the New World.[17]

Placentia Bay was not a formal diplomatic conference. There was no firm agenda, and no agreed result which the two sides were seeking to reach. As intuitive politicians, Roosevelt and Churchill were more interested in sounding each other out, and building their relationship.

Nevertheless, it would be strange to leave the conference without making a public statement. At their first encounter, on the previous day, Roosevelt had suggested to Churchill that they draw up a short joint communiqué. This would set out 'broad principles' to guide their conduct towards the war. There were echoes of the so-called 'fourteen points' which Woodrow Wilson, American president during World War I, had published upon US entry into the war in 1917. But, rather than a unilateral statement, it would be a combined effort. Churchill later called the text a 'simple, rough and ready wartime statement'.[18]

The same night, after dinner, the Prime Minister produced a first draft in his cabin. This set out five principles: no aggrandisement by either country as a result of the war; no territorial changes without the consent of the peoples concerned; freedom of speech and to choose forms of government; fair distribution of 'essential produce'; and an 'effective international organisation', to guarantee global security. Cadogan passed this text to Welles after the church parade on Sunday, and Churchill gave a copy to Roosevelt. The negotiation had started.

Back on the *Augusta*, Welles and his president read through the British draft. It was a good starting point. But two points raised concerns. The first was the commitment to an international organisation. This was code for rebuilding the League of Nations. The organisation had been the brainchild of Wilson. But, in his enthusiasm to embrace internationalism, the Democrat overreached himself. Back in the United States, a bloc of so-called 'irreconcilable' Republicans in the Senate had refused to ratify American membership. The isolationists who now opposed US entry into the war against Hitler were their ideological successors. Roosevelt feared that Churchill's wording would provoke them yet further. A more general reference would have to suffice.

The second point that caught Roosevelt's eye was the vague promise to ensure fair distribution of produce. Here, it was the Americans who wanted to be more specific, and the British who did not. Over the preceding months, both sides had been engaged in agreeing terms for Lend-Lease. The United States hoped to use these to bind the United Kingdom more clearly into a system for dismantling trade barriers after the war. At the Ottawa Conference in 1932, the British had introduced measures to protect trade within their empire, called 'Imperial Preference'. The Americans argued that it was discriminatory, and should be terminated.

Welles produced a revised draft. The challenge was to preserve an elegant turn of phrase while avoiding the political sensitivities. The text lengthened, with additional points on free passage of the high seas, abandonment of the use of force, and disarmament. This was presented to the British on Monday morning, at a meeting aboard the *Augusta* with Roosevelt, Churchill, Cadogan, Hopkins and Welles.

Churchill took the text, and read it aloud. He agreed at once to the first three points, on territorial aggrandisement, territorial changes and self-government. The Prime Minister reached the fourth point, on trade. He paused. Welles had reworked the wording. It now committed both sides to open their markets 'without discrimination and on equal terms'. Did this, Churchill asked, apply to Imperial Preference?[19]

'Of course,' responded Welles. The American diplomat could be cool and distant, 'a tall glass of distilled ice water', as one journalist described him.[20] But on this point he became animated. He launched into a long account of how global trade had collapsed since the Depression. It was necessary to restore 'collective sanity in world economics'. Roosevelt looked on, nodding.

Churchill responded with his trump card. Such a provision, he argued, would require prior consultation with the Dominion governments, in Australia, Canada, New Zealand and South Africa. This would take at least a week. To reinforce his point, he gave a lecture on British political history. In the 1900s, Joseph Chamberlain, the ambitious scion of a Birmingham business family and father of Neville, had torn the Conservative Party open with a campaign to introduce protective tariffs against rising competition from abroad. Churchill was one of the younger members who had left in protest. Even in the 1930s, the shadows of this debate still hung over Conservative politics. This was not the moment, he argued, to reopen the wound.

Hopkins, sitting alongside Roosevelt and Welles, listened carefully. This sounded ominous. Both Churchill and Welles were digging in. If stalemate ensued, the closer relationship between London and Washington that he had sought to build over the last year might buckle. A diplomatic way out was required.

It was 'inconceivable', Hopkins suggested, that the statement should be held up for consultation with the Dominions. Would another form of words avoid this hurdle?

Welles looked uncomfortable. The former social worker was letting the British off the hook.

Churchill grabbed at the opening. Perhaps, he suggested, a suitable qualification could be added. He offered the phrase 'with due regard for our present obligations'. Roosevelt welcomed the suggestion, and asked that Welles follow up separately with Cadogan to confirm the text. Sitting alongside their bosses, the two men kept silent. At their first encounter, aboard the USS *Arkansas*, Welles had sat at the head of the wardroom table with a pile of files, quizzing Cadogan on Britain's wartime diplomacy.[21] After this awkward start, their relationship had begun to gel. 'I have hobnobbed with him a lot,' noted Cadogan in his diary, 'and have tried to get through his reserve.'[22] Nevertheless, they both knew that this round had just gone to the British.

The Prime Minister resumed reading. After a few more sentences, he paused again. This time his attention was drawn to point seven, about international security. Welles had removed the reference, previously drafted by Churchill, to a new global organisation. The Prime Minister asked why.

It was Roosevelt's turn to react. Wilson, his predecessor as a Democrat in the White House, had seen his career derailed over the League of Nations. While the Republicans blocked American membership, Wilson was incapacitated by a stroke, and his presidency stumbled to an ignominious end. Roosevelt was determined not to fall into the same trap. In the Cabinet Room at the White House, he had displayed a portrait of Wilson over the mantelpiece. On occasion, working on draft speeches, he would look up at his predecessor, either for inspiration or as a warning.[23]

More specific wording on this point, Roosevelt stated, would not be wise. It was important to be realistic. Churchill recognised that he had reached the limits. He settled for a looser phrase, referring to 'a wider and more permanent system of international security'.[24]

It was time to break for lunch. Churchill returned to the *Prince of Wales*. That evening, after a further round between Welles and Cadogan to tie up the details, the text was sent by telegram to London for approval by the War Cabinet. Clement Attlee, deputy prime minister and leader of the Labour Party, was still awake and at his desk, despite the time difference. In Churchill's absence, he had taken over the reins of government with alacrity. He was, noted Private Secretary John Colville, 'like a child with a new toy it is longing to use'.[25]

At one o'clock in the morning, Attlee summoned his colleagues. Within two hours, a reply had flashed back to Placentia Bay. Leslie Hollis, a Royal Marines officer from the War Office secretariat, passed the decoded message to Churchill. He was in his cabin close to the ship's bridge, clad in his favourite dressing gown, decorated with dragons. Attlee was content.[26] The next morning, Cadogan found Churchill sitting in his bed, reading papers. He looked up as the Permanent Secretary walked in.

'Thank God I brought you with me, Alec,' said the Prime Minister. Cadogan was not an emotional man, but on this occasion he felt a flush of pride.[27]

At five o'clock on Wednesday 13 August, the *Prince of Wales* steamed out of Placentia Bay. Two American destroyers, *Mayrant* and *Rhind*, accompanied her. As the battleship sailed from Canadian waters, the clocks on board were put forward two hours.

By the following day, the flotilla was out on the high seas of the Atlantic. Waves battered against the ship, lifting and dropping the bow in continual motion. Thuds and clangs rattled through the innards. In the wardroom, officers gathered round the wireless set. The Roman Catholic chaplain, Father Driscoll, had wrestled with the wiring for much of the voyage. Finally, with a splutter, he coaxed the machine into life.

Over the airwaves came the nasal voice of Attlee, broadcasting from London. He announced that the Prime Minister and President had met. The exact venue remained a secret. Then Attlee read out the text of the joint declaration, later known as the Atlantic Charter. For most of the ship's crew, it was the first they had heard of what had transpired at the conference.

Among the dark naval uniforms, covered across the chest with yellow lifebelts, the mood was anticlimactic. Many had hoped that the United States might declare entry into the war. This seemed a poor substitute. Even Colville, listening to Attlee's broadcast back in London, thought it sounded rather tame.[28]

'Well,' said one officer after the broadcast had finished. 'I expect there was far more to it than just that!'

Sitting in one of the easy chairs, Morton allowed his thoughts to wander. The words of George Washington, at the Constitutional Convention in Philadephia in 1787, came into his mind. 'Let us raise a standard,' the President had declared, 'to which the wise and honest can repair: the rest is in the hands of God.'

Perhaps, Morton decided, this declaration was another kind of standard. It might just be the start.[29]

ONE

Getting Started

I've been around the world in a plane
Settled revolutions in Spain
The North Pole I have charted
But I can't get started with you.

Song by Ira Gershwin, popular during the
San Francisco Conference in 1945

Less than four months after Placentia Bay, the United States was at war. At dawn on Sunday 7 December 1941, Japanese aircraft staged a surprise attack against the US naval base at Pearl Harbor, in Hawaii. Within minutes, five US battleships had been sunk, eight damaged, and 188 aircraft destroyed.

The next day, at noon, Roosevelt appeared before Congress. Wearing the leg braces, and supported by his son James, the President walked to the same spot at the lectern in the Senate chamber where, in April 1917, Wilson had requested American entry into World War I. At that time, Roosevelt had been a vigorous 35-year-old. Now, as president and two months short of his sixtieth birthday, his invalid steps were slow and painful. The President had come to request that Congress declare war against Japan.

From the gallery, he was watched by a young British journalist. Alistair Cooke had studied as a student in America, and later become a naturalised US citizen. The outbreak of war was the biggest story yet of his career. All that morning, Cooke had hung around in the White House press room with the rest of the Washington journalist corps, jostling and smoking as they waited for news. When he learned that Roosevelt was about to address Congress, the Englishman rushed over to Capitol Hill, pushing his way past armed guards and Secret Service agents to gain access to the Senate chamber. As the President inched up the ramp that led to the lectern, grasping a hand rail to steady himself, the audience burst into applause. Spotlights blazed down, illuminating the scene. Cooke found himself deeply moved. It was, he reflected later, the embodiment of 'what a man can suffer, and what he can grow to by reason of it'.[1]

The news reached Churchill at Chequers, where he was spending the weekend with Harriman. The former banker had continued to serve as Roosevelt's personal envoy in charge of Lend-Lease since Placentia Bay. Initial, patchy reports came through on the radio with the nine o'clock evening news. Churchill and Harriman decided to stay up and wait for more details. Then Sawyers, the prime ministerial butler, came in. 'It's quite true,' he said. 'We heard it ourselves outside. The Japanese have attacked the Americans.'[2]

The next morning, Churchill decided to visit Washington. For the Prime Minister, the news had brought relief, and clarity. After all the trauma of Dunkirk and the fall of France, the long wait was over. American entry into the war opened the prospect that Britain might win, after all. 'He is a different man,' noted Charles Wilson, his doctor. 'The Winston I knew in London frightened me [...] now – in a night, it seems – a younger man has taken his place.'[3]

Four days later, Churchill sailed from the Clyde, aboard the battleship *Duke of York*. This new addition to the Royal Navy was a sister ship to the *Prince of Wales*. Earlier that autumn, the *Prince* had been dispatched to Singapore. On 10 December, following Pearl Harbor, Japanese bombers cornered her off the coast of Malaya. A chance torpedo crippled the port propeller, and further bombs hit amidships. In 90 minutes, she had sunk. Captain Leach and 840 of the crew who had made the trip to Newfoundland perished.

The *Duke of York* had better luck in crossing the Atlantic. The most perilous stretch was the first part, through the western approaches off Brest. At this point, close to the French coast, her course ran across the route taken by U-boats sailing out to attack Allied convoys. But the battleship pressed ahead, following a rapid, zig-zagging course to avoid detection in the heavy winter seas, and outstripping her escort of destroyers. Once past the Azores, the threat receded. Churchill retired to his cabin, gathering his thoughts for the visit ahead. Wilson passed the time in conversation with his fellow passengers, while the waves outside pounded against the ship's hull.

The prime ministerial party docked in Chesapeake Bay ten days later, on the afternoon of 22 December. Anxious to make dinner with the President, Churchill persuaded the White House to send a plane for the final leg to Washington. The British flew after dark, aboard a sleek Lockheed Lodestar. As they followed the line of the Potomac River, the travellers looked down at the American capital below them. In contrast to the darkness of blackout London, Washington was still bathed in light. Thompson, the aide who had purloined tinned turtle soup for dinner aboard the *Prince of Wales* at Placentia Bay, was transfixed.[4] At the White House, the windows had been darkened, as a security precaution, and dummy anti-aircraft guns installed on the roof, but the traditional Christmas tree still blazed with light on the south lawn.

Churchill stayed for two weeks. On Christmas Day, he attended church with Roosevelt, hearing the carol 'O Little Town of Bethlehem' for the first time. Then, on Boxing Day, he addressed a joint session of Congress. 'I cannot help reflecting', he noted, 'that if my father had been American and my mother British, instead of the other way round, I might have got here on my own.'[5] The house erupted with laughter. Back at the White House, Roosevelt encountered Churchill naked, emerging from a long, hot bath. 'The Prime Minister of Great Britain', quipped the latter, 'has nothing to conceal from the President of the United States.'[6] In the camaraderie of midwinter, the Anglo-American relationship was blossoming.

Arcadia, as this conference was codenamed, covered both military plans and alliance politics. But Roosevelt, as at Placentia Bay, wanted a gesture to dramatise the struggle in which America was now engaged. His solution was a typical mix of theatre and improvisation. On New Year's Day 1942, ambassadors of the 26 countries fighting against the Axis gathered in the Oval Office to sign a declaration. At the President's suggestion, they called themselves the 'United Nations' (a name supposedly agreed during the bathroom encounter), and committed to fight together for life, liberty, independence and religious freedom. Churchill delighted in quoting from Byron's *Childe Harold*: 'Here, where the sword united nations drew, / Our countrymen were warring on that day!'[7]

The American president and British prime minister signed first, along with the Soviet ambassador, Maxim Litvinov, and his Chinese colleague, T. V. Song. Others followed in alphabetical order, entering the Oval Office in turn. All except Litvinov had dressed in dinner jackets for the occasion.[8]

Roosevelt himself had written out the sequence on White House notepaper, amending with arrows to put the four main powers at the top.

The ambassadors signed the declaration at a desk that had been presented by Queen Victoria to President Rutherford Hayes in 1880. This was made with timbers from the ship HMS *Resolute*, which had been abandoned after becoming trapped in the ice while searching for the ill-fated Franklin expedition of 1845. As the ceremony took place, Fala, the presidential dog, snored gently on a sofa, while Eleanor Roosevelt, first lady, and her dinner guests watched from the door.[9]

The internationalist cause had not died with Wilson. To prepare the Paris Peace Conference, which negotiated the Versailles Treaty, Wilson had been supported by a group of some 150 scholars and experts. They were known as 'the Inquiry'. The head of research was Walter Lippmann, a liberal journalist who had served in the US Army Expeditionary Force to France. Many members travelled with Wilson to Paris.

In 1920, after the Senate vote against League membership, this group sought to keep the flame alive. They created the Council of Foreign Relations, which published a journal called *Foreign Affairs*, aimed at the liberal elite of Washington and New York. In the first edition, Elihu Root, who had been secretary of state under Teddy Roosevelt, argued that the United States had become a world power as a result of World War I, and needed to uphold her responsibilities.

These men did not believe the League had been doomed from the start. Rather, it had been crippled by American abstention, and a lack of teeth. With a new world war, there was a fresh opportunity. In December 1939, the diplomat Norman Davis, who served as undersecretary of state to Wilson, launched a private initiative with Hamilton Armstrong, editor of *Foreign Affairs*. With a committee drawn from Council members, they produced a series of private papers for the Roosevelt administration, entitled the 'War and Peace Studies', which echoed the work of the Inquiry. Territorial issues were handled by Isaiah Bowman, director of the American Geographical Society and a key adviser at the Paris Conference, while Allen Welsh Dulles, a diplomat who had worked on disarmament at the League, covered security matters. His brother, the lawyer John Foster Dulles, had also served as an adviser in Paris. Other key figures included Lippmann, and Anne

O'Hare McCormick, foreign correspondent of the *New York Times*, who had interviewed Hitler and Mussolini in the 1930s, and become the first woman to serve on the newspaper's editorial board.

The Old Executive Building stood on the intersection of Pennsylvania Avenue and 17th Street, opposite the west wing of the White House. This mansion, built in the 1870s, was home to the State Department. Seventy years on, it was showing its age. Offices were cramped and antiquated. In summer, the corridors were stifling, and in winter erratic central heating made the building an oven.

Cordell Hull, the 70-year-old secretary of state, occupied an office in the south-west corner. He was a veteran of the Washington scene. Born in a log cabin in Olympus, Tennessee in 1871, as one of five sons, Hull had worked his way up through the rough-and-tumble of Democrat politics in the South. In 1933, Roosevelt appointed him secretary of state, chiefly to anchor support from the southern wing of the party. By 1941, he had served longer in the role than any before him. An elegant, upright man, in a three-piece suit, with white hair in a neat parting, Hull was the archetype of a southern gentleman. Dean Acheson, who worked with him as one of the under-secretaries in the State Department, recalled a 'well-structured face [...] sad and thoughtful'.[10]

The Secretary was willing to engage with Davis and Armstrong. During his tenure, he had championed free trade, battling the protectionist currents of the 1930s. With the onset of war, Hull saw there might be a new opportunity. In 1939, he took on a researcher from the Council of Foreign Relations, Leo Pasvolsky, to advise him on what might be done.

They were an unlikely match. Pasvolsky was short, with a pipe, moustache and large bald head. Hull called him 'Friar Tuck', while a contemporary compared him to 'the third little pig in Disney's version of that fairy tale – the one whose house could not be blown down'.[11] They came from very different roots. Pasvolsky was a cosmopolitan immigrant, born in Pavlograd, Russia in 1893, who had fled after the revolution in 1905. In America, he worked his way through night school and Columbia University. Then, in 1919, he covered the Paris Conference for the *New York Tribune*, and moved into a career in Washington.

Pasvolsky found his new assignment frustrating. A long career in Washington had taught his boss to be cautious. Hull would plod through draft speeches sentence by sentence, checking for the slightest hostage to fortune. Welles treated him with ill-disguised contempt. The rest of the bureaucracy had fragmented between the geographical divisions which covered different parts of the world, like feudal baronies. Days went by in meetings which, Acheson recalled, 'gave the illusion of action, but often frustrated it by attempting to reconcile the irreconcilable'.[12] Career officials spent more time worrying about the arcana of diplomatic protocol than pursuing foreign policy.

Even after Pearl Harbor, the State Department struggled to find a role. Roosevelt preferred to bypass it altogether, working through men like Hopkins and Harriman as his personal envoys. The Old Executive Building, Pasvolsky concluded, was not promising ground in which to plant the Council's bold ideas. He would have to bide his time.

Beyond the avenues and mansion blocks of Washington a new breeze was blowing. The American people were at war. Alistair Cooke realised this with a jolt when he heard a radio newsreader calling San Francisco the 'Far Eastern Battle Zone'. For families across the country, foreign affairs had a new meaning. Twice, in living memory, America had tried to stay out of war, only to end up sending her men overseas. In 1940, the US armed forces had numbered just over half a million men. By 1943, this figure had risen to nine million. Cooke, touring across the country, watched young men enlisting. At Fort Knox, he saw couples taking a stroll together before the men embarked for a tour of duty overseas. The soldiers wore their uniforms gravely, as if carrying a new responsibility, while the women put 'a gentle face on the essential sadness'.[13]

In a radio address after Pearl Harbor, Roosevelt had said, 'We don't like it, we didn't want to get into it, but we are in it, and we're going to fight it with everything we've got.'[14] As Americans bade farewell to their menfolk, many asked how they could prevent it happening again. During 1942 and 1943, this debate gathered pace. During the Depression, Roosevelt had used the new medium of radio to deliver a weekly broadcast to the American people. He called them his 'fireside chats'. With America at war, the President needed an idea that the country could rally behind. Building a stronger international order, which would prevent war from happening again, was the answer. He used his radio broadcasts to fan the sparks of this debate. His intended audience was not just Democrats, among whom there had always been a streak of internationalism. Indeed, the vice-president, Henry Wallace, had been an outspoken advocate of the League. Rather, Roosevelt was reaching over to the other side of the political spectrum.

Since 1933, the President had enjoyed majorities in both presidential elections and Congress. But the pendulum was beginning to swing back. In the midterm elections, in November 1942, Republicans scored gains in both the House of Representatives and the Senate. With 37 seats in the latter, they were within reach of gaining overall control at the next elections, in 1944. Roosevelt looked vulnerable. The leader now seemed more popular than his party.

Yet the Republican Party faced challenges of its own. In the 1930s, the party had been dominated by isolationists. Arthur Vandenberg, senator for Michigan, had been a prominent member of the group. But, following Pearl Harbor, he changed his view. 'That day', he later wrote, 'ended isolationism for any realist.'[15] Vandenberg was joined by men like Wendell Willkie, who had stood for president in 1940, and Thomas Dewey, governor of New York and a hopeful for the nomination in 1944. However, on the other wing of the party, a diehard isolationist faction remained, led by Robert Taft, the senate minority leader from Ohio, whose father William had served as president and was a rival to Teddy Roosevelt. The internationalist cause, Franklin Roosevelt sensed, might drive a wedge between these halves of Republicanism, while providing a standard around which the rest of America could unite.

At Roosevelt's suggestion, Willkie made a global tour aboard a converted bomber, arguing for a 'new world idea'. His memoir, published in 1943 and entitled *One World*, became only the third non-fiction book in American history to sell more than a million copies.[16] Other Republicans joined in. Herbert Hoover, who had preceded Roosevelt as president, also wrote a book, calling for an effort to rebuild international law. John Foster Dulles led a commission formed by the Federal Council of Churches, which argued for a form of world government. With ideas like this in play, the President might just be able to forge the consensus in American politics which had eluded Wilson.

At the opposite end of Pennsylvania Avenue, the Senate was no stranger to new winds. Here, in the semicircular chamber on the north wing of the Capitol building, time moved at a different pace. Members sat at antique desks, each carved with the names of their forebears. In this auditorium the great debates over segregation and abolition had raged 80 years before, during the Civil War. It was a place where the past lived on. 'One or two' senators, recalled the journalist Allen Drury, who covered the chamber for United Press during the war, were 'still in tail-coats and possessed of flowing hair', and all were 'imbued with a massive sense of the dignity and power of being a Senator of the United States'.[17]

If the United Nations was to become a reality, it would have to pass through the Senate. Under the constitution, foreign treaties required ratification by a two-thirds majority. 'Thirty three senators have it in their power to wreck the treaty proposals of any administration,' advised a young British diplomat and academic, Isaiah Berlin, who had been assigned to the British Embassy in Washington. 'More than that number', he warned, 'are at present dubious of the desirability of establishing any real international system [...] the implications of which they have not thought out.'[18]

The principal committees sat on the third floor, in a corridor above the main chamber. In the panelled meeting rooms, deals were cut and legislation drafted before it reached the Senate floor. The committee on foreign affairs occupied numbers S116 and S117. In 1920, under the chairmanship of the Republican Henry Cabot Lodge, this committee had been instrumental in defeating Wilson. In 1943, it was 23 strong, with 15 Democrats, seven Republicans and one independent. But most of the Republicans were diehard isolationists, while only half of the Democrats could be relied on to vote with the administration.

Tom Connally, ranking senator from Texas, had taken over the chairmanship in 1941. Born in 1877, Connally was tall and broad-framed, with a shock of white hair, and often dressed in a wing collar and black bow tie. Berlin described him as 'a very typical, exuberant Southern gentleman', adding that he had the 'appearance and mannerisms of an old-fashioned actor'.[19] Though a Democrat, Connally saw himself as a watchful eye on the Roosevelt administration. When the President signed the formal declaration of war against Japan, on 11 December 1941, the senator contrived to be photographed standing behind the *Resolute* desk in the Oval Office, registering the exact time on his old-fashioned pocket watch.

Thirteen months later, in January 1943, Connally could sense change in the air. The new congressional session had opened that month with a fresh intake of congressmen and senators, elected in midterms the previous

November. In the corridors and dining rooms of Capitol Hill, excited newcomers asked how this, the Seventy-Eighth Congress, could rise to the expectations building across America.

At 38, Joseph Ball was the youngest member of the Senate. He had joined the chamber by an unusual route. Three years before, Ernest Lundeen, the incumbent for Minnesota, had died in an air crash. Harold Stassen, state governor and a moderate Republican, used his gubernatorial powers to appoint Ball in his place. It was a striking choice. Convention dictated that freshmen senators should keep their heads down. But Ball, a former journalist, was not conventional. In October 1940, as London was under bombardment from the German Luftwaffe, he used his maiden speech to call for American support to Britain, and a break with isolationism. Taft and his followers took note – here was trouble.

In the 1942 midterms, Ball was elected in his own right. Returning to Washington, he was determined to cause a stir. Days after the Seventy-Eighth Congress began, he assembled three co-sponsors, and tabled a motion on postwar foreign policy. This called for the United States to create a new international organisation, more muscular than the League, and complete with its own standing army. This trial balloon, as Berlin described it, was dubbed 'B2H2', after the first letters of the sponsors' surnames.

Ball had thrown down a gauntlet to his Texan colleague. While Connally was sympathetic to Ball's aims, his motion played with fire. Such forthright wording, which raised the spectre of the League, would be bound to draw a reaction from the isolationists. Taft, with an eye on the nomination in 1944, was looking to attack the administration. Roosevelt had asked Connally and fellow Democrats to keep the Senate off his back until the timing was right. To buy time, Connally resorted to the old tricks of the Hill. He buried the draft with procedural points and postponed a vote.

For much of 1943, this ploy worked. But then, in mid-September, challenge came from a new quarter, in the House of Representatives. William Fulbright, a freshman Democrat from Arkansas and an ardent internationalist, tabled a rival motion to B2H2. Within a week, it was carried in the House, by 360 votes to 29 against. Gallup polling suggested that public support for the motion was as high as 78 per cent.

The genie was now out of the bottle. The Senate could hardly remain silent while the House, a junior arm of the legislature, pronounced on foreign policy. 'God damn it!' thundered Connally to his staffers. 'Everyone is running around like a fellow with a tick in his navel, hollering about postwar resolutions.'[20]

The Texan veteran was not to be outdone. This new resolution was more nuanced than B2H2. It called for 'international machinery', rather than an 'organisation', and did not specify what form this might take. Connally spotted that, if he tabled his own motion in place of B2H2, which built on that in the House, he might wrest back the initiative. He therefore drafted a new text, which referred to an 'international authority'. This played to both sides of the debate. Internationalists could see it as matching the ambition set by Ball, while pragmatists could argue that it implied a looser arrangement between sovereign countries. In the last week of October, as autumn leaves turned on the poplar trees that lined Pennsylvania Avenue, Connally took the plunge and tabled his draft.

At the other end of the avenue, Hull and Pasvolsky watched closely. The previous August, Hull had finally managed to force out Welles, over a scandal prompted by allegations of homosexual conduct with a railroad steward. While Secretary and Deputy were at loggerheads, it would have been fatal to try making the case for an international organisation in the maelstrom of Washington politics. But now, with a clear hand, Hull was keen to move.

Pasvolsky saw his chance. Bypassing the geographical directorates, he assembled a new team. He wanted thinkers and doers. Scouting round Washington, he pulled in people that he could work with, such as Ralph Bunche, an academic and the first African American to gain a PhD in political science, and Alger Hiss, a lawyer and former assistant to the Supreme Court. His coterie eventually numbered over 100, concealed behind the anonymous title 'Division of Special Research'.[21]

Prior to his departure, Welles had prepared a draft charter for the new organisation. Pasvolsky used this as a starting point. Like Welles, he believed that the League had lacked a central driving body. Roosevelt talked about the United States, Soviet Union, United Kingdom and China acting as 'four policemen' to ensure order in the postwar world. Pasvolsky's answer was to give the organisation an executive committee, which would decide on security matters, and have permanent seats for the major powers. Other countries would sit on a general assembly. But Welles had argued for the new organisation to have a federal structure, with subsidiary regional organisations to underpin it. For Pasvolsky, this was anathema. The organisation must have sufficient authority, and that meant it must be global.

By early autumn, when the Fulbright Resolution was passed, Hull and Pasvolsky believed that the time had come to take the next step. If the new organisation was to be born, it would require support not just in the Senate, but in the wider world. And, for that, America needed the four policemen on board. It was time to go travelling.

The Foreign Office was housed in a grand neoclassical building, erected by the Victorian architect Charles Barry in the heart of London's government district, Whitehall. It was an unlikely art gallery for internationalism. British diplomacy was based on pragmatism. For centuries, her statesmen had sought to maintain a 'splendid isolation' for Britain and her empire from the European continent. It was a game that required cool heads rather than high ideals. However, during World War I, the Anglo-German artist Sigismund Goetze made an unusual bequest. At his own expense, he painted a series of huge murals around the main staircase. The result was unveiled in 1921, a year after the League was born.

Goetze's paintings depicted a Wagnerian allegory of the Versailles settlement. Britannia, joined by maidens dressed in togas to represent the republics of France, Italy and America, received tribute from her grateful allies. At her feet, a heap of discarded rifles and spiked helmets represented the fallen German Reich. Overhead, in the gold dome suspended above the ornate staircase, ran the inscription 'Let All The Nations Rejoice'.

Each morning, Anthony Eden climbed this staircase as he walked to his office in the north-west corner of the building. In this ornate room, decked in gilt with a view across St James's Park to Buckingham Palace, British foreign secretaries had watched the world go by since the days of Prime Minister William Gladstone in the nineteenth century. Above the entrance, Goetze had painted a Roman sibyl with a finger to her lips, commanding silence.

A handsome man with a neat moustache, Eden was born in 1897, the year of Queen Victoria's Diamond Jubilee. He was the son of landed gentry from Durham, in the north of England. Like his forebears, he was educated at Eton College, the historic establishment close to the royal castle at Windsor where British aristocracy had been educated for centuries. During his service in World War I, Eden was awarded the Military Cross, and became the youngest brigade-major in the British Army. Afterwards, he continued his studies at Christ Church, in Oxford University, where he received a double first-class degree in oriental languages.

Eden was elected to Parliament in 1923, at the age of 26. Just over a decade later, he became foreign secretary, when the incumbent, Sir Samuel Hoare, was obliged to resign over the Italian invasion of Abyssinia. Three years later, in February 1938, Eden himself resigned over the reluctance of Neville Chamberlain's government to confront Mussolini. In December 1940, he returned to his former job, when Churchill moved his predecessor, Lord Halifax, to be ambassador in Washington.

Eden and Cadogan, his permanent secretary, were pragmatists. They were not instinctively drawn to the internationalist vision. But they realised that it would be essential for America to remain engaged abroad after the war. In March 1943, Eden stayed in Washington for more than a fortnight, calling on Hull, Welles and Hopkins and spending the last three days at the White House with Roosevelt. He did not, Halifax reported to London, 'put a foot wrong'.

'Anthony,' announced the President one evening, 'you'll have to make a speech for us before you go home. Where shall it be?'

Eden ventured to suggest San Francisco, where he could emphasise Britain's commitment to the war against Japan, as well as that in Europe. But Madame Chiang Kai-Shek, wife of the Chinese nationalist leader, was leading a high-profile tour on the West Coast, and Roosevelt advised against.

'I know,' the President said after a pause. 'The State Legislature of Maryland will meet to hear you, and we will link you up to all the other state legislatures across the country.'

Eden was taken aback. His great-great-grandfather, Sir Robert Eden, had been the last colonial governor, and had become friends with George Washington after the War of Independence. The state coat of arms still contained the Eden family crest.

'Surely they don't want to be reminded of the colonial past?' Eden protested.

'Don't they just,' Roosevelt retorted. 'You'll see.'

A few days later, Eden visited Annapolis, capital of Maryland. He was given a rapturous welcome. The Foreign Secretary delivered his speech in the old statehouse, standing in front of a portrait of his ancestor. He felt, he recalled later, like a local boy who had made good.[22]

Eden was joined on the trip by Gladwyn Jebb, a fellow Old Etonian and rising star in the Foreign Office. Jebb had caught the eye of Cadogan, who brought him back from an assignment establishing the Special Operations Executive, a wartime sabotage organisation, to head a new department for postwar planning. Like Eden and Cadogan, Jebb believed in hard-headed diplomacy. Before the war, as a young official, he had thrived in the lively intellectual environment created by Sir Robert Vansittart, predecessor to Cadogan. Jebb served a posting in Rome in the mid-1930s, where he saw Italian fascism at first hand, and travelled privately in Germany. Together with men like Frank Roberts, who had joined the Foreign Office in 1930 and headed the German desk, Jebb became a sceptic of appeasement, as Chamberlain's policy was known. On the day that Chamberlain returned from Munich, Jebb watched from his first-floor office as the Prime Minister spoke on the steps of 10 Downing Street. He promised that the agreement had brought 'peace in our time'. Also watching was Sir Orme Sargent, deputy under-secretary, who acted as something of a mentor to Jebb and his contemporaries. 'You might think', lamented Sargent to his companions, 'that we had won a major victory instead of betraying a minor country.'[23]

Eden and Jebb returned from Washington convinced that Roosevelt was serious about creating an international organisation. But they also worried that the Americans were naïve about what it might achieve. Only a week later, news broke that the bodies of some 10,000 Polish officers had been discovered, bound and shot, in a forest at Katyn, in eastern Poland. Privately, the British realised that this was the work of the NKVD, Stalin's secret police. In September 1939, following the German invasion, the Red Army had occupied eastern Poland. When Eden first visited Moscow, in December 1941, Stalin had made clear that he expected to keep the gains he had made. Katyn was a brutal reminder that his regime would use every means available to meet his aim.

Eden and his officials, like their American colleagues, chose not to make a public outcry. They realised that, if the Americans really wanted an international organisation, they would all have to work with the Soviets. But, they also concluded, it would be a risky business. Britain would have to keep a close eye on what went on between her two allies.

TWO

Doing the Job

I do not like the job I have to do,
I cannot think my news will go down well.
Can I convince them of our settled view?
Will Stalin use Caucasian oaths and yell?

From lines composed by Cadogan and Field Marshal Wavell
en route to Moscow, 16 August 1942

Halfway round the world, in Moscow, autumn was in the air. Leaves were falling on the tree-lined boulevards of the Garden Ring, around the medieval centre and the Kremlin fortress, where Napoleon's Grande Armée had cut down limes for firewood during their brief occupation of the city in 1812. But in the American Ambassador's residence at Spaso House, the grounds already looked threadbare. Under the previous incumbent, William Standley, the gardens had been neglected. Only a few dead trees and bare shrubs remained in evidence.

Spaso House had seen jollier times. In the 1930s, the then ambassador, William Bullitt, was famous for his spectacular parties. At one, three performing seals from Moscow zoo entered the main ballroom as guests assembled, balancing a Christmas tree, bottle of champagne and tray of glasses on their noses. At another, bears, roosters, goats and sheep appeared, with masses of tulips flown in from Holland. Entranced, the Soviet writer Mikhail Bulgakov used the scene as a model for his novel *The Master and Margarita*.[1]

In autumn 1943, a new ambassador was coming. As the Red Army turned the tide against the German invaders, Roosevelt sensed a fresh phase in US–Soviet relations. To seize the moment, he dispatched Harriman. On 18 October, the former banker, a few weeks short of his fifty-second birthday, arrived in Moscow aboard a glistening C-54 transport plane. He had flown via Cairo and Tehran. It was a longer route than that which Hopkins had taken in 1941, but safer. With him came Kathleen, his lively 26-year-old journalist daughter. Together, they settled into the echoing and draughty house. Kathleen was appalled by the décor. Writing to her sister Mary, she moaned about the carpets, shaded 'sea-sick green-and-yellow'. In the spacious oval dining room, she complained, 'he sits at one end of the table and I'm half a mile away at the other.'[2]

On the flight over, Harriman was joined by Hull. It was the first time that the Secretary had travelled aboard an aircraft. As a first step in strengthening the partnership between the three Allied powers, Churchill, Stalin and Roosevelt had agreed that their foreign ministers should meet in Moscow. The elderly Hull was under medical orders not to travel, but had exploded at the suggestion that anyone else might replace him. To protect his cargo, the pilot was instructed to fly at low altitude. At Tehran, the plane took on a pair of Soviet aircrew to assist with navigation. They had orders to fly at maximum altitude so that the incoming plane could be recognised. For a few minutes, Russians and Americans engaged in agitated sign language, before compromise was reached.

The plane touched down in late afternoon. An autumn chill was already in the air. At the airport, Hull was greeted by his Soviet counterpart, Vyacheslav Molotov. Eden, who had also flown via Tehran, arrived a few minutes later. In front of the world's press corps, an honour guard of Soviet soldiers clad in shiny helmets and white gloves presented arms, and played a slightly out-of-tune rendition of the 'Star-Spangled Banner'. Hull beamed with pleasure. 'The old boy was in quite good spirits,' Eden noted in his diary, 'considering the ordeal.'[3]

Molotov was born in 1890, three years before Eden. He grew up in Kurkata, a village in rural Russia. From his early teens, he had gravitated to the communist cause. His family name was Scriabin, but, like many Bolsheviks, the young man adopted a pseudonym. Molotov translated as 'hammer-man' in Russian. Following the death of revolutionary leader Vladimir Lenin in 1924, Stalin assumed control. Molotov became his henchman. He and his wife Polina occupied a flat in the Kremlin next to Stalin and his wife, Nadezhda Alliluyeva. From 1930 he was chairman of the Council of People's Commissars: in effect, head of the government. Dour and pedantic, his colleagues dubbed him 'stone arse'. He wore wire-rimmed glasses, perched above his moustache, and, unusually for Soviet luminaries, a suit and tie. When he spoke, his voice had a slight stammer.

As he greeted Eden and Hull, the veteran Bolshevik had good reason to smile for the cameras. During the 1920s and 1930s, the Soviet Union had been an international pariah. When the Red Army invaded Finland in 1939, at the start of World War II, the League of Nations even voted to expel Moscow from membership. It was a final gesture of disapproval from an organisation which had otherwise proven powerless. Now, as common allies with the West, the tables were turned. The Red Army had driven back the German Wehrmacht, winning dramatic victories in the epic battle at Stalingrad the previous winter, and then in a vast tank confrontation at Kursk that summer. Meanwhile, in North Africa and southern Italy, American and British forces had succeeded in knocking Mussolini's forces out of the war.

For Molotov personally, the new tone was particularly welcome. Three years previously, in August 1939, he had concluded a non-aggression pact with Hitler's foreign minister, Joachim von Ribbentrop, which opened the door for Germany to attack Poland. In a secret protocol, the two powers agreed to divide the country between them. Now, as genial host, he could brush over the past. He thrived in the part, gathering his guests for a hearty welcome dinner at the foreign ministry's guest house in Spiridonovka Street, a few blocks from Spaso House. To mark the occasion, he even wore a newly designed diplomatic uniform, in black and gold braid with an ornate dagger. The Americans thought it looked like a Nazi outfit.[4]

The meeting lasted a fortnight. The weather was crisp and autumnal, reminding Harriman of his childhood in New England.[5] The first week was taken up with territorial questions in Europe. Aside from a decision to treat Austria, which had been annexed by Germany in 1938, as a separate state, most detailed issues were relegated for later discussion. At Eden's suggestion, the ministers agreed to create a European Advisory Commission for this purpose, staffed by their ambassadors in London. They also agreed a statement confirming that leading Nazis would be tried as war criminals after defeat. Progress seemed good. Reporting back to Churchill, Eden called it 'exceptionally smooth waters'.[6]

Hull had agreed with Roosevelt that he should come to Moscow with a plan to launch the new international organisation. He brought with him a draft statement, drawn up with Pasvolsky's help and agreed in advance with the British. This built on the United Nations declaration, signed nearly two years before. It included a commitment to 'establishing at the earliest practicable date a general international organization [...] for the maintenance of international peace and security'. At their third session, on 21 October, Hull presented his draft. His colleagues took note, and agreed to pass it to their deputies for more detailed negotiation.

While Hull awaited the outcome of his initiative, it was Eden's turn to make a move. The British were worried that, as the Red Army advanced towards Eastern Europe, Moscow would seek to establish a diplomatic stranglehold over the region. One potential vehicle would be to offer bilateral treaties with smaller countries, on terms dictated by the Soviets. Moscow was pressing the Czech government-in-exile, based in London, to agree such a treaty. This could be the first domino, the Foreign Office feared, in a Soviet diplomatic offensive that would lead to Poland. Eden wanted to see the Allies reach an agreement that the Kremlin would not conclude treaties without consulting London and Washington first. Eden called it a 'self-denying ordinance'.

On 24 October, the sixth day of the conference, the ministers gathered for their plenary session. It was three o'clock in the afternoon. They sat around a small round table, covered with a white cloth. Jugs of water and cigarettes in painted Russian boxes were laid out for the participants. In the middle stood a trio of little flags, with Stars and Stripes, Hammer and Sickle and Union Jack all neatly ironed into folds.[7]

Molotov, as chair, passed the floor to Eden. The Foreign Secretary set out his case. The United Kingdom was not opposed to such agreements in principle, he explained, including that between the Soviet Union and Czechoslovakia. But they wanted to avoid being played off against each another. Prior consultation between the major powers was the answer.

Molotov sensed his moment. Here was an opportunity to assert Moscow's sphere of influence, and to drive a wedge between the two Western allies. Turning to Hull, he asked if the United States had a view. For much of the conference, Hull had talked at length, in convoluted phrases. But on this occasion he had little to add. The septuagenarian said that he was not familiar with the details. He was happy to leave Eden and Molotov to judge.

The Soviet foreign minister turned back to Eden. Now that he had heard from their American colleague, did he still have concerns over the draft Czech treaty?

'I may be mistaken,' Eden began, 'but—'

'You are mistaken,' Molotov cut him short.

Realising he was outmanoeuvred, Eden withdrew. Molotov announced that he would straightaway send a telegram to Edvard Beneš, the Czech president exiled in London, and invite him to Moscow.[8] 'Eden could be tough when necessary,' recalled 'Pug' Ismay, Churchill's military chief of staff, who had joined him in Moscow. 'But [he could] also give way gracefully if the situation demanded it.'[9]

Having won his round with Eden, Molotov was ready to revisit Hull's declaration. Over the previous two days, their deputies had pored over the text. Andrei Vyshinsky, a hard-line Stalinist who had presided over the show trials of the late 1930s, represented the Soviet Union. A short man, with a barrel chest, ruddy complexion and round spectacles, he was seven years older than Molotov. As a young man Vyshinsky had taught Latin. At one moment a cheerful host, his mood could suddenly darken, and his eyes take on a cruel glint.

Vyshinsky succeeded in excising a line from the American proposal which barred the signatories from using military force without mutual agreement. Like Eden's self-denying ordinance, this could have constrained Moscow's room for manoeuvre in Eastern Europe. The word 'agreement' looked like a veto over the Red Army. At the Soviet diplomat's insistence, 'consultation' was inserted instead.

With this loophole closed, Molotov brought the draft back to plenary. Hull had previously insisted that the declaration be signed by Nationalist China, as the additional member of the 'four policemen'. Molotov now readily conceded the point. And, with that, he announced that the declaration had been agreed.

It was a moment of triumph for Hull. With the Moscow Declaration, as it was called, a path had been opened to secure Soviet participation in a new international organisation. But Molotov's rebuff to Eden had not gone unnoticed by the old southern gentleman. It was a worrying sign. In a break after the plenary session, Hull found himself talking with the Soviet foreign minister.

'Isolationism was almost your country's undoing, was it not, Mr Secretary?' asked Molotov.

Hull acknowledged that it was true. But, he observed, the same could be said for the Soviet Union.

Molotov smiled. It was indeed so.

Hull added a warning. 'After the war', he said, 'you can follow isolationism if you want, and gobble up your neighbours. But it will be your undoing. When I was young I knew a bully in Tennessee. He used to get a few things his way by being a bully and bluffing other fellows. But he ended up by not having a friend in the world.'[10]

Back in the United States, the press were ecstatic. 'Moscow Declaration Regarded as a Milestone in Human Progress,' declared the *New York Times*. Roosevelt too was elated. 'The Moscow accomplishments', he announced to a press conference, 'refuted predictions of cynics who thought [the] talks would be clouded with suspicion and would accomplish little.'[11]

Over on Capitol Hill, the news came as a relief to Connally. In the fortnight since Hull had left for Moscow, his gamble over a new motion had not fared well. Debate had staggered back and forth across the Senate chamber. Connally's clever wording had backfired. Ball and the supporters of his original B2H2 text thought the Texan's alternative lacked ambition. Having come so far, they were loath to throw their votes away on a compromise. Taft and his allies saw cracks opening among their opponents. From the White House, Roosevelt was watching with concern. A messy, premature debate on the Hill was exactly what he wanted to avoid.

On 1 November, hours after the Moscow Declaration was published, Connally rose to speak. The chamber fell silent. This communiqué that had just flashed around the world, he argued, buttressed his case. It was time to bring the matter to conclusion, and for the Senate to back what the four policemen had announced.

Ball sprang to his feet. Spotting that it included the prized word 'organisation', he pulled up his colleague. The Senate should be 'at least as clear and forthright', he argued, as Hull and his colleagues had been. Why not use the same language?

Connally was an old Senate hand. He knew when he had been outrun. In any case, Connally judged, he could afford to lower his guard. Now that Hull had shown his hand in Moscow, and promised the world a successor to the League, the administration's plans were hardly a secret. 'Organisation' it would be.

Four days later, on 4 November 1943, the motion passed by 84 votes. The Texan veteran had done his work.

Roosevelt was pleased at his secretary's visit to Moscow. For once, goodwill flowed between the White House and the Old Executive Building, on the other side of 17th Street. But the President was a politician who relied on intuition. If the United Nations was to become a reality, he needed to have Stalin on board. And, for that, he must meet the Soviet dictator face to face.

Presidential travel was a novelty. Before Wilson, no incumbent of the White House had visited Europe. The first time that Roosevelt crossed the Atlantic was to attend a conference with Churchill at Casablanca in January 1943. It was also the first time that any president had travelled by air.

Since Pearl Harbor, the President had wanted to meet with Stalin. A lengthy correspondence developed between them. But the latter had been reluctant to commit, arguing that his role as war leader prevented him from travel. Churchill had flown to Moscow and called on him in the Kremlin, in August 1942. For Roosevelt such a journey was impossible. Aside from his disability, he was required to be within ten days' round-trip travel time from Washington, so that he could sign and return congressional bills within the time limit required under the US constitution. He needed another meeting place. Different locations were mooted, even Alaska. Eventually 'Uncle Joe', as President and Prime Minister dubbed him in their own correspondence, agreed to meet in Tehran.[12]

On 13 November 1943, Roosevelt and his party left Chesapeake Bay aboard the USS *Iowa*. This was one of the new generation of American battleships, built to replace those lost at Pearl Harbor. While crossing the Atlantic, the President amused himself by watching films and observing the crew at drill. One morning, as he sat on the starboard deck, a torpedo was accidentally released by one of the escorting destroyers. Salt water had worked its way through the firing charge, and caused the detonation mechanism to short circuit. 'This is not a drill! Repeat – this is not a drill!' blared the ship's tannoys, as the vessel swung through a 90-degree turn and accelerated to 31 knots. Sailors scrambled to man the guns, and opened fire in the direction of the torpedo as it sped towards them. Anti-aircraft shells scudded at the underwater target, until, with a dull boom, the warhead was destroyed. As a former assistant secretary of the Navy, Roosevelt watched with fascination. Admiral King, who was travelling with the President, ordered an immediate investigation.[13]

The party arrived two weeks later, after an interlude in Cairo with Churchill and Chiang Kai-Shek, the Chinese nationalist leader. The final leg was by plane, crossing over the Levant and Iraq. Bethlehem, Jerusalem and the valley of the Tigris and Euphrates could be seen clearly from the air. Once in Tehran, the conference ran over four days, with a mixture of formal plenary sessions and informal dinners. Logistical arrangements were made by the Soviets, who had occupied the northern third of Iran, under a joint operation launched with the British the previous year to forestall Nazi subversion. Nervous at the risk from pro-German terrorists, and keen to prevent the British and Americans conferring among themselves, the Soviet delegation insisted on housing Roosevelt at a villa within their own compound.

The British delegation had flown by a similar route, aboard an Avro York aircraft. This was a modified version of the Lancaster bomber, rigged with such comforts for long-distance travel such as a galley that produced warm food. For Jebb, travelling alongside Eden, it was a homecoming. He had been posted to Tehran as a young diplomat in the 1920s, where he served under Harold Nicolson, the acting ambassador, and his wife Vita Sackville-West. He had enjoyed the posting, playing polo, shooting and learning Persian. When he and Eden arrived at the airport, Jebb was greeted by his old language teacher, Dabir-i-Hayyad, whose name translated as 'Felicitous Writer'. To his embarrassment, he found that he could not understand a word.[14]

The next day, 30 November, was a Sunday. At three o'clock in the afternoon, Stalin walked round to Roosevelt's villa. The sky was clear, with a mild autumnal sun. The Soviet leader was simply attired, in a khaki tunic with a single Order of Lenin on his chest. Roosevelt was accompanied by the diplomat Charles Bohlen. At 39, 'Chip', as he was known, was a seasoned Russia hand, who had served in Moscow under Bullitt during the 1930s. Stalin's interpreter, Vladimir Pavlov, completed the group.

'I am glad to see you,' said the President as he reached to shake hands. 'I have tried for a long time to bring this about.'[15]

Afterwards, Roosevelt signed a batch of congressional bills which had arrived by courier. Then he hosted a meal of steak and baked potatoes, cooked by his Filipino mess boys (who had only taken charge of the kitchen four hours earlier). He mixed the cocktails himself, with liberal quantities of vermouth, a little gin and ice. At first, Stalin offered no comment. When Roosevelt pressed him, the dictator replied, 'Well alright, but it is a little cold on the stomach.'[16]

Bohlen listened carefully. Though the Soviet dictator spoke a heavy Georgian-accented Russian, he used full sentences, which gave time to translate. He added short expressions, such as 'I could be wrong, but I think', which seemed to soften his impact. It was intended, Bohlen thought, to convey a certain humbleness of spirit, although he also wondered if it was a façade. On one occasion Bohlen approached him from behind, with a request from the President. Before he had time to look round, Stalin reacted with a curt 'For God's sake!' When he saw that it was an American who had interrupted him, and not one of his own staff, a flash of embarrassment crossed the dictator's face.[17]

Stalin could afford a show of humility. Two years earlier, as German forces threatened to overrun Moscow, all had seemed lost for the Soviet Union. 'Lenin founded our state and we've fucked it up,' he cursed to Molotov.[18] But now, as the year drew to a close, and the Red Army pushed the invaders back into Eastern Europe, new possibilities opened up.

For Stalin himself, it had been a long journey. He was born in 1878, four years after Churchill and three before Roosevelt, at Gori in Georgia. His family name was Djugashvili. The young Joseph, or 'Soso', as he was known, was scarred by smallpox at a young age, and injured his left arm in an accident with a carriage, leaving it shorter than his right. He trained as a priest, then joined the Bolsheviks. Like Molotov, he adopted a revolutionary pseudonym. Stalin meant 'man of steel' in Russian. When Lenin died in 1924, Stalin moved quickly to consolidate his power, eliminating his rivals, including Leon Trotsky, who had built up the Red Army as a defensive shield for the new Soviet state. Now, two decades later, the pockmarked former revolutionary was being courted by the leader of the free world.

Roosevelt was sounding Stalin out. The first meeting had gone well, but not covered any substance. The afternoon timing suited his purpose, in the lull between formal lunch and the full plenary session, which started at four o'clock. It added an air of seclusion, even intimacy. The next day, he decided to repeat the exercise.

Once more, they met at the President's villa.[19] Bohlen and Pavlov interpreted. This time, Roosevelt started with an unusual gesture. Leaning forward, he passed Stalin a clutch of secret papers produced by the US military. One was an assessment of the Yugoslav leader, Marshal Tito, while others covered the campaign against Japan. Stalin thanked him, and promised to return them later.

Following this gesture of trust, Roosevelt launched in. Could they speak freely, he asked, about the future of the world? Stalin nodded. The President continued. He wanted to talk about a new international organisation.

Stalin quickly interjected with a question. Would this be European in scope, or world-wide?

'World-wide,' replied the President. Drawing on the ideas of Pasvolsky and Welles, he set out how it might work. All those countries that made up the wartime United Nations could join. The number had swelled to some 40 since the Oval Office declaration. They would make up a general assembly. But, he added, the organisation needed direction. Therefore, a smaller executive committee would take the key decisions. Within this, the four policemen would have a special status, with permanent seats on the committee.

Stalin listened. Bohlen conveyed his president's ideas into Russian, with Pavlov nodding to verify the translation. Beforehand, Bohlen had worried at whether his command of the language was up to this assignment. During the opening plenary sessions, on military matters, he had stumbled at points over the more technical vocabulary. But Roosevelt was a considerate speaker, and had given the diplomat time to translate each sentence before starting the next.[20]

In the plenary sessions, Stalin had been brusque, even blunt. He had pushed Churchill for a date to launch a cross-channel invasion and relieve pressure on the Red Army. Writing that evening in his diary, Field Marshal Sir Alan Brooke, senior British military representative at the conference, complained that he would rather enter 'a lunatic asylum or nursing home' than carry on. But now, with Roosevelt, Stalin shared a different, more reflective side.[21]

Besides, the proposal was an opportunity. The League of Nations had been stacked against the Soviet Union. But this model was a different proposition. The USSR would sit as one of the great powers. In the years after the revolution, Western governments, including those in which Roosevelt and Churchill served, had tried to stamp out the Bolsheviks by intervention on the side of their opponents, the Whites, during the Russian Civil War. Now, they were offering them a share in running the world.

Stalin was curious about the executive committee. Would its decisions, he asked, be binding?

'Yes and no,' replied Roosevelt. The Council could make recommendations, but not compel sovereign countries, any more than the US Congress could be coerced by a foreign power. At the same time, the great powers should step in to counter aggression before it could gain momentum. If they had acted to close the Suez Canal in 1935, for instance, when Italy had invaded Abyssinia, Mussolini might have been thwarted. Warming to his theme, Roosevelt drew a sketch, with three circles to show the full membership of the United Nations, the executive council, and his four policemen.[22]

For Stalin, this was the reassurance he wanted. Sovereign countries would remain sovereign. He followed with more questions. How would smaller countries react? What about regional councils? Roosevelt ran through his answers.

It was already half past three. Over in the main Russian Embassy building, Churchill was waiting to start the next plenary session. With him, he had brought a ceremonial sword to honour the victory at Stalingrad, four foot in length and forged by the razor-manufacturing company Wilkinson with an inscription from King George VI. The presentation was scheduled to take place in a few minutes. An honour guard from the Royal East Kent Regiment, known as the Buffs, had drawn up with fixed bayonets. Opposite them stood a squad from the Soviet NKVD, in dark blue trousers and black boots. Stalin had dressed up for the occasion in an elaborate new uniform, complete with a single star of the Soviet Union on his chest. The dictator thanked the President, and hurried away to meet the Prime Minister.[23]

The conference was scheduled to finish two days later, on Wednesday 1 December. The US Air Force was anxious not to delay departure. The flight back across the mountains of southern Iran would need good weather. Forecasts suggested that conditions would worsen later in the week.

Roosevelt, however, had unfinished business. On the final afternoon of the conference, he met Stalin one last time. Once more, his villa was the venue. This time, Molotov and Harriman joined the group, along with Bohlen and Pavlov.[24]

The President quickly got down to business. In plenary, Stalin and Churchill had sparred over Poland. It was clear how seriously Stalin took the issue. So, after the group had found their places, Roosevelt dived straight in. He wanted, he said, to take the Soviet leader into his confidence, and talk American politics.

Roosevelt explained. He did not wish to run in the next presidential election, he said. But he might need to. The war might not be over in a year's time, when America would go to the polls. Equally, he understood that Stalin wished to see a revision of Poland's borders after the war. Personally, Roosevelt was sympathetic. However, with six or seven million American voters of Polish origin, he could not be seen to make a decision this side of the election.

Harriman and Bohlen looked on. This was dynamite. A week ago, the President had not even met the Soviet dictator. Now, he was hinting at a possible carve-up of Eastern Europe. Their British allies would be appalled, if they could witness this.

For Stalin, it was the moment for which he had been waiting. When the President finished, he responded. Western participants at the conference had noted how he spoke succinctly and to the point, never using a superfluous word. On this occasion, his comments were even briefer. Now that the President had explained his position, he said, he understood. Nothing more was said on the subject.

A few minutes later, Roosevelt brought up their earlier conversation, on the question of an international organisation. He hoped, he said, that reflection could continue.

Stalin took his cue. He had indeed been thinking it over, he said. He was now in a position to agree with the President. There should be an organisation, and it should be world-wide in scope.

The meeting adjourned. The Soviet delegation left the room. Their work was done.

As he walked away, Bohlen pondered what he had seen. At the start of his diplomatic career, in the 1920s, he had decided to specialise in the Soviet Union. It was an unfashionable choice in the State Department, at a time when the United States did not have diplomatic relations with Moscow. Bohlen had been taught the language by Russian exiles, and was posted to Latvia, in the Baltic, from where the Americans sought to keep track of events inside the Soviet Union. On one occasion he had even travelled up to the border, gazing down a dusty track at the barbed-wire fence and guard towers which separated him from the country on which he had based his career. Like Roosevelt, he believed in engagement with Stalin and the communist regime. He had leapt at the opportunity to accompany Bullitt in setting up an embassy in Moscow after relations were restored in 1934.

Here, at Tehran, he had been witness to the first encounter between an American president and a Soviet leader. It was a momentous occasion. But, he wondered, was this really the right way to go about it? Why had his president chosen to be so frank? Was he really prepared to support Stalin over Poland, or was he just playing for time?[25]

Roosevelt left the villa that night. He was driven in a staff car to the American military compound at Amirabad, which had been built as a transit point for Lend-Lease aid. The next morning, he reviewed a parade of some 3,000 soldiers and airmen, drawn up in ranks on the camp air strip. In the distance, snow could be seen on the Alborz Mountains behind Tehran. Then, at just after a quarter to ten, the presidential plane took off.

With him, in his papers from the conference, Roosevelt carried the sketch that he had drawn for Stalin. His plan was in business.

THREE

Leaving the Shadows

And so, leaning over the waters,
We will float away to oblivion,
And on earth then will cry for us only
Our own shadows which we leave behind.

From 'A Little Song', by Polish poet Krzysztof Baczynski,
who died aged 23 in the Warsaw Uprising[1]

The US Treasury Building lay on the corner of Pennsylvania Avenue and
15th Street. Its distinct classical façade, completed in the 1860s, faced across
to the White House, and, beyond, the Old Executive Office Building. In
front stood a statue of Alexander Hamilton, founding father of the republic
and first treasury secretary.

One hundred and fifty years after Hamilton, Henry Morgenthau held
the post. Like Cordell Hull, he had served through the duration of the
Roosevelt administration. Born into a prominent East Coast Jewish family,
Morgenthau's father, Henry Sr, was ambassador to the Ottoman Empire
during World War I, where he campaigned against the persecution of
Armenians. The Morgenthaus owned a farm in upstate New York, close
to the Roosevelts at Hyde Park. Henry Jr first met Franklin in 1913. More
than 20 years later, as political allies, they continued to enjoy a close
relationship.

For much of the 1930s, Cordell Hull had been in control of the foreign
economic agenda. Morgenthau concentrated on ensuring stable domestic
conditions to underpin the New Deal. With the onset of war, however, he
saw an opportunity to turn the tables. On the morning after the attack on
Pearl Harbor, Morgenthau announced the appointment of a new assistant
secretary to cover foreign economic issues.

His choice for the post was Harry Dexter White. The offspring of Lithuanian Jewish immigrants from Boston, White was born in 1892. His father's original surname, Weiss, had been Americanised at the time of his arrival. A short man with a moustache and rimless glasses, White worked in the family hardware business before serving as a soldier in France during World War I. But his real ambition was to be an academic. At the age of 30, he enrolled at college. Eventually, he earned a PhD from Harvard. Like his contemporary Pasvolsky, White moved to Washington during the early 1930s, where he caught Morgenthau's eye.

A week after his appointment, Morgenthau threw his new assistant secretary an assignment. How, he asked White, were currencies to be managed after the war?

The old system was broken. Before World War I, most countries had tied their currencies to a fixed value in gold, known as the Gold Standard. This had supported an era of globalisation, as European countries expanded into new markets and colonies around the world. But it was a system for capitalists, not workers. To maintain parity with gold, countries had to absorb economic shocks through lower wages and higher unemployment, rather than devaluation. As early as the 1890s, during agricultural depression in the United States, presidential candidate William Jennings Bryan delivered a speech to the Democratic convention with the cry, 'You shall not crucify man upon a cross of gold.' A few years later, the children's book *The Wonderful Wizard of Oz* offered an allegory on gold and its impact on America.

After 1918, with economies mired in debt and unemployment, the system became unsustainable. Britain had returned to the Gold Standard in the wake of World War I, when Churchill was chancellor of the exchequer, but was forced to abandon it again. Roosevelt took America off gold in January 1931. By the late 1930s, the Gold Standard was as broken as the League of Nations.

White saw his opportunity. An ambitious man, with a prickly temper and sharpness that his contemporaries found bruising, White shared his boss's determination to supplant the State Department in the foreign economic field. Assistant Secretary Dean Acheson, who held the equivalent portfolio under Hull, was a particular rival. As Washington settled into life on a war footing, and Churchill arrived to spend Christmas with the President, White set down to work.

* * *

John Maynard Keynes liked challenging orthodoxy. Born in 1883, son of a Cambridge don, the Englishman had grown up in the elegant, assured world of the late Victorian age. He was educated at Eton, a generation before Eden or Jebb, and then at Cambridge. After university, Keynes entered the Treasury, and, as a young official, attended the Paris Conference in 1919. He subsequently made his name with a virulent critique entitled *The Economic Consequences of the Peace*. During the 1920s, he belonged to the so-called Bloomsbury set, which included the writers Virginia Woolf, Lytton Strachey and E. M. Forster. In 1925, he surprised his friends by marrying the Russian ballerina Lydia Lopokova, whose father Fyodor was director of the famed Mariinsky Ballet in Leningrad.

By the 1940s, Keynes had entered the highest ranks of the British establishment. He was a senior adviser in the Treasury, peer in the House of Lords and a member of the Court, or governing board, for the Bank of England. And yet he remained an ambivalent insider. At Cambridge, he had dabbled in both atheism and homosexuality, and the rebellious streak continued through his adult life. 'Rather appalling, I feel, such respectability,' he wrote to his mother after his appointment to the Bank of England. 'It is only a matter of time before I become a Bishop or Dean of York.'[2]

Keynes and White came at the currency question from the same starting point. Both rejected the laissez-faire approach of the Gold Standard, or statist controls embraced by the Soviet Union, or Nazi Germany under Hitler's finance minister Hjalmar Schacht. Instead, they sought a middle way, which would allow countries to trade freely, but without the wrenching adjustments demanded by the Gold Standard. The answer that each identified was to establish a common international fund, to which governments would pay in, and which would then extend lending in hard currency to countries which found themselves in difficulties over the balance of payments.

Hard politics, however, were also at play. The British were engaged in a defensive game. The interwar years had left Britain's economy in a much weakened state. Sterling no longer enjoyed the dominant position as a global reserve currency which it had held in the nineteenth century. Since 1940, war had forced the British further into debt, and made them dependent on American Lend-Lease aid.

White and Morgenthau faced a different situation. The war had galvanised the American economy, raising output, shrinking unemployment, and restoring growth after the Depression. The United States seemed destined to dominate the postwar global economy. The dollar would supplant the pound. Others would want dollars to buy American goods. It was in Washington's interest to fix the rules under which they could obtain them.

Churchill and his government were cautious. At Placentia Bay, Churchill had offered only guarded support for the principle of trade liberalisation, which was the other side of the currency coin. He remained acutely aware that a powerful faction in the Conservative Party, led by the Canadian press magnate Lord Beaverbrook and Leo Amery, secretary of state for India, were wedded to Imperial Preference as a bulwark to safeguard the economic well-being of the British Empire.

Keynes understood the politics, but saw the economic realities too. As Lend-Lease aid poured across the Atlantic, the British economy was becoming a vast war machine fuelled by dollars. Adjustment back to peacetime would be impossible without further American assistance. And the price was to dance to an American tune on trade and currency liberalisation. So, during 1942 and 1943, Keynes made a series of visits to Washington to test the water. He found that he was pushing at an open door. White and Morgenthau were keen to draw the British into talks. By the autumn of 1943, the two sides were in serious negotiations.

Keynes and White made an odd couple. 'What absolute bedlam these discussions are!' noted James Meade, an economist from the British Cabinet Office, in his diary. 'Without any agenda or any prepared idea of what is going to be discussed they go for each other in a strident duet of discord.'[3] Keynes felt no compunction at showing his cleverness, and leaving others feeling snubbed. White, the outsider who had worked his way up the Washington system, saw in his negotiating partner all the qualities he despised in the English upper classes.

By October 1943, as Eden and Hull were preparing for their meeting with Molotov in Moscow, Keynes and White had agreed on the outline of an international fund. But Keynes had overstepped his brief. Back in London, Churchill was reluctant to authorise agreement. Behind the technicalities lay a blunt choice. If the British wanted American aid, they would need to commit to dismantling Imperial Preference. As Morgenthau put it to White, 'Is England going to play with the United Nations, or with the Dominions?'[4]

*　　*　　*

Like Morgenthau, Hull was in a waiting game.

After the meetings in Moscow and Tehran, Pasvolsky and Hull had hoped that momentum was building behind the United Nations. But in the early months of 1944 follow-up approaches to the Kremlin failed to gain traction. The Soviets seemed to have gone quiet. At the other end of Pennsylvania Avenue, impatience was mounting. In February 1944, Joseph Ball published an article with the headline 'Your Move, Mr President'. Now out of office, Sumner Welles produced a book entitled *The Time for Decision*, urging a push to set up the new organisation.

Not everyone agreed. Walter Lippmann, the celebrated newspaper columnist who had attended the Paris Peace Conference, took a different view. In 1943, he had written a book called *US Foreign Policy: Shield of the Republic*, which sold more than a million copies. This argued for bringing the Soviet Union into the Western alliance, as an insurance to keep the peace after the war. An international organisation, Lippmann believed, was no panacea, or substitute for a hard-headed partnership between the great powers. In the spring of 1944, he wrote a sequel, with the title *US War Aims*. It went further, suggesting that the price for peaceful relations with Moscow would be a Soviet *cordon sanitaire* in Eastern Europe.

Meanwhile, the long wait for the liberation of Europe was coming to an end. Plans for the cross-channel invasion, codenamed Overlord, were well advanced. It would be the most complex amphibious operation in military history. Over a million American servicemen had gathered in the United Kingdom. The American general, Dwight Eisenhower, led an international staff which prepared every aspect of the assault in painstaking detail. The exact date for the landings was kept a strict secret, with the code designation 'D-Day'. By April, naval forces were assembling in harbours and estuaries along the southern English coast, ready for the order to embark for France.

Hull and Morgenthau both knew that the moment was ripe. On 9 April, Hull delivered a radio address, announcing that America would host a conference to discuss the new international organisation, and inviting eight senators, including Connally and Vandenberg, to form a committee which would support the negotiations. A few weeks later, Morgenthau followed suit. The US Treasury sent out invitations to some 44 nations, including China and the Soviet Union, for a conference on the international fund. A few days later, on 29 May, Hull did the same for more private consultations on the international organisation, involving the Soviets, British and Chinese.

On the morning of 6 June 1944, Allied troops landed in Normandy, on the northern coast of France. 'The hopes and prayers of liberty-loving peoples everywhere march with you,' declared Eisenhower in a message sent to every member of his force. 'Let us all beseech the blessing of Almighty God upon this great and noble undertaking.'

The Mount Washington Hotel lay among the White Mountains, in upstate New Hampshire. The surrounding parkland was known as Bretton Woods. The hotel was built in 1902 by a coal and railroad magnate, Joseph Stickney. Along the main façade stood five octagonal towers, in an ornate Spanish Renaissance style. The view from the terrace below, a fifth of a mile in length, looked across to Mount Washington, the highest point in New England, and the Ammonoosuc River.

Here, on the afternoon of 1 July 1944, delegates of the United National Monetary and Financial Conference gathered for the opening ceremony. More than 700 assembled in the main hall, resplendent with stained glass, while Morgenthau delivered his welcome address. He read out a message from Roosevelt. 'Commerce is the life blood of a free society,' the President declared. Countries must allow the arteries of free trade to run again.[5]

A three-week ordeal of confusion, late nights and frantic bustle followed. White and Keynes co-chaired. Morgenthau hovered over proceedings, brokering deals in his suite of rooms, which were directly below those of Keynes (and thus vulnerable to disruption from Lydia's dancing exercises on the floor above).

The pressure told on Keynes' health, which had been in gradual decline through the war. On 19 July, he suffered chest pains after running up stairs to see Morgenthau. Rumours spread that it was a heart attack. Keynes' style of chairmanship also caused consternation. 'He knows this thing inside out,' complained Acheson, who attended from the State Department. 'When anybody says Section 15-C he knows what that is [...] Before you have an opportunity to turn to Section 15-C and see what he is talking about, he says, "I hear no objection to that", and it is passed.'[6]

Delegates drew up a charter for what was called the International Monetary Fund, and a parallel International Bank of Reconstruction and Development (later known as the World Bank). One major area of debate was over quotas, which dictated how much a country should pay in, how much it could borrow, and voting weights. As the principle contributor, the United States took the largest share, followed by the United Kingdom and the Soviet Union. In return, countries pledged to hold their currencies at a stable rate with the dollar, which would in turn maintain parity with gold. They also committed to lift controls, so that full convertibility was restored. America would, for its part, maintain the dollar's value. Where countries experienced major problems in their balance of payments, they could temporarily suspend convertibility, and borrow from the fund to tide over a period of adjustment.

If the Soviets agreed to join, it would be a powerful signal that Moscow was prepared to join Washington in rebuilding the new international order. All eyes were on the delegation from Moscow, led by deputy trade commissar Mikhail Stepanov. While the Soviets were keen to access potential American aid, they feared a capitalist trap. The highly technical subject matter didn't help. Their delegates were, as one American put it, 'struggling between the firing squad on the one hand and the English language on the other'.[7]

Even when the formal proceedings closed, on 21 July, the Soviet delegation reserved their final position until they had checked with Moscow. The question of quotas for the International Bank had become a last-minute sticking-point. The following night, as Morgenthau dressed for a celebratory dinner to mark the end of the conference, Stepanov sought him out.

'Mr Stepanov', announced the translator, 'has the answer from Mr Molotov, and that answer is that he is happy to agree to your proposition.'

Morgenthau paused, and checked his understanding. Stepanov explained that his government was prepared to meet its quota for participation.

Morgenthau broke into a smile. 'Well, you tell Mr Molotov', he beamed, 'that I want to thank him from the bottom of my heart.'[8]

Bretton Woods had shown what was possible. In a statement issued at the end of the conference, Keynes picked up on the mood. 'If we can continue in the larger task as we have begun in this limited task,' he declared, in a nod to the United Nations, 'there is hope for the world.'[9] That night, the economist was given a standing ovation as he entered the main hall. At the end of dinner, as he and Morgenthau left, a band struck up 'For He's A Jolly Good Fellow' and 'The Star-Spangled Banner'.

*   *   *

The War Office faced across Whitehall, a couple of hundred yards up from Downing Street and the Foreign Office. This neo-baroque building was erected in 1906, when British military strength stood at its zenith. Inside, two and a half miles of corridors and a thousand rooms contained the central nervous system for Britain's military effort across the globe. In front stood a statue of Field Marshal Alexander Haig, commander of the British Army on the Western Front during World War I. Cast in bronze, on horseback, he gazed down Whitehall to the Cenotaph, a simple classical obelisk erected by the architect Edwin Lutyens in 1920 to commemorate the war dead.

In late July 1944, Gladwyn Jebb took the short walk up Whitehall to the War Office. Jebb had come to brief the chiefs of staff. It was a serious assignment. The chiefs sat at the apex of Britain's war effort, with some five million men and women in uniform around the world.

Their head was Field Marshal Sir Alan Brooke, who had taken over from Sir John Dill in December 1941, and accompanied Churchill to Tehran. Brooke was an Ulsterman. He had served as a young artillery officer in World War I and commanded an army corps during the retreat to Dunkirk in 1940. He was joined by Admiral Sir Andrew Cunningham, the First Sea Lord, and Air Chief Marshal Sir Charles Portal, who led the Royal Air Force. Portal had been a fighter pilot on the Western Front, flying primitive biplanes, while Cunningham had commanded a destroyer that saw action in the Dardanelles campaign.

Brooke felt a deep responsibility in his role. Though not a religious man, his first reaction when Churchill offered him the job was to kneel and pray for divine guidance.[10] Over the years since, he had learned to be robust, including with the Prime Minister. 'When I thump the table and push my face towards him, what does he do?' lamented Churchill on one occasion. 'Thumps the table harder and glares back at me!'[11]

Jebb brought with him a paper entitled 'British Policy Towards Europe'. It contained a bombshell. The diplomat remained committed to working with the Americans on the United Nations. But, like Lippmann, he was a realist. Over the proceeding months, he had drafted and redrafted his paper, trying to imagine what Europe after the war would look like. Others offered advice, including Frank Roberts, who headed the Central Department, in charge of continental European affairs. Duff Cooper, the Conservative politician and former diplomat whom Churchill had removed from the Ministry of Information, provided views from his new role as liaison to the exiled French authorities in Algiers.

The meeting lasted 45 minutes. Jebb gave a short introduction. His thesis was simple. Co-operation between the great powers might work. But, equally, Europe could fall victim to what he dubbed *Machtpolitik*, or 'power politics', as the Soviet Union sought to establish its sphere of influence deep into the European continent. Picking up Duff Cooper's analysis, Jebb argued that Britain would need to gather together France and others into a defensive Western alliance. And, most unthinkable of all, a defeated Germany might also need to be a part.

When Jebb finished, the chiefs reflected on what they had heard. The mood was sombre. Was another war really around the corner? If so, commented Portal, then they might as well appoint their own successors there and then, to start planning for it. And what to do in the meantime?

That night, Brooke turned over this vision of the future in his head. If the Soviet Union was certain to be a threat, the prudent course was to start rehabilitating Germany now, while maintaining the guise of friendship with Moscow. It was an awesome prospect. Were the politicians, he wondered, up to the task?[12]

Chukotka was one of the most remote places on the planet. This icy peninsula stood on the far eastern point of Siberia, across the Bering Straits from Alaska. To the north lay the Arctic, and to the south the vast, frozen wastes of the Magadan region. In the 1940s, this desolate place was home to many of the labour camps where prisoners of Stalin's regime were detained. The largest in the region, named Sevvostlag ('North-East Camp', in the Russian acronym), housed 200,000 people.[13]

It was an unlikely spot for international diplomacy. But here, three weeks after the Bretton Woods Conference, the Soviet diplomat Andrei Gromyko found himself grounded. During wartime, the safest air route between Moscow and Washington was a gruelling five-day trek across Siberia and the Bering Straits. Soviet pilots called it the 'Mazaruk line', after Ilya Mazaruk, an aviator and Hero of the Soviet Union. American aircraft supplied under Lend-Lease were ferried from Fairbanks in Alaska across to the battlefront in Europe. A string of makeshift airstrips supported this traffic, including the tiny settlement of Uelkal on the southern coast of Chukotka. It was here that, in hurricane winds, the plane carrying Gromyko was forced to land.

Gromyko had just turned 35. Born to a peasant family in Byelorussia, on the western borders of Poland, he had joined the Communist Party as a student, moved to Moscow and become an economist at the Soviet Academy of Sciences. In 1939, he joined the Foreign Ministry. His first assignment was to head the department covering America.

Six months later, on the personal orders of Stalin, Gromyko was posted to Washington as deputy ambassador. Then, in August 1943, he was elevated to the top job. When Hull announced that he would host the United Nations Conference in Washington, Gromyko was the obvious choice to head the Soviet delegation.

It was a delicate assignment. A couple of weeks before, Gromyko had written a long paper for Molotov on relations between Washington and Moscow after the war. This mostly took an optimistic line. He judged that interests between the two powers would be compatible, although Eastern Europe might be a source of tension.[14] Venturing such judgements was the role of the diplomat. But, in Stalin's Soviet Union, it was wise to tread carefully. For those who overstepped the mark, the camps of Magadan were never far away. Ahead of the conference, Gromyko decided to return to Moscow and confirm his instructions in person.

On the way back, Gromyko and his colleagues were stuck in Uelkal for 24 hours. At one point, they ventured outside the airfield, braving the icy winds to visit a communal hut. There, sitting alongside the local Siberian inhabitants, they watched film clips of the war.

Great events were unfolding. On the plains of Byelorussia, where Gromyko had grown up, the Red Army had launched a vast offensive. It was codenamed Bagration, after the tsarist general who fought Napoleon. Some 400,000 German soldiers, from Army Group Centre, were captured. One column, of 60,000 men, was made to march through the streets of Moscow, and across Red Square, to imprisonment in Siberia. At the front, captured German generals and staff officers still held their heads high. But behind them their soldiers were a pitiful mob, dirty and unshaven. Soviet guards on horseback hastened them along. At the rear, trucks with tanks of disinfectant sprayed the streets. The invaders, like vermin, were being expelled from Russian soil.[15]

* * *

As a businessman, Edward Stettinius liked efficiency. The 43-year-old was born in Chicago, to a successful business family. He joined General Motors after World War I. Five years later he was a vice-president of the company, and by 1938 Stettinius had risen to be chairman of US Steel. During the war, Roosevelt brought him into government to run the Lend-Lease programme.

In September 1943, following Welles' departure, Stettinius joined the State Department as under-secretary. He set about introducing business methods to the moribund organisation, even drawing up an elaborate diagram to show how the different divisions should work together. But old hands were not willing to play along, and the initiative floundered.[16]

Handsome, with snowy white hair, dark eyebrows and teeth that flashed with his smile, Stettinius was a natural host. As a venue for the talks, Hull and Stettinius had chosen the elegant setting of Dumbarton Oaks, a classical mansion in Georgetown, on the outskirts of the capital. Originally built in 1801, the house was acquired in 1920 by Robert Woods Bliss, a former American diplomat, and his wife Mildred. They were enthusiastic patrons of the arts, and turned the house into a cultural centre.

The Washington Conversations on International Peace and Security, as the conference was titled, opened on 21 August. The main sessions took place in the music room, an ornate space decorated with Italian Renaissance tapestries. Here, before the war, the composer Igor Stravinsky had conducted a premiere of his *Concerto in E Flat*, later named after Dumbarton Oaks. Stettinius, anxious to make a splash in the media, brought in movie cameras to film the opening ceremony. Outside, the Washington summer was at its peak, while, indoors, bright arc lights blazed down. The delegates sweated through their introductory speeches.

The delegations were arranged around three sides of an open square. Stettinius presided. Gromyko represented the Soviet Union and Alexander Cadogan from the Foreign Office was there for the United Kingdom, along with Jebb and Cadogan's private secretary, Peter Loxley. Leo Pasvolsky sat next to Stettinius. This was the moment for which the émigré had been waiting.

The task before the delegates was to draft a charter for the new international organisation. Ahead of Dumbarton Oaks, the British and Soviets had signalled that they were prepared to accept Pasvolsky's draft as a basis. This followed the plan which Roosevelt had outlined to Stalin at Tehran. The new organisation would have a general assembly, with all participating countries, and a security council, to handle executive action on matters of peace and security.

Stettinius was optimistic. With brisk organisation, and genial hospitality, he hoped that Dumbarton Oaks could be as swift and successful as the Bretton Woods Conference had been. To break the ice, he organised an enthusiastic programme of social events.

On the first weekend, he took his guests up to New York. The delegates enjoyed a yacht trip in the harbour, and spent an evening at Billy Rose's Diamond Horseshoe, where they watched a performance by the Rockettes, a popular female dance troupe. While Gromyko made his excuses, Jebb and Cadogan came along for the ride. After the show, a beaming Stettinius took his guests backstage to meet the scantily clad chorus girls.[17] Asked to speak, the usually eloquent Cadogan offered a few awkward words. He was followed by a Soviet general, standing in for Gromyko, who cheerfully rose to the occasion. Among these beautiful girls, he declared, he had at last attained the paradise for which he had been fighting since the start of the war.[18]

Meanwhile, at the conference, progress was more mixed. During the first days, all had seemed well. Stettinius and Cadogan found that they could deal with Gromyko, if in a stilted way. They took to resolving awkward points during walks together around the spacious gardens. For the three delegation heads, it was easier to meet in a more limited group than the plenary sessions, which they called the joint steering committee. Stettinius hosted this group at his office in the library, rather than the larger music room.

Here, a week into the conference, Gromyko dropped a bombshell. On 28 August, the three delegations discussed voting arrangements in the security council. The conference had already agreed that the Soviet Union, United Kingdom and the United States should be permanent members of the council, along with China and France. In addition, Pasvolsky argued that they should be excluded from voting on any dispute to which they were a party.[19]

Gromyko interjected. Special arrangements would be required to address this point, he said.

Cadogan sensed that something was wrong. He looked at the Soviet diplomat, who at 35 was almost half his age. Would it be possible to resolve this during the conference, he asked?

His counterpart was non-committal. It might be possible to make a proposal, he suggested, weakly.

This was, Cadogan retorted, a serious matter. If it could not be resolved, progress would be very difficult. Pasvolsky agreed. There was, he added, no simple way to make special arrangements. As equal partners, the permanent members could not vote on disputes to which they were a party. This was crucial if the council was to be credible and effective.

A few minutes later, Gromyko dropped a further bombshell. The Soviet Union was comprised of 16 socialist republics. It followed, he said, that they should all have membership of the United Nations.

The room fell silent. Eventually, Cadogan spoke. He could, he said, make no comment. Stettinius agreed. There was nothing more to be said.

The Soviet position was dynamite. Gromyko's second demand, in particular, looked like a blatant attempt to pack the new organisation with extra Soviet votes. That afternoon, Stettinius rushed to the White House. He met Roosevelt soon after five o'clock, alone. 'My God!' exclaimed the President, when Stettinius explained the news.[20]

If news leaked, public furore could kill off the whole project. James 'Scotty' Reston, a celebrated journalist with the *New York Times*, had already broken a series of well-sourced stories on what was happening at Dumbarton Oaks. Back at the State Department, Stettinius locked his papers in a safe. In correspondence, he simply referred to Gromyko's demand for extra votes as the 'X Matter'.

While deadlock loomed at Dumbarton Oaks, in Europe the tide of the war was flowing fast. After two months of gruelling combat, Allied forces had broken out of the bridgehead established at D-Day. In mid-August, they liberated Paris. Tank columns raced towards the German border and the Rhine. It looked as if the war might be over in a matter of weeks.

Meanwhile, on the Eastern Front, tragedy unfolded. Following the German invasion of Poland in 1939, an underground resistance movement had formed, called the Home Army. It was under the command of General Tadeusz Komorowski, who reported to the Polish government-in-exile based in

London. But in Moscow the Soviets played host to a separate administration, led by communists. After news of the massacre at Katyn had broken in 1943, the London Poles severed links with the Soviet Union. Two rival governments-in-exile watched each other, from opposite sides of war-torn Europe.

As Soviet forces entered Poland from the east, the Home Army decided to make a move. On 31 July, some 40,000 resistance fighters launched an uprising in Warsaw. Their plan was to seize control, and establish a government before the Soviets could forestall them. It was a tragic miscalculation.

The Soviets slowed their advance, eventually halting on the bank of the Vistula River. The Home Army initially gained control of a large area in the centre of the city, but were then beaten back by savage German counter-attacks. Conditions inside the enclave became desperate. The Soviets stalled attempts by the Western allies to airdrop relief supplies.

Watching events from Moscow, Ambassador Averell Harriman despaired. Earlier in the summer he had been joined by a new deputy at the embassy. Born in 1904, George Kennan was from the same generation as Bohlen. The two men had studied Russian together, and served in Moscow under Bullitt. Harriman had been keen to have one of these Soviet specialists on his staff. After Tehran, Roosevelt had asked Bohlen to join him in the White House as a special adviser on the Soviet Union. The State Department assigned Kennan to Harriman.[21]

Harriman and Kennan found themselves plunged into handling the diplomatic fallout of the uprising. The British and American governments hoped that some compromise might be possible between the London Poles and Stalin. But Harriman's efforts failed to bear fruit. Late one night, Kennan saw his ambassador return from one particularly difficult round of talks at the Kremlin. He looked shattered.[22] Harriman and his daughter Kathleen had started their posting in high spirits. She had even competed alongside the Soviet downhill ski team. But reality was catching up with them. Kennan was more sanguine. His first encounter with Russia, a decade before, had left him with a dark view of the Soviet mind. The confrontation over Warsaw did not surprise him. There was, he wrote in his diary, little choice but to 'bow our heads in silence before the tragedy of a people who have been our allies, whom we have saved from our enemies, and whom we cannot save from our friends'.[23]

* * *

Back at Dumbarton Oaks, Stettinius decided to try upping the ante. On the morning of Friday 8 September, he accompanied Gromyko to a call on the White House. It was, as he recorded in his notes, 'our biggest and last remaining gun'.[24]

They met Roosevelt in his bedroom, on the first floor. The President had been briefed by Stettinius in advance. He decided to adopt a homespun approach. The voting issue, he explained, reflected an Anglo-Saxon sense of fair play. Under the common law tradition, parties to a dispute were barred from sitting in judgement. So husbands could not sit in jury on their wives, and vice versa.[25]

Gromyko respected Roosevelt. The diplomat had first seen the President when he spoke at the formal opening of the new National Gallery in Washington, in March 1941. He had admired the way that the polio victim walked to the podium and delivered his speech. Like Alistair Cooke, the British journalist, Gromyko saw in Roosevelt's struggle with the disease a triumph of the human spirit.[26]

As the President spoke, Gromyko listened respectfully, and said that he would report back.

Roosevelt could see that Gromyko was stuck. When a difficult point had come up earlier in the conference, Cadogan had quickly realised that Gromyko would not dare stray a 'hair's breadth' from his instructions.[27] The same was true now. The President asked if a message from himself to Stalin would help. Gromyko replied that this was a decision for Roosevelt.

Roosevelt understood. When Gromyko had left, he summoned Bohlen. This task needed someone who understood the Soviet mind. Together, they crafted a cable making a personal plea to Stalin.

While the delegates waited to hear the outcome, Stettinius took Cadogan, along with the Chinese delegation, on an excursion in the Virginia countryside. Sixteen limousines conveyed the party, with police escorts and sirens wailing. The group drove up into the hills for lunch, followed by a retinue of photographers snapping pictures. In the afternoon they stopped at Monticello, the house that had belonged to the revolutionary leader Thomas Jefferson, and then Montpelier, where James Madison had lived. Stettinius led them with boyish enthusiasm. 'Okay, boys!' he boomed as he strode around, and 'Now, boys, we'll go along here!' The climax was a buffet supper at the former steel magnate's own house, called Horseshoe, which dated back to the eighteenth century. His wife, three sons and their Dalmatian dog greeted the party, along with an African-American quartet singing Negro spirituals. Stettinius proudly showed off his turkey farm, which contained over 1,000 birds, and a state coach in the stables which was said to have belonged to the German Kaiser Wilhelm II.[28]

The following Wednesday, 13 September, Gromyko reported back to Stettinius and Cadogan. His instructions had come through from Moscow. There was no change in the Soviet position.

Stettinius spoke first. The news, he said, came as a great blow. It was difficult to see how public opinion could accept a United Nations in which countries could sit in judgement on their own disputes. Cadogan agreed.

Pasvolsky was sitting beside Stettinius, unusually taciturn.

'The Ambassador's statement', he commented, looking at Gromyko, 'alters the whole situation.'[29]

That night, the usually optimistic Stettinius felt low. He talked over the impasse with Joseph Grew, a veteran diplomat who had served at the Paris Peace Conference and was ambassador in Tokyo at the time of Pearl Harbor. Negotiations were always like this, Grew said. He encouraged the Secretary to persevere.[30]

For another two weeks, Stettinius and Pasvolsky tried to find a way through. A sub-committee, called the 'Formulations Group', was formed with Jebb and Andrei Sobolev, Gromyko's deputy. But no progress was forthcoming. Tempers started to fray. 'You can't have an international organisation without us,' Gromyko said bluntly in a private conversation with Stettinius. 'We can't have one without you.'[31]

After the success of Bretton Woods, Dumbarton Oaks was coming unstuck. Stettinius decided to cut his losses. On the afternoon of 27 September, he visited the White House, and briefed Roosevelt. With no agreement forthcoming on the key issues, it was time to park talks until the President could engage directly with Stalin. Roosevelt agreed. Presidential elections were looming, in early November. There was no more that could be done. Nonetheless, Roosevelt said he was optimistic. Hopkins, who was also present, congratulated Stettinius. It was, he said, a magnificent job.[32]

The next day, Stettinius brought the talks to a close. He announced that the United States would publish the draft charter anyway. On the question of voting, the text would simply be silent. The 'X Matter', as Stettinius had called it, would also remain secret. In the circumstances, it was the best that could be done.

That weekend, Cadogan flew back to London, his suitcase loaded with American luxuries for his wife, Theodosia. After six weeks away, it was good to be back. Their first granddaughter, Lavinia, had been born ten days before.[33]

On the same weekend, after 63 days of resistance, Komorowski ordered the men and women of the Home Army to surrender. From Warsaw's population of a million people, a quarter had been injured or killed.[34]

'The fate of the world', wrote the Polish poet Kazimierz Wierzynski, 'has been written in the fate of one city.'[35]

FOUR

Drawing Up Account

When the time comes to draw up our account,
To reckon what the enemy must pay,
We shall remember all.

From 'The Reckoning', a wartime poem by
Soviet writer Anton Prisheletz[1]

Fala, Roosevelt's four-year-old Scottish terrier, was about to enter the election campaign.

In June 1944, the Republican convention picked Thomas Dewey, governor of New York, to run against Roosevelt. Dewey was a moderate and internationalist, who opposed the isolationist wing of the party led by Robert Taft. In the primaries, his electoral machine quickly knocked out potential rivals, including Wendell Willkie, who had run in 1940. After 12 years out of power, the Republicans were determined to mount a serious challenge for the White House.

It looked as if they might have a chance. Writing in his regular newspaper column, Walter Lippmann concluded that Roosevelt looked 'weak and exhausted'.[2] In early August, following a tour of Pearl Harbor and Alaska, the President had given a campaign speech at Bremerton shipyard, on the Pacific Coast. It had been a lacklustre performance. Standing on the foredeck of a naval destroyer, in a strong wind, he struggled to control his papers and keep his balance. Afterwards, he collapsed in the captain's cabin, drenched in sweat. Across the country, voters started to wonder if the President was up to the job.

Roosevelt's campaign team was worried. Hopkins summoned back Robert Sherwood, presidential speechwriter, from a visit to the battlefront in France. At the midterms in 1942, large numbers of Democrat voters had failed to register. Polling suggested that this was happening again. A small turnout would work in the Republicans' favour.

In mid-September, Roosevelt had travelled up to Quebec in Canada for a conference with Churchill. On his return to Washington, his campaign swung into action. The press had been buzzing with rumours, planted by the Republicans, that after the Alaskan trip Roosevelt had sent his destroyer back to pick up Fala, who had supposedly been left behind on the Aleutian Islands. The filmmaker Orson Welles spotted that the story might make a good joke on the campaign trail, and wrote to the President with the suggestion. Fala was a constant companion in the White House, and had become famous across America. Roosevelt seized on the idea.[3]

A week later, on 23 September, Roosevelt gave a speech to the International Brotherhood of Teamsters. The union was one of the largest blue-collar organisations in America, and a backbone of the Democratic Party. His remarks were broadcast by radio across the country.

'Fala resents this!' he declared. 'I am accustomed to hearing malicious falsehoods about myself but I think I have a right to object to libellous statements about my dog.' The audience erupted with laughter. Afterwards, telegrams and letters poured in to the White House from around the country, addressed to Fala. Roosevelt was back in the fight.[4]

In the corridors of the Foreign Office, officials and ministers were drawing their own conclusions from Warsaw and Dumbarton Oaks. The advance towards Germany had ground to a halt. In mid-September, a bold attempt to seize a bridge over the Rhine by airborne assault failed, at Arnhem in the Netherlands. Meanwhile, the Red Army continued its advance into Eastern Europe, sweeping through Romania and Bulgaria. Jebb's dark warnings about Soviet *Machtpolitik* looked prescient.

Churchill decided to try his luck with a visit to Moscow. At midnight on 7 October, the prime ministerial party took off from RAF Northolt in an Avro York. The journey took 34 hours, travelling to Naples, then on to Cairo, across the Aegean, Dardanelles, Black Sea, and over the Crimea into Russia. On the instructions of King George VI, Eden took a separate flight – Churchill had designated the Foreign Secretary as his successor in case of death. It was a wise precaution. On the flight, the prime ministerial doctor,

Charles Wilson, found his charge dozing with an oxygen mask and lighted cigar in his lap, moments from combustion.[5]

The party arrived in Moscow on 9 October. The aircraft initially landed at the wrong aerodrome, 30 kilometres away. When it finally reached the right destination, there was a brief panic when the landing undercarriage jammed.[6] Churchill was driven to Molotov's dacha, or country retreat, some 20 miles outside the city, while Eden lodged at the British Embassy, an ornate nineteenth-century mansion on the opposite bank of the Moskva River to the Kremlin.

The visit lasted for ten days. On the first night, Churchill and Eden met with Stalin and Molotov, at the Soviet leader's quarters in the Kremlin. Arthur Birse, the embassy interpreter, joined them. Birse had originally worked in Russia as a businessman before the revolution. He joined the British Army at the outbreak of war, already 50, and was assigned to act as a translator in the Intelligence Corps. His opposite number was Pavlov, the same man who had worked with Bohlen. Outside, the first chill of autumn was descending. After years of war, Moscow was coming back to life. Camouflage had been dismantled from the walls of the Kremlin, and workmen were restoring the red-brick mausoleum in Red Square where Lenin's body was embalmed.

The Prime Minister made his pitch. Soviet forces were entering the Balkans, he said. But the British were also active in the region, with special agents and, since October, a military mission in liberated Greece. To avoid tension, he suggested the two powers should agree a simple division of interests.

To illustrate his point, Churchill took out a pen. Writing down a list of countries, he added percentages next to them. Romania would be 90 per cent under Soviet influence, with 10 per cent for the UK and USA. Bulgaria would be split 75 against 25, while Yugoslavia and Hungary would both be 50–50. Greece would be 90 per cent for the UK.

Birse translated, taking hurried notes as he did so. He had already performed the role for Churchill at Tehran, a year before. At one point, he had translated between Churchill and Stalin for seven hours without a break. It was, he later reflected, rather like a musician working with a composer's score. The interpreter had to stay true to the words that his boss had spoken, but give them cadence and tone in another language.[7]

On this occasion, little interpretation was required. Churchill passed the paper across to Stalin. The Soviet leader paused, then, with a blue pencil, made a large tick. The paper remained on the table. Both men were silent.

After a long pause, Churchill spoke. 'Might it not be thought rather cynical', he observed, 'if it seemed we had disposed of these issues, so fateful to millions of people, in such an offhand manner? Let us burn the paper.'[8]

Birse and Pavlov watched each other. As with Bohlen, they worked alternately, each translating from his mother tongue into that of the other. Occasionally Stalin would snap under his breath at his compatriot, telling him not to dawdle. Birse could sympathise with the pressure. At such moments, the exact choice of word was crucial.[9]

'No,' replied Stalin. 'You keep it.'

Churchill left for the night. 'I have had very nice talks with the Old Bear,' he wrote to his wife Clementine a few days later. 'Now they respect us here and I am sure that they wish to work with us.'[10] A couple of nights later, Churchill hosted Stalin for dinner at the British Embassy. It was the first time that Stalin had set foot in the ornate building, which was originally built by Pavel Kharitonenko, a nineteenth-century industrialist who made his fortune from sugar beet in the Ukraine. Over dinner, he gestured to a full-length portrait of King George V hanging on the dining-room wall. The bearded monarch had often been compared in appearance to the last of the Romanov tsars. 'Is that our Nicholas II?' asked Stalin.[11]

In return, Stalin hosted Churchill at the Bolshoi Theatre, in his first appearance at the venue since the start of the war. The Red Army Choir gave a rousing performance of patriotic songs and dances. Harriman and his daughter Kathleen accompanied them. When the audience saw the two leaders, they burst into applause. The sound was, Kathleen later told her sister, 'like a cloudburst on a tin roof'.[12]

On the night of 17 October, Churchill and Stalin held a final meeting. They dined on pork, and talked until four o'clock in the morning. The atmosphere mellowed. Stalin reminisced about his days spent in exile in Siberia, and joked about Churchill's support for the Whites in the Civil War. It was, they agreed, another era.

'A man's eyes should be torn out', concluded Stalin, 'if he can only see the past.'[13]

* * *

Fala had put his master back in the race. But Dewey had other lines of attack.

At the meeting with Roosevelt in Quebec, Treasury Secretary Henry Morgenthau had persuaded Churchill to sign up to a plan. White had drafted the text for him. It was entitled 'Program to Prevent Germany from Starting World War III'. This called for a punitive settlement after the war, dismantling German industry and reducing her economy to an agricultural base. Though the link was not made explicit, Morgenthau implied that it was the price for an American commitment to provide Lend-Lease during the period between the defeat of Germany and that of Japan, when the British hoped to start shifting their economy back to a peacetime footing. When they heard what had happened, both Cordell Hull and Henry Stimson, secretary of war, were appalled.

Days after Quebec, news of this so-called Morgenthau Plan had leaked. In Berlin, propaganda chief Joseph Goebbels seized on the story. As American forces crossed the German border, along the edges of the Rhineland, resistance stiffened. Stories started to circulate in the American press that the Morgenthau Plan was to blame. Roosevelt was forced to back away from the proposal. But the electoral damage was done. On 18 October, in a speech at the Waldorf-Astoria in New York, Dewey lambasted Roosevelt and Morgenthau for creating what he called a 'first-class cabinet crisis', and putting the lives of American servicemen at risk.

Roosevelt was determined to hit back. The fight with Dewey had breathed energy into him. On 21 October, he travelled to New York. He spent four hours touring around all five boroughs of the city in an open-topped car, despite steady rain and the autumn chill. Some three million people turned out to watch. On Ebbets Field, home ground of the Brooklyn Dodgers, the President stepped from the car, and walked to a lectern, while onlookers cheered. Six days later Roosevelt visited Philadelphia, then Chicago, where he spoke at Soldier Field, the huge football stadium on the Near South Side. Standing next to his boss, speechwriter Robert Sherwood gazed out at the vast crowd of 100,000 people, illuminated in the darkness by searchlights. As each line of the speech reverberated through loudspeakers, waves of applause rolled back from across the ground.[14]

On the evening of 7 November, the President and his entourage returned to Hyde Park, the Roosevelt country estate in upstate New York. The candidate listened in the library as results came in on the radio. By late evening, it was clear that he had won, with 36 states and 432 votes in the electoral college.

It was a victory, but not a landslide. In the popular vote, Dewey had scored a credible 22 million, against 25.6 million for Roosevelt. Compared to his earlier victories, in 1932, 1936 and 1940, this was a much reduced majority. Lippmann, like many of his readers, had decided to back Roosevelt more through Dewey's shortcomings than real conviction. The *New York Times* only endorsed him with 'deep reluctance and strong misgivings'.[15]

Cordell Hull was tired. In late October, he had been admitted to the Bethesda Military Hospital outside Washington with tuberculosis and diabetes. His wife thought that the spat with Morgenthau over Germany had weakened him.

With the election over, Hull decided that the moment had come. On 27 November, Roosevelt announced that his secretary of state had tendered his resignation. It was a painful moment. 'The end of a long career is at hand,' noted his friend, Assistant Secretary Breckinridge Long, 'ending not in satisfaction, as it should, but in bitterness.'[16]

Roosevelt had a successor in mind. James Byrnes was a former senator and Supreme Court judge. During the war he ran the Office of War Mobilisation, which oversaw the domestic war effort. But Hopkins advised against. He recommended Stettinius instead. The businessman would, he reasoned, not stand in the way of Roosevelt's personal diplomacy with Stalin. The President agreed. On the first day after Hull's departure, the former steel executive stepped up to his new role.

Dumbarton Oaks was supposed to be a stepping stone. Originally, Stettinius and Pasvolsky had envisaged that the next stage would be a wider conference to negotiate the charter, in the same mould as Bretton Woods. Stettinius had even discussed possible venues with Roosevelt. Both men were keen on French Lick, a small spa town in southern Indiana, where Roosevelt had announced his first run for the presidency in 1931. But deadlock at Dumbarton Oaks had knocked this plan off track.

With the election over, Roosevelt was keen to meet with Stalin. During November and December, the two men exchanged suggestions on a possible location. Eventually, they settled on Yalta, a resort in the Crimea, on the Black Sea.

On 20 January 1945, Roosevelt took the oath as president again. It was the first inauguration held under wartime conditions, and a more modest affair than previous occasions. The ceremony was held on the south portico of the White House, rather than the Capitol, where presidents had been inaugurated since the days of Abraham Lincoln. Three days later, the presidential party set sail from Newport News, a naval base in Virginia, aboard the heavy cruiser USS *Quincy*. The ship had taken part in the D-Day landings: her eight-inch guns had provided covering fire for American troops landing on the beach codenamed Utah, at the western end of the assault zone. The voyage lasted nine days, following a zig-zag course to avoid U-boats. While aboard, Roosevelt celebrated his sixty-third birthday. A tea party was held in his quarters, with his daughter, Anna Boettiger, acting as hostess. First the commissioned officers presented him with a cake, then the warrant officers, then the enlisted men. In the end, five cakes were laid out on the table, with a single candle for the President to blow out.[17]

The flotilla landed at Malta on 2 February, where the President held a brief meeting with Churchill. Then, early the following morning, his party set off by air, aboard a newly modified C-54 transport plane. Nicknamed the *Sacred Cow*, it was the first aircraft dedicated for presidential use, with a sleeping area, radio telephone and retractable elevator to lift Roosevelt in his wheelchair.

Nearly 12 hours later, they arrived at Saki airfield, in the Crimea. Roosevelt was met by Molotov, and, sitting in an American military jeep, inspected a Soviet honour guard. The drive to Yalta, some 90 miles away, lasted three hours, snaking across the Crimean Mountains, which separated the coast from the interior. Soviet soldiers lined the route every few hundred yards. Roosevelt travelled in a Packard limousine loaned by Stalin. Anna, worried about his father's fragile health, shooed away his entourage and travelled alone with the President.[18]

The British journey was marred by tragedy. The support party flew from RAF Lyneham, bound for Malta, in two transport aircraft. The diplomat Gladwyn Jebb travelled aboard one, which was diverted to Naples. The second came down in the sea off Lampedusa, where it hit a submerged reef. Thirteen out of 20 passengers on board were killed, including Peter Loxley, Cadogan's private secretary who had been at Dumbarton Oaks, and Captain Barney Charlesworth, an aide to Brooke.

The British party was devastated at the loss. Pierson Dixon, the principal private secretary to Eden, had been responsible for drawing up the delegation list. Racked with guilt after the tragedy, he found it difficult to sleep.[19]

The Livadia Palace was an unusual choice of venue for a Soviet leader. The villa was built in the years before World War I for the last Russian tsar, Nicholas II. It stood on a promontory above the Black Sea, in Italian Renaissance style, with ornate colonnades overlooking shady garden courtyards. After the revolution in 1917, Nicholas' mother, the Dowager Empress, fled to the palace. She was later rescued by the Royal Navy. In July 1942, following the capture of the Crimea, the German general Erich von Manstein was awarded a field marshal's baton at a ceremony in the grounds. Dixon thought that the landscape came from another era. It had, he noted in his diary, a 'strangely melancholy character'.[20]

The Americans were allocated rooms in the palace. As at Tehran, the British were given separate quarters, in the neighbouring Vorontsov Palace, some 30 minutes away. Roosevelt took a suite on the first floor, close to the ballroom where plenary sessions were held. Admiral King was assigned to the former boudoir of the tsarina. Kathleen Harriman had travelled down from Moscow by train in advance to oversee preparations. 'I never quite realised that so many things could go wrong in so many ways,' she lamented in a letter to her sister.[21] Birse found his interpretation skills pushed to the limit. In between working sessions, he was required to negotiate with the Russian domestic staff over one headache after another.[22]

When he arrived at Yalta, Bohlen found a letter from Kennan in the diplomatic pouch. Writing from Moscow, his friend expressed concern at the way that the United States was acquiescing in Soviet expansion across Eastern Europe. The United Nations was a lost cause. Why not just make a clean break and recognise different spheres of influence? Bohlen scribbled a hasty reply. Such a view was 'naïve'. The American public had no appetite for confrontation with Moscow. 'Quarrelling with [the Soviets] would be so easy,' he concluded, 'but we can always come to that.' In the meantime, the challenge was to find a way of making the relationship work.[23]

At four o'clock on the afternoon of 4 February, Stalin drew up at the Livadia Palace, for a private meeting with Roosevelt before the main conference began. As at Tehran, he was accompanied by Molotov and Pavlov.

The Generalissimo walked upstairs to meet Roosevelt. The President was waiting in what had been the tsar's antechamber, together with Bohlen. Entering the room, Stalin broke into a smile, and shook Roosevelt warmly by the hand. He sat down next to the President on a divan, under a painting of a frozen Russian landscape. Robert Hopkins, son of Harry and a photographer with the US Signals Corps, snapped a picture of the scene.[24]

The two leaders launched into a discussion of the military situation. Joking, Roosevelt reminded Stalin of his dinner that he had hosted at Tehran, when both men teased Churchill with pointed jokes. Stalin had offered a toast to the execution of 50,000 German officers, which had almost prompted Churchill to walk out. Perhaps his host would like to do the same again. The British, the President added later, liked to 'have their cake and eat it'. Bohlen explained the phrase to Stalin.[25]

Immediately afterwards, the two men went through to the ballroom for the first plenary session of the conference. Churchill, Roosevelt and Stalin sat at a large, round table, flanked by their foreign ministers, interpreters and military staff. There were some 15 seats in all. More junior participants occupied a second circle of chairs, or hung around in the adjoining rooms, hoping for an excuse to join the main conference. Harriman called this condition 'conference fever'. James Byrnes, the former senator, had joined the American delegation at Roosevelt's request, and proved to be a particular victim. On one occasion, when he was excluded from the plenary, Anna was obliged to soothe his bruised feelings.[26] Eventually he inveigled himself into the room. Hopkins sat silently in the second row, watching Roosevelt, and occasionally passing him scribbled notes with advice.[27]

On the second day, discussion turned to Germany. The conference confirmed that after defeat the country would be placed under Allied military government, including the French, in four separate occupation zones. But what then? Stalin wanted a tough approach: he argued that Germany should be broken up, and some $20 billion in industrial plant and other assets be stripped as reparations for the Allies. Churchill took a more lenient view: recalling the aftermath of World War I, he said that he was 'haunted by the spectre of a starving Germany'. If the horse was to pull a cart, it needed to be given fodder.[28]

The leaders agreed to delegate further discussion to Stettinius, Molotov and Eden. This group resumed the following morning. Stettinius signalled movement towards the Soviet position. The United States, he said, was keen to issue a communiqué that week. On reflection, he was content to include the word 'dismemberment', which Stalin had requested and which could be taken to imply the break-up of Germany.[29]

Molotov seized his moment. This was, he said, entirely acceptable.

Eden had little choice but to agree. In London, he had predicted to Cadogan that only Stalin had a clear view of what he wanted, and would dominate the conference. Now it seemed all too true.[30] With agreement reached, Stettinius adjourned the session. He hosted cocktails in his room before lunch. The mix of lemon and vodka that he offered to his guests was, he told them, called a White Lady.[31]

Roosevelt looked tired. The election campaign and long journey to the Crimea had taken a toll. Churchill's doctor, Charles Wilson, watched from a distance with professional interest. It was, he thought, a case of hardening in the brain arteries. At points the President seemed weary and disengaged. Like Wilson, Portal was concerned. Roosevelt's mind was, he confided to his diary, 'not what it was'.[32]

Over the winter, the President had tried on a new compromise over the voting issue with Stalin. This would retain the veto for executive decisions in the Security Council, but not procedural ones. The permanent members would not be able to block discussion, but they could prevent the Council taking action. Harriman had originally floated the proposal with Stalin in early December, but met with polite indifference.

With the issue of Germany settled, Roosevelt decided that the time had come to try again. The third plenary session of the conference opened at the usual time of four o'clock in the afternoon. Stettinius gave an update on the discussion about Germany. Then Roosevelt asked to discuss the United Nations. He introduced the topic with an impassioned appeal. He was not so optimistic, he said, as to believe in eternal peace. But 50 years without war should be feasible and possible. Stettinius followed him. He outlined the same proposal which Harriman had presented to Stalin.[33]

The Generalissimo listened. He needed to study the document in further depth, he said. The issues went beyond simple voting rules. As long as the three leaders were alive, they would not engage in aggression. But, in ten years' time, they might no longer be around. A new generation would take power, who did not remember the horrors of the war. And the risk remained that the country might be isolated, just as the Soviet Union had been expelled from the League of Nations over the invasion of Finland. The Western powers had 'isolated us', Stalin reminded his colleagues, in the manner of a crusade.

Churchill leapt to respond. 'We were very angry,' he explained. Britain and France were all alone.

'How could you guarantee that such a thing could not happen again?' replied Stalin.

The temperature was rising. At moments like this, Bohlen noted, it helped that the conference had several subjects to resolve. When the leaders became stuck on one topic, they could always switch to another. It allowed them to maintain a cordial atmosphere.[34] Alongside Germany and the United Nations, the conference was due to discuss Poland, and the potential entry of the Soviet Union into the war against Japan.

The President employed this tactic now. The plenary had, he sensed, covered as much ground on the United Nations as it could at this stage. He suggested that the delegates turn to Poland. At Tehran, the President had hinted at a possible deal with Stalin, once the presidential election was over. That point had now come.

Roosevelt introduced the discussion. The United States was, he said, furthest away in distance from Poland. Perhaps that meant he could bring some perspective. Moreover, he added, in a nod to his earlier conversation with Stalin, there were six or seven million Poles in the United States. He was prepared to accept a revision of the eastern border between Poland and the Soviet Union. But public opinion in the United States wanted to see a representative government in Warsaw.

Churchill agreed. He too was prepared to accept a revision to the eastern border, along the line which Lord Curzon, the British foreign secretary after World War I, had proposed in 1919. But, like the President, he wanted to create a sovereign and independent Polish government. For Britain, he explained, it was a question of honour. The British had gone to war to defend Poland in 1939. The country must emerge from the war 'mistress in her own house and captain of her soul'.

Stalin suggested a brief intermission. When the leaders reconvened, he spoke in response to what Roosevelt and Churchill had said. The Soviet dictator deliberately used short sentences. It gave the interpreters time to translate his words. As Pavlov communicated what Stalin was saying, the British and Americans strained to follow the train of thought.

For the Soviet Union, the Generalissimo began, Poland was a question of both honour and security. The country was a corridor, through which German forces had passed twice in the last 30 years. It was in the Soviet Union's interests that Poland itself was strong enough to close this corridor. Stalin turned to the question of a government. Churchill, he noted, had made a slip of the tongue when he talked about creating a Polish government. 'I am called a dictator and not a democrat,' he quipped, 'but I have enough democratic feeling to refuse to create a Polish government without the Poles being consulted.'[35]

It was a quarter to eight in the evening. The plenary had run for almost an hour. Hopkins quietly passed a note to his boss, suggesting that they adjourn. When Stalin had finished speaking, Roosevelt announced that the session was over for the day.

Stalin's offer had sounded reasonable. But the diplomats around the table were sceptical. Over the past three years, as Harriman and Cadogan well knew, attempts to broker a deal between the different Polish governments-in-exile had proven futile. Now, with the Red Army occupying Poland, the chances of success were even slimmer. In his diary that night, Dixon lamented that Stalin sounded 'sincere, and as always [...] hyper-realistic'.[36]

Roosevelt, however, refused to give up. Back in his quarters, he asked Bohlen to draft a letter to Stalin. They should summon to Yalta both the Soviet-backed Poles, who were based in the eastern Polish city of Lublin, and those from London. In his text, Bohlen tried using the argument that he had given to his friend Kennan. 'Our people at home', the letter warned, would 'look with a critical eye' at any failure to reach agreement between allies.[37]

The next afternoon, on 7 February, it was Stalin's turn to make a move. Two days into the conference, the Soviet leader had found his rhythm. 'The most impressive of the three,' commented Cadogan in a letter to his wife. 'Very quiet and restrained [...] never uses a superfluous word.'[38] Gromyko noted how his boss accumulated knowledge and insight on the other players. 'His memory worked like a computer', he recalled, 'and missed nothing.'[39]

The plenary opened at ten past four in the afternoon. Roosevelt suggested that the leaders resume discussion on forming a new Polish government. 'I think we want something new and drastic,' he added, 'like a breath of fresh air.'

A few minutes later, Stalin responded. The Generalissimo had received Roosevelt's letter from the night before. He was open to the idea of bringing the different Polish factions to Yalta for discussions. However, he had only read the letter an hour and a half before the plenary started. In the time available, he had not been able to reach the key players by telephone. While his colleagues continued the search, why not revert to discussion on the United Nations?

At Stalin's request, Molotov then gave a formal response to Stettinius' proposals on voting. The Soviet Union could now agree. 'We believe', he announced, 'that the decisions taken at Dumbarton Oaks and modifications suggested since by the president will secure collaboration by nations great and small after the war.' There was, added Molotov, only one question left, about the position of the Soviet republics. It would only be fair to give Byelorussia, Ukraine and Lithuania, as those who had suffered most in the war, seats at the general assembly. Just as the countries of the British Commonwealth had progressively grown towards self-government, so might the Soviet republics.

Roosevelt had what he needed. It was, he responded, 'a great step forward'. The immediate priority was to hold a founding conference. They should move quickly, as early as March.

Seated to Roosevelt's left, Churchill now entered the fray. Before the conference, Eden and Cadogan had struggled to engage their prime minister on the details of the United Nations. But now Molotov's reference to the Commonwealth had sparked his interest. Defaulting to the tactic he had used at Placentia Bay, the Prime Minister claimed that he needed to consult the Dominions before giving agreement. And the timetable that Roosevelt described sounded ambitious. In March, the Allies would still be waging war. Some nations at a conference would be 'screaming in agony', he said, while others would be 'calmly weighing the problems of the future'.

Hopkins, sitting behind Roosevelt, sensed a problem. He scribbled a note and slipped it to his boss: 'Perhaps we better to wait till later tonight what is on his mind.'[40]

Roosevelt proposed a short break. Details, he said, could be tied up by foreign ministers.

A few minutes later, discussion resumed. With a deal on the table over the United Nations, Roosevelt suggested that they return to Poland.

Molotov took the floor. Reading from a text, the Soviet foreign minister set out an alternative to what the President had proposed. A committee, comprising of Molotov, Harriman, and Archibald Clark Kerr, the British ambassador in Moscow, would oversee formation of a government. This would be based on the Lublin Poles, but include some of the London exiles. At the same time, Poland would gain new borders, with the Curzon Line to the east, and, to the west, annexation of German territory up to the Stettin and Neisse rivers. 'We are still trying to telephone the Polish leaders,' he added, 'but without success.' In their absence, the plan that he had described should meet what the President wished to achieve.

Roosevelt and his team could see this was the best they would get. 'We are making real progress,' responded the President. He would study the proposal further.

Churchill, stalling, asked if Poland could really absorb so much German territory. 'It would be a pity', he mused, 'to stuff the Polish goose so full of German food that it got indigestion.' There was a school of thought in England that was shocked at the idea of transferring millions of people by force.

Stalin reassured him. The Germans, he noted in a laconic tone, had already fled.[41]

The Yalta Conference was now on the home stretch. For many delegates, the physical and mental strain had been considerable. Dixon was struggling with the double burden of heavy meals and insufficient sleep. Along with Eden, Cadogan and Birse, he would break away when he could for walks in the gardens and on the mountainside around the Vorontsov Palace. The discomfort was increased by the lack of bathrooms. Long queues formed outside the few facilities available. The British delegation was guarded by a detachment of Royal Marines. These soldiers eventually found a *banya*, or Russian steam bathhouse, to wash themselves. Somewhat to their surprise, they were beaten with birch twigs by elderly Russian *babushki*, in traditional fashion.[42]

Over the remaining four days, the various strands fell into place. On the United Nations, the founding conference was set for 25 April (a date proposed by Jebb, because it was his birthday).[43] Over reparations from Germany, Roosevelt suggested a compromise, at Hopkins' suggestion. The communiqué from Yalta would refer to the figure of $20 billion, but only as a Soviet proposal. At a private meeting on 8 February, Stalin gave Roosevelt and Harriman a commitment that, after Germany was defeated, the Soviet Union would enter the war against Japan, in return for territorial gains in the Far East.

That night, Stalin hosted a final dinner for the three leaders. The Americans counted some 45 toasts over the evening, which meant each course was often cold by the time it arrived on the table. Much to his relief, Cadogan managed to duck the occasion. The Soviet leader paid elaborate tributes to his two comrades. Roosevelt, replying, talked of a family among the leaders. Kathleen Harriman proposed a toast on behalf of Anna Boettiger and Mary Churchill, daughter of the Prime Minister, as the ladies present.[44]

As the toasts became more verbose, the interpreters struggled to keep up. When Churchill talked about the 'broad sunlight of victorious peace', Birse was almost stumped to find an equivalent phrase in Russian. Meanwhile, Bohlen fortified himself with several glasses of vodka.

Eventually, Stalin took pity. Rising to his feet, he offered a toast to the trio of intrepreters, who, he said, had 'worked while we were enjoying ourselves'. On them, the whole conference relied. Walking round the table, he clinked glasses with each of the three men in turn.

Churchill chipped in. 'Interpreters of the world unite,' he cried. 'You have nothing to lose but your audience!' Stalin broke into hearty laughter. His colleague's parody of the communist slogan had tickled his sense of humour.[45]

The conference broke up on 11 February. Roosevelt left first, on a flight to Alexandria in Egypt. Churchill flew via Athens. His plane passed over the Dardanelles, and then the Greek island of Skyros. Looking out of the windows, the party spied the tomb where the English poet Rupert Brooke had been buried before the landings in 1915. Churchill rejoined Roosevelt at Alexandria, where they dined together once more aboard the USS *Quincy*.

Brooke had a more lonely duty to discharge. At Athens, he peeled away from the prime ministerial party, and took his own flight back to Malta. The plane arrived in the late afternoon. The field marshal went straight to Mdina, in the centre of the island.

There stood the Imtarfa Cemetery, a small burial ground for British serviceman. Carrying a wreath, he walked up to the grave where the body of Barney Charlesworth had been laid to rest a few days before, following the air crash off Lampedusa.

In silence, Brooke remembered their last moments together, as they parted at RAF Northolt. 'See you in Malta,' had been the Ulsterman's final words to his aide. The two men had travelled a long path together. Charlesworth had been awarded the Military Cross in World War I. In 1939, already in his late forties, he re-enlisted. He fought alongside Brooke in the Dunkirk campaign. Afterwards, as his aide, Charlesworth had become a trusted confidant. Death now divided them.

Brooke placed his wreath on the grave, then returned to his car. Later that night, he boarded his plane for the flight to England. The field marshal was no stranger to grief. He had lost his first wife, Jane, in a driving accident 20 years before, when he himself was behind the wheel. The war had brought many more moments of tragedy. As a keen amateur ornithologist, Brooke often found that he could draw consolation from the changing seasons and the beauty of nature. But, on this occasion, the blow had gone deep. The loss of his friend hung over him like a black cloud.[46]

FIVE

Furling the Flags

Till the war-drum throbb'd no longer, and the battle flags were furl'd
In the Parliament of Man, the Federation of the World.
There the common sense of most shall hold a fretful realm in awe,
And the kindly earth shall slumber, lapt in universal law.

From 'Locksley Hall' by Alfred, Lord Tennyson,
carried by Truman in his wallet

Less than two months after the Yalta Conference, Roosevelt was dead.

On his return to Washington, the President addressed Congress. For the first time, he did so seated. At times his voice was unsteady, and his hand shook as he reached for a glass of water. In late March, speechwriter Robert Sherwood joined him with Anna Boettiger for lunch on the terrace above the south portico of the White House. The President seemed quiet and withdrawn. Shaken, the staffer slipped away after the meal.[1]

The end came quickly. On Thursday 12 April, Roosevelt was resting at his private country retreat in Warm Springs, Georgia. At one o'clock that afternoon, while reading papers and posing for a portrait, he collapsed. Two hours later, he was pronounced dead. The cause of death was a cerebral haemorrhage. Fala, who had been sleeping quietly, suddenly rushed outdoors, and barked wildly into the distance.[2]

News quickly passed back to the White House. At just after five o'clock, the press secretary, Stephen Early, reached the Vice-President on the phone. Harry Truman was on the Capitol, sharing a drink with the speaker, Sam Rayburn. Early sounded tense. The Vice-President should, he said, come to the White House at once. Truman left immediately. He returned to his office, fetched his hat, then ran through the basement to reach his official car, losing his Secret Service bodyguards in the process.

It would be the last time in eight years that he managed to give them the slip.

Harry Truman's journey to the White House had begun in Missouri. He was born in 1884, the eldest of three children. His parents were smallholding farmers. Following Irish-American tradition, they gave Harry a middle initial, 'S.', to reflect that of his two grandfathers, Anderson Shipp Truman and Soloman Young. When Harry was six, the family moved to Independence, the fourth largest town in the state.[3]

Truman worked on the farm, then the railroad. In 1917, he enlisted in the army, and served as an artillery captain on the Western Front. After the war, Harry married Bess Wallace, who also came from Independence, and to whom he had first proposed six years earlier. He started a haberdashery business, but it folded in 1921, a victim of the postwar slump. The next year, Truman became involved in politics. With the backing of Tom Pendergast, who dominated the Democrat political machine in Kansas City, Truman ran for state-level positions. In 1934, he secured a seat in the US Senate.

Ten years later, Truman found himself propelled to the forefront of national politics. Senior party figures in the Democratic National Committee were wary of giving another term to Henry Wallace, who had served as Roosevelt's vice-president since 1941. Wallace came from the left of the party, and was seen as a liability. They persuaded the President to take on Truman instead.

Truman occupied the post for less than three months. It was largely a ceremonial role. He saw Roosevelt alone on just two occasions. Truman did not attend the conference at Yalta, and was not briefed on what had been agreed with Stalin. His most newsworthy moment came in mid-February, when he was snapped at a Washington Press Club event playing the piano for servicemen, while the actress Lauren Bacall serenaded him from a perch on top of the instrument. The double act by Vice-President and glamorous Hollywood icon was an instant hit. Bess was not amused.[4]

Truman arrived at the White House at 5.25 p.m. He was taken to Roosevelt's private quarters, on the second floor. There, he was met by Early, Anna and the President's widow, Eleanor.

Eleanor stepped forward. 'Harry,' she said, 'the President is dead.'

For a few moments, Truman could not speak. Eventually, he asked if there was anything he could do for the former first lady.

Eleanor looked back at him. 'Is there anything we can do for you?' she answered. 'For you are the one in trouble now.'[5]

Early put out a press statement at 5.47 p.m., announcing the death. As the news spread, people reacted with shock. Ted Achilles, a mid-level official at the State Department, noticed the Stars and Stripes being lowered from the flagpole on the White House lawn. It was not yet sunset, when the flag was usually taken down, and Achilles wondered for a moment what was happening. That he saw the flag halt at half-mast, and realised something was wrong.[6] Silent groups began to gather on Pennsylvania Avenue. In Berlin, where it was already past midnight, Goebbels reacted with glee. Immediately, he phoned Hitler, and ordered champagne for his staff.[7]

A few minutes later, Stettinius arrived at the White House. His face was covered in tears. Les Biffle, secretary to the Senate, followed. Truman asked them, along with Early, to summon the cabinet. He also authorised use of a government plane for Eleanor to travel to Warm Springs.

Over the next hour, senior members of the administration and Congress gathered. The group assembled in the Cabinet Room. Morgenthau, Stettinius and Rayburn were there, along with Henry Stimson, secretary of war, James Forrestal, secretary of the navy, and Admiral William Leahy, the White House chief of staff. Wallace, who had taken the role of commerce secretary following the election, was also present. Stettinius made a brief speech on behalf of the cabinet, pledging their support.

Truman was joined by Bess and their only daughter, Margaret. He sat silent in a chair, holding Bess' hand. Stettinius sat down next to them, and the two men talked quietly about what had happened. The Secretary observed that human beings found an inner strength at such moments. Truman agreed.[8]

At just after seven o'clock, Chief Justice Harlan Stone called for silence. He and Truman stood at the north end of the long cabinet meeting table. In his left hand, Truman held a Gideon Bible, which the White House Chief Usher had produced from a desk drawer. Stone prompted him to raise his right, and take the oath.

'I, Harry Shipp Truman,' began the Chief Justice.

'I, Harry S. Truman,' repeated the Vice-President, correcting his middle name.

'... do solemnly swear ... so help me God.'

Truman looked across to the mantelpiece. On the wall hung the portrait of Wilson which Roosevelt had placed there. Below, a clock showed the time. It was 7.09 p.m.[9]

As the cabinet dispersed, Stimson drew Truman aside. There was, he said, a matter of great importance, which he must discuss with the President soon. It regarded a new explosive device. Truman looked blank. It was the first that he had heard of the atom bomb.

The United Nations Conference was due to start in less than a fortnight.

As a member of the Senate, Truman had seen Roosevelt prepare the ground. He had himself voted for the resolution tabled by Texan senator Tom Connally 18 months before. Only a few weeks prior to Roosevelt's death, the Vice-President delivered a speech in Jefferson City, Missouri. 'America can no longer sit smugly behind a mental Maginot line,' he warned, in a reference to the obsolete defences which had failed to protect France in 1940.[10]

His conviction ran deep. In his wallet, Truman carried a passage from 'Locksley Hall', by the Victorian poet Alfred Tennyson. As a teenager at high school, Truman had copied down the verse. 'For I dipt into the future, far as human eye could see,' it ran. 'Far along the world-wide whisper of the south-wind rushing warm / With the standards of the peoples plunging thro' the thunder storm / Till the war-drum throbb'd no longer, and the battle flags were furl'd / In the Parliament of Man, the Federation of the World.'[11]

On the night that he took the oath, Stettinius and Early asked Truman if the conference should go ahead. Truman confirmed that it should. It was his first decision as president.

On the evening of Thursday 12 April, Harriman was hosting a farewell party at Spaso House for one of his staff. It was a lively occasion, and guests were still dancing after midnight. At one o'clock in the morning, the embassy duty officer called Kathleen. He had heard about Roosevelt's death on a radio broadcast. Quietly, she drew her father aside to break the news. Harriman looked sombre. He asked his assistant, Robert Meiklejohn, to break up the party, and withdrew to his study. There, he called the foreign ministry. Molotov was still awake, and hastened round to meet the

Ambassador. When Harriman received him, the foreign minister seemed deeply moved. Despite the late hour, he lingered, talking about the role that Roosevelt had played in the war.

The following evening, Harriman called on Stalin. In silence, the Soviet leader held his hand, evidently distressed. Then he offered the Ambassador a seat. He would, he said, give Truman all the support he could, in continuing Roosevelt's cause.[12]

Since Yalta, relations between Moscow and Washington had soured. The tripartite commission, on which Harriman sat with Molotov and Archibald Clark Kerr, had made little progress over Poland. In late March, 16 former leaders of the Home Army had been lured out of hiding, only to be deported in secret to Moscow. To add to the tension, the Soviet foreign ministry had announced that Molotov would not go to the United Nations Conference, leaving Gromyko to represent the Soviet Union instead.

Harriman seized his moment. As a mark of respect, he suggested, might Stalin reconsider, and send Molotov to San Francisco? The Ambassador offered to put a plane at his disposal, even to paint it with a red star. Stalin agreed, but declined the offer of transport.[13]

Two days later, on Sunday 15 April, a simple memorial service was held at the American Embassy. Molotov attended, at the head of a full array of senior Soviet officials and military leaders. The embassy choir led the congregation with 'O God Our Help In Ages Past'. It was the same hymn that Roosevelt and Churchill had sung together on the foredeck of the *Prince of Wales* at Placentia Bay.

Harriman read out a prayer that Roosevelt had himself composed on the eve of D-Day. 'Grant us brotherhood in hope and union,' ran one line, 'not only for the space of this bitter war, but for the days to come which shall and must unite all the children of the earth.'[14]

Two days later, Harriman flew back to Washington. He travelled in a B-24 Liberator bomber. Over 18,000 of these craft were produced, the most of any type in the war. The journey took 49 hours, flying via Italy and North Africa. It was a record time for the American diplomat. He was anxious to meet the new president and brief him before Molotov's arrival. Like many Americans, he wondered whether the little-known senator from Missouri was up to his new job.[15]

Barely a week had passed since Roosevelt's death. For Truman, his first days as president were spent in a whirl. Roosevelt's body was brought to Washington on Saturday 14 April, for a funeral service in the White House. He was buried the following day at Hyde Park, the Roosevelt family home in upstate New York. That night, Truman scrabbled to prepare an address to Congress, due the following day. On the Tuesday, he held a first briefing session with the Washington press corps. More than 300 packed into the Oval Office. And that night he gave a radio address to the nation, again rushing to draft the script in time.

In between these public engagements, Truman faced other calls on his time. There were briefings with his cabinet and military staff, congressional figures, visits to the Map Room, as Roosevelt's wartime command centre in the basement was known, and correspondence with Stalin and Churchill. Over the preceding weeks, both Western and Soviet armies had launched massive offensives into Germany. The race to reach Berlin was on. As Truman scuttled around the White House, rushing from one appointment to another, his bodyguards struggled to keep up – they were used to protecting a president in a wheelchair.[16]

Friday 20 April brought the heaviest schedule of appointments yet. Morgenthau was the first of the day. He brought with him three US marines. They were veterans from the bloody assault on the Japanese-held island of Iwo Jima, which had concluded a month earlier. During the battle, a group of six soldiers raised the Stars and Stripes over the devastated battlefield. The moment had been captured in a shot by the celebrated war photographer Joe Rosenthal, and became an instant media hit. The trio were the only survivors from the flag party.[17]

Later in the morning, Truman met Dr Stephen Wise, chair of the American Zionist Emergency Council. As the Allies advanced into Germany and Poland, they had discovered the full horror of the concentration and extermination camps, where millions of Jews and other victims of Nazi oppression had been murdered. On 11 April, American forces had entered Buchenwald, near Weimar. Four days later, the British liberated Bergen-Belsen. Gruesome images flashed around the world, of emaciated survivors and mass graves. Pressure was growing for the United Kingdom, which governed Palestine under a mandate established after World War I, to allow more Jewish refugees to return to their historic homeland.

Wise left just before noon, after a 15-minute meeting. He was followed by Harriman and Stettinius. They were joined by Bohlen.

The Ambassador briefed Truman. Soviet policy was pursuing two conflicting strands. Stalin wanted co-operation with the United States after the war, not least to secure financial assistance. But he was pursuing a strategy in Eastern Europe which was potentially in collision with this goal. At worst, it amounted to a 'barbarian invasion'. The best course, Harriman advised, was to stand firm.

Truman agreed. 'The Russians need us more than we need them,' he observed.

The Ambassador found himself reassured, but also concerned. It was clear that Truman was learning fast. He had absorbed his brief, and had read up on the Yalta agreements. But he was also unsure of himself. At several points in their conversation, the new president said he was not equipped for the job, and lacked experience.

Harriman felt he must say something. As he stood to leave, he drew the President aside. Frankly, the Ambassador said, he had feared that Truman would not be up to speed. Hence his hasty return to Washington, ahead of Molotov. But what he had seen left him greatly relieved.[18]

Truman needed moments like that. The week had been an ordeal. The new president had found the address to Congress on Monday afternoon particularly daunting. 'Have confidence in yourself,' Alben Barkley, the veteran Democrat senator from Kentucky, told him. 'If you do not, the people will lose confidence in you.'[19]

On the same day that Harriman met Truman, the Senate held a debate. It was the last opportunity for members to voice their views ahead of the San Francisco Conference.

At Yalta, Roosevelt and Stettinius had agreed that the United States should field a substantial delegation. This would include senior members of Congress from both sides of the aisle. Senators Connally and Vandenberg headed the list. They were joined by Democrat Sol Broom from New York, who chaired the House Foreign Relations Committee, and Republican Charles Eaton, of New Jersey. From outside Congress, Harold Stassen, the 37-year-old former Republican governor of Minnesota was included, and John Foster Dulles, the lawyer who had attended the Paris Peace Conference in 1919.

Across America, excitement was building. Archibald MacLeish, a poet and assistant secretary at the State Department in charge of public relations, orchestrated a major campaign. A pamphlet about the Dumbarton Oaks proposals was distributed to over a million homes around the country, along with a film entitled *Watchtower Over Tomorrow*. In the run-up to the conference, many cities took part in a Dumbarton Oaks week, with town hall meetings and rallies.[20]

Connally spoke briefly. The Senate should not expect perfection, but the delegation was determined to try. Tears filled his eyes as he sat down. His Republican counterpart, Arthur Vandenberg, followed. He paid tribute to his Texan colleague. Then, turning to the rest of the chamber, he offered a plea. 'Once more', he declared, 'I am asking that your prayers for this great enterprise shall fail neither it nor us.'

As the Republican sat down, a wave of applause broke around him. Senators sprang forward to shake Vandenberg and Connally by the hand, and clap arms around their shoulders. Twenty-six years after Wilson had sailed to Paris, America was going to another peace conference.[21]

Molotov arrived in Washington on the afternoon of Sunday 22 April. His journey, flying by C-54 across Siberia and the Bering Straits, had taken two days longer than Harriman's. The foreign minister stayed at Blair House, the official government guest facility on Pennsylvania Avenue. Harry and Bess Truman were also in residence. Amid the rush, Eleanor had yet to move out from the White House.

The following day, Molotov called on Truman in the Oval Office. It was five-thirty in the afternoon. The room was still as Roosevelt had left it, with prints of the Hudson Valley and models of ships displayed around the walls. Gromyko accompanied him, together with Pavlov. Harriman joined on the American side, along with Bohlen and Leahy from the White House.

Over dinner the night before, the two men had enjoyed an amicable first encounter. Truman had confirmed that he would stand by the commitment made at Yalta for territorial concessions in the Far East following Soviet entry into the war against Japan.

At this meeting, Truman was more businesslike. He quickly launched into his remarks. It was, he said, a matter of deep disappointment that the Soviet Union had not been able to engage in consultation with the London

Poles. The failure of the three allies to carry out what they had agreed at Yalta cast doubt on their unity of purpose. In his last message to Stalin, Roosevelt had made the same point.

Molotov turned ashen. The Soviet Union was, he said, committed to co-operation. In the past, the three great powers had managed to work together. They did so by treating each other as equals, and not by one or two countries imposing their will on the third.

Truman cut him short. He rose to his feet. 'That will be all, Mr Molotov,' he said. 'I would appreciate it if you would transmit my views to Marshal Stalin.'

Molotov filed out of the room. The Americans looked at each other. Bohlen, who once again had acted as interpreter, felt exhilarated. This was different to Roosevelt. At last, a president had stood up to the Soviets. Leahy had a similar reaction.

Harriman, however, was worried. What, he wondered, would Molotov tell Stalin? Where was this heading?

As he drove away with Molotov, Gromyko too was puzzled. He had met Truman as vice-president, and liked him. But something seemed to have changed. The man in the Oval Office was different, more strident. He didn't seem to be interested in listening.[22]

SIX

A Sentimental Journey

Gonna take a sentimental journey
Gonna set my heart at ease
Gonna make a sentimental journey
To renew old memories.

From 'Sentimental Journey', performed by Les Brown and
Doris Day, US number one hit in summer 1945

Ed Stettinius liked San Francisco. Lying in his bed at Yalta one night, he had dreamt of the wide bay and the Golden Gate Bridge. This, he decided, was where the United Nations Conference should take place.

The State Department laboured to make Stettinius' vision a reality. While Pasvolsky focused on policy, his colleague Alger Hiss, a former lawyer and journalist, handled logistics. Hiss assembled a secretariat, staffed by more than 1,000 officials, along with security personnel and interpreters. Special trains and military transport aircraft were chartered to bring the delegates to San Francisco. A printing centre was established for conference documents, capable of turning out half a million pages a day. Graphic experts designed a logo for the new United Nations, with a map of the world, flanked by olive branches, and coloured white on a light blue background. Washington gossip had it that Stettinius chose the colour to match his own snow-white hair.[1]

The delegates assembled in San Francisco on Wednesday 25 April. They included some 37 foreign ministers and five prime ministers. As the conference opened, news broke that American and Soviet troops had met on the Elbe River at the heart of Germany. The end of the war in Europe was at hand.

That evening, Stettinius hosted the opening ceremony, at the San Francisco Opera House, which had been completed in 1932, in a Beaux-Arts style, as a monument to servicemen from World War I. An audience of more than 3,000 gathered in the main auditorium. The celebrated Broadway designer Jo Mielziner had created a set specially for the occasion. Four gold columns were ranged along a curtain of light blue cloth, symbolising the four freedoms which Roosevelt had proclaimed at his inauguration speech in 1941. Behind them stood a half-moon of flags, from all 46 nations at the conference. Against this backdrop, a troop of US servicemen marched onto the stage. They were followed by the Secretary of State, together with Earl Warren, governor of California, and Roger Lapham, mayor of San Francisco. Hiss accompanied them.

Stettinius called for a minute of silence, in memory of the war dead. Then he introduced Truman. The President spoke over a radio link-up from the White House. 'You', he declared, 'are to be the architects of the better world.'[2] Afterwards, Stettinius addressed the delegates. 'San Francisco is a symbol in our history,' he noted. 'To us the West has always meant the future.'

The audience applauded. It was not just diplomats and politicians who had come to San Francisco. Movie stars and celebrities had flocked to the city, including such popular figures as Orson Welles and Rita Hayworth. In one encounter, the journalist Alistair Cooke found himself sharing a hotel lift with film star Groucho Marx.[3]

Among them was a young naval officer called John Fitzgerald Kennedy. Aged 27, Kennedy was the son of Joe, who had served as American ambassador to London in the early years of the war, and was a noted supporter of appeasement. The younger Kennedy had joined the navy in 1941, and commanded a torpedo launch in the Pacific War. When his ship was rammed and sunk by a Japanese destroyer, Kennedy rallied the survivors and swam to a nearby island. He towed one wounded crewman with a lifejacket strap clenched between his teeth. At San Francisco, Kennedy wrote for the *Chicago Herald-American*, and threw himself into the social scene. On one occasion, onlookers recalled watching the young naval officer and Eden jostling for a dance with the American heiress Viscountess Harcourt.[4]

That evening, after the opening ceremony, Stettinius hosted a meeting of the American delegation. The venue was his penthouse suite on the fifth floor of the Fairmont Hotel, a few blocks north of the Opera House. It was a wood-panelled room, lined with leather-bound books.

The time was almost nine o'clock. Stettinius had just come off the phone with Truman, debriefing the President on the day's events. Outside, dark had descended across the Bay area. As Stettinius addressed the group, faces lengthened. It was already clear that the conference was running into difficulties.

The problem was Molotov. After his bruising encounter with Truman, the Soviet foreign minister had arrived in San Francisco determined to throw his weight around. In Berlin, the Red Army were edging closer to Hitler's headquarters at the centre of the city. Defeat was imminent. Everyone wanted to see the Soviet foreign minister, the man of the hour. 'He holds the centre of the stage,' wrote the young British journalist, Michael Foot, 'and other delegations pirouette around him.'[5] Kennedy thought that he was more like a player running with the ball in a game of American football, and daring others to tackle him.[6]

Molotov had several lines of attack. Under terms agreed at Yalta, countries attending the conference were required to declare hostilities against the Axis countries by 1 March. Argentina had favoured Germany for much of the war. The military junta under General Juan Perón only made its declaration in late March. But the Latin American participants were united behind Buenos Aires, and Stettinius needed their support. At the same time, the Polish issue remained unresolved.

How to respond? Stettinius asked for views.

Vandenberg spoke first. That morning, he had speculated in his diary over what might lie ahead. 'I don't know if this is Frisco or Munich,' he wrote. 'At what point is it wisest to stop appeasing Stalin?' The senator now shared his concerns with his colleagues. What would happen, he asked, if the United States held firm?[7]

Harold Stassen interjected. He was a trim man, with dark, receding hair and a high, domed forehead. After the 1942 midterms, he had resigned his office to serve on the staff of Admiral William Halsey, commander of US forces in the South Pacific. He took a practical view. This, he said, was the veto issue all over again. The Soviets were seeking to gain an armlock over proceedings.

He was followed by John Foster Dulles. The veteran lawyer's white hair was brushed back in a tidy parting. Round wire-rimmed glasses framed his face, with eyebrows raised as if asking a question. Dulles was not a man to give ground lightly. To do so now, he said, would be an unacceptable blow to American prestige.

Stettinius looked around the room. The delegation had reached a decision. They would face down Molotov. Afterwards, Vandenberg reflected on the evening's events in his diary. 'We might as well', he concluded, 'find out now whether Russia intends to work in decent co-operation.' If not, both sides would simply be stuck in a perpetual row.[8]

That weekend Cadogan took a break. He had managed to obtain a ticket for the San Francisco Symphony Orchestra. Yehudi Menuhin was in town, playing Beethoven's Violin Concerto. Birse also tried to attend, but found that it had sold out. Then, on the Sunday morning, Cadogan attended a service at the city's cathedral. The Bishop of California presided, while Stettinius read the lesson. When the collection was carried to the altar on gold plates, laden with dollar bills, the bishop leaned back and burst into a rendition of 'The Star-Spangled Banner'. Afterwards, Stettinius posed for photos at the lectern, first gazing at the Bible, then upwards to heaven.[9]

On the Monday, Hitler committed suicide at his bunker in Berlin. Soviet soldiers overran the last Nazi defences, and hoisted the Hammer and Sickle flag over the Reichstag parliament building.

As the Nazi regime collapsed, Molotov continued his diplomatic offensive. At a meeting of the conference of the executive committee, he called for Argentina to be barred, unless Poland was also admitted. The vote was defeated, by nine to three. Undeterred, Molotov escalated his case, to the steering committee, and then to a plenary session. Quoting Roosevelt's own words, he called Buenos Aires the 'headquarters of the fascist movement' in the western hemisphere.

Stettinius intervened, and called for a vote. Molotov's proposal was defeated, by 31 to 4. The Soviet foreign minister had been outgunned.

Kennedy's newspaper column was billed as a plain-speaking take from an ex-serviceman. 'Diplomacy', he reminded his readers, 'might be said to be the art of who gets what and how.'[10] By this definition, Stettinius had succeeded. But inside the American delegation victory tasted bittersweet. At his suite in the Fairmont, along the corridor from Stettinius, Harriman looked on with concern. It was right, he believed, to stand up to the Soviets.

The Yalta agreements were not being upheld. But Argentina's participation seemed an odd case on which to fight.

Worse news was to come. On the evening of 3 May, as he greeted guests arriving for dinner at the Soviet Consulate, Molotov mentioned casually to Stettinius that the 16 Polish leaders arrested in March had been taken to Moscow for trial. As the Soviet foreign minister turned away to welcome Eden, his American counterpart remained standing on the spot, a smile fixed on his face, unsure what to do.[11]

At ten o'clock the following night, Stettinius met with Eden and Molotov at his penthouse. Harriman, Cadogan, Gromyko, Bohlen, Pavlov and Birse were all present. The atmosphere was tense. Anne O'Hare McCormick, the veteran *New York Times* reporter, later commented that the 'temperature dropped like a plummet' as news of the impending trial spread around the conference.[12]

Eden said that he was shocked. Stettinius nodded in agreement. Molotov said little, but looked uncomfortable. 'A perfectly disgraceful performance,' Cadogan concluded gloomily in his diary afterwards. 'How can one work with these animals? And if one can't, what can one hope for in Europe?'[13]

As the meeting broke up, Birse sought out Pavlov. The two men had formed a close working relationship during the war years. At the end of each meeting, they would sit down together to compare notes and double-check their translation for the record.

When Molotov saw his colleague moving towards Birse, he pulled him back. 'Why are you helping the other side?' he asked Pavlov. As he slipped away, the Soviet interpreter shot Birse an uncomfortable look.[14]

In the early hours of Monday 7 May, at Eisenhower's headquarters in Reims, France, Colonel-General Alfred Jodl signed a document of surrender on behalf of the German High Command. News swept around the world.

In London, Churchill addressed the House of Commons. Roars filled the chamber. Order papers were thrown into the air. Afterwards, the Prime Minister led members across Parliament Square, for an impromptu service of remembrance at St Margaret's, the parliamentary church in the shadow of Westminster Abbey.

That evening, more than a million people took to the streets. Crowds filled Whitehall, Piccadilly, and thronged the Mall, outside Buckingham

Palace. The young princess Elizabeth slipped out of a side-gate with her sister, Margaret, and two young Guards officers to join the celebrations. Groups danced up and down, singing such popular wartime songs as 'Roll Out the Barrel' and 'Hang Out the Washing on the Siegfried Line'.[15]

In San Francisco, the British delegation was staying at the Mark Hopkins Hotel, on the adjoining block to the Fairmont. At midday, they congregated in the glass-fronted bar on the nineteenth floor, called Top O' The Mark. The group fell silent as King George VI came on the radio, delivering an address to the Commonwealth. 'We shall have failed and the blood of our dearest will have flowed in vain', he declared, 'if the victory which they died to win does not lead to a lasting peace, founded on justice and goodwill.'

The British sang their national anthem, and looked for a drink to toast their sovereign. But the cabinets were locked. As a precaution, the San Francisco city authorities had imposed a 24-hour ban on alcohol sales.[16]

Molotov left San Francisco on 9 May. With victory in Europe, he was needed back home. Ambassador Andrei Gromyko took over as head of the Soviet delegation.

The conference was moving into a new phase. Now that the modalities had been agreed, discussion shifted to the detail of the charter text. Gromyko faced a challenge. The draft agreed at Dumbarton Oaks gave the Security Council supremacy over regional bodies, and power to veto action taken by them. This reflected Pasvolsky's conviction that the new organisation must be a truly global body. But the Soviets wanted a safeguard to protect agreements between Moscow and the states of Eastern Europe. It was the same point on which Eden and Molotov had clashed in Moscow nearly two years before.

Molotov was not the only participant who wanted to safeguard regional agreements. The Latin American countries, fired by their victory over Argentina, took the same view. In February, as the price for attendance at San Francisco, they had secured a commitment from Washington to a pan-American defensive alliance in the western hemisphere, under a treaty signed in the Mexican city of Chapultepec. Led by Lleras Camargo, the 39-year-old foreign minister of Colombia, the Latin Americans argued that this was essential to underpin the doctrine announced by President James Monroe, more than a century before, to defend the western hemisphere against outside intervention.

The US delegation was torn. For a whole day, on Monday 7 May, debate rattled backwards and forwards in the penthouse suite at the Fairmont.[17]

Vandenberg sympathised with the Latin Americans. The Monroe Doctrine had been a buttress of American foreign policy for over a century. Pasvolsky took the opposite view. The United Nations was supposed to mark an end to territorial deals of the kind which had undermined peace after World War I. 'We will convert the world into armed camps,' he warned darkly, 'and end up with a world war unlike any we have yet seen.'

Dulles offered a compromise. The charter did not infringe on the inherent right of states to engage in their own self-defence. This could be managed on a collective basis, as well as individually. Described in these terms, regional agreements might be acceptable.

At the Paris Conference, the core issues had been resolved in small daily meetings between Wilson and Lloyd George, together with their French and Italian counterparts. Twenty-six years later, Stettinius adopted the same approach. As the conference moved into a third week, he started to do more business in his penthouse suite, with Eden and Gromyko, along with the French and Chinese representatives. They became known as the Big Five.

At a meeting with this group on 12 May, Stettinius unveiled Dulles' compromise. Eden claimed to be outraged. It was 'regionalism of the worst kind'. The whole concept of a world organisation would be undermined. Cadogan and Jebb looked on, nodding approval.

Gromyko took note. He would need to study the proposal more closely. Sensing the mood, Stettinius suggested that the delegates break, and reconvene that evening.[18]

Afterwards, Eden, Cadogan and Jebb stayed behind with the Americans. At once, the tone of the conversation changed. Stettinius and Vandenberg explained their problem, while Eden confided that the British were more sympathetic than he had been prepared to admit in front of Gromyko. He described the problem of Soviet *Machtpolitik*, which Jebb had identified a year before. Sitting at the Foreign Secretary's side, the British diplomat suggested a modification. Dulles' proposal was earmarked for chapter eight of the charter, on regional organisations. Alongside this, Jebb offered a new article for chapter seven, which covered enforcement action by the Security Council. This would reinforce Dulles' point, by stating that member states enjoyed an 'inherent right of self-defence, either individual or collective', even if the Council had failed to respond to an act of aggression.[19]

That evening, at six o'clock, Stettinius reconvened a meeting of the Big Five. With the British proposal now in play, positions started to converge. Gromyko commented that Jebb's text was much nearer the ideals and principles of the United Nations as he understood them. Dulles added an explanation about the treaty of Chapultepec. Pasvolsky looked on in silence. Regionalism was back on the table.

Nonetheless, Vandenberg was worried. Stettinius was an excellent manager. He had delivered the conference with only two months' notice. But he was not a leader or a politician. Rumours were circulating that Truman had decided to replace him. Since Roosevelt's death, the post of vice-president was vacant. Under the constitution, the Secretary of State was now second-in-line to the President. Truman needed a figure with more political authority in the post. Byrnes was said to be in the running. Vandenberg decided that he must act.

In a quiet moment, he drew the Secretary of State aside. The Latin Americans had been raising more difficulties, on the grounds that Jebb's draft did not refer explicitly to Chapultepec. He should, the senator advised, show a firm hand, and seize the problem. It was time to look like a secretary of state.[20]

Stettinius took heed. He called Truman, and secured his personal commitment to call a conference that autumn, which would conclude a pact, to be known as the Organization of American States. Then, in the afternoon, he went back to the Latin Americans, and told them to back down. Connally weighed in alongside him. 'Trust us!' he declared, as his face reddened with the effort. 'We're in the western hemisphere as much as you.'[21] Over the next few days, negotiation moved back to the Big Five, as Stettinius hammered out a deal with Gromyko. 'It shows what he can do,' noted Vandenberg warmly in his diary. 'I hope that he continues to be secretary of state.'[22]

'The same passions and selfishness that produced the Treaty of Versailles,' Kennedy warned his readers, were at work in San Francisco.[23]

Edward Wood, 1st Earl of Halifax, had lived through the consequences of failure at Versailles. Born in 1881, to a landed family in Yorkshire, Halifax was a close contemporary of Churchill. During the interwar years, he served as viceroy of India and then, following Eden's resignation, as foreign secretary. In 1940, the aristocrat was the main voice within the cabinet to urge a possible truce with Hitler after the defeat of France. Churchill later moved him to be ambassador in Washington, where he served throughout the war. A slender man, born with only one hand, Halifax was an enthusiastic huntsman. It was an image which brought mixed reactions. 'Are we going to war for the sake of a lot of English fox-hunters?' asked one American journalist soon after his arrival.[24]

Eden and Halifax travelled to San Francisco together, along with the Labour leader, Clem Attlee. But, by mid-May, it was clear that the wartime coalition back in London was unravelling. From Conservative ranks, Brendan Bracken and Lord Beaverbrook encouraged Churchill to dissolve Parliament and call an early election, even before the war with Japan was over. They hoped that the victory over Germany would give the party an edge. Attlee had already returned to London, and Churchill was insistent that Eden should do the same. The Foreign Secretary was loath to leave San Francisco while the outcome of the conference still hung in the balance, but eventually bowed to his leader's wishes. He left Halifax and Cadogan to lead the British delegation.[25]

On Saturday 26 May, the two men joined Stettinius, Gromyko and the others in the Fairmont suite. The conference had come under strain from a new direction. Herbert Vere Evatt, the abrasive Australian foreign minister, was mobilising the smaller nations against the Big Five. Their grievance was over voting on the Security Council. Giving the Big Five a veto, as permanent members, would leave the smaller countries in a weaker position. Momentum was gathering. Under the rules of the conference, two-thirds of delegations could propose an amendment to the charter. Technically, the Big Five could decide to block it – but such a step would risk blowing the whole conference apart.

The meeting began at 9.15 p.m. For the first half hour, Gromyko was silent. Eventually, he weighed into the discussion. There were, he said, very important questions at stake. Under the proposal made by Stettinius at Yalta, the veto could not be exercised over procedural questions, only substantive matters. But what if the Council had to decide whether an issue was procedural or substantive? Would the veto apply then?[26]

The British and Americans exchanged nervous glances. The implication was huge. In Moscow, Harriman and Kennan liked to joke that, in dealing with the Soviets, 'you had to buy the same horse twice.'[27] By seeking to expand the veto, Gromyko was pulling at the other end of the rope to Evatt. The whole edifice of the Charter might collapse.

Like Gromyko, Halifax had remained silent until now. He looked at his Soviet counterpart. At moments like this, the aristocrat could be forbidding. Isaiah Berlin, the young academic who worked in his embassy, and who had come to San Francisco to help with translating Russian texts, called him the 'Headmaster'.[28]

Halifax chose his words carefully. He had not, he said, been present at Yalta. But he thought this issue had been resolved. He looked across at Stettinius, Jebb and Cadogan, who had all been in the Crimea. If not, Halifax added, they were in for trouble.

On Friday 1 June, nearly a week later, the group met again. It was nine o'clock in the evening.

Gromyko had checked his position with Moscow. After opening pleasantries, he returned to the veto question. His government's position was as he had set out at the previous meeting. Stettinius looked around at his colleagues. There was little to say. Halifax could only respond that he needed to reflect.[29]

'We all knew', Vandenberg wrote in his diary that night, 'that we had reached the zero hour of this great adventure.'[30] In a letter to his wife, Cadogan described it as the moment that the storm burst. 'It's simply arguing about words, on the surface,' he mused. 'But it is of course a symptom of something much deeper – Russian suspicions and unwillingness to co-operate. How to cure those, I really don't know.'[31]

The next morning, Stettinius spoke over the phone with Truman. They were both clear that there could be no compromise. It was, Truman said, 'something neither I nor you nor the American people can take.' There was only one card left for the Americans to play. Halifax had suggested a direct approach to Stalin. Truman and Stettinius decided to give it a shot.[32]

In the days of Bullitt, when Bohlen and Kennan had first worked in Moscow, security at the American Embassy had been lax or non-existent.

An undercover check by the Federal Bureau of Investigation found serious irregularities. The communications room, where cables were decoded, was frequently left unlocked. Soviet visitors wandered freely around the building. Later searches revealed scores of listening devices, concealed in walls. During wartime, procedures were tightened up. Only selected personnel had access to the communication room, and code books, labelled Brown or Blue according to the level of classification, were kept in a locked safe.[33]

In the early hours of 3 June, a telegram arrived from San Francisco. Once the cable had been decrypted, Harriman read through the contents. It contained instructions from Stettinius. In detail, the Secretary of State set out the veto issue, and how deadlock had been reached at San Francisco.[34]

Harry Hopkins was staying with Harriman at Spaso House. After Yalta, the former social worker had drifted out of contact with Roosevelt. His cancer had worsened. News of the victory in Europe found him in his bed, at home in Georgetown. But Truman had summoned him back to duty. The President had agreed to meet with Churchill and Stalin in July at Potsdam, outside Berlin. It was essential to broker a solution over the Polish issues in advance. Hopkins had been dispatched to Moscow.

He was accompanied by Bohlen and Louise, his third wife. A former editor of *Harper's Bazaar* magazine, the Washington socialite caused a stir among Soviet officialdom. Generals and bureaucrats jostled to chat with her over dinner. One morning, a government truck pulled up at Spaso House. Soldiers produced gifts of precious stones and furs. Her husband, horrified at what would happen if the American press got hold of the story, had to hustle them away.[35]

The American had made good progress with Stalin. At their first meeting, he described the circumstances of Roosevelt's death. Stalin nodded, noting that Lenin too had suffered a cerebral haemorrhage. Bohlen thought that the Generalissimo was milder than on previous occasions, perhaps out of deference to his old wartime comrade.[36]

Three days after Stettinius' instructions came, the American held his sixth and final meeting with Stalin. Harriman accompanied him, and they were joined by Molotov. It was six o'clock in the evening. After a brief introduction, Hopkins and Harriman explained the issue. Stalin turned to his companion. 'What is all this about, Molotov?' he demanded. Listening in, Bohlen noted the formal use of the surname. Stalin was keeping his foreign minister as a distance. Molotov launched into a complex explanation of the decision taken at Yalta. At moments like this, under pressure, his stutter would worsen, and a lump would appear on his forehead.[37]

'Molotov, that's nonsense,' Stalin interjected. Bohlen understood, but did not translate. Stalin turned back to Hopkins. The American position, he said, seemed correct, but he wished to check.

Hopkins pushed home his advantage. The situation was urgent, he said. They should resolve it that night.[38]

In San Francisco, tempers were wearing thin. The conference was now into its seventh week. The veteran reporter Scotty Reston had got hold of the story about Hopkins' mission. It was front-page news. Delegates waited, while press speculation mounted.

What if Hopkins failed? Stettinius held a tense conversation over the phone with Pasvolsky. The émigré suggested adjourning the conference.

'We can't do that,' snapped Stettinius. 'We are going to have a charter and we are going to find an answer and I have complete confidence.'

'All I have confidence is that we have to do a lot of hard work,' replied Pasvolsky.[39]

The news reached Stettinius first, flashed back on the encrypted cable traffic from Moscow. Less than 24 hours after the encounter between Hopkins and Stalin, Stettinius ushered Gromyko into his suite. There was, he said, some news that he wished to pass on. As a long-standing colleague, he wanted Gromyko to know first.

As Stettinius described what had happened, the Soviet diplomat turned a deep shade of red. He had been overruled.

The next morning, Stettinius called a meeting with the American delegation. He had received a written message from his Soviet counterpart. Connally read out the text. 'You have convinced us,' it read, 'and we have agreed. We shall find solutions to all remaining problems in the same spirit of goodwill and mutual understanding.' The statement ended with a word of hope for the future: 'This is what counts, and is going to count in the long run.'

The delegation cheered. That night, Vandenberg recorded the scene with triumph in his diary. 'We have discovered (I hope) that we can get along with Russia,' he added, 'if and when we can convince Russia that we mean what we say.'[40]

Stettinius had a visitor. It was the morning of 21 June. The charter had been agreed. In four days' time, Truman was due to arrive in San Francisco to attend the formal signing ceremony. George Allen was a Democratic Party operative and friend of the President. He had come to California to make arrangements, and break some bad news.

The two men sat in the penthouse room at the Fairmont. 'You've done a magnificent job here,' said Allen. 'The only thing that can happen to you is something bigger than secretary of state—'

'George, what are you talking about?' Stettinius interrupted.

Allen explained. Truman envisaged that Stettinius might move across to be the first US ambassador to the United Nations. 'There really isn't anybody else,' he added.

Stettinius said that he would think about it. The two men walked over to the window. As they looked out over the city, Stettinius ran over the offer in his mind.

'I entered the government service out of love of my country,' he said. 'I will be the easiest man to deal with that Truman ever dealt with.'[41]

The *Sacred Cow* gleamed as it descended through the clouds towards Hamilton Air Base. When the aircraft had taxied to a halt, the door opened, and Truman stepped out. A battery of guns fired 21 rounds in salute. The president waved as he descended from the plane. He was dressed in a lounge suit and a grey Stetson hat. Stettinius waited to greet him.

The Secretary ushered his president to an open-topped car. Together, they drove into the city. It was Truman's first major public appearance since becoming president. More than a million people had turned out to line the streets. On one of the towers of the Golden Gate bridge hung a banner with the word 'WELCOME!'

That evening, Stettinius took Truman up to the penthouse suite at the Fairmont. Walking round the table in the main room, he pointed out the places where the various delegates had sat during their meetings. The two men sat down. Stettinius ordered a martini, and Truman an Old Fashioned whisky cocktail.

'Well,' said the President, 'you certainly have done a grand job here. Are you satisfied with what I am planning?'

Stettinius sidestepped the question. Truman pressed him. 'You are the only one I can turn to to carry out this thing,' he said.

The Secretary paused. There were, he said, various conditions that he wished to make. Truman said that he would meet them.

Stettinius looked at him. 'Mr President,' he said, 'do you really believe that you can do this thing and put Byrnes in without its appearing publicly like a kick in the pants for me?'

'I sincerely believe that it can be done that way,' replied Truman.[42]

The signing ceremony took place in the Veterans Building, across the street from the Opera House. Mielziner had swathed the stage in blue cloth, surrounded by flags of the United Nations. On the walls behind, the theatre contained a series of eight murals by the Anglo-Welsh painter Frank Brangwyn, which he had originally painted for the Panama–Pacific International Exposition in 1915. In a Beaux-Arts style, these were grouped around the themes of earth, air, fire and water, and depicted timeless aspects of human existence: hunting; catching fish; treading grapes; and kindling fires.

In the centre of the stage stood a large round table, covered in blue velvet. The charter was laid out, printed in five official languages: English, French, Russian, Chinese and Spanish. Leaving nothing to chance, Mielziner's crew inserted pink slips of paper between the leaves of the charter text, with delegation names. Individual signatures were then marked in pencil outline, which could be removed by special rubber eraser once signed in ink. In the wings of the theatre, a room was made available where delegates could practise their signatures on a mock-up of the charter.[43]

Each delegation entered in turn, starting with China, as the first victim of fascist aggression. The Chinese delegates signed with their own traditional ink and brushes.

At 3.15 p.m., Truman led the American delegation onto the stage. He was joined by Stettinius, Connally, Vandenberg and Stassen. While Stettinius sat down at the table to sign, Truman stood to his right, hands clasped behind his back, beaming at the audience. He looked down. Stettinius' hands were shaking. The cameras rolled. When the Secretary of State had finished, the President reached over and clasped his hand.[44]

Afterwards, delegates walked over to the Opera House, where Truman gave the closing address. He announced Stettinius' appointment, and congratulated the delegates. 'History will honour you,' he added as his hands chopped the air, palms facing inwards in his characteristic gesture. 'The successful use of this instrument [...] will tax the moral strength and fibre of us all.'[45]

Others followed. Halifax used his speech to deliver a warning. The United Nations was not an 'enchanted palace'. There was no guarantee that it would bring harmony between nations. Jotting in his notebook, Kennedy had similar thoughts. 'Musn't expect too much,' he wrote. 'Things can't be forced from the top.'[46]

When the speeches had ended, the band struck up 'The Star-Spangled Banner'. That evening, Stettinius flew back to Washington, along with Vandenberg and Halifax. The former secretary had become close to the Ambassador. Vandenberg was amazed to hear the reserved Halifax and Stettinius address each other by their first names, which both shortened to 'Ed'.[47]

When they arrived in Washington, the Senate Foreign Affairs Committee had turned out at the airport to greet them. 'It seemed', noted Stettinius in his diary, 'as if school were over and everyone was going home for vacation.'[48]

SEVEN

Force to Break

Batter my heart, three-person'd God, for you
As yet but knock, breathe, shine and seek to mend;
That I may rise and stand, o'erthrow me, and bend
Your force to break, blow, burn and make me new.

Sonnet by John Donne, quoted by Robert Oppenheimer
at the Alamogordo test, July 1945

'Operated on this morning,' read the telegram. 'Diagnosis not yet complete but results seem satisfactory and already exceed expectations.' The date was Monday 16 July 1945. At 7.30 p.m., a private cable reached the US delegation at the Potsdam Conference. It was sent by George Harrison, president of the New York Life Insurance Company, and assistant to Henry Stimson, the secretary of war.

President Truman had arrived at Potsdam the previous day. He crossed the Atlantic aboard the cruiser *Augusta*, the same warship which had carried Roosevelt to Placentia Bay. Byrnes travelled with him, as the new secretary of state. With the war in Europe at an end, the journey was quicker and more direct, with no need to follow a zig-zagging course to avoid U-boats. The vessel docked at Antwerp. From there, the President and his entourage drove to Brussels, and then, flying aboard the *Sacred Cow*, to Berlin. After passing over Frankfurt, the party entered airspace above the Soviet occupation zone in Germany. Twenty P-47 Thunderbolt fighter planes escorted them along an air corridor, ten miles wide.[1] In mid-afternoon they touched down at Gatow airport, where Truman was met by Stimson, Harriman and Gromyko.

Under the system agreed at Yalta, Berlin was sub-divided into separate occupation zones for each of the four Allied powers. Potsdam was just outside the city boundary, in the Soviet zone. The Red Army was therefore responsible for preparing the conference. Plenary sessions would take place at the Cecilienhof, a sprawling country house built for Crown Prince Wilhelm in a half-timber English style. To brighten things up, a giant star of red geraniums, 24 feet wide, was planted across the courtyard lawn.[2] The leaders were accommodated in nearby Babelsberg, a small town spread along the pine-wooded shores of Lake Gribnitz. It had been home to the German movie industry, and survived the war relatively intact.

Their accommodation, 2 Kaiserstrasse, was a stucco mansion overlooking the lake. Truman was not impressed. Large chimneys concealed the roof, and the interior was dark and gloomy. 'Make the place look like hell but purely German,' wrote the President in his diary.[3] Truman occupied a suite of rooms on the second floor, shared with Leahy, while Bohlen and Byrnes were on the floors below. As at Yalta, facilities were limited. 'The bathroom and bathing facilities were wholly inadequate,' lamented an official in the White House log book.[4] Churchill was installed nearby, in a house previously owned by a director of Deutsche Bank, while Stalin was a mile away down the same road.[5]

On the Monday afternoon, Truman and his entourage set off on a tour of Berlin. Seated in the back of an open-topped Lincoln with Leahy and Byrnes, he drove along the autobahn into the centre. Uniformed Soviet female police directed the traffic with flags. By the side of the road the US 2nd Armored Division was drawn up in formation, to salute their commander in chief. Nicknamed 'Hell on Wheels', the unit had fought in North Africa, Italy and then across Europe from Normandy to Berlin. Tanks were parked side-by-side, stretching for a mile and a half along the road. It took Truman's motorcade 22 minutes to drive the full length.[6]

Further into the city centre, the destruction increased. The Unter den Linden was littered with rubble and twisted street lights. The fragrant scent of limes, remembered by those who had visited Berlin before the war, was replaced by the stench of burning and open drains. The party visited the Reich Chancellery, where Hitler had lived and worked. They were shocked at the destruction. In the state rooms, chandeliers still hung from the ceiling, but water dripped down from burst pipes, onto floors littered with broken concrete and marble. The walls were covered with crude graffiti left by Soviet troops. Below, the cellars concealed a warren of half-flooded bunkers and gun emplacements.[7]

Leahy was both awe-struck and fascinated; the Admiral remembered his first experience of naval gunnery, at the bombardment of Guantánamo, in Cuba, during the US–Spanish war of 1898. Soviet artillery had blown shell holes in the side of buildings, whereas British and American bombing had collapsed whole structures into rubble. He and his colleagues were moved at the sight of long lines of refugees, old men, women and children, walking along the roads. 'That's what happens', commented Truman, 'when a man overreaches himself.' That evening, over dinner back at Kaiserstrasse, the mood was subdued. Each man pondered on what he had seen.[8]

Stimson had no need to explain the meaning of the cryptic telegram to his president.

Three months before, during the week after Roosevelt's death, he had first briefed Truman on the atomic secret. Their meeting took place on 25 April, the same day that the United Nations Conference opened in San Francisco. Stimson met Truman in the Oval Office. They were joined by General Leslie Groves, head of the Manhattan Project, as the secret programme to develop the bomb was known.

Stimson was born in 1867, just two years after the end of the Civil War. As a child, he heard his great-great-grandmother recount her own childhood conversations with George Washington.[9] While a student at Yale, he spent a summer trekking in the hills of Montana, with the Blackfeet Indians. Stimson learned to track, shoot, canoe and make camp. It was the start of a lifelong love for the American wilderness. 'Selfishness cannot be easily concealed,' he wrote of life in the West. 'The importance of courage, truthfulness and frankness is increased.'[10]

After Yale, Stimson attended Harvard Law School, and then worked as a junior lawyer for Elihu Root, who later served as secretary of war under Teddy Roosevelt. Stimson himself took over the post in 1911, under President William Taft, and served for two years. In 1929, he returned to the cabinet, as secretary of state under President Herbert Hoover. Though a Republican, he stayed on in the Roosevelt administration, serving once more as secretary of war. Dressed in an old-fashioned style, with wing collar and pocket watch in his waistcoat, he projected integrity and moral authority. One journalist described him as a 'granite statue to the ancient virtues'.[11]

Stimson had prepared a type-written document. He passed it to the President, and asked him to read it. 'Within four months', the report began, 'we shall in all probability have completed the most terrible weapon ever known in human history.'

Truman read on, in silence. The paper described the bomb's capability, and the impact that it might have on international affairs and ending the war. When he had finished, Groves produced another, more lengthy, report, describing the Manhattan Project. The President protested, but both men urged him to read his way through the document. 'We can't tell you this in any more concise language,' they explained. 'This is a big project.'[12]

At Stimson's suggestion, Truman authorised a private group, called the Interim Committee, to analyse the implications of this new weapon. It was chaired by the Secretary of War, along with Groves, Byrnes and William Clayton, under-secretary at the State Department. They were joined by James Conant, president of Harvard University, and Robert Oppenheimer, the 41-year-old scientist who led the secret research laboratory at Los Alamos, in New Mexico, which had designed the bomb.

During May, this group wrestled with questions over the bomb's use. They came to the unanimous view that it should be used to end the war with Japan, and dropped without warning, to achieve maximum effect. A separate committee, staffed by air force officers, drew up a list of potential targets.[13] This included the cities of Hiroshima, Yokohama and Kokura. The ancient capital of Kyoto was also listed, but, at Stimson's insistence, dropped in favour of Nagasaki, a port on the southern end of the Japanese islands.

The Potsdam Conference opened on the afternoon of Tuesday 17 July. The three delegations assembled in the main reception room of the Cecilienhof. They sat around a table 12 feet in diameter, larger than those at either Tehran or Yalta. Truman, Byrnes, Leahy, Bohlen and Joseph Davies, former ambassador to Moscow, sat in the US delegation, while Stalin, Molotov, Vyshinsky, Gromyko and Pavlov represented the Soviet Union.

For the British, Churchill and Eden were joined by Labour leader Clem Attlee. Following the decision to dissolve the wartime coalition, a general election had taken place in Britain a fortnight before, on 5 July. The results would take three weeks to be counted, as postal ballot papers returned from servicemen overseas. In the meantime, the Prime Minister had invited his opponent, and former wartime deputy, to watch proceedings. Attlee sat to Churchill's left, looking on in silence. Cadogan and Birse completed the delegation. The outcome of the election, as Churchill confided to his doctor, hung like 'a vulture of uncertainty in the sky'.[14]

Truman was the newcomer to the group. Nevertheless, Stalin and Churchill appointed him to preside over plenary sessions. Birse thought the new president conducted himself like a company chairman, polite but determined.[15] At their first session, Truman outlined how the conference should function. As at Yalta, detailed matters would be handled by foreign ministers.

'We shall have nothing to do,' joked Stalin.

'I don't want to discuss,' retorted Truman. 'I want to decide.' He added a suggestion that the plenary sessions should subsequently start earlier, from four in the afternoon rather than five, as had happened on the first day.

Both Stalin and Churchill preferred to work at night and rise late. But they fell in with Truman's proposal. 'I will obey your orders,' quipped the Prime Minister.[16]

The conference faced three, interconnecting issues: Poland; Germany; and the war with Japan. On the first of these, Harry Hopkins' mission to Moscow had made some headway in forming a new Polish government, although a question remained over demarcation of the western Polish border with Germany. Following the end of hostilities, the Soviets had transferred responsibility to Warsaw for territory up to the western Neisse River. This amounted to unilateral annexation. Churchill and Truman came to Potsdam determined to stand firm. Over Germany, the Allied powers had established separate occupation zones, but they still faced questions over how the country should be administered, and what arrangements should be made for reparations.

After the first couple of days, it became clear that the conference was making only slow progress. Truman confided in a letter to Bess that he was 'sick of the whole business'.[17] Churchill, for his part, found the new president's brisk approach to working through the agenda rather disconcerting. When Truman brought the second day's plenary to a close after just two hours, Churchill was, observed Cadogan, like a child with its toy taken away from it.[18]

For Eden, other anxieties weighed on his mind. In late June, his eldest son, Simon, had gone missing with an RAF flight over Burma. Agonised, Eden and his wife, Beatrice, waited for news. The tension was all the harder to bear amidst the strains of the election campaign.

Two days into the conference, a telegram arrived from the air force chief, Charles Portal. Dixon brought it to his boss, who was working in the garden. A search party had found the crashed aircraft in the jungle. All the crew were dead. Pilot Officer Simon Gascoigne Eden was among them, a few months short of his twenty-first birthday. A volume of Shakespeare's *Henry V* was discovered among his personal effects.

That night, Eden dined with the rest of the delegation. Though he seemed composed, inside the pain was hard to bear. Father and son had been close. Simon had followed the same path through Eton and Oxford, where he studied for a year before joining the RAF. 'Life seems desperately empty,' confessed the Foreign Secretary in his diary.[19]

At noon on Saturday 21 July, a full report of the atomic test arrived by courier from Groves. That afternoon, in the study at Kaiserstrasse, Stimson shared the account with Truman and Byrnes. He read it out aloud, taking an hour to do so. In simple, unvarnished words, Groves described the explosion, at Alamogordo, in the New Mexico desert. The initial flash, he wrote, was as bright as 'several suns at midday'. A fireball rose 10,000 feet into the air, followed by a dust cloud four times that height. Half a mile from the epicentre, a steel and concrete tower, built to test the effect on multi-storey buildings, was ripped from its foundations.[20]

When Stimson had finished, Truman said that the news had given him an entirely new feeling of confidence. Here, in his hands, was the means to bring the war to an end. Later that afternoon, at the plenary session, he seemed to radiate authority. 'It was apparent', noted one member of the American delegation, 'that something had happened.'[21]

That evening, Stalin hosted dinner for his fellow leaders. Outside, the midsummer twilight lingered late into the evening. A couple of days before, Truman had given a piano concert at Kaiserstrasse, with a US Army sergeant on the keyboard. The Soviet dictator decided to match him. The celebrated pianist Vladimir Sofronitsky was flown in from Moscow, along with two female violinists. Sofronitsky, who was married to the daughter of the Russian composer Alexander Scriabin, had received the Stalin Prize in 1942. It was only the second time that he had performed outside the Soviet Union. The ensemble played a programme of Liszt, Tchaikovsky and Chopin.

Truman was entranced.[22] As a boy, he would rise at five in the morning to practise the piano. In adulthood, it became a source of relaxation.[23] Earlier that afternoon, after his meeting with Stimson, the President had played on the piano at Kaiserstrasse. Leahy and Byrnes accompanied him for an impromptu sing-along. 'I can't say that the singing was very high quality,' recalled a State Department official who interrupted them, 'but the piano-playing was rather good.'[24]

The following night, a thunderstorm erupted over Potsdam. An 80-year-old lime tree came down outside Churchill's villa. The roots were ripped up, bursting a water main. Charles Wilson, the prime ministerial doctor, called in the morning. He found his charge lying in bed, deprived of water for his bath. Sawyers was mopping up a spilt glass of pineapple juice from the bedside table. When the butler had been dismissed, Churchill confided news of the Alamogordo test to his doctor. 'It is the second coming,' he said in a solemn voice. 'It gives the Americans the power to mould the world.'[25]

Byrnes had a similar thought. The Washington veteran had built a career from cutting deals in the corridors of Capitol Hill. He reckoned that he could see the outline of a bargain with the Soviets. On the morning of Monday 23 July, Byrnes met Molotov in his study at the Cecilienhof. They were joined by Bohlen and Pavlov. Byrnes made his proposal. Rather than seeking to extract reparations from Germany as a whole, each of the four occupying powers should do so from their own zone. To compensate for greater industrial output in the western zones, some surplus would be transferred to the east. At the same time, the United States would accept revision of the Polish border to the Western Neisse. Molotov undertook to discuss the proposal with Stalin.[26]

That night, it was Churchill's turn to host dinner. He was determined to trump the previous occasions. An RAF band was drafted in to provide music and invitations were sent out. The Royal Engineers had constructed a special table, but the Prime Minister feared that it was not large enough. Wilson and Tommy Thompson, the prime ministerial aide, conducted a trial. They sat in chairs and, rather self-consciously, checked for elbow room while Churchill looked on. Eventually, the prime minister ruled that only 28 would fit around the table. Too many guests had been invited. Two members of the British delegation were quietly stood down.

At the end of the evening, Stalin suggested that his companions autograph the menu. Others rushed to follow suit. 'This means signing 28 menus,' grumbled Churchill. Sawyers was summoned to bring extra fountain pens. A general melee ensued. Even Field Marshal Alan Brooke entered the fray, warmly shaking hands with Stalin. Afterwards he sat down with Wilson and reminisced. During their journeys together to the wartime conferences, the two men had not always seen eye-to-eye. But now, as the long struggle was coming to an end, the Ulsterman showed a warmer side. 'I have felt that every day of this war', he confided, 'was taking a month of my life.'[27]

Meanwhile, events in the Far East were gathering pace. That night, another telegram arrived from Harrison. 'Operation may be possible any time from 1 August, depending on state of patient and condition of atmosphere.' The following morning, Tuesday 24 July, Stimson called on Truman in his study at Kaiserstrasse. Both men knew that the moment had come. The instruction was passed to George Elsey, a junior naval officer, who transmitted it on to Washington.[28]

A specialist unit, the 509 Composite Group, had been training in use of the bomb. Later that day, an order flashed from Washington to General Carl Spaatz, commander of strategic air forces, authorising them to drop it on Japan at any time after 3 August, when the conference at Potsdam would be complete. 'It seems to be the most terrible thing ever discovered,' Truman wrote in his diary. 'But it can be made the most useful.'[29]

At the end of the plenary session that afternoon, Truman drew Stalin aside. Birse and Churchill, dressed in a tropical RAF uniform, watched from a discreet distance. To increase the impression of informality, Truman asked Bohlen to hang back, too. While Pavlov interpreted, the President broke news of the bomb to Stalin. The United States had, he explained, acquired 'a new weapon of unusual destructive force'. Stalin seemed disinterested. He hoped, he said, that the Americans would make good use of it against the Japanese.

'How did it go?' asked Churchill afterwards, as he and Truman waited for their cars outside.

'He never asked a question,' replied the President.[30]

That night, Churchill slept badly. His mind was troubled by morbid dreams. He imagined that his life was over, and that his dead body lay under a white sheet on a table in an empty room. In the morning, he recounted the scene to Wilson. 'Perhaps this is the end,' he mused.[31]

Election results were due the following day. Churchill and Attlee attended a final plenary session together, before flying to London. 'I'll be back,' said the Prime Minister, as he rose to leave. Stalin offered one last quip to his old sparring-partner. Pavlov translated. 'Judging by the expression on Mr Attlee's face,' he said, 'I do not think that he is looking forward avidly to taking over your authority.'[32]

Attlee was not expecting to win. Labour had seen two short periods in government, in 1924 and then between 1929 and 1931, but as a minority in the House of Commons. At the last general election before the war, in 1935, the party had managed respectable gains, rising to a total of 154 seats. But the step to a full majority still looked too great. Attlee later confided to Colville, the private secretary who had worked with him while Churchill was at Placentia Bay, that he had expected to reduce the Conservative lead to 40, at best.[33]

As the results came in, however, it was clear an earthquake had taken place. Labour had more than doubled its seats, with close to 400 Members of Parliament. The Conservative share had collapsed, to 190. Brendan Bracken and Harold Macmillan, Conservative MP for Stockton, had lost their seats, along with 188 of their colleagues. British politics had been thrown upside down.

Churchill was stunned. 'I have no automobile, no place to live – what shall I do?' he lamented to Ismay.[34] At a glum lunch in Downing Street, his wife, Clementine, suggested that defeat might be a blessing in disguise. 'At the moment', Churchill retorted, 'it's certainly very well disguised.'[35]

That evening, Churchill drove to Buckingham Palace, to resign his office to King George VI. Half an hour later, Attlee drew up in a modest Hillman motor car, chauffeured by his wife. Afterwards, the new prime minister joined a victory rally of his MPs at the Methodist Central Hall, a large auditorium on the opposite side of Parliament Square to the House of Commons.

A couple of hundred yards away, Churchill returned for a final night to the underground bunker from where he had directed the war effort. Clementine retired to bed with a migraine. Churchill dined alone with Bracken and his daughter Mary. In the 1930s, when Churchill had last found himself out of office, he had taken up painting. The hobby had languished during the war, though Churchill had managed some canvasses on a holiday at Hendaye, in the south of France, before Potsdam. The former prime minister announced that he would resume his pastime. Mary duly produced a painting from the holiday. In silence, they sat and gazed at it.[36]

Attlee was born in 1883, a year before Truman. The son of a solicitor, who rose to be president of the Law Society, he enjoyed a comfortable, middle-class upbringing in Putney. In the years before World War I, he became involved in social work at a youth club in the East End of London, through his old school, Haileybury. It was a formative experience for the privileged young man. In later life, he would describe his shock at hearing boys talk of going home to an empty table for dinner.[37]

During the war, he had served in the Dardanelles campaign, where he was wounded, and in France. Afterwards, Attlee returned to the East End. He became mayor of Stepney, then entered Parliament. In 1931, the minority government splintered between those led by Prime Minister Ramsay MacDonald, who opted to stay on in a coalition with the Conservatives, and the majority of the Labour Party, who returned to opposition. Four years later, in the wake of the 1935 general election, Attlee was elected leader. He presided over a party bruised by the experience of holding office. 'It was especially good for us,' he later reflected. 'It gave us a sense of pace and a sense of proportion [...] with that great mass of Tories opposite you, you learned to grin and bear it.'[38]

Attlee presided over a team of big political beasts. Ernie Bevin, a former trade union leader, had held the role of minister of labour during the war, while Herbert Morrison, previously leader of the Greater London Council, was home secretary. Hugh Dalton had led the Special Operations Executive, with Jebb, and then become president of the Board of Trade. They were joined by Stafford Cripps, who had been ambassador in Moscow early in the war, then overseen aircraft production.

With the election won, the political manoeuvring began. Morrison had stood for the leadership in 1935. He now angled for the party to hold another vote, rather than accept Attlee as prime minister. Bevin swung his support behind Attlee, and Morrison's initiative collapsed. But the episode complicated formation of a new cabinet. Previously, Attlee had envisaged that Bevin would be chancellor of the exchequer. He now concluded that giving both Bevin and Morrison a domestic portfolio would invite further trouble. So, in a last-minute switch, he sent Bevin to the Foreign Office, and Morrison became lord president. Dalton moved to be chancellor instead. He had expected to be foreign secretary, and even, on Attlee's advice, packed a light suit in readiness for the trip to Potsdam.[39] Waiting back at the conference, where he was holding the fort, Cadogan sniffed in a letter to his wife than it was all 'rather untidy'.[40]

Bevin learned of his appointment at five in the afternoon. Four hours later, he arrived at the Foreign Office. He was met by Dixon, who had spent an emotional afternoon packing up with Eden, after five years in the job. They spoke for an hour, sitting in an empty office. That night, Dixon took an official car home, and presented his son, Piers, with a souvenir from Berlin. It was a chunk of the marble top from Hitler's desk in the Reich Chancellery.[41]

Attlee and Bevin arrived in Potsdam on Saturday night. It was the first time that Bevin had flown in an aircraft. After dinner and brief consultation with Truman and Byrnes, they went into a plenary session, which opened at 10.30 p.m. Attlee offered a few words of apology at the delay. Bohlen thought that, despite the diffidence, there seemed a new strength to him.[42] The new prime minister sat in the chair which Churchill had occupied only days before, smoking his pipe and nodding while Bevin spoke. His foreign secretary embraced the role with gusto. 'I'm not going to have Britain barged about,' he had declared to Ismay, when Churchill's former chief of staff came to meet them at Gatow airport.[43]

The conference was entering a final stage. Having authorised use of the bomb against Japan, Truman was anxious to wrap up and head back to Washington. The next day, he and Byrnes held a private meeting with Molotov. Byrnes outlined his deal in more detail. Over the next 24 hours, this was firmed up in meetings of the foreign ministers. Under an agreement called the Potsdam Protocol, Germany would be governed on a four-power basis, with reparations largely drawn from each occupation zone. The German–Polish border was settled along the Western Neisse. The British, still adjusting to the change of government, found themselves sidelined. 'Jimmy B is a bit too active,' Cadogan recounted to his wife, 'and has already gone and submitted proposals to Molotov which go a bit beyond what we want at the moment.'[44] Squeezed into a chair behind Attlee and Bevin, Dixon scrabbled to follow drafting of the final communiqué.[45]

Early on the morning of Thursday 2 August, Truman left Kaiserstrasse. He boarded the *Sacred Cow* at Gatow, and flew to England. The plane was due to land at St Mawgan airport, in Cornwall. But fog forced a diversion to

Harrowbeer, a small RAF station some ten miles north of the naval base at Plymouth, where the *Augusta* was waiting.[46]

King George VI had travelled to Plymouth to meet the President. He hosted a lunch of fish and lamb chops aboard the cruiser HMS *Renown*. Byrnes, Leahy and Halifax joined them. As the waiters served food, the Secretary of State started talking about the atom bomb. The King intervened. 'I think', he suggested, 'that we should discuss this interesting subject over our coffee.' Later, when the party could speak freely, Leahy argued that the bomb would not work. He had been an explosives expert in the US Navy, and was sceptical about the Manhattan Project. George VI disagreed, and offered him a bet.[47]

By mid-afternoon, Truman had put to sea, aboard the USS *Augusta*. Four days later, on Monday 6 July, the President was taking lunch with members of the crew, in the mess. Captain Graham, an officer from the map room, interrupted them. He passed across a decrypted message, along with a map of Japan. Graham had circled the city of Hiroshima in red. 'Results clear cut,' read the signal. 'Successful in all respects.'

Truman shook Graham's hand. 'This', he exclaimed, 'is the greatest thing in history.'[48]

News flashed around the world. The next day, Andrei Sakharov was walking to his local bakery, near Dinamo metro station in Moscow. The young Soviet physicist was 24 years old, and had recently moved back to the capital after spending the war at a research laboratory in Ulyanovsk, 500 miles to the east. He stopped to glance at a newspaper. When he saw the story, his legs almost gave way. 'My fate and the fate of many others', he later recalled, 'had changed overnight.'[49]

Stalin's nonchalant reaction when Truman told him about the bomb had been a front. For more than three years, NKVD agents in the United States had targeted the Manhattan Project, which they referred to using the codename 'Enormoz'. By the end of 1944, they had three spies inside Los Alamos. The most significant was Klaus Fuchs, a German scientist who had fled to England before the war, and who formed part of the British team assigned to work alongside Oppenheimer and the Americans. Before the Potsdam Conference, Fuchs had tipped off his handlers that a test explosion was imminent.[50]

The leading Soviet atomic physicist was Igor Kurchatov. His team was based at a secret facility, called Laboratory No. 2, and he was given access to information gathered by the NKVD. Yet, compared to the American effort, the Soviet programme was modest.[51]

In February 1945, the NKVD had assessed that the Americans were a year or more away from obtaining the bomb. The Alamogordo test threw Stalin's calculations. After his conversation with Truman at Potsdam, the Generalissimo had vented his frustration with Molotov and Gromyko. The Soviet Union must, he declared, remove America's monopoly.[52]

In mid-August, Stalin summoned Kurchatov and Boris Vannikov, commissar for munitions. 'Hiroshima has shaken the world,' he told them. 'The balance has been destroyed.' A few days later, the State Defence Committee issued a secret decree, instructing that work be accelerated. Vannikov was appointed to head a new First Chief Directorate, while Kurchatov led the research. The programme was codenamed Task Number One. The scientists would have everything that they needed. 'If a child doesn't cry, the mother doesn't know what he needs,' Stalin told Kurchatov. 'Ask for whatever you like.'[53]

Overall responsibility for Task Number One was entrusted to NKVD chief Lavrentii Beria. Stalin had brought his fellow Georgian to Moscow in 1938, to oversee the purges of thousands of officials and military officers, which had tightened his grip on power. By 1945, Beria was at the height of his influence. When he joined a dinner with Roosevelt and Churchill at Yalta, Stalin introduced his colleague as 'our Himmler', in a reference to the head of the Nazi secret police.[54] Beria knew how to scare the government machine into action. On one occasion, Gromyko saw Deputy Foreign Minister Andrei Vyshinsky receive a phone call in his office. The former prosecutor leapt out of his chair, and cringed as he spoke into the handset.[55]

Beria's vast security establishment swung into action. Within days of the atomic explosions, NKVD agents from the Soviet Embassy in Tokyo visited Hiroshima. They collected photos and samples, including a burnt human hand.[56] On 22 August, instructions were sent to Colonel Zabotin, head of the military intelligence cell at the Soviet Embassy in Ottawa. 'Take measures to organise acquisition of documentary materials on the atomic bomb!' they ordered. 'The technical process, drawings, calculations ...'[57]

EIGHT

The Half-Open Door

But in real life, right now,
You hear how I am calling you.
And that door that you half opened
I don't have the strength to slam.

From 'Cinque' by Anna Akhmatova, inscribed by her
on a book given to Isaiah Berlin in January 1946

It was 10.15 p.m. on 23 August. Japan had surrendered a week before. At the Prime Minister's residence in Downing Street, senior members of the Labour Government gathered for an emergency meeting.

The group met around the long cabinet table, built in the time of William Gladstone, 70 years before. On the wall above the main fireplace hung a portrait of Robert Walpole, the first man to hold the office of prime minister, in the early eighteenth century. Attlee chaired, with Bevin, Dalton, Morrison and Stafford Cripps, president of the Board of Trade. The meeting was joined by Halifax, the economist John Maynard Keynes and Edward Bridges, the cabinet secretary.

Labour was facing its first crisis. A few days before, Dalton had circulated a paper by Keynes. The two men had known each other since Dalton studied at Cambridge before World War I, where he formed a close friendship with the young poet Rupert Brooke.[1] Keynes' paper was entitled 'Our Overseas Financial Prospects'. It made bleak reading. Britain had ended the war in a desperate plight, with debts more than twice the size of GDP. Drastic economies would be required, and assistance from the United States, or Britain would face what Keynes called a 'financial Dunkirk'.[2]

The clock was ticking. When Churchill had met Roosevelt and Treasury Secretary Henry Morgenthau at Quebec, a year before, they agreed that

Lend-Lease would continue during the period between the defeat of Germany and that of Japan. That transition period was now over. On 20 August, the US authorities had given notice that aid shipments would be terminated with immediate effect. For the British, it came as a hammer-blow. 'The dollar sign is back in the Anglo-American equation,' warned a telegram from the embassy in Washington.[3]

Attlee and his team faced a dilemma. In 1942, the economist William Beveridge had published a report on social policy. It was highly popular with the wartime public, selling more than half a million copies. Labour had embraced Beveridge's ideas, and developed ambitious plans to deliver a new National Health Service, social insurance and universal education after the war. Expectation that they could deliver was a major reason for the landslide election victory. But, if Keynes' sums were right, how were they to pay for it all? Failure would condemn Attlee's government to the same fate as that of Ramsey MacDonald 15 years before.

The previous fortnight had seen an odd mix of emotions flow through Britain. There was elation that the war was finally over, but it was coupled with exhaustion and anxiety at the future. One poll suggested that 57 per cent of respondents were depressed, and just 32 per cent cheerful.[4] The atom bomb cast a shadow over victory for many. 'The lynch-pin that had been underpinning the world had been half wrenched out,' reflected Charles Wilson, Churchill's doctor. 'I thought of my boys.'[5]

Attlee invited Keynes to brief the meeting.[6] The economist's advice was simple. The British had no choice but to seek support from the Americans. It would need to be a loan, and probably on commercial terms. To complete the deal, London might even need to throw in some extra concessions, such as military bases in overseas territories. But it should be possible. 'I can almost hear those coins jingling in my pocket,' commented Bevin. But, he added, 'I'm not sure it's really there.'[7]

In relief, Attlee and his cabinet seized at the opening. They agreed, as Halifax put it, to 'turn Keynes loose' in Washington and see what he could get.[8] The next day, Attlee announced the visit to the Commons. His government had a plan.

Ernie Bevin was made of different stock to his predecessor, Eden. Born in 1881, the year before Roosevelt, he was the illegitimate son of a village woman from Exmoor, in Somerset. His mother died when he was seven. He worked from the age of 11, first as a farm hand, then a dock worker in Bristol. Physical labour turned him into an imposing barrel of a man. Bevin, as Attlee later put it, had learned 'the power of voice, fists and feet'.[9]

The Foreign Office had not worked with his like before. At his first encounter with Jebb, Bevin sat in silence for a few moments, scowling. 'Must be kinda queer for a chap like you', he interjected, 'to see a chap like me sitting in a chair like this.'

When Jebb ducked the jibe, Bevin threw him another taunt. 'Ain't never 'appened before in 'istory,' he remarked, in his broad Somerset accent, glancing at the Etonian diplomat through his thick spectacles.

This time, Jebb sprang to the challenge. He pointed out that Thomas Wolsey, chancellor to King Henry VIII, had come from equally humble roots.

'Well,' replied Bevin, impressed. 'I must say, I never thought of that.'[10]

It was a typical exchange. Bevin liked to have a feel for the people he worked with, in a rough-hewn and intuitive way. 'E.B. really takes on too much, sees too many people and throws out too many ideas,' concluded a weary Dixon, at the end of one particularly gruelling day.[11] He was, recalled another official, like an 'elephant which never really sleeps, but grunts, twitches and paws the ground during the night'.[12]

Bevin inherited a difficult portfolio. There was a strong faction within the Labour Party who thought that Britain should not seek confrontation with the Soviet Union. Yet Attlee and Bevin had few illusions about dealing with Stalin. At Potsdam, Attlee spent more than two weeks observing the Soviet dictator. He was, he later recalled, a 'slippery customer', rather like a Renaissance potentate.[13] Bevin had learned to distrust communists during his years in the trade union movement. As a steward for the Dockers' Union, he found that most captains offered to do business over a drink, but the Soviets would withhold hospitality until agreement was reached.[14] In their early weeks in office, both men were determined to follow the course set by Churchill and Eden. 'How fat Anthony has grown,' joked one Labour MP, when he saw the rotund Bevin at the dispatch box in the House of Commons.[15]

September brought Bevin's first test. London was to host the Council of Foreign Ministers. This body, comprising of representatives from the United States, United Kingdom, Soviet Union, France and China, had been established at Potsdam. It was supposed to act as a forum for negotiation of peace treaties with the Axis satellite countries – Italy, Bulgaria, Rumania, Hungary and Finland. The group was also charged with overseeing Germany, and eventually concluding a peace treaty. On 11 September, Bevin welcomed his guests to Lancaster House, a Regency palace on the opposite side of St James's Park to Whitehall. They gathered in an ornate gallery on the first floor, with views across the park to Buckingham Palace.

The group had a newcomer. Georges Bidault was the foreign minister of France. During the war, the British had not enjoyed an easy relationship with their neighbours. Bevin had himself been present at a particularly fraught meeting on the eve of D-Day between Churchill and Charles de Gaulle, leader of the Free French forces. The two met in the Prime Minister's official train, drawn up in a siding at Droxford, in Hampshire, close to where the invasion fleet was embarking on the south coast. In a conversation made even more difficult by Churchill's insistence on speaking French, de Gaulle refused to associate himself with the liberation that was being launched.[16]

Nevertheless, the political imperative to preserve relations between Britain and France remained. After the liberation in August 1944, the Conservative politician Alfred Duff Cooper went to Paris as British ambassador. On the first night of the Lancaster House meeting, he dined with Bevin, Bidault and Attlee. To his amusement, he found himself translating Bevin's dirty stories into French, while Attlee looked on with embarrassment.[17]

The practical problem for the Council was who could make peace with whom. The Allied countries had not all been at war with the same foes: China never declared war against Germany; and France, defeated in 1940, had not technically been at war with those Axis countries which entered the war afterwards. On the opening day of the conference, Bevin proposed a pragmatic way round this problem. All the participants could take part in discussion on peace agreements, but only those who had actually been at war could sign them.

During the war, Molotov had travelled more frequently and further afield than Stalin, with visits to London and Washington, as well as his journey to San Francisco. The two men established a pattern of close consultation. When he was in negotiations, Molotov would report each night by telegram to Stalin, who would send back instructions. At the end of the first day in London, Molotov updated the Generalissimo on events. Recognition of pro-Soviet governments in Romania and Bulgaria had emerged as a sticking point. Stalin encouraged his subordinate to stand firm.[18]

Molotov took note. But he was hopeful of making progress. A week into the conference, he and Bevin dined together, then engaged in a late-night singing session. While the Foreign Secretary gave a rendition of 'Cockles and Mussels' and Byrnes' Irish-American aide sang 'Danny Boy', Molotov launched into 'Roll Out the Barrel'.[19]

A few days later, the atmosphere changed. Molotov had briefed Stalin on the decision to allow all participants to take part in negotiating peace treaties. The dictator exploded. He sent back a reprimand, through Molotov's deputy, Andrei Vyshinsky. 'You must adhere to the decisions of Potsdam,' he declared, switching to the formal pronoun in Russian, as a clear mark of disapproval. Molotov wrote straight back: 'I admit that I committed a grave oversight,' he confessed. 'I will take immediate measures.'[20]

On the following morning, Molotov changed tack. The Soviet delegation asked to delay the plenary session. Bevin and Dixon hurried over across the park from the Foreign Office, anxious to learn what had happened. They found Molotov and Byrnes in a private conversation in the Soviet delegation room, with Bohlen and Pavlov. Molotov explained: the Soviet Union believed, on reflection, that the decision to involve China and France in discussions violated the agreement reached at Potsdam.[21]

Bevin rejected the change outright. It was the Soviet attitude that was holding the conference up, not procedural rules. Molotov was arguing for harmony, but only in line with his own interpretation of what had been agreed. To change now would, he said, 'destroy the Council of Ministers and make it a farce'. Byrnes supported him.

Molotov refused. He might find it difficult, he replied, to proceed on this basis.

Over the next week, all three sides went round the same arguments. Tempers flared, and the conference edged towards collapse. 'Imagine the most difficult and suspicious characters that you have ever known,' commented the French ambassador, René Massigli, over lunch with Harold Nicolson during one break in proceedings. 'Multiply the first and treble the second – and you have some idea what this conference is like.'[22]

Molotov was beginning to get under Bevin's skin. John Foster Dulles watched from his seat with the American delegation. Molotov was, he thought, like a bull-fighter, planting darts in his victim. He realised that it was a deliberate tactic.[23] On 30 September, Molotov offered a new barb. 'Eden was a gentleman,' translated Pavlov. 'Bevin is not.' A few minutes later, Bevin responded in kind. Listening to Molotov, he declared that the Soviet foreign minister's arguments sounded like those used by Hitler. Molotov went pale, and rose to leave. He was only persuaded to return to the table from his position standing at the door, when Bevin offered to withdraw his remark.

Sensing that the game was over, Dixon passed his boss a note, and suggested that they break for a farewell glass of champagne. Two days later, the conference adjourned.[24]

Secretary of War Henry Stimson returned from Potsdam a tired man. His first days in Washington were absorbed with arrangements for the atom bomb and surrender of Japan. Two days after the attack on Hiroshima, at five in the morning, Stimson experienced sharp pains in his chest. A team of military doctors examined him, and advised rest. That afternoon, he broke the news to Truman. He confessed that he felt like a deserter in the middle of battle.[25]

The two men agreed that Stimson should take a holiday. On 12 August, as discussion on terms for the Japanese surrender swirled around Washington, the Secretary of War and his wife Mabel flew up to Highhold, their estate on Long Island. The next day they travelled on to St Hubert's, a country club in the Adirondack Mountains of upstate New York.

Stimson stayed there for three weeks, resting and listening to news over the radio. His thoughts wandered over the events of the preceding months, and in particular the bomb. At Potsdam, Stimson had met Stalin for a private conversation. They talked about life in the outdoors. The Generalissimo told him he believed that Russians and Americans shared something in common. Now, surrounded by the mountain scenery that he loved, Stimson pondered the future. Over a secure telephone link to Washington, Stimson chewed over his ideas with Harriman and McGeorge Bundy, his assistant.[26]

The Secretary decided that the time had come to step down from public service. In early September, he returned to Washington, and called on Truman. Stimson presented a handwritten letter of resignation. As they talked, the Secretary mentioned his thoughts on the atom bomb. Truman encouraged him to set them down on paper.

A week later, Stimson presented his memo to the President. It was a proposal to put the bomb under international control. 'Civilisation', the Secretary argued, 'demands that some day we shall arrive at a satisfactory international arrangement.' While the United States still held a monopoly on the new technology, there was a unique opportunity to shape that deal under terms set by Washington. The Americans should approach the Soviet Union and reach an understanding. 'The only way', the Secretary wrote, 'you can make a man trustworthy is to trust him.' It was a dictum that Stimson had learned at Yale, some 60 years before.[27]

Under Roosevelt, cabinet meetings had been held on a Friday. Truman continued the tradition. Friday 21 September was Stimson's seventy-eighth birthday, and his last day as secretary for war. The President arranged a ceremony to mark the occasion in the White House Rose Garden. He presented Stimson with the Distinguished Service Medal. Afterwards, the cabinet walked inside, to the long room where Truman had taken the oath of office five months before. When they had taken their places, the President invited Stimson to lead a discussion on his paper. After the Secretary had finished speaking, Truman went round the table. Henry Wallace was enthusiastic. Failure to give the Soviets this knowledge, he argued, would make them an embittered and sour people. Acheson, representing Byrnes, was also supportive. However, Fred Vinson, who had taken over from Morgenthau as treasury secretary, and James Forrestal, from the Navy Department, were opposed. The bomb, declared Forrestal, was the property of the American people. To share it with Moscow would amount to appeasement. 'We tried that with Hitler,' he added darkly.[28]

Truman drew the discussion to a close, inviting his colleagues to submit further views on paper. Stimson thanked the group, and left Washington for Highhold.[29]

The same weekend, Truman travelled down to Jefferson Island, in Chesapeake Bay, for a gathering of Democrat congressmen and senators. Under Roosevelt, these informal conferences had become a regular event. Truman continued the tradition with gusto, playing poker on the porch of the island clubhouse with his old colleagues.[30]

The President returned to find Washington in high excitement. News of the cabinet discussion had leaked. Scenting division within the administration, the press latched onto the story that Wallace favoured a soft line with Moscow. To calm the furore, Truman put out a statement. He called on Congress to create a new Atomic Energy Commission, which would ensure civilian control over the bomb, and declared that the administration would explore the scope for international co-operation, through the United Nations. [31]

Journalists were quick to spot the potential contradiction between these two commitments. A week later, during a visit to Caruthersville, Missouri for the county fair, Truman was tackled once again. Did his statement, one correspondent asked, mean that America would not share the secret of the bomb?

Truman tried to draw a distinction. The scientific theory was understood around the world. But only America, he argued, had worked out how to engineer an actual bomb. Other countries would 'have to do it on their own hook, just as we did'.[32]

A few weeks afterwards, in October, Stimson suffered a major heart attack. He survived, and settled into a long period of convalescence. In his youth, Stimson had loved riding. Incapacitated by his condition, he settled instead for touring the estate at Highhold in an Army surplus jeep, shooting or fishing, and swimming in the sea.[33]

'I liken them to bees,' Keynes advised the cabinet after one of his wartime trips to Washington. For weeks, American officials would buzz around without pattern or purpose. Then, when the queen bee in the White House gave off a signal, they would swarm together in a 'compact, impenetrable bunch'. In negotiations, it meant that the outcome remained fluid until the last minute.[34]

The British economist had arrived in Washington with high hopes of securing a loan. Halifax and Keynes led for the UK, with his old sparring partner, Harry Dexter White, on the US side, along with Vinson and William Clayton from the State Department. By late September, however, it was clear that the Americans were playing tough. They queried the figures that Keynes presented, and insisted that a loan on commercial terms was the best on offer. With the war over, neither the US Congress nor public was minded to offer charity to the British. A poll suggested that 60 per cent of Americans were opposed to a loan for the UK.[35]

A fortnight into the talks, Halifax, Keynes, Clayton and Vinson established an inner group, which met in private at Blair House, opposite the White

House. In this private setting, Clayton and Vinson put a deal on the table.[36] They suggested that the US would be prepared to lend up to $5 billion – but there were conditions attached. The loan would bear interest, and Britain must follow through on the commitment she had made at Bretton Woods to make sterling fully convertible. Keynes was interested. Quick calculations suggested that a loan of this size might just be enough. Halifax suggested throwing in American use of military bases in the UK as a sweetener. With a deal in the air, Keynes and Vinson circled each other 'like a bedroom scene in a Noel Coward play', as one member of the British delegation described it.[37]

As the weeks went on, Keynes' health deteriorated. 'Very nervy and difficult to deal with,' wrote one colleague in his diary. 'He is quite exhausted and the effects are not easy for the rest of us.'[38] At night, back at their hotel, Lydia would soothe the pains in her husband's chest with ice cubes provided by room service.[39]

Keynes and Halifax were not just negotiating with the Americans. They had to be able to sell a deal back to London. Their task was complicated by the highly technical subject matter. Dozens of telegrams flowed across the Atlantic each week. Those from Washington to London were labelled 'Baboons' by the British delegation, supposedly because Leo Crowley, the hard-spoken Irish-American who had taken over from Stettinius as administrator of Lend-Lease, looked like an ape. The replies from London were called 'Nabobs'.

'Foreign Secretary, have you got the telegram?' asked Dalton at one evening meeting around the cabinet table in Downing Street.

'I've got 'undreds,' replied Bevin, shuffling his papers in despair. Sir Edward Bridges, cabinet secretary, sidled round the table and rearranged the documents.[40]

Attlee's cabinet was divided. Aneurin Bevan, who was responsible for establishing the National Health Service, led a left-wing faction which wanted to play tough. The mainstream, around Attlee and Dalton, with measured support from Bevin and Cripps, saw the necessity of accepting a loan, but balked at the price. On the night of Tuesday 6 November, debate dragged on until after midnight. Eventually the cabinet agreed to deal. 'We took on the assault in successive waves,' noted Dalton in his diary. 'No doubt it would be much more satisfactory if there were a better practical alternative, but in fact there isn't.'[41]

*   *   *

For five years before becoming prime minister, Attlee had watched Churchill do the job. At times, the conduct of cabinet meetings left him in despair. Churchill failed to read papers in advance, and monopolised the discussion with long monologues. When he took over, Attlee was determined to take a different approach. 'A fairly egocentric cabinet minister can get along,' he later concluded, 'but an egocentric prime minister can't.'[42]

Nonetheless, there were some issues that only the Prime Minister could decide. Within weeks of taking office, it was clear that the atom bomb was in this category. During the war, Roosevelt and Churchill had agreed that scientific co-operation over atomic energy should continue into peacetime. The British watched Truman's public statements with concern. Events were drifting in an unwelcome direction. 'American public opinion is inclined to look on the bomb as an American possession,' warned one official, 'and Congressional opinion will certainly incline to the view that it ought to remain one.'[43]

These public developments were matched by worrying events in private. In early September cipher clerk Igor Gouzenko defected from the Soviet Embassy in Ottawa. He brought with him details of NKVD espionage against the Manhattan Project. However, to dismantle the spy network that Gouzenko had exposed, public prosecutions would be required. The British were willing to take this step, whereas the Americans feared that it would further sour relations with Moscow.[44]

Attlee decided that he must visit Washington. He flew on Friday 9 November. During the journey, he amused himself by reading *Wisden*, the cricket almanac, and quizzing his staff on match statistics. There were, he thought, similarities between picking a well-balanced cricket team and forming a cabinet.[45]

On arrival in Washington, the Secret Service sped Attlee to the White House in a motorcade. The next day, Sunday 11 November, President and Prime Minister attended an Armistice Day commemoration at Arlington National Cemetery. Together with William Mackenzie King, prime minister of Canada, they laid wreaths at the tomb of the Unknown Soldier while a bugler played the 'Last Post'. Afterwards, the three men retired to the US Navy yacht *Sequoia*, moored on the Potomac River. Halifax and Byrnes accompanied them, along with Sir John Anderson, a Conservative politician who had served as Chancellor of the Exchequer during the war, and whom Attlee had asked to stay on and handle atomic matters. The location allowed discussion to take place in private. When one British official attempted to take notes on the conversation, Byrnes insisted that he destroy them.[46]

The British quickly ran into a problem. Their hopes had been pinned on the secret wartime agreement between Roosevelt and Churchill. But it became clear that the Americans had no record of this undertaking. And, regarding the Gouzenko case, Truman offered no clear view. The Americans were themselves embroiled in debriefing another defector, Elizabeth Bentley, who had recently turned herself in to the FBI with details of a Soviet spy ring in Washington.[47]

Anderson and Groves were obliged to negotiate a new memorandum. Alongside this, the president and two prime ministers agreed on a more lengthy public statement, pledging to establish a UN commission on atomic energy, with a view to placing international controls on the new technology. On 13 November, Attlee addressed a joint session of Congress. 'Man's material discoveries', he warned, 'have outpaced his moral progress.'[48]

Attlee travelled back through Ottawa. En route, he learned that Truman had decided not to take action over Gouzenko. 'It makes me despair,' wrote Bevin when he heard the news.[49]

Once Attlee was back in London, negotiations on the loan resumed. By early December, the British concluded that the terms on offer were the best that they could get.[50] Dalton was informed that agreement had been reached by Burke Trend, his private secretary, while taking a bath at the chancellor's residence in 11 Downing Street. The civil servant sat on the lavatory seat, reading the Baboon reporting telegram out loud, as Dalton gestured and splashed with a large sponge.[51]

The loan would need to be approved by Parliament, along with British participation in Bretton Woods. Attlee and Dalton decided to put the vote through quickly, before Christmas. With a large majority, Labour easily won. But the debate had an ugly feel to it. Twenty-nine Labour MPs staged a rebellion, together with many Conservatives. They included the former journalist Michael Foot, who had been at San Francisco, along with fellow recently elected members Barbara Castle and Jim Callaghan. Robert

Boothby, Conservative MP for Aberdeen and former parliamentary aide to Churchill, spoke for many when he dubbed the loan an 'economic Munich'.[52]

As the debate took place, Keynes was aboard the liner *Queen Elizabeth*, travelling back across the Atlantic. In his cabin, he listened to the radio with mounting anger. The economist had persuaded himself that failure to obtain the loan might produce unrest and even civil strife in Britain. 'He thought of the amiable life of the Sussex countryside,' recalled one colleague, 'of cultivated gentle people all over England, living modestly, loving books and music, disseminating sweetness and light.' All this, Keynes believed, was hanging in the balance.[53]

After the Commons, the bill had to pass through the House of Lords. Here, Labour could not rely on a majority. Beaverbrook and others who had championed Imperial Preference might try to derail the vote. The *Queen Elizabeth* docked at Southampton on Monday 17 December, after a voyage of six days. Keynes travelled direct to London, just in time to catch the first day of the debate. On the following day, he spoke. It was, Attlee later said, one of those moments when a single individual can swing the argument. He used a cricketing metaphor to illustrate his point: 'A leader has to be ready to go out and hook one off his eyebrows over the pavilion.'[54]

When Keynes spoke to an audience, it was, recalled one Canadian diplomat who had watched him the previous summer, 'like a great conductor taking over'. His argument 'soared and fluttered and hovered'.[55] On this occasion, Keynes let rip with all the passion and frustration that had built up over his autumn in Washington. Addressing his opponents, he demanded to know if they could offer a viable alternative. Together, he claimed, the loan and Bretton Woods represented hope for a better world. 'I beg those who look askance at these plans', he concluded, 'to ponder deeply and responsibly where it is they think they want to go.'[56]

The vote was carried by 90 votes to 8. The following evening, Dalton hosted dinner at the Savoy. Exhausted, Keynes was obliged to lie on a sofa for much of the meal. He was 'brilliant, ironic and gay', Dalton recalled, 'but terribly tired'.[57]

Bohlen was enjoying his holiday. In early December, he had slipped away from Washington to visit his mother in South Carolina. She was originally from New Orleans, and proud of her French ancestry. Her father had been a senator, and served as American ambassador in Paris at the end of the nineteenth century. His daughter had accompanied him, acting as his hostess. Later, she would delight in taking her own children back to the country that she loved. 'Look,' she told them on one trip, as she pointed to a herd of cows. 'You must admit that they are prettier than cows in America.'[58]

The phone rang. It was Byrnes. The Secretary had been reflecting over the Thanksgiving weekend. Ever since the breakdown of the Council of Foreign Ministers in London, he had been turning over in his mind how to get relations with the Soviets back on track. As he talked with Bohlen, he explained his solution. At Yalta, the three leaders had agreed that their foreign ministers should meet every three months. In principle, this commitment still stood. Byrnes wanted Bohlen to come with him to Moscow.

The diplomat raced back to Washington. He and Byrnes flew to Paris, and then Frankfurt, where they picked up a Soviet navigator and radio-operator. As the plane left Germany, they received news of a weather front over Moscow. The pilot was American, and decided to push ahead. However, unable to communicate with his crew, he lost his bearings in the heavy cloud. The plane drifted off course to the north, then to the east.

The aircraft was due to land at Vnukovo airfield, to the south of Moscow. Deputy ambassador George Kennan was waiting, along with Vyshinsky. Snow lay thick on the ground. As the minutes ticked by, the Deputy Minister became increasingly agitated. Eventually the aircraft emerged from the clouds, and came in to land.

The Secretary stepped out to greet the welcoming party, but he was clad in just a thin coat and ordinary shoes. Bohlen had remembered the Russian winter, and taken the precaution of acquiring winter clothing from the US Army before leaving Washington. Horrified, Kennan bundled the Secretary into a car. They rushed to Spaso House, where Kathleen Harriman plied him with soup and drinks.[59]

Byrnes had not consulted his British colleague before proposing the meeting to Molotov. When Bevin found out, he was furious, and threatened not to come. But his officials eventually talked him into making the journey. The party suffered an equally difficult flight. Ice on the wings forced a second plane, carrying the support staff and Permanent Secretary Alexander Cadogan, to abort and return to Berlin. Dixon was left without his usual entourage of secretaries.[60]

Notwithstanding the weather, Byrnes was determined that the meeting should succeed. Following Truman's pledge for international co-operation over atomic energy, the Secretary wanted to agree a way forward with Moscow. To advise him, he brought James Conant, president of Harvard University, who had been closely involved with the Manhattan Project. In advance, Harriman had prepared the ground. The Soviets agreed to a compromise over the question of involvement in drafting treaties which had caused the break in London. At their first meeting, as a sign of goodwill, Byrnes presented Molotov with a watch and signed photo of himself.[61]

It had not been an easy autumn for his Soviet counterpart. In October, Stalin had left Moscow for a long vacation at Sochi, on the Black Sea. Molotov was left in charge, but the Generalissimo kept a close eye. The foreign press buzzed with rumours that Stalin was ill, and Molotov close to assuming control. At a reception in the Kremlin to mark the anniversary of the Bolshevik Revolution, Molotov appeared to suggest that he was prepared to lift censorship in the Soviet Union.[62]

News reached Stalin. He sent back a telegram to Beria, along with Anastas Mikoyan and Georgy Malenkov, fellow members of the Politburo. It contained a blistering reprimand for Molotov. Stalin instructed the trio to read out the contents to their colleague. As he listened, Molotov was reduced to tears. In a grovelling reply back to Stalin, he pleaded for forgiveness. 'I shall try through deeds to regain your trust,' he promised, 'in which every honest Bolshevik sees not only personal trust, but also the trust of the party, which is dearer to me than my own life.'[63]

The meeting with Byrnes gave Molotov an opportunity to set the record straight. Kennan watched both men around the meeting table. Molotov, he thought, looked like a poker player who knew he had the stronger hand. Byrnes, by contrast, was an intuitive operator. 'He plays his negotiations by ear, going into them with no clear or fixed plan,' lamented Kennan in his diary. 'His weakness in dealing with the Russians is that his main purpose is to achieve an agreement.'[64] Nor was Byrnes interested in keeping Washington abreast of what he was up to. After the first conference session, Harriman asked if he should draft a reporting telegram. Byrnes was scathing. 'The President has given me complete authority,' he told the Ambassador. 'I can't trust the White House to prevent leaks.'[65]

Older Soviet hands looked on with concern. Harriman became exasperated, at one point pulling Dixon aside to apologise for his boss's behaviour.[66] Kennan hosted dinner for Bohlen and Isaiah Berlin, the British academic who had served in Washington during the war, and recently transferred to Moscow for a stint at the embassy. Berlin was Russian by birth. His family came from Riga, on the Baltic, but had emigrated before the revolution. 'The Russians view a conflict with the Western world as quite inevitable,' he told his American colleagues. To expect a different attitude was wishful thinking.[67]

On 23 December, Byrnes called on Stalin at the Kremlin. Bohlen and Harriman accompanied him. They were ushered through a series of chambers, until they reached Stalin's office. The Soviet leader had just celebrated his sixty-seventh birthday. When Byrnes asked how he had spent his vacation, he said that he had been reading the Secretary's speeches. His guest was tickled at the compliment.[68]

Afterwards, the Secretary returned to Spaso House, for drinks and banter with his entourage. He was due at the Bolshoi Theatre, for a special performance of Prokofiev's *Cinderella*, hosted by Molotov. The ballet had been written a few years before, but staging was delayed by the war. Waiting at the theatre, Kennan eyed his watch nervously. The production was due to start. Spotlights shone on the empty official box, where the ministers were due to sit. Eventually, half an hour late, the Secretary arrived.[69]

The conference ran on over Christmas. A few days before the end, Stalin hosted dinner for the three ministers at the Kremlin. Molotov was in a good mood, and ventured a joke.

He looked across at Conant. If the scientist 'had a bit of the atom bomb in his pocket', he said, he should bring it out there and then.

Stalin cut him short. 'This is too serious a matter to joke about,' he interjected. 'I raise my glass to the American scientists and what they have accomplished. We must now work together to see that this great invention is used for peaceful ends.'

Harriman and Bohlen watched Molotov's reaction. Though humiliated, he never altered his expression.[70]

A few minutes later, Byrnes tried another tack. He raised his glass, and offered a toast that those 'whom war hath joined together, let not peace put asunder'. He waited while the interpreters translated his words into Russian. But Stalin and Molotov looked on with blank expressions. With no equivalent phrase in the Soviet marriage ceremony, the joke was lost in translation.[71]

Byrnes and Bevin left Moscow a few days later. The final round of talks had only concluded at 3.30 a.m. – four hours later, Molotov and Vyshinsky waved off the Secretary of State at the airport. Exhausted, Byrnes slept through the first leg of his flight home, as far as the Azores.[72]

As the Secretary made his way home, Isaiah Berlin prepared for another journey. His posting to Moscow was due to end. The journey back to the West would take him by train to Leningrad, and then Helsinki.

On his way home, Berlin wanted to pay a final farewell to someone who had come to symbolise his own complex relationship with the country of his birth. In the autumn, he had made contact with the poet Anna Akhmatova, a leading figure of the Soviet literary scene. Akhmatova had seen her first husband executed in the 1930s. Her son, Lev Gumilev, had only been released from captivity in the Gulag for service in the army. During the war, she and other writers had been afforded greater freedom. Now, that was receding again. At their first meeting, in November, Berlin and Akhmatova had spent a long night together at her flat in Leningrad, locked in conversation and mutual fascination. She was, he recalled, 'a stately, grey-haired lady' with 'an expression of immense sadness'.[73] Berlin was entranced.

On the afternoon of 4 January, he called at Akhmatova's apartment. It was in the Fontanny Dom, formerly a palace of the Sheremetev family in tsarist times. Here, the poet had lived through the ordeal of the wartime siege. Berlin presented her with a copy of *The Castle* by Franz Kafka, in English, and a collection of verse by the Sitwells. In return, she gave him several volumes of her own poetry, with dedications inscribed inside. One was a short poem composed after their first meeting. 'Sounds die away in the ether,' Akhmatova had written, 'And darkness overtakes the dust. / In a world become mute for all time, / There are only two voices, yours and mine.'

Berlin took his leave. At the Finland station, where Lenin had arrived before the revolution in 1917, he boarded a train for Helsinki. When he reached the border, a customs official searched his belongings. The woman picked up the books, and leafed through one of them. She saw the inscription inside, and bowed for a moment in respect. Then, closing the volume, she waved the academic-turned-diplomat on his way.[74]

NINE

Slackened Sail

Of those Rich Lights, Great Halifax shin'd there;
In Pow'rs whole Constellation, None more fair;
In Calms or Storms, in every varying Gale;
The Furl'd, the Hoysted, or the Slacken'd Sail.

Verse on George Savile, 1st Marquess of Halifax (1633–95),
sent by Keynes to Halifax, January 1946

'This afternoon I saw Mr Jebb running', reported one newspaper correspondent, 'with a very *strong* expression on his face!'[1]

Gladwyn Jebb was indeed a man in a hurry. At the age of 45, the British diplomat was acting secretary-general of the United Nations. London was due to host the first meeting of the General Assembly. At San Francisco, Halifax had picked out Jebb, and he asked Cadogan to second him for the job.[2] Following ratification of the charter, Jebb took over from the American diplomat Alger Hiss as head of the UN secretariat.

Through the autumn of 1945, he laboured to set the new organisation in motion. Jebb borrowed an office at Church House, close to the Houses of Parliament. He quickly assembled a team to help him: Brian Urquhart, a former British paratroop officer who had tried to warn his superiors before the disastrous operation at Arnhem; David Owen, a civil servant and former private secretary to Stafford Cripps; and Ben Cohen, a Chilean diplomat. They were joined by two Chinese diplomats, Victor Hoo and Wellington Koo. 'They didn't know whether they were coming or going,' ran one ditty popular among the team, 'Koo, Hoo, Cohen and Owen.'[3]

Problem after problem sprang up. On one occasion, Owen and Urquhart found themselves juggling the competing demands of a delivery of typewriters, a pair of cleaners and the foreign minister of Yugoslavia, Stanoje Simic.[4] Jebb valued people who were decisive. His colleagues learned to walk into the boss's office, and ask for a steer. 'I greatly preferred people who stood up to me,' he later reflected, 'and could never abide having dealings with nervous assistants.'[5] In November, the team ran a dress rehearsal, with a mock debate about the fate of penguins in Antarctica.[6] It was becoming clear that the role of a permanent secretary-general would be crucial. The appointment would be one of the first issues for the new organisation to decide. 'Unless he is a man of quite exceptional character,' mused Jebb in a letter to his predecessor, Hiss, 'he will find himself in the loony bin long before his five year period is up.'[7]

The General Assembly opened on 9 January 1946, with a banquet hosted by King George VI. The following day saw the first working session. The venue was the Methodist Central Hall, where six months earlier the Labour Party had celebrated victory. With money tight, the British could not afford the elaborate staging provided by Mielziner in San Francisco. However, the Ministry of Works did supply chairs covered in light-blue cloth, and erected a podium in front of the huge Victorian organ which dominated the hall.[8]

The American delegation had, like Keynes a month before, crossed the Atlantic aboard the *Queen Elizabeth*. Stettinius led, in his new post as ambassador to the United Nations, along with Vandenberg, Dulles and Connally. On the quay at Southampton, the delegates were greeted by the Lord Mayor of the city, dressed in traditional three-cornered hat and fur-trimmed coat.[9]

Byrnes travelled separately, by air. On the eve of the first meeting of the Security Council, he met with Stettinius at his hotel. He would, he said, leave his predecessor to run the show. The only issue of concern to him was the appointment of a secretary-general. 'I might like to fool about with that a little bit,' he warned.[10]

The delegation was joined by a newcomer – Eleanor Roosevelt. The months since her husband's death had been a difficult time. Bereavement was compounded by the discovery that Franklin had spent his final hours in the company of a long-standing friend, Lucy Mercer Rutherfurd. Early in their marriage, Roosevelt had conducted an affair with Rutherfurd. Eleanor had only agreed to a reconciliation when her husband pledged not to see his lover again. Although the reunion on the eve of his death was apparently platonic, the news was devastating to his widow.

The former first lady had moved to a cottage in upstate New York. She christened the spot Val-Kill, or 'waterfall stream' in Dutch. There, she lived with Fala. The dog, like his mistress, found the adjustment hard. He would sit in the dining room, watching the door in expectation that his master would return. On one occasion, General Eisenhower came to visit. As his motorcade approached the drive, with police escort sirens wailing, Fala's ears pricked up. He thought it was the President.[11]

Eleanor had joined the delegation at Truman's suggestion. At first, she struggled to find a role. 'My contribution,' she wrote to her daughter, Anna, 'beyond the fact that I am Pa's widow and by my presence seem to remind them of him, is very insignificant.'[12] Watching the proceedings, she worried that Byrnes was too cordial with the other delegations, and Vandenberg too arrogant. To provide some balance, she took to hosting tea for female delegates at Claridge's hotel. They were 16 in number, and enjoyed the more informal atmosphere.

The horse-trading over the appointment of a secretary-general was in full flow. Gromyko and Vyshinsky, representing the Soviet Union, argued for Simic, the Yugoslav foreign minister. The Americans and British preferred Lester Pearson, Canadian ambassador to the United Nations. Faced with a stand-off, Byrnes and Vyshinsky cut a deal. They settled on Trygve Lie, a Norwegian socialist who had also been foreign minister for his government-in-exile (and who was dubbed 'Tricksy Lie' by British wags).[13] On 29 January, as the General Assembly closed, Jebb left his seat to make way for his successor, and rejoined the British delegation.[14]

A couple of days later, as the conference was winding down, the Norwegian called on Stettinius. He thanked the American for his support and told him it was a great honour. He confessed that he felt very bewildered. 'I don't quite know where to turn,' he added.

Stettinius assured him that the United States would support him. After the meeting, though, he worried at what he had heard. Lie would clearly need a lot of help.[15]

Harry Hopkins was nearing the end. Following his mission to Moscow the previous summer, the former social worker had retired to his home on Fifth Avenue in New York. He managed a final trip back to Washington in the autumn, to receive the Distinguished Service Medal from Truman. At home, he fretted over what to do with the clutter that he had accumulated through a lifetime in government service. Money was tight, and Hopkins still had a keen eye for a deal. On one occasion he asked Robert Sherwood, his old associate, to track down an art dealer who could value a set of etchings inherited from his first marriage. When the former speechwriter arranged an introduction, Hopkins spent a whole afternoon grilling his visitor on the auction business.[16]

His body, however, was worn out. In November, Hopkins was admitted to hospital, with suspected cirrhosis of the liver. 'I dislike having the effect of a long life of congenial and useful drinking,' he wrote in a last letter to Churchill, 'and neither deserve the reputation nor enjoy its pleasures.' When Harriman called on Stalin in mid-January, bidding farewell at the end of his tour in Moscow, the Soviet dictator asked him to pass on his best wishes to Hopkins.[17] However, it was too late: Roosevelt's former aide was slipping into unconsciousness. He died on 29 January, the same day that the General Assembly closed in London.

The funeral took place on 1 February, at St Bartholomew's Church on Fifth Avenue. Halifax travelled up to New York for the occasion, along with Secretary of the Navy James Forrestal, Supreme Court Judge Felix Frankfurter, Eleanor Roosevelt and a host of other Washington luminaries. The church was decked out in flowers, with creepers festooned around the choir. Halifax later described the scene to Churchill. It was, he thought, rather overdone, like something in a Botticelli picture. After the service, the congregation processed out as the organist played the 'Battle Hymn of the Republic'. Louise, Hopkins' widow, struggled to hold back her tears.

Crowds lined the pavement outside, waiting to pay their final respects. As he left the church, Forrestal turned to thank the rector, who was standing next to the door.

'Well,' replied the priest, 'I think we have given him a good send-off.'[18]

Three weeks later, George Kennan walked into the cipher room of the US Embassy in Moscow. It was a Friday evening.

Harriman had left his post a month before. Kennan stayed on as acting ambassador. The previous 18 months had been both an exhilarating and a gruelling experience. Kennan admired Harriman, but struggled to keep pace. The two men often worked late into the night together. 'He wanted to know everything about everything,' his deputy recalled. On occasion, Kennan would stumble home from the office in the early hours of the morning, only to be interrupted with a call to his bedside phone from his boss.[19] With Harriman now gone, and Moscow in the depths of winter, the

American diplomat had collapsed with a cold, sinus trouble and toothache. He retreated to his bed, to wade through the telegram traffic.

One cable, marked no. 284, caught Kennan's attention. The Soviet Union had announced that it would not, after all, join the International Monetary Fund and the World Bank established at Bretton Woods. A few days afterwards, Stalin delivered a speech at the Bolshoi Theatre. This appeared to argue that the wartime alliance had been a temporary arrangement, and that the inherent tensions between communism and capitalism would now re-emerge. In Washington, Harrison Freeman Matthews, director of the Office of European Affairs, thought it was a turning point. What, he asked Kennan, was the connection between the two events?[20]

Since his arrival in Moscow, Kennan had written a series of long analyses on the Soviet Union. His first was entitled 'Russia – Seven Years Later', and surveyed how the country had changed since his last posting. When Harriman travelled to Washington that summer for consultations, he took a copy with him, but offered no comment back to Kennan.[21] His deputy's evaluation of the Soviet character, dark and realistic, was not in tune with the official view. But, with Harriman gone, Kennan could now speak his mind. 'You're in charge now,' Harriman told him as he left. 'You can send all the telegrams you want.'[22]

As he read cable 284, Kennan decided the moment had come. 'They had asked for it,' he said later. 'Now, by God, they would have it.'[23]

State Department telegrams were supposed to be short and crisp. Kennan ignored the rules. Lying in his bed, he dictated to his secretary, Dorothy Hessman. The text ran to 8,000 words. Kennan then dragged himself to his feet and took his draft to the cipher room. There, the duty clerk, Martha Mautner, translated it into code. To fit the standard cable template, the text was divided into five parts. It was, Kennan thought, like the structure of a Protestant sermon from the colonial era. Mautner gave it the reference number 511.

Kennan's thesis was simple. The Soviet Union, like Russia before it, was a cynical and opportunistic power, focused on advancing its own interests. This historical tendency was exacerbated by an 'atmosphere of Oriental secretiveness and conspiracy' inside Stalin's regime. But, unlike Hitler, the Soviets would not take unnecessary risks. Washington could afford to stand firm. Americans, Kennan told his colleagues, should 'have courage and self-confidence to cling to our own methods and conceptions of human society'.[24]

While Kennan held the fort in Moscow, Harriman had travelled back home. On the way he visited Japan, where he called on the commander of the US occupation forces, General Douglas MacArthur. On his return to Washington, Harriman was awarded the Medal of Merit by Byrnes. 'I want to live my life,' he told reporters after the ceremony. 'Five years is a long time and I want to get to know this country again.'[25]

The former ambassador read Kennan's dispatch. It was, he thought, rather slow going. Nevertheless, he sent his erstwhile deputy a brief message of congratulation. He also passed the text to Forrestal. The Secretary of the Navy seized on what he read. In Washington, the mood was darkening. A few days before, news of the Gouzenko case had broken in public. Now, in Kennan's telegram, Forrestal had found an explanation for why hopes of co-operation with Moscow were flawed. He ordered hundreds of copies to be printed, distributing it to his cabinet colleagues, newspaper editors, and as required reading for his own officials. The cable spread across Washington, where it quickly became known as the 'Long Telegram'.[26]

At the State Department, Matthews was delighted. 'Heartiest congratulations and best wishes,' he wrote back to Kennan. 'I cannot overestimate its importance to those of us here struggling with the problem.'[27]

Life out of office did not suit Churchill. Since defeat the previous July, he had drifted through the motions in his new role as leader of the opposition. That December, at a dinner organised with younger Conservative MPs, he sat bored and silent. 'They are no more than a set of pink pansies,' he moaned to a colleague afterwards.[28] His doctor, Charles Wilson, began to worry for his state of mind. Churchill had suffered from bouts of depression throughout his life, which he called his 'black dog'. In the wake of electoral defeat, the symptoms returned. 'I'm finished,' he muttered to Brendan Bracken on frequent occasions, 'I'm finished.'[29]

In October, Churchill received an unusual invitation. Westminster College, in Fulton, Missouri, was not a familiar name on the diplomatic circuit. But the president, Franc McCluer, was ambitious to put his institution on the map. He contacted Truman through Harry Vaughan, an old friend of the President, and sent him a letter addressed to Churchill. It was an invitation to deliver a lecture at the college. Truman forwarded the letter to the former prime minister with a covering note in his own handwriting. 'This is a wonderful school in my home state,' he wrote. 'Hope you can do it, I'll introduce you.'[30]

Churchill had already planned to spend the winter in Florida. The prospect of combining it with seeing Truman again was enticing. He accepted, and used the holiday to compose his speech.

The prospect of a break was appealing to Truman, too. His first months in office had been exhilarating, with the end of the war, Potsdam and the United Nations. Since then, life as president had settled into a grinding rhythm. 'I'm trying to do what he would like,' Truman would tell visitors, pointing to a portrait of Roosevelt in the Oval Office.[31] But across America, the strains were growing. As servicemen were demobilised, and defence contracts expired, the economy stuttered. Strikes broke out. Inside the White House, Truman struggled to assemble a team of his own. Byrnes, in particular, rankled. The Secretary of State had not kept the President informed during his visit to Moscow. When he returned, he delivered a radio broadcast on the outcome of the conference, without reporting to Truman first. The President tried to give Byrnes a dressing down, but it wasn't clear that the message had sunk in.[32]

The party set off on Monday 4 March, travelling aboard Roosevelt's old presidential train, the *Ferdinand Magellan*. The journey from Washington to Missouri lasted 18 hours. Churchill worked his way through five scotches before dinner. When the meal was finished, the former prime minister turned to Truman.

'Harry,' he said, 'I understand from the press that you like to play poker.'

The President was delighted, and challenged Churchill to a game, along with Vaughan, Charlie Ross, his press secretary, and Clark Clifford, the new White House naval attaché. Churchill changed into his favourite siren suit for the occasion. While the former prime minister was out of earshot, Truman turned to his staff with a grave expression. 'The reputation of American poker is at stake,' he declared. 'I expect every man to do his duty.'

They did as asked. At one point, Ross nursed a hand with an ace and an ace-in-the-hole. Churchill only held a jack. As Ross raised the stakes, an unsuspecting Churchill chose to match him. By the time they finished, in the early hours of the morning, he had lost $250.[33]

The next morning, Truman and Churchill arrived in Fulton. The town was bursting with anticipation. After lunch with President McCluer, an academic procession led across to the college gymnasium, where the speech would take place. Churchill wore the scarlet gown and black cap of Oxford University, while Truman was dressed in a lounge suit. Inside the gymnasium was a platform festooned with garlands and bouquets of flowers. A lectern stood at the centre, with the presidential seal. It was a new design, commissioned six months before. On Truman's instructions, the eagle's head was turned to face the right claw, which held an olive branch. The left clutched arrows, as a symbol of war.

Churchill called his speech 'The Sinews of Peace'. There was, he said, a special relationship between Britain and America. The challenge was to use it for the good of the world. 'Opportunity is here now, clear and shining for both our countries,' he declared. 'To reject it or ignore it or fritter it away will bring upon us all the long reproaches of the after-time.' Working through the United Nations, there was a chance to renew partnership with the Soviet Union, and build a 'temple of peace'. But the moment risked slipping away. A shadow had fallen over Europe, cast by what Churchill called an Iron Curtain dividing east from west.

When the former prime minister finished, his audience burst into applause. Sitting behind him on the podium, Truman clapped enthusiastically.

The President had told his friend beforehand that the text was 'admirable, and [...] would make a stir'.[34] Yet it was strong stuff. That night, the columnist Walter Lippmann and his wife dined at the house of Dean Acheson, assistant secretary at the State Department, along with the diplomat Charles Bohlen and Henry Wallace, secretary of commerce. The speech dominated dinner conversation. Acheson stood by Churchill, arguing that the time had come to stand up to Soviet expansionism. Wallace argued the opposite. By upping the rhetoric, America risked exactly the outcome it was seeking to avoid. Lippmann agreed. Later, in a letter to a colleague, he called the Fulton speech an 'almost catastrophic blunder'.[35]

On his way home, Churchill stayed in New York. Protestors gathered outside his hotel. 'Winnie, Winnie, go away!' they chanted. 'UNO is here to stay.'[36] Inside, Churchill received a visit from Walter Bedell Smith, who had been Eisenhower's chief of staff during the war. Bedell Smith was earmarked to succeed Harriman as ambassador in Moscow, and wanted to hear Churchill's advice before he took up his posting.

Bedell Smith found Churchill in his bathtub. It was the first time that the former prime minister had encountered unpopularity in the United

States. He was clearly disturbed. But he was also unrepentant. 'Mark my words,' he told his visitor. 'In a year or two, they will say "How right Churchill was".'[37]

A few days later, in mid-March, the United Nations arrived in New York.

Until a permanent home was established, the General Assembly and Security Council rotated between different venues. Following the inaugural session in London, it was the turn of New York. In mid-March, Trygve Lie travelled across the Atlantic aboard a converted Lancaster bomber, accompanied by Brian Urquhart. Temporary premises were made available at Hunter College, a private university on the junction of Park Avenue and 68th Street. The gymnasium was assigned for use by the Security Council. The delegates jostled to find their places in unfamiliar surroundings. Writing to his old boss Jebb, Urquhart described the scene: it was, he said, 'a cross between a music hall and a rather large night club'.[38]

The Security Council was facing its first crisis. During the war, the United States, Britain and the Soviet Union had occupied Iran to forestall Nazi infiltration. In doing so, they had committed to withdraw their troops from the country after the end of hostilities. The deadline fell on 2 March, six months on from the formal surrender of Japan. American forces had pulled out at the beginning of the year, and the British followed suit. But the Soviets remained, arguing that the Red Army was required to protect minorities in the northern province of Azerbaijan, which was adjacent to the Soviet republic of the same name. Talks were held in Moscow to resolve the crisis, with the Iranian prime minister, Ahmad Qavam. They proved fruitless; Qavam and his government decided to up the ante, and make a formal appeal to the Council to resolve the dispute.

Stettinius was nursing difficulties of his own. Following his meeting with Molotov in Moscow, Byrnes was keen to make progress over international control on atomic energy. With his encouragement, Truman appointed Bernard Baruch, a former Wall Street banker, as his representative at the United Nations to handle the initiative. The appointment had not been cleared with Stettinius first, and he was left feeling sidelined.

Once in New York, Byrnes met Stettinius to co-ordinate their approaches on Iran. The Secretary had delivered a speech to the Overseas Press Club in Washington a few weeks before, in which he committed the United States to pursue the issue at the United Nations. He warned Stettinius that he wanted to argue the case at the Security Council in person.[39]

The Council session opened on 25 March. Alongside Stettinius, Gromyko served as ambassador for the Soviet Union, and Cadogan represented the United Kingdom. The three men who had brought the United Nations to life through the long journey of Dumbarton Oaks and San Francisco were thus reunited. They sat at a mahogany table, drawn up in a horseshoe shape. Together with the five permanent members, Australia, Brazil, Egypt, Mexico, the Netherlands and Poland filled the remaining seats. In the background, a camera filmed the opening proceedings. It made a sound, Urquhart thought, like that of scrambling eggs.[40]

In Moscow, there were signs that Qavam might be close to a deal. Gromyko pressed to postpone discussion for a fortnight, until the situation became clearer. However, Byrnes was not prepared to wait. Gromyko, too, was in little mood for compromise. Stettinius floated the idea of accepting postponement for just a few days. 'I don't need any help,' his Soviet counterpart snapped back angrily.[41]

Under the UN charter, decision on the agenda was a procedural matter. The veto did not apply. It was this very point which Gromyko had resisted at San Francisco, only to see Stalin concede it to Hopkins. Now, he found himself caught in the exact bind which he had sought to avoid. When the Soviet diplomat proposed that the Council vote on whether to include Iran on the agenda, only Poland supported him.[42]

With Gromyko overruled, the Council proceeded to discuss events in Iran. The following afternoon, debate rolled on for two hours. Byrnes argued that they must act. Otherwise, he said, the Council would 'die in its infancy of inefficiency and ineffectiveness'. Gromyko tried again to close down discussion, with a vote for postponement. Again, he was defeated.

There was only one option left to the Soviet ambassador. He rose to his feet. Carefully, he packed his papers into his briefcase. Then, together with his advisers, he walked out of the gymnasium.[43]

Without the Soviet Union, the Council was stuck. The remaining members wanted to resolve the Iranian issue. But they needed Gromyko at the table. For the first time, the Security Council had fallen hostage to a walkout.

The solution came by another route. A few days later, Qavam and his government announced that agreement had been reached with Moscow. The crisis was defused. Troops would be withdrawn by May, and the position of the Azeri population in northern Iran respected. The Soviets had, it seemed, backed down. However, the Security Council had played little part in resolving the dispute. 'It is degenerating into a tiltyard,' Cadogan warned in a dispatch to Bevin. 'I see little chance of its being used for any other purpose.'[44]

Stettinius had made his mind up. A few weeks later, he travelled to Washington, and went to call on Truman in the Oval Office. The President looked tired and grey. Byrnes sat in on the meeting.

'Well,' said Truman. 'This is awfully bad – every time I get a good man in place and everything begins to click, then he wants to up and leave me.'

'Mr President,' Stettinius ventured, 'if things had worked out as you and I had planned them in San Francisco a year ago, I would not be here today resigning.'

Both Truman and Byrnes were silent. 'Well,' said Truman a few moments later, 'I am terribly sorry.'

'Mr President, this is an extremely sad moment for me,' replied Stettinius. 'I have had my heart in this work.'

'I know you have,' said Truman.[45]

It was Keynes' first visit to Savannah, in Georgia. He liked the southern city. With spring, the streets were lined with purple azaleas and bathed in sunshine. It was, he told the local press, like a beautiful woman, with a face 'concealed behind a veil of delicate lace'.[46] He and Lydia stayed on nearby Wilmington Island, at the General Oglethorpe Hotel.

Savannah had been chosen by Vinson for the inaugural meeting of the International Monetary Fund and the World Bank. With ratification of the Bretton Woods agreement now complete, in all signatory countries except the Soviet Union, the new organisations could be established. Arrangements needed to be made for location of headquarters, recruitment of permanent staff, and appointment of executive directors, representing the main shareholder countries. To welcome the delegates to Savannah, Vinson gave a reception at the General Oglethorpe, and treated them to an impromptu rendition of 'My Old Kentucky Home'.[47]

Just before his departure for America, Keynes had attended the opening of the Royal Opera House, at the company's new home in Covent Garden. As chairman of the trustees, Keynes was due to welcome King George VI and Queen Elizabeth to the event. But, waiting in the foyer, he suffered a minor heart attack, and was barely able to complete his duties. Afterwards, Keynes managed to enjoy the performance. It was the ballet *Sleeping Beauty*, with Margot Fonteyn in the role of Princess Aurora. Seeing artistry restored on the stage after wartime was a powerful emotional experience. 'All the grace and elegant things', he wrote, 'had not entirely vanished.'[48]

At the conference, it became clear that the new Bank and Fund would operate under strong American influence. Vinson insisted that they be based in Washington, with the United States as the largest shareholder. Concerned by what he saw, Keynes gave a speech at the final dinner of the conference. The economist recalled the christening party in the first act of *Sleeping Beauty*. The Fund and the Bank were like a pair of baby twins. Universalism, Courage and Wisdom should be their godmothers. No malicious fairy must put a spell on them, lest they grow up as politicians, with every decision twisted by calculation of national interest. 'I don't mind being called malicious,' Vinson was alleged to have retorted. 'But I do mind being called a fairy.'[49]

Harry Dexter White was in the audience. Before Savannah, Truman had nominated him for the post of US executive director at the Fund. But a shadow was falling over the Treasury official. The FBI investigation sparked by the defection of Elizabeth Bentley had exposed a high-level spy ring in Washington. White appeared to be a member. John Edgar Hoover, director of the Bureau, warned Truman against pursuing the appointment. The President had opted to go ahead, but placed White under surveillance.[50]

The next morning, Keynes and his wife travelled back to Washington, for the return journey to England. His health was not good. Twenty years earlier, the couple had acquired a country home at Tilton in Sussex, at the foot of the South Downs. It had become a treasured retreat. Keynes loved the walk up to Firle Beacon, a vantage point with views across to the English Channel. On their return from America, they returned to Tilton for a rest. Too weak to make the ascent, Keynes was driven up onto the Downs on Easter Sunday. He managed the walk back down, all the while in animated conversation with Lydia about the poetry of Alexander Pope. But the next morning, he suffered another heart attack. This time it was fatal. He died with his wife at his side, a few weeks short of his sixty-third birthday.[51]

TEN

Early Stirrings

There is some soul of goodness in things evil,
Would men observingly distil it out;
For our bad neighbour makes us early stirrers;
Which is both healthful and good husbandry.

Shakespeare, *Henry V*, Act IV, Scene I, quoted by Kennan
to Naval War College, October 1946

Georges Bidault had waited a long time for this moment. It was France's turn to host the Council of Foreign Ministers. After the humiliation of defeat in 1940, the long years of occupation, and the abortive meeting in London the previous autumn, Paris was back at the centre of international diplomacy.

The French Foreign Minister was 46. In 1940, he had served as a sergeant in the French Army. He was assigned to an engineer regiment, and sent to the front in horse-drawn wagons that had seen service in the war with Prussia in 1870. 'No one, not even the officers, knew or cared about what was going on,' he recalled. 'That day was the moment of truth.'[1] Bidault was taken into captivity by the Germans. Later he was released and became a leader of the underground resistance against German occupation inside France. In August 1944, following the liberation of Paris, he walked up the Champs Élysées in a victory parade alongside de Gaulle.

The Council opened on 25 April 1946. Bidault, as host, was determined to lay on an impressive show. Jacques Domaine, head of protocol at the French Foreign Ministry, met delegates at Le Bourget airport. They were driven through the Paris streets in motorcades, each car travelling at high speed with two police motorcyclists in front blowing whistles. The Paris traffic was thick with bicycles. As they sped along, Byrnes and his wife feared they might cause an accident. The Secretary tried to persuade their chauffeur to slow down, but to no avail.[2]

Bidault greeted his guests at the Palais du Luxembourg, in the 15th arrondissement. This ornate residence had originally been built in the seventeenth century for the mother of King Louis XIII. Guests entered through the magnificent Escalier d'Honneur, which led up to the main reception rooms. Members of the Garde Républicaine stood on either side, resplendent in brass cavalry helmets, with drawn sabers.

Behind the display, France was a weakened and divided country. The old Third Republic had collapsed with defeat by Germany and occupation. In the wake of liberation, de Gaulle formed a provisional government. Elections in October 1945 then returned delegates to a constituent assembly, tasked with drawing up a new constitution. But the vote split between communists, socialists and the Mouvement Républicain Populaire, a centre-right party led by Bidault. De Gaulle was suspicious of sharing power with communist ministers. In January 1946, he resigned, gambling that without him France would be ungovernable.

The stage was set for a series of weak governments, as the socialists and Bidault's Mouvement struggled to hold the ring, while the communists became increasingly alienated. In early May 1946, a national referendum rejected the draft constitution by a narrow margin. The following month, Bidault took over leadership of the provisional government. 'France', he recalled, 'had to improve institutions and look for new men.'[3]

The Council was an opportunity for Bidault to show that, notwithstanding these strains at home, he could deliver on the international stage. At Moscow, Byrnes and Harriman had reached agreement with Molotov that France could take part in the negotiation of peace treaties with all the former Axis powers. The stage was now set to draw up these with Bulgaria, Finland, Hungary, Italy and Romania as the minor Axis states. Further down the track was the much more difficult question of what to do about Germany. When asked about what to expect, Byrnes quoted a Negro spiritual, 'Standin' in de Need of Prayer'.[4]

The treaties were less complex than those agreed at Versailles after World War I. There were no major border changes to be decided. Even so, the negotiations could still be tortuous. Discussions over the frontier between Italy and Yugoslavia, around the Adriatic port of Trieste, were particularly difficult. Senator Arthur Vandenberg had accompanied Byrnes to Paris, along with his colleague Tom Connally. He looked on as the Secretary laboured away. 'We spent an entire afternoon throwing commas and colons at each other,' he lamented in his diary at one point. 'It was a day's total loss.'[5] The two senators took to drawing doodles to pass the time.[6]

A week into the conference, Bevin proposed a break to mark the May Day public holiday. He left for a sight-seeing trip to Fontainebleau, while Pierson Dixon, his private secretary, collapsed for an afternoon slumber. That Friday, Bevin and Duff Cooper hosted a reception for the delegates at the British Embassy. The Ambassador and his wife, Lady Diana, had quickly found themselves at home in the magnificent building on the Rue du Faubourg Saint Honoré. Duff Cooper had brought his collection of books from England, and set about creating a library. On the night of the party, a chestnut tree was floodlit in the garden, while Bevin led dancing in the ballroom. The gathering only broke up at two in the morning.[7]

Under the approach agreed between Byrnes and Molotov in Moscow, the Council would draft the outline of peace treaties, then put them to a wider conference of all those countries which had fought against the Axis powers. After a month of laborious negotiation, the Council was ready to move to this second phase. Invitations were issued, and an announcement given to the press.

Hours later, crisis struck. Molotov declared that the wider conference could not take place until rules of procedure were agreed. Bevin was exhausted, and suffering from toothache. The delegates had been up until one o'clock the night before, arguing over conference details. Now the Foreign Secretary snapped. 'I've 'ad enough of this, I 'ave,' he shouted at Molotov, and rose, waving his fists. Bohlen watched, entranced. 'For one glorious moment', he recalled, 'it looked as if the foreign minister of Great Britain and the foreign minister of the Soviet Union were about to come to blows.'

Byrnes intervened, and the incident was smoothed over. Eventually, the session wrapped up at close to nine o'clock. It had, commented Bevin, been a 'most unfortunate' day.[8]

Gilda was America's third atom bomb. The device dropped on Hiroshima was a cylinder, nine feet long, containing a gun barrel that fired two charges of uranium together. *Gilda* was a compact sphere, which used a different

1. Placentia Bay, 1941 – Churchill and Roosevelt at Church Parade on HMS *Prince of Wales*.

2. Placentia Bay, 1941 – Churchill and Blackie the Cat.

3. Tehran, 1943 – Stalin and Harry Hopkins. Interpreter Vladimir Pavlov stands between them, while Molotov looks on from behind. On the right, General Marshall and British ambassador Archibald Clark Kerr shake hands.

4. Tehran, 1943 – Sword of Stalingrad presentation. To the left, Alan Brooke and his fellow Chiefs of Staff look on.

5. Malta, 1945 – Edward Stettinius, Alexander Cadogan and Averell Harriman.

6. Yalta, 1945 – Harry Hopkins, press secretary Stephen Early and Charles Bohlen.

7. White House, 12 April 1945 – Harry Truman takes the oath of office, with Bess at his side, and watched by the Cabinet.

8. San Francisco, 1945 – Molotov, Stettinius and Eden debate a point. Behind Eden sits Clem Attlee, engrossed in reading.

9. San Francisco, 1945 – Senator Arthur Vandenberg signs the UN Charter. Behind him stand Truman, Stettinius, Tom Connally and, to the right, Harold Stassen.

10. Potsdam, 1945 – James Byrnes meets Andrei Gromyko and Andrei Vyshinsky at Gatow airport.

11. Potsdam, 1945 – Ernie Bevin argues his case, flanked by Cadogan and Attlee, filling his pipe. Interpreter Arthur Birse takes notes.

12. Fulton, 1946 – Truman applauds Churchill at the end of his 'Iron Curtain' speech. Clark Clifford stands between them, in naval uniform.

13. White House, 1947 – Marshall takes the oath as Secretary of State, administered by Chief Justice Fred Vinson. Truman looks on.

14. Harvard, 1947 – Marshall on the steps of the Widener Library, flanked by University President James Conant and General Omar Bradley (in uniform).

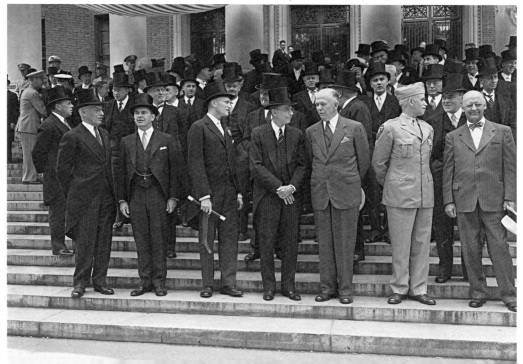

15. Lake Success, 1947 – Eleanor Roosevelt listens to simultaneous interpretation.

16. Washington, 1949 – Dean Acheson signs the NATO treaty, watched by Truman.

method to obtain critical mass for the nuclear reaction: a ring of explosives compressed a core of plutonium from all sides. The name was taken from the film starring Rita Hayworth, which was released in February 1946. Hayworth played a beautiful femme fatale, who enjoyed a tumultuous relationship with her husband, a small-time gambler, and his associate.

The rivalries around Hayworth's atomic namesake were equally complicated. The Manhattan Project had been led by the army, while the air force was responsible for dropping the bomb in action. With the war over, Forrestal was eager for the navy to take a greater role. Truman was committed to rapid demobilisation, and scaling back military spending. In December 1945, the President had announced his intention to bring all three armed services, together with the marines, into a single department of defense. Forrestal was strongly opposed. The bomb offered a way to safeguard the navy's position.

Meanwhile, Bernard Baruch had other ideas. At the age of 76, the former financier saw his appointment by Byrnes as representative to the United Nations for atomic matters as a chance to crown a lifetime of influence in business and politics. Baruch had started out on Wall Street as an office boy. By the age of 30, he had become a millionaire from trading sugar. During World War I, he was an adviser to Wilson, and attended the Paris Peace Conference. International control over atomic energy, he commented, offered an opportunity to 'go towards the light at the end of the tunnel – eternal peace'.[9]

During the spring of 1946, a group led by Acheson and David Lilienthal, former director of the Tennessee Valley Authority, had drawn up plans for how such control might work. They were joined by Conant, Groves and John McCloy, who had served as deputy to Stimson during the war. The group envisaged progressive internationalisation of the atom bomb. A UN agency would be established, and gradually assume control of nuclear materials.

Baruch was not interested. 'The Western Union doesn't take messenger boys at my age,' he told Acheson.[10] The plan struck him as unrealistic, and unlikely to win support. In Congress, Brien McMahon, the Democrat senator for Connecticut, had proposed a bill which would impose a blanket prohibition against sharing of all restricted data on atomic energy. The financier decided that an equivalent hard-headed approach was required at the United Nations. With Byrnes' support, he secured approval from Truman for an alternative proposal. This focused on gradual disarmament, rather than international control. The United States would retain control of the bomb until other countries committed not to develop atomic weapons of their own.[11]

Plans for *Gilda* were well advanced. Forrestal decided to push ahead with a dramatic display of the new device. The location chosen was Bikini Atoll, a remote archipelago in the Pacific captured from the Japanese during the war. The test was codenamed Operation Crossroads. During June 1946, 47,000 personnel laboured to make the final preparations. Ninety-five ships were assembled at the atoll, to simulate the impact of an atomic attack on a naval anchorage. They included decommissioned German and Japanese vessels. At the centre of the fleet was the USS *Nevada*, a veteran battleship which had survived the attack on Pearl Harbor. Her decks were painted orange, for use as an aiming point to drop the bomb. Eight B-17 bombers were adapted with remote-control flight equipment, so that pilots could guide them as unmanned drones over the test area to collect samples and photos.

Back in New York, on 14 June, Baruch launched his plan. He spoke at the UN Atomic Energy Committee, in the same gymnasium at Hunter College where Gromyko had staged his walkout. 'We are here', Baruch announced, 'to make a choice between the quick and the dead.' Fashionable New York society had turned out to listen, and the plan was given a warm reception in the press. 'Better foreign inspectors at Oak Ridge,' commented the *New York Times*, in a reference to one of the production facilities developed under the Manhattan Project, 'than foreign bombs over our cities.'[12]

Three days later, Gromyko tabled a counter-proposal. The Soviet Union agreed with the ambition of disarmament, but wanted a more ambitious timetable. As a model, Gromyko took the Hague Convention on poison gas, which had been agreed in 1925 to ban the weapon after widespread use in World War I. Parties would commit themselves to destroy stockpiles of atomic bombs within three months. In practice, this meant unilateral disarmament for the United States. A few weeks later, Gromyko stayed at Baruch's house on Long Island. The two men talked about their rival proposals. The gap, they both recognised, was unbridgeable.[13]

On 1 July, *Gilda* was detonated. It was the first atomic explosion to take place in peacetime. The test was conducted in front of a large panel of military observers from other countries, including the Soviet Union. In a pointed gesture, British personnel were denied privileged access to the test data.[14]

Forrestal had flown to Bikini for the occasion. After the explosion, he boarded a small launch, and entered the lagoon where the *Nevada* and other ships had been moored. The Secretary of the Navy was joined by Admiral William Blandy, who had overseen preparations. They approached the USS *Skate*, a submarine which had been ripped open by the bomb. Geiger counters started to click rapidly, signifying intense levels of radiation. The party beat a rapid retreat.

Later, Forrestal put out a statement. 'The US Navy', he declared, 'will continue to be the most efficient, the most modern, the most powerful in the world.'[15]

Meanwhile, in Paris, Byrnes was getting impatient. Three days had passed since the dinner at which Bevin lost his temper with Molotov. It was July, and Paris was sweltering in the summer heat. The Council of Foreign Ministers was still unable to agree whether the wider peace conference should go ahead.

Negotiations were stuck over the question of what voting rules to use. Eventually, Bidault gathered his colleagues into his office at the Palais du Luxembourg. It was a closed session, with only the key players present. After nearly six hours, the ministers thrashed out a compromise. Relieved, Byrnes and Bohlen emerged to brief the rest of their delegation.[16]

Nevertheless, at this rate, the Council would take years to complete its job. Byrnes could not afford to wait that long. Before the journey to Paris, he had been diagnosed with heart problems. The Secretary had agreed with Truman that he would step down later in the year. Before he did so, Byrnes wanted to finish the job of making peace. The Council needed to step up the pace, and start talking about Germany.

Since defeat in May 1945, Germany had been administered by the four powers. They operated under the system agreed at Potsdam. Within each zone, military commanders exercised supreme authority. Matters affecting Germany as a whole were decided jointly, by an Allied Control Council. Special arrangements covered Berlin, where the city administration was shared between the Allied powers. In individual states, local German politicians, who were judged not to have links to the Nazi Party, were appointed as minister-presidents. Major Nazi war criminals, including Luftwaffe chief Hermann Goering, were tried by an international tribunal with judges from the four powers, based in the city of Nuremberg.

During the first year of occupation, these arrangements proved moderately successful. General Lucius Clay, who as deputy to Eisenhower was responsible for day-to-day administration of the American zone, struck up a working relationship with his Soviet counterpart, General Vassily Sokolovsky. The two men would dine and watch a film together with their wives. Sokolovsky was an avid reader of English novels, especially Jane Austen, and enjoyed engaging in conversation with his Western colleagues.[17]

Nevertheless, the occupation faced enormous strains. Some six million refugees fled from the eastern provinces of Germany, in Prussia and Silesia, which had been transferred to Poland. Huge numbers flocked to the western zones, preferring to take their chances under the British and Americans. In the major cities, orphaned children roamed the streets. Economic production collapsed. Touring the British zone in March 1946, the British Jewish writer, Victor Gollancz, was appalled at what he saw. Daily food intake had fallen to 1,000 calories, barely more than that given to concentration camp inmates. Child mortality had increased dramatically since the end of the war. 'The plain fact is', he wrote, 'that we are starving the Germans.'[18]

As the occupation continued, differences emerged between the four powers. In London, frustration was mounting. Britain could ill afford the cost of a prolonged occupation. Both the Soviets and French, on the other hand, favoured a tough approach. France had been invaded by the Germans three times in living memory, in 1870, 1914 and 1940. French national security, so the orthodoxy ran, required that Germany be kept weak by occupation. To suggest any alternative was, as one British diplomat put it, 'like talking kindly about the devil in the Vatican'.[19]

Within the Foreign Office, thinking was moving towards abandoning a four-power approach, and running the western zones of Germany as a separate enterprise instead. This so-called 'western option' had a strong advocate in Sir Orme Sargent, who had taken over from Cadogan as permanent secretary in January 1946. Sargent was sceptical about working with Moscow, just as he had been over compromise with Germany at the time of Munich.[20]

Byrnes believed that this went too far. It was, he thought, still possible to hold Germany together and work with the Soviets. His model for a peace treaty was based on a proposal that Vandenberg had made to the Senate a year before. In London, nine months later, Byrnes floated the idea with

Molotov. He suggested a deal between the four Allied powers which would leave Germany neutral for 25 years. Byrnes repeated the suggestion to Stalin when he visited Moscow in December 1945. The Generalissimo sounded interested. 'If you decide to fight for such a treaty,' he told the Secretary, 'you can rely on my support.'[21]

Encouraged, Byrnes had sent a draft text to Molotov in February 1946. He received no response. At the end of their first week together in Paris, he tabled the text as a formal proposal.[22] But, when he raised the topic with Molotov and Vyshinsky over dinner, they stonewalled. To add to the air of menace, Soviet bodyguards stood outside the door of Byrnes' hotel suite as they dined, even barring his wife from returning to her room.[23]

For the next two months, Molotov held back from giving Byrnes an answer. Meanwhile, back in Moscow, the draft treaty was circulated around the government system for views. The conclusion was almost unanimous: Byrnes' plan was a ploy. Neutrality was meaningless. One official declared that it would lead to a 'military renaissance' of Germany under American leadership. The Soviet Union could not afford the risk.[24]

In mid-July, Molotov finally gave his response. He told his colleagues that he wished to make a statement in response to Byrnes' proposal. The Soviet Foreign Minister produced a text, and began to read. The treaty, he said, was motivated by the interests of world peace and security. But the provisions that it included were inadequate to meet this aim. It needed radical revision.[25]

The next day, Molotov delivered a further statement. 'The spirit of revenge', he began, 'is a poor counsellor in such affairs.' The Soviet Union did not wish to see the destruction of Germany, but rather the birth of a democratic and peace-loving state. Moscow was prepared to listen to the aspirations of the German people. The Allies should concentrate on establishing a trustworthy and peaceful government in Germany first. Only once this had been done would it be possible to conclude a peace treaty.[26]

Unknown to the other participants, Stalin had personally vetted the text. An earlier draft had stated that once reparations had been paid, the Red Army might withdraw from Germany. But Stalin removed the reference. 'We at the present stage', he told his foreign minister, 'cannot limit the time of occupation.'[27]

Byrnes could see that the chances of reaching a treaty that year were receding. When Molotov had finished speaking, he offered a few words in response. The Council had, he noted, been engaged in negotiating peace treaties for the minor Axis countries since the previous September. They did not know how much longer it would take. Was it not possible to begin preliminary discussions on Germany in parallel?

Molotov refused. It was too soon to take this step.

That evening Byrnes discussed what he had heard with Lucius Clay, commander of the US occupation zone, along with Connally and Vandenberg. Local elections were due to take place in Germany later in the autumn. It was a first, tentative step towards the reintroduction of democracy. In the Soviet zone, a grassroots communist party was growing under the leadership of Walter Ulbricht, a former cabinet-maker who had spent the Nazi period exiled in Moscow. The group surmised that Molotov was making a play for German public opinion, in the hope that voters would lift the communists into power.

Clay argued for a fresh start. At the start of the occupation, the Americans had adopted a draconian approach, reflecting the influence of Henry Morgenthau's abortive plan to reduce Germany to a pastoral state. Clay disagreed with this stance, and, over the first year of occupation, sought to present a more human face. At his initiative, orders to American military units were transmitted uncoded over the airwaves, so that ordinary Germans could listen in.[28] Rules on so-called 'fraternisation' between American soldiers and German civilians were relaxed. Now he saw an opportunity to go further. He sent a paper to Byrnes, with ideas for moving towards more self-government in the western zones.

In early September, Byrnes travelled to Berlin, along with Vandenberg. He wanted to see the country for himself, and consult with Clay. Together, Secretary and Senator travelled across Germany to Stuttgart, riding aboard a train that had belonged to Hitler. Byrnes and his wife used a lavender-tiled bathroom built for the Nazi dictator. 'Look who's here!' shouted out one American soldier as they passed. 'Hi, Jimmy!' The party were shocked by the devastation. It was 'past comprehension,' wrote Vandenberg in his diary. 'There certainly won't be any "German menace" again in my lifetime.'[29]

They arrived in Stuttgart just before noon on 6 September. Byrnes met the minister-presidents for Württemberg, Bavaria and Hesse at the train station, still scarred with bomb damage. Stuttgart was home to the German motor manufacturers Daimler and Porsche, whose factories had been heavily targeted by British and American bombers. By the end of the war, some 4,500 inhabitants of the city had been killed, and 15 million cubic metres of rubble lay in the streets.

Together with Clay, Byrnes and the minister-presidents went to the Opera House. Known as the Grosses Haus, it was one of the few public buildings still standing in the city. The nearby Kleines Haus, where Richard Strauss had staged the premiere of his opera *Ariadne auf Naxos* in 1912, had been destroyed. As Byrnes walked up to the stage, a US military band played the song 'Stormy Weather'.[30]

Flanked by Clay, Vandenberg and Connally, with the Stars and Stripes hanging against the theatre safety curtain behind them, Byrnes delivered a speech on American policy towards Germany. It was his riposte to Molotov. The country should not become a 'pawn or a partner in the military struggle for power between the East and the West', nor be subject to a long 'alien dictatorship'. Byrnes jabbed with pointed finger to emphasise his points. 'I want no misunderstanding,' he said. 'We will not shirk our duty. We are not withdrawing.'

At the end of the speech, the audience erupted with applause. When the clapping had died away, the band played 'The Star-Spangled Banner'. Hearing the American national anthem, Vandenberg later told Byrnes, had never before given him such a thrill.[31]

Harry Truman was feeling the strain. The journey with Churchill to Missouri had been a welcome interlude. Back at the White House, issues piled onto his desk. Days were filled with meetings. Each night, the President would plough through hundreds of pages of paperwork. In May, America was brought to a standstill by a national coal and railroad strike. Midterm elections to the House and Senate loomed in the autumn. It would be the first national poll since Truman had taken over. 'Mr President,' read one telegram from an irate voter, 'Zero Hour is here. Who is to rule our nation?'[32]

Truman stood firm. When he demanded new powers from Congress to break the strike, the trade union leaders stepped back from the brink and returned to work. But the boost to the President's authority was short-lived. Within his cabinet, deep differences were emerging over how to handle the Soviet Union. While Navy Secretary James Forrestal favoured a hard-line approach, Henry Wallace, secretary of commerce, took the opposite view.

To gauge what his officials were really thinking, Truman asked Clifford and George Elsey, the assistant who had overseen redesign of the presidential seal, to conduct a private survey of opinion across senior levels of the administration about the reality of working with the Soviets.

On 12 September, Wallace was due to give a speech at Madison Square Garden, New York. The Commerce Secretary ran through his draft with Truman first. However, under pressure of work, it was a hurried meeting, and the President had not focused on the detail.

Assuming that he had presidential authorisation, Wallace circulated the text in advance to journalists. The speech was a loosely disguised rebuttal to that given by Byrnes in Stuttgart only days before. 'The real peace treaty we need', it argued, 'is between the United States and Russia.' Wallace added that Truman had read the text and endorsed it. At a press conference on the afternoon before the speech was delivered, one journalist threw the President a question. Did Truman stand behind what the Secretary intended to say?

Truman walked into the trap. He had, he said, approved the whole speech.

Scenting blood, others piled in. Was the speech a departure from Byrnes' policy?

No, Truman continued. They were exactly in line.[33]

As Truman's staffers, Ross and Clifford were still learning the media game. Ross himself had not read the speech. After the press conference was over, he failed to spot the implications. Even when William Clayton, acting as secretary of state during Byrnes' absence in Europe, suggested that Wallace should be asked to withdraw, he did not see the urgency. That evening, Truman, Ross and Clifford settled down for a game of poker at Clifford's Washington home.[34]

The next morning they awoke to a shock. The Washington press had seized on the story. Truman found himself in a firestorm. Byrnes reacted with fury, and threatened resignation if Wallace was not sacked. The Secretary of Commerce dug in. The two men had been potential rivals to Truman for the nomination as vice-president in 1944. Now they were locked in a stand-off. Vandenberg issued a statement from Paris, where he was attending the international conference to conclude the peace treaties negotiated that summer. 'We can', he warned dryly, 'only co-operate with one secretary of state at a time.'[35]

Truman found himself in a position that he loathed. To be successful, he wrote to his daughter Margaret, a president must be a 'liar, double-crosser and an unctuous religio, a hero and a whatnot'.[36] For almost a fortnight, he tried to find a way of bridging differences between the two men. But it was impossible. Then, in a fit of temper, he wrote an angry private letter to Wallace, demanding his resignation. The following morning, Truman realised the potential damage if the letter leaked. On his instructions, Clifford quietly retrieved it. Wallace replied in short, measured terms, offering his resignation, and pledging to 'continue to fight for peace'.[37] Nevertheless, the wounds remained – Truman's administration was weakened. His personal poll rating fell to a new low of 32 per cent.

A few days later, Clifford presented the President with the report that he and George Elsey had written. It made for bleak reading. Most officials, they reported, believed that the Soviet Union and the United States were embarked on a collision course. Moscow's goal, the report concluded, was 'in direct conflict with American ideals'.[38]

At seven o'clock the next morning, Truman called Clifford.

'How many copies of that memorandum do you have?' asked the President.

Clifford had ordered for 20 copies of the top-secret report to be printed, and planned to distribute them around the administration.

'I want them all,' responded Truman. 'I think you'd better come down now, Clark [...] if this got out it would blow the roof off the White House, it would blow the roof off the Kremlin.'

The President took the copies, and locked them in his personal safe.[39]

The midterm elections in November 1946 brought heavy losses for the Democrats. Campaigning under the motto 'Had Enough?', Republicans gained a majority in both houses. After the long years of Democrat ascendancy under Roosevelt, the pendulum seemed to be swinging back.

In the 12th congressional district of California, a former naval officer, Richard Nixon, defeated the incumbent Democrat by a margin of over 15,000 votes. Among the small new intake of Democrats, former naval officer and journalist John F. Kennedy secured a seat for Massachusetts. In Michigan, where Vandenberg was re-elected with a margin of more than half a million votes, the senator celebrated with his wife and daughters. As results flowed in from across the country, Republican Party grandees flocked in to join them. Vandenberg looked set to be a key power-broker in the new Congress. One staffer played 'Hail to the Victors Valiant' on a piano. It was the marching song for the University of Michigan.[40]

Truman cast his vote back where his career had begun, in Independence, Missouri. That night, he returned to Washington aboard the *Ferdinand Magellan*, playing poker with Ross and a group of reporters. At each stop, election results were passed to the travelling party. Truman seemed calm. When Margaret handed him a slip of paper with the latest scores, he smiled. 'Don't worry about me,' the President said. 'I know how things will turn out and they'll be alright.'[41]

The following morning, Dean Acheson knew where he needed to be. Over the last 18 months, the Under-Secretary had become close to the President. During Byrnes' long absences abroad, Acheson had endeavoured to steer the ship, and maintain cordial relations between the Old Executive Building and the White House. He and Truman came from very different backgrounds. Acheson was the son of a bishop in the Episcopalian Church. Educated at Groton and Yale, with a bristling moustache and tailored English suits, the 53-year-old was the epitome of East Coast sophistication. But he had developed a deep respect for Truman. The President, he believed, combined integrity and common sense. On one occasion, when Acheson intervened to defuse a row with the Soviet Embassy, Truman pulled him aside in the Oval Office. He reached across his desk, and picked up a gold-coloured frame. It contained a picture of Bess. On the back, she had written: 'Dear Harry, May this photograph bring you safely home from France – Bess'. The inscription was dated 1917.[42]

The *Ferdinand Magellan* was due to arrive at Union Station. The vast, vaulted terminal was built 40 years earlier, to serve the Pennsylvania and Baltimore railroads. In Roosevelt's administration, it had been a tradition for cabinet members to greet the President here as he returned to Washington after an election victory, and escort him to the White House. But, on this occasion, only Acheson turned up.

As a solitary figure stepped from the train, book under one arm, the Under-Secretary stepped forwards to greet his president.

Truman had a smile on his face.

The first step towards constructing an atomic bomb was to build a nuclear reactor. The Manhattan Project had reached this milestone in December

1942, with a prototype housed in a squash court at the University of Chicago. Soviet nuclear scientist Igor Kurchatov had long wanted to match the American achievement. During the war years, however, his team struggled to acquire the necessary raw materials. Calculations suggested that 500 metric tons of graphite, and 50 of fissile-grade uranium, would be required to build a pile of sufficient mass.

After Hiroshima, and with NKVD chief Lavrentii Beria in charge, everything changed. The NKVD constructed a vast network of secret facilities across the Soviet Union and Eastern Europe. Uranium ore was mined as far afield as the Harz Mountains of Germany and along the Kolyma River in Siberia. A plant at Elektrostal, outside Moscow, processed the rock into round slugs, for insertion into the reactor. Kurchatov and his colleagues were inundated with supplies.

The team worked at a secret complex called Laboratory No. 2 in a Moscow suburb. Under a house in the grounds, they dug a pit to house the reactor. It was seven metres deep. Using the same approach as the Americans, the Soviet scientists built up graphite blocks into a pile. They had estimated that 76 layers would be required, but by number 58 it was clear that the count of neutrons was increasingly rapidly. When the sixty-first was reached, the reaction was ready to begin.

The date was 25 December 1946. It was six o'clock in the evening. Kurchatov ordered all staff to leave the building, except for his immediate assistants. Slowly, they removed the cadmium rods which controlled the speed of the reaction. Red lights flashed on the gamma-ray monitors, and the rate of clicks increased from the neutron counters. The reaction was gathering pace.

'Well,' Kurchatov said, 'we have reached it.' He ordered his team to reinsert the control rods. For the first time, the Soviet Union had generated nuclear energy.

A few days later, Beria came to inspect the facility. Once again, Kurchatov and team activated the reactor. On the control panel, clicks and flashes grew more urgent. 'It's started,' shouted the scientists.

'Is that all?' asked Beria, as he peered into the pit containing the pile of graphite. 'Nothing more?'[43]

ELEVEN

Something Brewing

When we gathered on Mondays with Oscar Ross Ewing
It was certain that something momentous was brewing;
But of 'side' and false pride he completely did lack,
So we called him by nothing more pompous than 'Jack'.

'Ode to the Wardman Park Monday Night Club',
composed by Leon Keyserling in 1973

It was a cold and icy morning in January 1947. The reporters huddled in a shed at Union Station for warmth. With them stood Colonel Marshall Carter, an aide to General George Catlett Marshall.

More than two months had passed since Truman arrived at the same spot after defeat in the midterm elections. Battle-lines were forming up in Washington, with an eye to the presidential elections the following year. Few commentators thought that the incumbent would be re-elected. The press pack was looking to anoint alternative contenders.

Just after nine o'clock, the Statesman Limited train from Chicago pulled into the station. Carter dashed along the platform. He spied his boss. Marshall was wearing a camel-hair coat with a fur collar. As he stepped out of the door, Carter pulled him aside with an urgent message.[1]

Marshall had recently passed his sixty-sixth birthday. An upright man, with light blue eyes and a serious expression, the General was the offspring of an old Pennsylvania family. He had graduated from Virginia Military Institute, and served in the US Army for more than 40 years, until his retirement at the end of World War II.

Along with Secretary of War Henry Stimson, Marshall had overseen the largest mobilisation of American manpower ever known. On the eve of D-Day, Marshall received news that his own stepson, Allen Brown, had been killed in action. He bore the news with characteristic fortitude. 'He was a big man in every sense of the word,' recalled Ismay, who worked with him in joint Anglo-American staff meetings. 'He carried himself with great dignity.'[2] At home, Marshall was a man of simple tastes. He went riding for exercise along the Potomac each morning, and limited his vices to a weakness for maple candy and pulp fiction.[3]

After the war, Truman had dispatched Marshall to China, to mediate between communist and nationalist forces in the civil war. It was a thankless mission. In the summer of 1946, Eisenhower visited Marshall at his residence in the nationalist capital Nanking. He brought an invitation from Truman. Following Byrnes' decision to step down as secretary of state, the President was looking for a successor. Would Marshall take on the job?

The General accepted, but asked to remain in China for a final shot at brokering agreement between the two sides. Eisenhower and he agreed a set of codewords with which to communicate over the appointment. Truman was thrilled when he heard the news. 'This', the President declared, 'gives me a wonderful ace in the hole.'[4] For Marshall, the benefits were less clear-cut. The salary was not generous, and a return to duty would mean that his army pension would be cut in half. The General had been offered up to half a million dollars to write his memoirs. He had declined. An honest account would damage senior public figures, Marshall reasoned, and, after a lifetime of service, he would not contemplate such an act of disloyalty.[5]

Marshall had flown back from China in early January, just as Truman announced his appointment to succeed Byrnes. He and his wife, Katherine, had stopped in Hawaii for a vacation, then travelled on to Chicago. Severe weather delayed their arrival in Washington.

Monday 20 January 1947 was Byrnes' last day in office. His final act was to sign the five peace treaties that he had negotiated on behalf of the United States. A few weeks earlier, *Time* magazine had hailed him as 'Man of the Year'. But a lasting peace in Europe remained elusive. Without agreement over Germany, a settlement over the minor Axis countries was only a halfway house. Lippmann called it an 'attempt to govern the moon in order to regulate the sun'.[6]

As Marshall stepped from the train, Carter slipped his boss a note. It was from James Shepley, a trusted contact who worked for *Time*. Marshall was a respected figure on both sides of the political divide. A few days earlier, confirmation of his appointment had been swept through the Senate without the usual committee hearing. But Shepley had picked up rumours that Vandenberg saw Marshall as a potential candidate for the presidency, and thus a political threat. Any such perception would cast a shadow over his post from the start.[7]

Marshall realised immediately that he must take action. Throughout his career, the General had been scrupulous in maintaining political neutrality. He even refused to cast a vote in elections. Standing on the platform at Union Station, he gathered the shivering reporters around him. After he had answered a few standard questions, he called them to order. 'I'll give you something,' the General said.[8]

'I think', Marshall continued, 'this is as good a time as any to terminate speculation about me in a political way.' He went on. 'The office of secretary of state is non-political, at least under present conditions, and I am going to govern myself accordingly.'[9] Throughout his time in office, Byrnes had been coloured by suspicion that he harboured presidential ambitions. Now, with a single shot, Marshall had changed the equation. 'By taking himself out of the presidential campaign of 1948,' Reston told his readers, 'General Marshall has simplified his job.'[10]

Having made his statement, Marshall drove to the White House. In a brief ceremony, he took the oath of office. Fred Vinson, the former treasury secretary whom Truman had appointed as chief justice the previous summer, conducted the ceremony. Byrnes was also present. Afterwards, Marshall walked across to the Old Executive Building with Acheson. He turned to his new colleague.

'Will you stay?' he asked the Under-Secretary.

'Certainly,' Acheson replied.[11]

'Gentlemen, don't fight the problem. Solve it!'[12]

In the weeks that followed, Acheson and his colleagues became used to Marshall's favourite dictum. The General had found his new department in disarray. 'Lawyers aren't organisers,' he later recalled. 'They didn't have any organisation [...] and you couldn't get your fingers on the damn thing.'[13] Marshall moved to introduce military efficiency. He designated Acheson as his deputy, and Carter as his chief of staff. All issues were to come through them. 'You didn't make jokes with the Secretary,' recalled one official. 'He was a man who, when he made decisions, everybody knew nothing small and calculating went into the decision.'[14]

Spotting his moment, Acheson raised a question which had been festering for the last six months. The State Department had swollen almost fourfold since the start of the war. The Old Executive Building was too small and antiquated; 3,200 employees were now spread across 17 different buildings around Washington. New premises had become available at the old War Office building. This purpose-built office was in the Foggy Bottom district of Washington, a few blocks to the north-west of the White House. Was it time to move?

Marshall asked for the reasons against.

'Tradition,' answered Acheson.

'Move!' ordered the General.

Four months later, the migration was complete.[15]

The State Department had become used to what one official later described as 'policy lag'. American diplomacy followed events, rather than leading them. Acheson warned Marshall that his shake-up might induce a spate of heart attacks. Carter predicted that it would take six months for things to fall into shape.[16]

In fact, the new regime quickly settled down. Under Byrnes, the department had experimented with holding a morning meeting each day, to co-ordinate business. But, with the Secretary frequently out of town, it had not taken hold. Acheson revived the practice. Every morning, at 9.30, the main division heads would gather in his office. Acheson chaired, supported by Carter and Clayton. It became known as the 'prayer meeting'. Participation became a badge of pride, and junior officials competed to gain seats at the table.[17]

Arthur Vandenberg had a new job. With a Republican majority, the Michigan senator became chairman of the Foreign Relations Committee, and president of the Senate. Normally, the Vice-President would preside over Senate meetings. With the post vacant, the role fell to Vandenberg. Each morning, a government Cadillac would collect him from his lodgings at the Wardman Park Hotel. He occupied an ornate office with crystal chandeliers next to the Senate chamber. When Truman gave a formal dinner in his honour, a Marine Corps band and singers from the Metropolitan Opera in New York provided music.[18]

It was the Eightieth Congress since the foundation of the republic. Expectations were running high. With success in the midterms, the Republicans were a step closer to winning the White House in 1948. Vandenberg and his fellow senator Robert Taft were both potential nominees for the Republican ticket. Taft saw himself as a conservative traditionalist, committed to upholding what he called the 'American Way of Life'. The New Deal, he believed, had been in conflict with the original principles of the founding fathers who established the republic. Bureaucracy and social interventionism would stifle American enterprise. In the wake of the strikes the previous year, Taft wanted to curb union power. He co-sponsored a bill with Fred Hartley, a Republican congressman from New Jersey, to tighten rules on picketing, secondary strikes and closed shops.

Vandenberg struck a different tone. While Taft sought to put distance between Republicans and Democrats, Vandenberg championed bipartisanship. Days before Byrnes retired from office, he shared a platform with the Secretary for a last time, at the Cleveland Foreign Affairs Forum. His speech called for a 'permanent American foreign policy [...] which serves all America and deserves the approval of all American parties'.[19]

The Democrats faced a similar choice. Two years on from Roosevelt's death, they needed to define a new direction. At the Wardman Park Hotel, a group of younger members started to gather for regular meetings on a Monday night, over drinks and a steak dinner. Their host was Oscar Ewing, acting chairman of the Democratic National Committee. The circle included men like Leon Keyserling, vice-chairman of the President's Council of Economic Advisers, and David Morse, assistant secretary of labor. They saw themselves as liberals, who wanted neither a retreat back to the era of the New Deal, nor to compete head-on with Republican conservatism. The group agreed to formulate common positions, and support each other in advocating them within the Truman administration.

Clark Clifford was their link to the White House. The former naval aide had become one of Truman's most trusted advisers. Clifford came from St Louis, in the Midwest. It helped him relate to the President's own Missouri roots. At six foot tall, with blond good looks, he projected a steadiness which the President needed. 'Clark's key to success with Harry S. Truman', Keyserling later wrote in a ditty, 'was simply that both were so very human.'[20]

* * *

'Christ it's bleeding cold!' wrote the Oxford undergraduate Kingsley Amis to his contemporary, Philip Larkin. 'Life here is quite impossible.'[21]

Britain was in the grip of the worst winter since 1880. At the end of January 1947, temperatures plummeted. Readings as low as -21 degrees Celsius were recorded; the River Thames froze over.

Britain ran on coal. With the country snowbound, distribution collapsed. The railways became blocked by snowdrifts. Power stations were forced to ration output. Electricity was only available for five hours a day. Pipes froze. At their home on Mount Street, in London, Gladwyn Jebb and his wife Cynthia sat shivering, wrapped in eiderdowns and hot water bottles. A visit to Harrods, which had its own power generator, provided a brief respite.[22] In Parliament and at Buckingham Palace, staff were reduced to working by candlelight.

The fuel shortage presented Attlee's government with its worst crisis yet. In 1946, economic recovery had looked in prospect. Labour pressed ahead with its plans for the National Health Service and social security. Swathes of the economy, including the railways and coal mines, were brought under public ownership. A sense of satisfaction spread through Attlee's cabinet. In January 1947, just before the cold struck, they presented Attlee and his wife with an engraved salver to mark their silver wedding anniversary. The Downing Street cook made an iced cake, in the shape of the number 25.[23]

Now all that was cast into doubt. Unemployment leapt from 400,000 to 1.75 million in the space of a few weeks.[24] 'It will take us months and months to recover from this disaster,' lamented Harold Nicolson in his diary.[25]

With the crisis, hard choices beckoned. The British Empire had ended the war with strategic commitments far beyond her straitened financial circumstances. Across the Middle East, Asia and the Pacific, there were some 140,000 soldiers, 78,000 RAF personnel, and naval forces including two battleships, five aircraft carriers, 20 cruisers and 40 destroyers. Britain was providing military support against a communist insurgency in Greece, maintaining a UN mandate in Palestine, and facing mounting ethnic and sectarian strife in India. Occupation of Germany and Austria required a further 280,000 personnel. Through their first 18 months in government, Attlee and Dalton had tried to persuade Bevin and the Chiefs of Staff that their commitments were unsustainable. They made little headway.[26]

A further burden was added in October 1946. Following the Bikini tests, Truman had signed into law the bill tabled by Senator McMahon, which prohibited sharing of atomic technology. The door was firmly closed on co-operation with the United States. With a small inner circle of ministers, meeting in a committee under the anonymous title GEN 75, Attlee weighed up whether Britain should build its own bomb. Dalton and Cripps flinched at the cost. It was Bevin who swung the issue. At one key discussion, he made an impassioned plea. They needed to have the bomb with a 'bloody Union Jack flying on top of it'. Without that, he argued, British foreign policy would always be subservient to the United States.[27]

'There are occasions', Attlee reflected in his retirement, 'when if you hesitate and go slow things will get not better but worse.'[28] February 1947 was one of them. As snow lay outside Downing Street, Attlee and Dalton pushed the cabinet into a series of dramatic choices. Britain would have to scale back. The government agreed to give India independence, no later than June 1948. Attlee dispatched a new viceroy, Lord Louis Mountbatten, to prepare the ground. Responsibility for Palestine would be handed over to the United Nations. And British aid to Greece and Turkey would be terminated at the end of March. The British Empire was entering its final chapter. When Attlee announced the decision to the House of Commons, Churchill dismissed it as 'Operation Scuttle'.[29]

It was a grey Friday afternoon in Washington. At the State Department, Acheson was holding the fort. Marshall had left at lunchtime to travel down to New Jersey. He was due to attend the bicentennial commencement ceremony at Princeton University that weekend. In the corridors, files were being packed into crates, ahead of the move to Foggy Bottom.[30]

A message arrived. It was from the Private Secretary to Lord Inverchapel. Archibald Clark Kerr, as Inverchapel was known before his elevation to the peerage, had moved across from Moscow to Washington the previous summer, in succession to Halifax. The Ambassador had an urgent, formal note to hand over to the Secretary of State.

Acheson agreed that, in Marshall's absence, the Ambassador's private secretary might pass an advance copy to Loy Henderson, head of the Office of Near Eastern Affairs in State. The son of a church minister from Arkansas, Henderson had served in the Red Cross in World War I. He married a

Latvian woman, and joined the Foreign Service as a Russian specialist. A few years older than Kennan and Bohlen, he served with them in Riga, and then under Bullitt in Moscow.

Inverchapel's note arrived at three o'clock, together with a supporting paper. They were, Acheson later recalled, 'shockers'.[31] Inverchapel conveyed details for the withdrawal of British aid from Greece and Turkey, where the army was mobilised on a semi-permanent basis against the Soviet threat. Henderson and John Hickerson, head of the Europe division, went straight to Acheson. 'We're right up against it now,' commented the Under-Secretary.[32] All three men were clear that the American response would have to be immediate. Acheson instructed his colleagues to work through the weekend.

By Sunday evening, the staff work had been done. Henderson and Hickerson assembled a set of papers, outlining the scale of needs posed by both countries, and the case for America to fill the gap left by the departing British. They gathered at Acheson's house in Georgetown, and briefed him on their work. Before turning in for the night, the trio downed a couple of martinis, to the success of their enterprise.[33]

The following morning, Marshall met Inverchapel. Then, at lunch in the White House, he briefed Truman, Forrestal and Robert Patterson, who had succeeded Stimson as secretary of war. The problem had, he said, been 'dumped in our lap'.[34] Support to Greece and Turkey would cost an estimated $250 million. Yet the group was clear that America had no choice but to accept the challenge. A communist take-over in Greece would, commented Forrestal, mean 'the world cut in half'.[35]

Expenditure on this scale could not be met within existing allocations. It would require a specific authorisation. Since the Eightieth Congress had opened the previous month, Republicans had been engaged in a showdown with the administration over the budget. They were, joked the senator Henry Cabot Lodge, cutting expenditure 'like a man wielding a meat axe in a dark room'. Truman had submitted a proposal for $41 billion, covering the year 1947. The Senate was only prepared to authorise $37 billion.[36]

Three days later, on Thursday 27 February, Truman, Marshall and Acheson invited a delegation from Congress to the White House. All the heavyweights were present: Vandenberg, Connally, Speaker Joseph Martin and leaders of the various budget committees. Only Taft was absent.

Truman invited Marshall to speak. This was, the Secretary argued, 'the first crisis in a series'. The Soviet Union was seeking to expand its influence in the Middle East and more widely. The choice was between 'acting with energy or losing by default'.[37]

Vandenberg was suspicious. The senator disliked this 'crisis method', as he called it. The administration would confront Congress with urgent requests for support which could not be turned down.[38] He had not been briefed on Greece in advance. It felt as though he was being bounced.

The other senators and congressmen were also not convinced. One commented that it sounded like 'pulling British chestnuts out of the fire'. They peppered Marshall with questions: What exactly was involved? How much would it cost? In their internal discussion beforehand, Hickerson had called for a pitch to Congress which would 'electrify the American people'.[39] But Marshall's explanation had been dry and analytical. Acheson sensed the mood slipping away. Under his breath, the Under-Secretary caught his boss's attention.

'Is this a private fight?' he asked. 'Or can anyone get into it?'

Marshall motioned to Truman. The Under-Secretary, he said, wished to speak.

Before entering government, Acheson had trained as a lawyer. He served as a junior staffer to Louis Brandeis, the celebrated Supreme Court judge. Whereas civil law taught the general, he later reflected, 'training in the common law concentrates one's attention on the specific.'[40]

Acheson took the floor. He started his pitch with the general, and worked up to the specific. For nearly two years, since the end of the war, Byrnes had led the search for peace. It had proven fruitless. Meanwhile, communist influence was expanding. Greece lay at the intersection of the Mediterranean, Europe and the Middle East. Like apples rotting in a barrel, communist takeover in Athens could spread eastwards, to Turkey and Iran, southwards, into Egypt, and west, to Italy and France. The Soviets risked little, and could make great advances in return. Far from pulling chestnuts out of the fire, America had to face the reality that Britain was close to bankruptcy. Only the United States could act.

Acheson finished. Silence fell. Then, at last, Vandenberg turned to Truman.

'Mr President,' he said. 'If you say that to Congress and the country, I will support you, and I believe that most members will do the same.'[41]

*   *   *

In early March, Truman travelled to Mexico. It was the first time that an American president had made a state visit to its southern neighbour.

He returned to Washington, which was still recovering from a late-winter downfall of snow, on Thursday 6 March. During his absence, Acheson, Leahy and Clifford had worked on a message for Congress. At Clifford's urging they had decided to upgrade the format to a set-piece speech, before a joint session of both Senate and the House.

Truman was not a natural public speaker. He preferred to interact with people in person, shaking hands on the campaign trail or trading votes in the Senate. On a podium, he could sound hollow. His voice became more high-pitched, accentuating his Midwestern vowels. He chopped his hands up and down for emphasis, while rocking on the balls of his feet. It was a far cry from the assured, patrician style of Roosevelt. The president, ran one popular Washington joke, missed a cabinet meeting because his limbs were too stiff from trying to put his foot in his mouth.[42]

Clifford knew that this speech would be crucial. Joseph Jones, speechwriter in the State Department, produced an initial draft.[43] Clifford and Elsey then spent a Sunday in the White House, scrubbing the text. They read sections aloud to each other, trying to put it in words which would sound authentic to Truman.

The core was a request to Congress for $400 million in support for Greece and Turkey. Jones followed Acheson's approach, and put this in a broader context. His text contained a passage calling for 'the United States to give support to free peoples who are attempting to resist subjugation [...] [and] work out their own destiny'. But, for Elsey and Clifford, the draft felt too bureaucratic. They hit on a simple reformulation. Truman had grown up with the language of the Bible.[44] His first address to Congress after Roosevelt's death had concluded with a prayer from the Book of Solomon. The two men decided to break down the key passage into three sentences, each starting with the words 'I believe'. They dubbed it the 'credo'.[45]

The speech was due to take place two days later, on Tuesday 12 March. It was to be a joint session of Congress, held in the House of Representatives. As the congressmen took their places, Bess Truman struggled to find a seat, until an aide came to help her. At 12.45 p.m., Speaker Martin called the audience to order. Then Vandenberg entered, as senate president, leading a procession of senators who had walked through from their own chamber at the other end of the Capitol building. They were followed by the President and members of his cabinet.

Truman mounted the podium, his speech in a black folder under his arm. 'Mr President, Mr Speaker,' he began, acknowledging Vandenberg and Martin seated behind him.

The President, himself a former senator, launched into his speech. 'The gravity of the situation which confronts the world today', he declared, 'necessitates my appearance.' Truman continued, making the same case that Acheson had outlined in the Oval Office a fortnight before. Failure to act in Greece would have far-reaching effects, in both the West and the East.[46]

The speech went on. Truman spoke for more than 15 minutes. Building to a climax, he delivered the credo that Clifford and Elsey had composed.

'I believe that it must be the policy of the United States to support free peoples.

'I believe that we must assist free peoples to work out their destiny in their own way,' he continued, hands chopping up and down.

'I believe that our help should be primarily through economic and financial aid.'

As Truman ended his remarks, the audience burst into applause. The President reached across to shake hands with Vandenberg and Martin. Then, as the clapping continued, he flashed a smile at Bess, and offered a slight bow.[47]

Previous speeches by Truman had not left much of a mark. This time was different. It was, the *New York Times* wrote afterwards, a speech that had changed American foreign policy 'in the space of twenty-one minutes'.[48] The *Washington Post* called it 'one of the most momentous ever made by an American Chief Executive'.[49] Within a few days, Washington commentators were calling it the 'Truman Doctrine', and comparing it to that of Monroe more than a century before.

Lippmann was uneasy. In rushing to take action, he warned his readers, the administration had bypassed the United Nations. It was an opportunity missed. Working through the organisation that Roosevelt had created would have 'answer[ed] the charge that we are doing what we have so often charged others with doing'.[50] At a Washington dinner party a few weeks later, Lippmann clashed with Acheson. The two heavyweights engaged in heated argument, words and gestures flying. Guests looked on in shocked fascination. Lippmann worked his way through cigarette after cigarette. The next morning, with a throbbing head and dry throat, he resolved to quit smoking.[51]

In Moscow, Molotov read Truman's speech with interest. He discussed it with Nikolai Novikov, the Soviet ambassador who had taken over in Washington when Gromyko moved to New York.

'The president is trying to intimidate us, to turn us at a stroke into obedient little boys,' Molotov told his representative. 'But we don't give a damn.'[52]

TWELVE

Across the Harbour Bar

Then with a song upon our lips, sail we
Across the harbor bar — no chart to show
No light to warn of rocks which lie below,
But let us yet put forth courageously.

From 'At Graduation 1905', by T. S. Eliot, recipient of
an honorary degree from Harvard in 1947

Moscow was having a spring clean. The city was due to host the fourth meeting of the Council of Foreign Ministers. At the Moskva Hotel, just opposite the American Embassy, the rooms had all been refurbished. The doormen were dressed in new, elaborate uniforms. A sparkling line of new Zis taxi cabs appeared outside.

Three days before Truman delivered his speech to Congress, Marshall arrived in the Soviet capital. He travelled in a C-54, accompanied by Charles Bohlen, his assistant Marshall Carter and John Foster Dulles, the Republican expert on foreign affairs. Vyshinsky met them at the airport, along with Bedell Smith, who had served as ambassador since the previous spring – he wore a bowler hat for the occasion. Marshall, who had served in uniform alongside Bedell Smith for much of his army career, was unimpressed at this civilian garb.

The American delegation stayed at Spaso House. Bedell Smith handed over his ambassadorial bedroom to Marshall. The ballroom, where Kathleen Harriman had broken the news of Roosevelt's death to her father, had been turned into a typing pool for the secretaries. The dining room, still in the drab colours that Kathleen had loathed, had become a canteen. Bedell Smith's wife dispensed meals on trays for those who could not break away from their desks.[1]

The delegation settled into a routine. Marshall would study his papers each morning, clad in a blue Chinese robe. He had brought a record player with him, and listened to classical music as he worked.[2] At around 10.30 a.m., the delegation would gather to prepare for the Council. Marshall and Carter sometimes went off to take exercise on the Lenin Hills, to the south-east of the city centre. It was here that Kathleen had practised her downhill skiing. An NKVD detail would follow them at a distance, and the streets emptied of pedestrians as they passed.[3] Bedell Smith was, in any case, rather self-conscious about his appearance. A few days into the conference, the soldier-turned-diplomat visited a Soviet barber. He spoke no Russian, and the barber no English. When Bedell Smith asked, in sign-language, for hair tonic, the barber misunderstood and applied red hair dye. Despite repeated washing, the ambassador was left with a distinctive tinge to his neat side-parting.[4]

Bevin had a more leisurely journey to Moscow. In Paris the previous summer, the Foreign Secretary had collapsed with heart trouble. His doctor had given him use of his sailing boat, moored on the Hamble estuary near Southampton, for a period of convalescence. Long-distance travel by aircraft was forbidden, so for this trip, Bevin opted to travel by train.

En route, he and Bidault had met at Dunkirk, to sign a new treaty between Britain and France. The British ambassador to France, Alfred Duff Cooper, joined them; the treaty was largely his initiative. Bidault had chosen the venue, as a place resonant with the wounds of defeat in 1940. Dunkirk was still in ruins, and largely deserted. The signing ceremony was held in the prefecture, one of the few buildings left intact. Afterwards, both delegations walked on the beaches where the evacuation had taken place seven years before. 'We gazed on the desolate sight of a derelict sea coast under a winter sky,' Cooper noted in his diary, 'and shivered.'[5]

From Dunkirk, the journey to Moscow took four days. At Brest-Litovsk, on the old Polish border, Bevin and his colleagues changed over to a Soviet train. It ran on a broader gauge of track than those in Western Europe. Bidault came by the same route. Once in Moscow, the British party were guests of Sir Maurice Peterson, who had taken over as ambassador when Archibald Clark Kerr moved to Washington.

Peterson and his wife were animal-lovers. They kept a brood of chickens in the attic, to supply them with eggs. The family dog was an elderly

Scottish Terrier called Brindle. One night at dinner, Bevin was offered what looked like dog biscuits with the cheese. He asked Lady Peterson if this was indeed the case.

'As a matter of fact they are, Secretary of State,' she replied. 'But we like them.'

Bevin paused. Silence fell, as they sat in the ornate dining room where Stalin had admired the portrait of George V. Then he ventured a question.

'I 'ope I'm not depriving Brindle of his dinner?' asked the Foreign Secretary.

'That's quite all right,' replied the Ambassador's wife. 'Brindle won't eat them.'[6]

The Council met at the Hall of Aviation Industry, near the Moskva Hotel. Molotov played host. 'Hand covering chin, elbow on table, slowly nodding his head,' Carter described in a letter home to his wife. 'Completely poker faced.'[7] Beside him sat Vyshinsky. The other ministers sat at opposite points of a circular table, flanked by four or five assistants. Carter hovered at a smaller table behind, ready to run errands.[8]

Marshall had come to Moscow with modest hopes. With the other peace treaties signed, he believed that it might just be possible to launch negotiations on the treaty over Germany which had eluded Byrnes. What he found dismayed him. Molotov and Bevin spent much of the first week trading blows over a report on the Allied occupation. During the second week, discussion moved onto the principles which should underpin a treaty. Here, more serious divisions opened up. While Molotov and Bidault continued to argue that the Germans should pay heavy reparations, Bevin warned that it would leave an 'economic cesspool in the middle of Europe' and sow the seeds of the next war.[9] 'It's a little difficult', commented one member of the American delegation in a letter home, 'to see where we go from here.'[10]

The Council dragged on through March, and into April. The Western delegates took the opportunity to see Prokofiev's *Cinderella* at the Bolshoi, and the ballet *Romeo and Juliet*, which the composer had completed before the war, and then re-choreographed. But the conference itself was heavy going. Charles Kindleberger, an economist in the American delegation, described it to a colleague back in Washington as 'snail-like'.[11]

'Where are we?' asked Bevin during one particularly tedious session.

'God knows,' replied Bidault.

'I didn't know that he was a member of the Council of Foreign Ministers,' the British Foreign Secretary shot back.[12]

The Western foreign ministers took it in turns to call on Stalin in the Kremlin. Bidault was invited to do so first. It was a calculated nod to the French. De Gaulle had signed a bilateral treaty with Moscow in the autumn of 1944, as a snub to the British and Americans. The Soviets still hoped to prise Paris away from London and Washington. 'It is better to be two against two than three against one,' Stalin assured Bidault when they met.[13]

Bevin went next. Like Bidault, he called on Stalin late at night. The Soviet dictator was in a friendly mood. When Eden had first visited Moscow in December 1941, he had launched negotiations on an Anglo-Soviet treaty of friendship. It was time, Stalin suggested, to renew this. 'The thing for you and me to do is keep the ball bearings greased,' he declared, 'so that there won't be friction when we do meet.'[14]

Marshall held back. He wanted to see how his talks with Molotov played out before meeting Stalin. As he got the measure of his opposite number, Marshall became more skilled at anticipating his attacks and countering them. On one occasion, Molotov claimed the US Department of Commerce had seized a vast number of German patents from the US occupation zone. Advised by Kindleberger, Marshall calmly produced a memo prepared by the department, which noted that such material had been made publicly available in the United States. Amtorg, the Soviet procurement agency based in Washington, was the largest customer. Molotov had been caught out. Vyshinsky burst into laughter, while his boss looked grim.[15]

Eventually, on 15 April, Marshall went to the Kremlin. It was ten o'clock at night when the American party arrived. Marshall was accompanied by Smith and Bohlen. It was the first time that the American diplomat had seen the Soviet dictator since Byrnes' visit to Moscow almost 18 months before. He looked tired and careworn. On the Soviet side, Molotov and interpreter Vladimir Pavlov were present, along with Nikolai Novikov, ambassador in Washington. They met in a wood-panelled conference room, next to Stalin's own office.

Marshall recalled their wartime partnership. He reminded Stalin of the discussion at Tehran, four years earlier, when he had briefed the Allied leaders on plans for the D-Day landings. Even at that moment of high tension between the Allies, Marshall and Stalin had enjoyed a cordial relationship. When the arguing was done, the Generalissimo had wrapped his arm around the American's shoulders in solidarity.[16]

Marshall then steered conversation back to the present. He spoke for almost an hour. 'I went at Mr Stalin hot and heavy,' he recounted to a friend a couple of months later, 'and minced no words whatsoever.' During the war, he said, the American public admired the Soviet Union. But that goodwill was now fading, as a result of Soviet attacks and obstructionism. Six weeks in Moscow, Marshall said, had led him to the conclusion that the Soviets were not serious about a treaty over Germany.

Molotov interjected. It was Britain and America, he declared, who had violated the common approach agreed at Potsdam.

Marshall glowered. He pointed his figure at Molotov, and looked at Stalin. 'There is', he stated flatly, 'not one word of truth in what that man says.'[17]

The Soviet dictator sat impassive throughout. Bedell Smith and Bohlen watched as he doodled on his notepaper with a red pencil, drawing wolves' heads. It was a favourite pastime. During one of the wartime conferences, the British Royal Marine, Leslie Hollis, and Admiral Cunningham from the Royal Navy spotted that Stalin had left a sketch on the table. At the end of the working session, both men raced to bag the souvenir. Hollis beat his naval rival by a whisker.[18]

When Marshall had finished, Stalin spoke in response.

It had, he conceded, been a difficult period for the Soviet Union since the end of the war. Losses had been greater than first appreciated. Perhaps the Soviet bureaucracy had made mistakes. Nevertheless, it was important to proceed carefully. Napoleon had divided Germany, only to lay the seeds of subsequent reunification and the rise of Prussia. Naturally, the former Allies had differences of view. They should 'have patience and not become depressed'. The Soviet Union, he assured Marshall, would not turn negotiations over Germany into some kind of game.

It was approaching midnight. Marshall thanked Stalin, and took his leave. As they rose from their places, Bedell Smith glanced at his watch. The meeting had lasted 88 minutes.[19]

A week later, on Thursday 24 April, Molotov hosted a final plenary session. It was the forty-third of the conference, and produced no more movement than the previous occasions. That evening, Stalin entertained his visitors to a farewell dinner at the Kremlin, in the great hall of Catherine the Great. After drinks with members of the Politburo, the Generalissimo led them into the main dining room. It boasted an ornate vaulted ceiling, with gold lacquer on the cornices and elaborate chandeliers. He was dressed in a simple military uniform, while Molotov wore a dark blue suit.

Wartime dinners had been lengthy and liquid affairs. At Yalta, both Brooke and Cadogan privately vented at the late nights and large quantities of vodka.[20] This occasion was more restrained. Bedell Smith noted that the meal lasted for little more than an hour, and the food was relatively modest. Andrei Zhdanov, Politburo member in charge of ideology, was on a diet, and confined himself to soup and water.

There were five toasts during the dinner. Stalin began, with a tribute to Truman and Marshall. Molotov followed, proposing a toast to Bevin and Marshall. Then, in a deliberate insult, he offered a separate toast to Bidault. The Frenchman reddened, but kept his counsel.

After dinner, Stalin led his guests down a blue-carpeted curving staircase, to a private cinema. The seats were laid out in pairs, so that each Westerner was hosted by a member of the Politburo. On a small table in front stood chocolates, cigarettes and a double magnum of champagne.

The group watched a recent Soviet film, called *The Stone Flower*. This movie was shot in colour, on Agfa film captured in Germany. It had won an award at the inaugural meeting of the Cannes Festival in the previous September. The plot was based on a Russian folk tale, about an orphan craftsman called Danila, and his quest to find the perfect malachite with which to carve a flower.

The group broke up at midnight. By Soviet standards, it was an early night. When Bevin, Byrnes and Molotov had dined at the Kremlin 16 months before, the meal lasted until three o'clock in the morning.[21] As they drove back through the darkened Moscow streets to Spaso House, an air of gloom hung over the Americans. Bedell Smith had arrived in the Soviet Union believing that the wartime partnership could be kept alive. Now, he was not so sure.[22]

The ministers left Moscow the next morning. Vyshinsky came to the train station to bid farewell to Bevin. The British Foreign Secretary was in a cheery mood. After seven weeks in Moscow, he was glad to be going home.

'The more we are together, together, together,' he sang. 'The more we are together, the merrier we shall be.'

'What a jolly man!' commented Vyshinsky with a sneer.[23]

Marshall's flight home lasted two days. During a stop-over in Berlin, he conferred with Clay and General Robertson, the British military commander in Germany. His meeting with Stalin had made a deep impression. Like Bedell Smith, he believed it right to try finding a way through with the Soviets. But now that seemed to be impossible. Stalin was content for Europe to drift. The Moscow Conference had provided clarity. Dulles later compared it to 'a streak of lightning that illuminated a dark and stormy scene'.[24]

Marshall and his colleagues arrived home at lunchtime on Saturday 26 April. While still in Moscow, he had decided to continue the pattern established by Byrnes, and deliver a radio broadcast on the results of the conference. This took place on the Monday evening. It was the first that Marshall had given as secretary of state. The General was not a natural public speaker, but his calm, factual style worked well on radio. It was not, he said, a time for what Lincoln had called 'pernicious abstractions'. Concrete solutions were needed. 'Disintegrating forces are becoming evident,' Marshall warned. 'The patient is sinking while the doctors deliberate. So I believe that action cannot await compromise through exhaustion.'[25]

The next day, Marshall summoned Kennan. The diplomat had returned from Moscow the previous autumn. At the suggestion of Forrestal, he had taken up a one-year post at the National War College. This new facility was created by the Navy Secretary to prepare officers for senior command positions. It was a happy period for the Kennan family, with Annelise, his Norwegian wife, and their two young children. They lived in a house provided by the army, with tennis courts and a swimming pool. At weekends the family would retreat to East Berlin, the 235-acre farm which Kennan had acquired in Pennsylvania. Tending the property became an ongoing project.

Kennan called on Marshall in his new office at Foggy Bottom. It was a bare room with a high ceiling on the sixth floor. A portrait of Stimson hung on the wall. Leather-backed chairs with armrests stood on either side of the desk, for visitors. A single blotter and stand for pens lay on the surface between. It was kept clear of papers.[26]

The General explained. When he arrived at State, he had found an organisation without a central policy capability. 'You can't operate and plan at the same time,' Marshall later observed. 'You just had a hit or miss affair going on around there.' He wanted Kennan to create a new policy team.[27]

Kennan's assignment to the War College was due to run until June. Marshall instructed the diplomat to cut it short. Time was running out to stem the drift in Europe. If the State Department did not seize the initiative, others would act instead, including in Congress. As Kennan rose to leave, Marshall offered one final piece of advice. 'Avoid trivia,' he told the diplomat.[28]

The Policy Planning Staff was launched a week later. Marshall believed that quality of people was more important than numbers. Operating at breakneck speed, Kennan assembled a small team around him. They included Charles Bonesteel, a colonel from the US Army, and John Paton Davies, who had served with Kennan in Moscow. The group were based in a suite adjoining Marshall's office. Knowing that he was weaker on economic issues, Kennan tried to fill the gap. He approached Paul Nitze, a former banker who had served with the Board of Economic Warfare during the war, then moved across to work with Clayton in the Office of International Trade Policy. However, Acheson, who had clashed with Nitze, blocked the appointment. 'George, you don't want Nitze,' he warned. 'He's not a long-range thinker, he's a Wall Street operator.'[29]

During his year at the National War College, Kennan had delivered a series of lectures. They acted as a mould for his thinking. The posting in Moscow had led him to conclude that co-operation with the Soviet Union would not work. But nor, he believed, was confrontation the right course. With the invention of the atomic bomb, total war threatened the end of civilisation. Strategists needed to revert to the world of the eighteenth century, in which statesmen manoeuvred for long-term advantage without risking all on the battlefield. Kennan turned to the historian Edward Gibbon, whose history of the Roman Empire he had read during the war. The Soviet Union, he believed, was doomed to overreach itself in the same way. For Americans, the key was to have strategic patience.[30]

Like Lippmann, Kennan was dubious that the Truman Doctrine offered the right answer. The rhetoric of Clifford and Elsey's credo was too sweeping. He preferred to take a different tack. His advice was presented to Marshall on 23 May. The paper was given the reference PPS/1, as the first product of the new planning staff. An aid programme for Europe should, Kennan argued, be more practical in focus. It should require the European recipients to work together, be limited to four or five years, and involve direct aid, not loans. Above all, decisive action was needed. Europe must have 'the impression that the United States has stopped talking and begun to act'.[31]

Lippmann was coming round to a similar viewpoint. A few weeks earlier, he wrote a column, under the banner 'Cassandra Speaking', a pseudonym that he used only for the most serious pronouncements. Europe, he warned, was collapsing. America must be ready to contemplate assistance 'on a scale which no responsible statesman has yet ventured to hint at'. It would amount to a new programme of Lend-Lease.[32]

Four days after Kennan submitted his paper, Clayton offered his own memo to Marshall. Aged 67, the Assistant Under-Secretary was born in Mississippi. He had left school at 13, and entered the cotton business, rising to head the largest cotton trading company in the world. Clayton entered government service during the war. He worked for Wallace, but clashed with the then vice-president, and moved across to the State Department under Stettinius. A generation older than Harriman or Acheson, Clayton was an imposing six foot three inches, with white hair swept back and a robust, businesslike manner.

Clayton had returned from a visit to Europe the previous week. Over lunch with Nitze at the Metropolitan Club, he recounted what he had seen. He was particularly struck at how the link between countryside and cities was breaking down. Farmers were hoarding produce, reluctant to sell while city dwellers had nothing to offer in return.[33] He had started to record his thoughts on the flight back over the Atlantic. Back in the office, he finished his draft.

'It is obvious', the paper began, 'that we grossly underestimated the destruction to the European economy by the war [...] Europe is steadily deteriorating.' Demand had collapsed. Export industries were caught in a catch-22 situation, unable to earn the dollars that they required to pay for raw materials. The problem was compounded by the constraints on industrial output in Germany imposed by the occupation. Grants, perhaps of six or seven billion dollars a year, were required. The key would be to mobilise public support in the United States. The President and Secretary should make a 'strong spiritual appeal', and ensure 'the American people are taken into the complete confidence of the administration and told all the facts'.[34]

This was what Marshall had wanted. Kennan and Clayton had framed the debate. He gathered together his key advisers. Acheson, Clayton, Kennan and Bohlen were all present. At Marshall's invitation, Clayton introduced the discussion. The General canvassed views around the room. On the broad strategy, there was no disagreement. All believed that a major aid programme was required. As Marshall himself observed, it would be folly to 'sit back and do nothing'. The questions were more tactical. How to deal with the Europeans? And how to handle Congress?

The group agreed that European governments themselves would need to take responsibility. Bohlen talked about laying the foundations for an economic federation in Europe, three or four years down the track. The more difficult question was whether to invite the Eastern Europeans and the Soviets to participate. Kennan argued to 'play it straight'. Bohlen agreed, but thought it a gamble. Acheson noted that it would take several months to secure agreement from Congress. The Americans would need to negotiate with the Europeans first, to establish momentum.[35]

Marshall did not offer his own verdict. 'The general was an orderly man,' Kennan recalled. 'He had asked us for a recommendation and he had received it.' He wanted to reflect in private before taking a decision. In closing the meeting, he reminded his officials to guard against leaks.[36]

The General did not take long to decide. The next day, he mentioned to Acheson that he had been invited to receive an honorary degree from Harvard, in Cambridge, Massachusetts. James Conant had first made the offer to Marshall more than two years before. But, during the war, the general had turned down all such honours, as a matter of principle. The only exception was when Harriman persuaded him, on the eve of D-Day, to accept a Soviet medal presented by Gromyko.[37] After the war, Conant renewed the invitation once more, but Marshall declined, on the grounds that he was absent on his mission in China. Undeterred, Conant made a third attempt, at the time that Marshall was appointed secretary of state. He added an offer to stay overnight at the President's lodge. The main degree ceremony, known as the Commencement Exercises, was held in the morning. In the afternoon, Marshall would have an opportunity to address the Harvard Alumni Association.[38]

Would it make a good platform from which to launch the new initiative? Acheson was sceptical. He was a member of the Yale Corporation, which served as the governing body for his old university. He had seen many commencement speeches. They were, he told Marshall, a ritual to be endured without hearing.[39] But Marshall had made his mind up. He issued an instruction to Carter, asking for a draft to speak for ten minutes, covering the situation in Europe. 'Irritation and passion', he warned, 'should have no part in the matter.'[40] He also dropped a line to Conant. If academic costume was required for the occasion, he told the president, his hat size was 7½ plus, and height six foot one inch.[41]

Carter passed on the request to Bohlen, along with the papers prepared by Clayton and Kennan. Bohlen wove together a script, using text from both sources. Marshall tinkered with the draft on the flight up to Massachusetts. He made some further changes that evening, at Conant's house.[42] The result was then typed out in a clean version, on seven crisp sheets of paper.

As he did so, Marshall realised that the text had not been cleared with Truman. But he decided to press ahead anyway. 'The Secretary', noted one official later, had 'tremendous power of decision, and his batting average [was] phenomenally high.'[43]

Commencement Day brought a clear, blue sky over Cambridge. It was Thursday 5 June. Some 8,000 students and wellwishers had gathered in the university's Tercentenary Theatre. This open space was named after the three-hundredth anniversary of the university foundation in 1636, and dotted with maple, beech and hickory trees. On one side lay the Widener Library, built in memory of a Harvard graduate who perished aboard the *Titanic*, and at the other the Memorial Church, which was constructed in 1932 to commemorate those alumni killed in World War I.

At 9.30 a.m., a bell tolled in the Memorial Church tower. The University Marshall and the Sheriff of Middlesex County, followed by Conant, led a procession of university dignitaries into the Tercentenary Theatre. Marshall wore a plain, light grey suit. Among candidates for honorary degrees, he was joined by Omar Bradley, the general who had commanded American ground forces at D-Day, and the atomic scientist Robert Oppenheimer. The poet T. S. Eliot and typeface designer William Dwiggins also joined the group.

Following the Commencement Exercises, lunch was served at the university's Fogg Museum. Then, at two o'clock, the Alumni Association gathered in Harvard Yard, a leafy quadrangle adjacent to the Tercentenary Theatre.

Conant offered a brief introduction. That morning, in conferring an honorary degree on Marshall, he had compared the General to George Washington, as America's first soldier-statesman. The audience erupted with applause when they heard the citation. Now, it was the General's turn to speak.

Marshall came to the podium. He offered a few words of thanks to Conant. The award had, he said, left him almost overwhelmed. Then, turning to the prepared text in front of him, he started to read. His voice took on a more sombre tone.

'I need not tell you gentlemen', he began, 'that the world situation is serious.'

Marshall set out the facts of the case. The European economy had become dislocated. He painted the same vivid picture which Clayton had described to Nitze. Farmers were ceasing to sell foodstuff to cities. The chain of production and commerce was at risk of disintegration.

Turning to the question of what America should do, Marshall used language drawn from Kennan's paper. 'Our policy is directed not against any country or doctrine,' he declared, 'but against hunger, poverty, desperation and chaos.' In such circumstances, America must act. It should not do so in a piecemeal way, or just to alleviate the problem, but seek to provide a solution. Nor, Marshall added, should the United States draw up an aid programme unilaterally. 'This is the business of the Europeans,' he concluded. 'The initiative, I think, should come from Europe.'

This line completed the script that Marshall had prepared. Soon after he had taken office, Marshall had tried speaking without notes, at a briefing with journalists. It was not a success. The Secretary had strayed beyond his brief, and given out more of a story than intended. Afterwards, Acheson and Carter gave their boss a lecture on the importance of sticking to a clear script. Marshall was crestfallen, but took the advice.[44]

As he completed his prepared remarks, a ripple of applause started among the audience. But, seizing the moment, Marshall decided to take a chance. Removing his glasses, he looked up from his notes, across the lawns of Harvard Yard. The audience fell silent again.

It was a final thought, added on the spur of the moment. 'To my mind,' he said, 'it is of vast importance to our people to reach some general understanding rather than react to the passions and prejudices of the moment.' This was the same advice that he had offered to Carter, in preparing the speech. 'The whole world's future', he added, 'hangs on a proper judgement, hangs on a realisation by the American people of what can best be done, of what must be done.'[45]

THIRTEEN

Impatient Dawn

From out this world of stars and mists and motion
The dawn – impatient of the time allowed –
Probes sharply down the canyons of the cloud
To find the fragments of an empty ocean.

From 'Homeward Bound At Dawn Over Mid-Atlantic',
composed by George Kennan, September 1947

Bevin was a poor sleeper. His overweight, over-worked body found it hard to settle. Lack of exercise, poor diet, smoking and alcohol had taken a toll. Bevin suffered from a weak heart, damaged liver and high blood pressure. Alexander McCall, his doctor, claimed that he could not find a single organ that was healthy, except for the feet. In his quest to keep the ailing Foreign Secretary on the road, McCall became a regular member of the team. 'This is Alec,' said Bevin when he introduced the doctor to King George VI. ''E treats me be'ind like a dartboard.' During the Moscow meeting of foreign ministers, Bevin twice had attacks of pain in his chest. McCall took to hovering at the back of meetings, just in case.[1]

On the night of 5 June 1947, Bevin was sitting in bed at his flat in London. Over the radio came a programme called *American Commentary*. This weekly feature was usually presented by American journalists, talking about events in their own country, and became popular in Foreign Office circles. But Joseph Harsh, who had been scheduled to appear, was away touring US military bases in Europe. His place was taken by Leonard Miall, a BBC correspondent based in Washington.

A couple of days earlier, Miall had lunched with Acheson, along with Malcolm Muggeridge from the *Daily Telegraph*, and René MacColl of the *Daily Express*. The trio were tired of seeing important news stories leaked to

Walter Lippmann, Scotty Reston and other leading American journalists. They hoped to establish a channel to Acheson.

The Under-Secretary arrived with a hangover. 'If those limeys offer me sherry,' he muttered to his press aide, 'I shall puke.'

'Now,' said Muggeridge, greeting his guest. 'We won't have this horrible bad habit of having some strong liquor before lunch. Sherry?'

Revived by a dry martini, Acheson warmed up. He warned the British that a major initiative for American aid to Europe was coming. 'As soon as you get a copy,' he advised, 'telephone the whole thing to London. It does not matter what hour of the night it is; wake up Ernie and put a copy in his hands.'[2]

Miall decided to make the Harvard speech his story. When Marshall had finished redrafting, on the eve of the commencement ceremony, his aides phoned through a text from Conant's house to Acheson. Miall managed to secure an advance copy from the State Department press office. Because Marshall was due to speak in the afternoon, and *American Commentary* was scheduled for broadcast at 5.30 p.m. East Coast time, Miall had to record his comments in advance. He chose to focus on the question of what should happen next. 'The ball has now returned,' he reflected. 'Washington will watch eagerly to see the reaction across the Atlantic.'

As he listened to Miall's broadcast, Bevin thought that it sounded as though Marshall himself were speaking across the airwaves. It was, he later said, a 'lifeline to sinking men. It seemed to bring hope where there was none.'[3]

Britain was in need. Under the terms of the loan negotiated by Keynes, exchange controls on sterling must be lifted by mid-July 1947. After the disruption of a harsh winter, however, demand for dollars to pay for imports far outstripped earnings from exports. A currency crisis loomed. Delivering his annual budget in April, Dalton tried to rally MPs with a quotation from Cromwell. 'Well, your danger is as you have seen,' the parliamentarian had told his Ironside soldiers during the Civil War. 'But I wish it to cause no despondency; as truly I think it will not; for we are Englishmen.'[4]

The next morning Bevin strode into his office overlooking St James's Park. 'Get me Marshall's speech,' he instructed his staff. 'I want Bidault on the telephone.'

Duff Cooper was having a busy patch. Over the years of his marriage to Diana, the ambassador had enjoyed a string of liaisons with other women.

His posting to Paris offered more possibilities. Earlier that spring, he launched into a new affair. This time, his lover was Susan Mary Patten, wife of a diplomat at the American Embassy. They began the relationship at the end of May, with an evening alone at the Dorchester Hotel in London. But life was taking its toll. Duff Cooper suffered from weakened kidneys and liver, with poor circulation and bouts of numbness in his feet and thighs. His doctor prescribed a diet of fish, chicken and vegetables, alongside baths and exercise. 'Although he clearly won't follow it,' commented Diana in a letter to their son, John Julius, 'it must take the gilt off the gingerbread.'[5]

On the evening of Monday 9 June, Duff Cooper received a telegram from Bevin. It was marked 'Most Immediate Top Secret'. The Ambassador was instructed to sound out Bidault over the Harvard speech. Duff Cooper called on the French Foreign Minister the next morning. He found Bidault, like Bevin, keen to engage.[6]

A week later, Bevin himself came over to Paris. He was met at Le Bourget airfield by Duff Cooper. The two men drove to the British Embassy, where Diana served tea. That night, Bidault came for dinner, along with a team of his officials.[7]

The Frenchman brought an unwelcome message. Bidault and Paul Ramadier, the socialist prime minister, faced a difficult moment in domestic politics. At the end of May, they had engineered a split with the communists. Party leader Maurice Thorez and four of his colleagues resigned from ministerial office. Now outside the government, they were plotting revenge. At the same time, de Gaulle had launched a new political movement, called the Rassemblement du Peuple Français, around a core of his old wartime associates.

Against this backdrop, Bidault had to play the Marshall initiative carefully. It was essential that Paris be seen to engage with the Soviets in good faith. Bevin and Duff Cooper realised that it would mean a delicate diplomatic balancing act. While the Soviet Union should be given a genuine opportunity to take part, it must not lead to delay or obstruct the American initiative.[8]

Back in England that Friday, Bevin's private secretary, Pierson Dixon, took his boss to Eton College. Dixon's son, Piers, was a pupil at the school, and had been angling for Bevin to address the Political Society. Jebb had spoken to the same audience a few weeks before. Bevin took the privileged surroundings in his stride. When one young man asked if he expected Moscow to respond to Marshall's offer, Bevin was doubtful. 'The Tsar

Alexander still hasn't answered Castlereagh's questions,' he noted, referring to Russia's diplomatic manoeuvres during the Napoleonic Wars. Afterwards, Bevin gave Dixon and his son a lift back to their home in Egham. He came in for a nightcap, along with his bodyguards and drivers.[9]

In Moscow, Molotov had indeed read Marshall's speech with interest. On his own, translated copy, he jotted down short notes. The statement that the initiative must come from Europe caught his particular interest. His instinct was to accept. After all, the Soviet Union had benefited from Lend-Lease during the war. Why not, as one member of Molotov's secretariat later put it, 'accept the proposal and [...] minimise its negative aspects'?[10] On 21 June, Stalin authorised Molotov to meet with Bevin and Bidault for exploratory discussions.[11]

As Bidault made preparations to host Molotov in Paris, Assistant Secretary William Clayton arrived in London. He found England in a state of excitement. The previous summer, test cricket had resumed after the war. South Africa was the visiting side for 1947. The opening match had been played at Trent Bridge in Nottingham while Bevin was in Paris. South Africa managed an impressive start, but were forced to a draw when the talented English batsman Denis Compton scored 163 runs in his second innings. After the wartime years, it lifted the national mood. 'The sight of Compton in full sail', wrote the cricket commentator Neville Cardus, was 'a propulsion of happy sane healthy life'.[12] Attention was now fixed on the second match in the series at Lord's Cricket Ground, in St John's Wood.

A couple of miles south of Lord's, Clayton held a series of meetings at Downing Street with Attlee, Dalton, Bevin and Cripps.[13] On Marshall's instructions, he brought a tough message with him.[14] The British hoped that they might take on a privileged role, as co-sponsors of the aid programme with the Americans. 'Britain with an Empire', Bevin argued, 'was on a different basis.' But Clayton was firm. The UK would not be treated as a special case. London's value to Washington was rather in galvanising a common European position. Bevin retorted that this would scotch the 'little bit of dignity that we have left'. The American was unimpressed. But he also gave a private assurance: if it proved impossible to bring the Soviet Union on board, the United States would proceed with aid to Western Europe alone.[15]

The day after Clayton left London, Bidault hosted Bevin and Molotov in Paris.[16] It was less than three months since the trio had parted company in Moscow. They met at the Quai d'Orsay, home of the French Foreign Ministry. Built in the 1850s, as part of Emperor Napoleon III's modernisation of central Paris, the ornate edifice overlooked the banks of the Seine. Here, in the grand Salon de l'Horloge, plenary sessions of the Paris Conference had taken place in 1919.

Bidault met his colleagues in the more intimate Salon des Perroquets. It was named after antique tapestries hanging on the walls. Despite the grand setting, the atmosphere was tough. On the first day, the three men became bogged down in familiar arguments about the agenda. 'This is going too slow,' commented Duff Cooper in his diary. 'We have got nowhere so far.'[17] Even once discussion moved onto the substance, Molotov was cautious. The Americans, he argued, should provide more details. Did Bevin or Bidault know any more? Bevin, concealing what he had learned from Clayton, played dumb.

Molotov was feeling the strain. He slept badly on his first night in Paris, kept awake by crying from the four-month-old baby of a junior NKVD officer at the Soviet Embassy.[18] Then, on the morning of 30 June, a coded telegram arrived for Molotov from Vyshinsky.

The Soviets enjoyed a privileged window into Western thinking. In the years before the war, NKVD agents had recruited a group of young British men as agents. Several of the group had met as students at Cambridge University in the late 1920s and early 1930s. The leading lights of the group were Kim Philby, who had joined the British Secret Intelligence Service, and Guy Burgess, a flamboyant journalist who entered government service during the war. A third member, Donald Maclean, worked in the Foreign Office. In the years after the war, Maclean was serving at the embassy in Washington, while Burgess was private secretary to Hector McNeil, minister of state and deputy to Bevin.

Drawing on these sources, the NKVD had obtained a report of Clayton's meetings in London. Molotov saw immediately that he faced a trap.[19] If the British and Americans had already agreed to keep the Soviets out of an aid programme, there was no reason to enter into serious negotiations.

During his previous stay in Paris, Molotov had been careful to keep in close step with Stalin. When the French placed him in the second row at a military parade, he stormed off in protest. Later he checked with Stalin that he had done the right thing. 'You behaved absolutely correctly,' the Generalissimo had replied. 'The dignity of the Soviet Union must be defended in great matters but also in minutiae.'[20] On this visit, with the stakes so high, Molotov could not afford to put a foot wrong.

In the plenary discussion that day, Molotov opted to play defensive. He increased his demands. There should be no collective European programme, and a firm commitment that the future of Germany remained a matter for all four Allied powers. Bevin retorted that it amounted to asking for a blank cheque. As he watched the two men arguing, Duff Cooper concluded that the game was over.[21]

Molotov was coming to the same view. That night, Molotov cabled back to Stalin, advising that the French and British were 'in dire straits' from an economic perspective, and beholden to America for support. In these circumstances, the Soviet Union should not follow suit.[22] As Molotov drafted his cable, Bevin met with Jefferson Caffery, American ambassador in Paris. The conference had, he told Caffery, 'to all intents and purposes broken down'.[23] The only question left was who would be able to pin the blame on whom.

The remaining uncertainty was Bidault. The next morning, Dixon picked up rumours that the French might be wavering. Bidault summoned the French cabinet, and, for a few anxious hours, the British delegation awaited further news. Later that afternoon, the Frenchman came back with a counter-proposal. A European aid programme should be linked to a new initiative on Germany, which would put coal from the Ruhr mines at the service of the French economy.

Molotov undertook to reflect. But he realised that Bidault was simply playing to French domestic opinion. 'Our stand differs radically from that of Britain and France,' he cabled to Stalin. 'We can hardly expect any joint decisions.'[24]

On the next and final day, the two sides split apart. Bevin and Bidault announced that they would press ahead without Moscow. Britain and France would issue a joint invitation to other European countries to take part in talks on Marshall's proposal. Molotov responded with a stern warning. The aid programme, he declared, risked 'splitting Europe into two groups'.[25]

At four o'clock the following morning, the Soviet Foreign Minister and his entourage left Paris.[26] In his diary, Duff Cooper reflected on the news. 'We have done all we could to prevent this,' he wrote, 'the Western Bloc which I have always advocated has at last been manufactured in Moscow. *Tant mieux*.'[27]

* * *

Eleanor Roosevelt had been troubled by the Truman Doctrine. 'It all seems', she commented in a private letter to Acheson, 'a most unfortunate way of doing things.'[28] But Marshall's speech filled her with hope. America had discovered a way to resist Soviet expansionism without ideological conflict.

Her encounter with the United Nations in London the previous year had left Roosevelt with a taste for international diplomacy. With Truman's encouragement, she was appointed to the Commission for Human Rights. At San Francisco, the signatories to the UN Charter had agreed to draft an international statement of human rights, which, for the first time, would be universal in scope.

Four days after the Harvard speech, Roosevelt was at Lake Success. It was a new temporary home for the United Nations, in upstate New York. She had been elected chair of the drafting group appointed by the commission to produce a draft text. Among the eight members were Charles Malik, from Lebanon, and René Cassin of France, the lawyer and veteran of World War I, who had led an international movement of veterans during the interwar years to promote peace.

The commission was supported by a division of the United Nations secretariat led by John Humphrey, a Canadian lawyer. Humphrey had surveyed different national legal traditions. They stretched from the English Bill of Rights to the American and French revolutionary declarations, to those from the Soviet Union and Latin America. He and his team combined these into a list of 48 fundamental rights, which they believed were global, regardless of race or religion.

The group faced a monumental task. Was this the right list? And should respect for these rights be made a binding international obligation? To do so might infringe national sovereignty, and drag the commission back into the debate from San Francisco about balancing international co-operation with the sovereign independence of countries.

During these opening discussions, Roosevelt took soundings. The British, represented by a young lawyer named Geoffrey Wilson, wanted a binding text. But Vladimir Koretsky, representing the Soviet Union, was cautious. Roosevelt could see that in the wake of the Truman Doctrine she must tread carefully. During an earlier visit to Britain, an American soldier had asked her how to handle the Soviets. 'Have convictions; be friendly; stick to your beliefs; and work as hard as they do,' was her reply.[29]

She sensed that a non-binding declaration was as far as Koretsky could go. And the US Senate, also concerned to safeguard its sovereignty rights, might share his view.

Cassin was a firm interventionist. 'I have always thought that a life is incomplete', he wrote in his diary during wartime exile in London, 'if, to a great love, a man was incapable of adding a great work [...] which would survive us.'[30] Watching the occupation of France, he had seen how laws could be twisted to terrible ends. In the summer of 1945, Paris had been shocked at the haggard spectacle of survivors returning from the concentration camps. At the Gare de l'Est, one group had stood in a line and sung 'La Marseillaise' in broken voices. Bystanders were reduced to tears.[31]

The French veteran believed that national law must be anchored on international principles. But it might also be possible to square this with Koretsky's concerns. The answer was to aim for a declaration, rather than a binding convention, which under international law would have moral but not legal force. Working with a small drafting sub-group, alongside Roosevelt, Wilson and Malik, he took Humphrey's list, and reordered it into a text. As inspiration, Cassin drew on the Declaration of the Rights of Man, made in the French Revolution, and the Napoleonic Code. 'All men, being members of one family,' read the first article, 'are free, possess equal dignity and rights, and shall regard each other as brothers.'[32]

Bevin was enjoying his trips to Paris. On 11 July, he flew over to Le Bourget for the third time in just over a month. Bevin and Bidault were hosting a conference of European countries on the Marshall initiative. The Harvard speech had invited Europe to come up with its own plan for economic recovery. It was now for the conference to decide how that should be done. Duff Cooper and Bidault came out to the airfield to meet Bevin, but the plane was delayed and they were obliged to wait for an hour and a half.[33]

That night, the Foreign Secretary gatecrashed a party at the British Embassy for the Cardiff Business Men's Club. The group were on their way to Czechoslovakia, for a goodwill mission. Bevin gave an impromptu speech, which was greeted with hearty cheers. Dinner followed. By the end of the evening, the Foreign Secretary was on very lively form. When Lady Diana suggested that he might call it a night, he flung his arms around her in the embassy lift and offered a kiss. It was, she confessed in her diary afterwards, like trying to resist a 'mountain-weight of lava'. In desperation she looked around for Dixon, but the Private Secretary had already left for bed.[34]

The conference opened the following morning, in the main dining room at the Quai d'Orsay. Invitations had been sent out to 22 countries, including, from the east, Czechoslovakia, Poland, Hungary, Bulgaria, Romania and Yugoslavia. Molotov's initial instinct, reflected in a cable sent to Soviet ambassadors in these countries on 5 July, was to encourage them to go ahead and accept. With her satellites present, the Soviet Union might sabotage proceedings from a distance. Nevertheless, this approach carried risks. In Poland and Czechoslovakia, communists only shared power in coalition governments, and did not enjoy complete freedom of manoeuvre. They might be tempted to ignore Moscow's warning and accept American aid anyway.[35]

Two days later, the official line changed. When Stalin learned that the Czechs were leaning towards accepting the invitation, he was enraged. A Czech delegation, led by the communist prime minister, Klement Gottwald, was summoned to Moscow. At a late-night audience, Stalin gave them a dressing down.[36] The Czechs had no alternative but to withdraw. 'I went to Moscow as the foreign minister of an independent sovereign state,' lamented the Czech Foreign Minister, Jan Masaryk. 'I returned as a lackey of the Soviet government.'[37] In a cable, Bedell Smith called it 'nothing less than a declaration of war'.[38]

Without the Eastern Europeans, there were 16 countries left around the conference table. They spanned the continent, from Iceland to Turkey. Despite the disparate nationalities, decisions flowed easily. By the end of the second day, it was clear that the conference was already on the home straight. The next day was the French public holiday of Bastille Day, and Bevin decided to give himself a break. Leaving his officials to wrap up the details, he slipped out to watch the traditional military parade along the Champs Élysées. In the evening, he dined at the embassy. Afterwards, Lady Diana took him on a tour of Paris by night. This time, Dixon came along as well. The carload stopped for a drink at a café in Montmartre. One of the dancing partygoers recognised Bevin, and called on him to give a speech. He did so, and was greeted with cheers. The group returned to the embassy at two in the morning, in high spirits.[39]

The conference wrapped up the following day. Marshall's initiative was in business. The ministers had agreed to establish a Committee of European Economic Co-operation (CEEC), which would take forward the detailed work of drawing up a plan for economic recovery. Robert Marjolin, a senior French Treasury official, would be chair, along with Oliver Franks, a British philosophy don who had been permanent secretary in the British Ministry of Supply during the war.

As Bevin travelled back to London, Lady Diana reflected on her encounter in the lift with the former trade unionist. She decided to keep it to herself. 'There's life in the dear old dog,' she wrote in her diary. He had 'courage and character and humanity, and a lot of other nice things'.[40]

Bevin returned to lengthening shadows in London. Earlier in the month, the national mood had been lifted by news of the engagement between Princess Elizabeth and Prince Philip of Greece, a young naval lieutenant who had served in the war. Pressures were mounting on the Labour Government, though: alongside the impending economic crisis, arguments had broken out over nationalisation of the steel industry, as well as the National Health Service. In India, the British were engaged in final preparations for independence. Philip's uncle, Lord Louis Mountbatten, had committed to hand over power by mid-August, a full year ahead of the timetable originally proposed by Attlee. But violence between Muslim and Hindu communities was spiralling out of control.

These strains took a toll on the cabinet. Earlier in the summer, Attlee and his colleagues had managed to put on a united front at the annual party conference, held in the seaside resort of Margate. However, the obligation under the US loan negotiated by Keynes to float sterling imposed a relentless timetable. On the same day that Bevin flew back from Paris, the government lifted exchange controls on the pound. A run on the currency followed – $106 million left the country in the first week, then $126 million in the second.[41] At this rate, Dalton calculated, the reserves would be dry by November. The Chancellor was hanging on his nerves, taking sleeping pills at night and Benzedrine to get through the day.[42]

Ministers started to mutter about the leadership. As they travelled back from a conference with the Miners' Union in Durham, Dalton sounded out Bevin in the back of his ministerial car about taking over the premiership. The Foreign Secretary was non-committal. Parliamentary aides set about briefing rival versions of what was said.[43] Four days later, tempers flared during a late-night meeting of the key players in Downing Street. Bevin arrived from dinner in a truculent mood. Attlee struggled to keep order while he and Morrison quarrelled. 'Where do we sleep tonight – in 'ere?' the Foreign Secretary asked as he finally lurched out after midnight.[44]

Parliament rose at the end of July. The run on sterling continued. Attlee left for his usual holiday in North Wales, while Bevin went to Dorset and Dalton to Sussex. Morrison was left holding the fort in London. In mid-August, he summoned his colleagues back for a crisis meeting. They agreed that there was no choice but to reinstate exchange controls. Beforehand, Dalton and Cripps had had a private word with Bevin, sounding him out again on the leadership. Again, he declined. 'It's all this intriguing I won't do,' he said afterwards to Christopher Mayhew, his parliamentary under-secretary. 'What happened to Lloyd George and Asquith? The public gets to know you're an intriguer.'[45] Attlee, he added, was the best prime minister that Labour could have. Anyone who wanted to get rid of him was a fool.[46]

The plotting continued. Dalton and Cripps tried a new tack. Attlee could move to the chancellorship, while Bevin went to No. 10, Dalton took over at the Foreign Office and Cripps was in charge of economic planning. They probed Morrison for support, but he was non-committal. Cripps decided to make a direct approach. On the evening of 9 September, he went to see Attlee. 'S.C. at least has courage and clarity,' wrote Dalton in his diary.[47]

Sitting together in Downing Street, Cripps presented Attlee with an ultimatum. He argued that the economic situation was critical, and outlined the new division of jobs which he and Dalton had drawn up. Attlee listened calmly. 'Most reasonable,' he commented. Then he picked up the phone on his desk, and asked the No. 10 switchboard to connect him to Bevin.

The Foreign Secretary came on the line. 'Stafford's here,' said the Prime Minister. 'He says you want to change your job.'

Bevin said this was not the case.

'Thought not,' replied Attlee. He replaced the handset. Without Bevin on board, the plan outlined by Cripps and Dalton was unworkable.

Attlee then turned the tables on Cripps. If the economy was what he cared about, why not take on an enlarged portfolio as Minister for Production, co-ordinating work across Whitehall? It was impossible to turn down.

Rather sheepish, Cripps returned to the Treasury and debriefed Dalton. The coup had failed.[48]

* * *

Oliver Franks liked to solve problems. A clergyman's son, he had been born in 1905, in a village outside Birmingham. Franks was educated at Bristol Grammar School, and at home, where he devoured his father's books on theology and poetry. 'He had a mind', recalled one teacher, 'that was so logical it was frightening.'[49]

At the age of 22, Franks was elected a fellow of Queen's College in Oxford, where he had studied classics. Ten years later, he was appointed to the Professorship of Moral Philosophy at Glasgow University, a post once held by the economist Adam Smith. After the outbreak of war, he took leave of absence to work as a civil servant. It was a different kind of education. Whitehall revolved around meetings. Franks tried to draw conclusions from what he saw. If the participants could only agree on what needed to be done, and not how to do it, the meeting failed. Getting that right, he figured, was the key.[50]

Franks had not wanted to come to Paris. With the war over, he had returned to Oxford as master of Queen's. University life was, he later wrote, 'frisking like a lamb in green pastures'. But Bevin had worked with him in the war, at the Ministry of Supply, and wanted him back. Within days of Marshall's speech, he had persuaded his former colleague to become a civil servant again.[51]

It was clear that Franks and Robert Marjolin, his French co-chair, faced an uphill task. Under the approach agreed by Bevin and Bidault, each member of the CEEC was supposed to present a national plan for recovery, which would then be amalgamated into a collective proposal for the Americans. But the committee soon ran into deadlock. Many of the 16 countries had unrealistic expectations of what they might receive, or different views about how to stimulate the European economy. Italy wanted more freedom for workers to migrate abroad, while Belgium argued for greater free trade. Deep differences existed over whether to rehabilitate Germany, too. As the conference opened, in mid-July, the British and Americans broke the news that Clay and Robertson had reached agreement to lift controls of industrial output in their occupation zones, now combined into a single entity called 'Bizonia'. The French feared that it was a first step towards restoring Germany as a great power. Bidault felt bitterly let down, and wrote private letters of protest to Bevin and Marshall.[52]

In some cases, even the grasp of the basic economic picture was shaky. One French official confessed that his figures were no more than intelligent estimates.[53] The Greeks were in a similar position. When a British official found his Greek counterpart filling out numbers late at night, the latter admitted that no one in Athens had a clue what the real statistics were.[54] A first count of the bids from each of the 16 countries added up to a staggering $29 billion. When Isaiah Berlin came over to help Franks, he despaired. The Europeans, he commented, were like 'lofty and demanding beggars'.[55]

In Washington, General Marshall's new deputy was watching the work of the CEEC intently.

When Marshall arrived at the State Department, he had agreed with Acheson that the former lawyer would stay on for six months. After that, Acheson would return to his private practice. To succeed him, Marshall chose Robert Lovett, the 52-year-old former banker who had served as deputy secretary to Stimson during the war. His father and Harriman's were business associates. The young Lovett became a friend of the Harriman family, and close to Averell's mother, Mary. One summer, during a long train trip together in the Midwest, she sawed a piece of hardened wood in two, and gave Robert one half to use as a paperweight. It sat on his desk during his years at the Pentagon.[56]

Acheson and Lovett had studied at Yale together, and remained friends in adult life. They worked hard to ensure a smooth handover. 'I've known Bob since college,' Acheson told Vandenberg at Lovett's confirmation hearing in the Senate, 'and I hope you will be agreeable to accept his services.'

'Welcome,' replied the Senator. 'May God have mercy on your soul.'[57]

Even so, departure came as a wrench for Acheson. The regulars at his morning meeting presented him with a silver tray. It was inscribed with their names, including Clayton, Bohlen, Henderson and Hickerson. Public life, Acheson later wrote, was an existence beyond the ordinary. Leaving it was like coming off a drug.[58]

Lovett found a team who were worried. A request for aid on the scale that the CEEC was contemplating would have no chance with Congress. The decision to cede responsibility to the Europeans for drawing up the plan, for which Kennan had argued back in May, now looked like a risky gamble. What the team called the Marshall Plan was, as one official quipped to a colleague, like a 'flying saucer – nobody knows what it looks like, how big it is, in what direction it is moving, or whether it really exists'.[59]

America, Lovett warned the general, might be confronted not with a single, co-ordinated plan, but with 'sixteen shopping lists'.[60]

Kennan and Lovett hit on a solution. In Paris, Franks had already formed a close working relationship with Clayton. The southerner had spent much of the summer in Geneva negotiating a General Agreement on Trade and Tariffs to expand the process of liberalisation begun at Bretton Woods. In his speech at Harvard, Marshall had talked about providing 'friendly aid' to help the Europeans draw up a plan. It provided a hook. Lovett dispatched Kennan, Nitze and Charles Bonesteel, the US Army colonel seconded to the Planning Staff, to Paris. They called themselves the 'Friendly Aid Boys'.

Clayton and Kennan met with Franks. They laid out seven guidelines for how the CEEC should assemble its plan, including a commitment to free trade and integration across different European economies. The direction was welcome. Franks excelled as a persuader and organiser. But sometimes, observed one Oxford contemporary, he needed to be set the problem.[61]

Franks was intrigued by Kennan. There was, he recalled, a 'combination of rational, lucid exposition with controlled passion'.[62] The American seemed to be a man who agonised within himself before reaching a decision.

It was a shrewd observation. Kennan came from the Midwest, in Milwaukee, Wisconsin. Though educated at the prestigious Princeton University, he felt an outsider in the company of East Coast men like Bohlen and Acheson. Kennan wrestled with intense inner feelings. In his diary, he jotted down his thoughts and snippets of conversation. He even recorded details of his dreams, before they faded from memory. Reflection brought insight. His mind would settle, he wrote on one occasion, 'like the waves in a swimming pool when the last swimmer has left'.[63]

During 1947, Kennan had found little time for his diary. The pressures of the National War College and Policy Planning Staff had got in the way. It had been an intense period. During the weeks leading up to the Harvard speech, Kennan worked around the clock. One evening, he walked around the block at Foggy Bottom to clear his mind, tears of strain and nervous tension streaming down his face.[64] A few weeks later, he committed an awkward error of judgement. Kennan published an article in *Foreign Affairs*, under the pseudonym 'Mr X', with a precis of the Long Telegram. The Washington press quickly identified the author, and Kennan was obliged to make an embarrassed apology to Marshall. He felt, he wrote later, as though he had dislodged a mountain boulder, and watched it plunge into the valley below, 'shuddering and wincing at every successive glimpse of disaster'.[65]

Flying back from Paris, Kennan was at last able to return to his diary. Looking out of the plane window, he saw the dawn breaking through the clouds above the Atlantic. He began to write, putting the spectacle before him into verse.

'The dawn', he begun, 'probes sharply down the canyons of the cloud / To find the fragments of an empty ocean.' Then, turning to his own situation, he wrote of the 'home-bound pilgrim', engaged in an 'endless flight', with 'no final landing field'.

The composition ended with an appeal for happiness: 'Content / Be he whose peace of mind from this may stem: / That he, as Fortune's mild and patient claimant, / Has heard the rustling of the Time-God's raiment / And has contrived to touch the gleaming hem.'[66]

Meanwhile, at the CEEC in Paris, Franks and his team laboured on. Otto Clarke, a former journalist and colleague from the Ministry of Supply, pulled together a first draft of the report. The British dubbed it a 'torso'. Limbs were added over the days that followed. The final document was 690 pages long. Under Franks' guidance, the committee had managed to reduce the total request for aid to $19.3 billion.

On 22 September, ministers from the 16 countries came to Paris for a formal signing ceremony. Bevin attended, along with Cripps. The next morning, Franks ate breakfast alone at the Hotel Crillon, where he had stayed for the last two months. He felt exhausted. As the strain caught up with him, tears started to run down his face.

He was found by Edward Hall-Patch, Bevin's principal adviser on economic issues. Hall-Patch commandeered a car, and the two men drove out of town, to Chartres. They visited the great thirteenth-century cathedral. For an hour, Franks sat in the darkened interior. The clergyman's son was lost in his thoughts. Afterwards, the two men enjoyed a good lunch, and drove back to Paris, much restored.[67]

FOURTEEN

The Giant's Strength

O, it is excellent
To have a giant's strength;
but it is tyrannous
to use it like a giant

Shakespeare, *Measure for Measure*, Act II, Scene II,
quoted by Harold Nicolson to Vita Sackville-West
in October 1947, in reference to the Soviet Union[1]

The American Embassy stood on Mokhovaya Street, in the centre of Moscow. Opposite, across the expanse of Manezh Square, lay the high brick walls of the Kremlin. Beyond was Red Square, with the squat mausoleum containing Lenin's embalmed body. Inside the embassy, junior diplomats tried to figure out what was going on at the centre of Soviet power. They pored over newspapers and watched the line-up of senior leaders at public parades, speculating about who had risen or fallen in the hierarchy.

Bedell Smith was dubious about such activity. When his staff offered their latest theories, he was reminded of the Marquis de Custine, a French traveller who visited Moscow more than a century before. The Frenchman described a country where the truth was wrapped in the shadows. 'We have the weakness of chattering,' he concluded. 'They have the force of secrecy.'[2]

In the summer of 1947, a new story appeared in the press. Stalin was going on a road trip. It was 14 years since he had last toured the country. The Generalissimo set off on 16 July, accompanied by Nikolai Vlasik, his chief bodyguard. They travelled in a convoy of Zis 110 limousines. Stalin headed south to the cornfields of Kursk, scene of the climactic tank battle in 1943. From there, he drove to Kharkov, then down to Yalta. The party embarked on a naval cruiser, the *Molotov*, which had served in the wartime siege of Sevastopol, on the Crimea. This warship took them on the short voyage around the Black Sea coast to Sochi, close to Stalin's retreat at Ritsa.[3]

Stalin left Moscow politics in a state of tension. A year before, he had elevated a shadowy secret policeman, Viktor Abakumov, to head the NKVD, under the new title Ministry of State Security. The new protégé was a brutal operator. Abakumov liked to administer beatings to his victims personally, in his office. To protect his valuable Persian carpets, a bloodstained mat was unrolled across his office floor. It was an appointment intended to unsettle Beria. The Georgian retained overall control of the state security apparatus, including the atom bomb, but Abakumov reported direct to Stalin.[4]

The Generalissimo used a similar ploy against Molotov. Andrei Zhdanov was born in 1896, six years after the Soviet Foreign Minister. Like Molotov he grew up in a middle-class household. His father was an inspector of schools for Mariupol, in the south-eastern, Russian-speaking region of Ukraine. But unlike Molotov, Zhdanov only joined the party after the revolution. In 1934, Sergei Kirov, party boss in Leningrad, was murdered in mysterious circumstances. Stalin moved Zhdanov into the post. As German forces surrounded Leningrad in the autumn of 1941, Molotov was sent to inspect the city defences. He found his fellow Politburo member holding himself together with heavy drinking and cigarettes.[5]

After the war, Stalin brought Zhdanov to Moscow. His brief was to oversee party and cultural matters, as the regime's leading ideologue. During the war, the Kremlin had needed artists and writers to build public support. With victory achieved, Zhdanov was ordered to clamp down. 'We could never quite get round to you during the war,' joked Stalin to one Soviet filmmaker. 'But now we'll give you the full treatment.'[6]

In August 1946, Zhdanov delivered a speech to the Writers' Union in Leningrad. Soviet literature had, he argued, become enslaved to the West. Anna Akhmatova and the satirist Mikhail Zoshchenko received particular denunciation. The poet whom Isaiah Berlin had so admired was, declared Zhdanov, 'half-nun, half-harlot'.[7] In the months that followed, Zhdanov and Stalin widened the campaign to attack musicians and scientists. They hounded Dmitri Shostakovich, the celebrated composer who had written a symphony from inside besieged Leningrad, along with Sergei Prokofiev. Zhdanov was himself an amateur pianist, and lectured Shostakovich on how to produce music that would better appeal to the masses.

Zhdanov was also responsible for communists abroad. Since the early days of the revolution, the party had maintained an international network, alongside diplomatic contacts for government business. These were originally run through the Communist International, or Comintern. In 1943, as a gesture of solidarity with his wartime allies, it was dismantled by Stalin. But the structures remained in place, with institutes in Moscow and a network of agents around the world. Party and foreign ministry provided what Harriman called a 'double-barrelled gun' to deal with the outside world.[8]

In August 1947, Stalin summoned Zhdanov to Ritsa. Events in Western Europe worried the Generalissimo. Immediately after the war, he had condoned a gradualist strategy for the seizure of power by communist parties abroad. In conversations with Thorez and others, Stalin encouraged them to form 'popular front' coalitions with other left-wing parties as a stepping stone to eventual communist control.[9] But events in Paris over the summer left this strategy outmanoeuvred.

Stalin ordered Zhdanov to pursue a fresh tack. The Comintern was to be reactivated under a new name – the Information Bureau of the Communist Parties, or Cominform. The two men agreed that Zhdanov should host a meeting of European communist leaders, and present them with a plan. In a memo sent a few weeks later, Zhdanov fleshed out the details. Comrades would be instructed to reject 'American serfdom', and recognise the error of their previous ways.[10]

On 22 September, Zhdanov arrived in Szklarska Poręba, in Poland. He was accompanied by his Politburo colleague Georgy Malenkov. Twenty years before, this picturesque Silesian mountain village had hosted the first winter games of the International Workers Olympiad. Athletes from Czechoslovakia, Hungary, Finland and Germany took part. Events included cross-country and downhill skiing. No medals or national symbols were permitted, only the red flags of the socialist movement.

The two leaders stayed at a hunting lodge. The facility had been used by the Nazi leader Hermann Goering. When Lower Silesia was transferred to Poland, the Polish State Security Service turned it into a sanatorium.[11] To keep in touch with Stalin, Zhdanov and Malenkov communicated in coded telegrams. They used their old revolutionary aliases, Comrades Sergeev and Borisov, while Stalin was called Filippov.

Communist leaders came to the gathering from around Europe. They met behind closed doors. Zhdanov delivered the main speech. In a phrase introduced to his draft by Stalin, he warned that the world was dividing into 'two camps', with capitalist and communist blocs implacably in conflict. The divide stretched beyond Europe, to encompass the struggle fought by such countries as Indochina and Indonesia against their colonial overlords. Capitalist America was seeking to dominate the world. Co-habitation with non-communist parties must come to an end.

The French communist leader, Maurice Thorez, did not come to Szklarska Poręba. He sent his deputy, Jacques Duclos. In debate Zhdanov, supported by the Yugoslav Milovan Djilas and Ana Pauker, the Romanian communist leader, rounded on the Frenchman. Djilas reminded his colleagues that parliamentary elections were one means to take power. There were other options. 'Is it useful to disclose your own cards to the enemy?' asked Zhdanov. 'The law of the class struggle is such that only the law of force counts.'[12]

Duclos was a week short of his fifty-first birthday. A veteran of World War I, he had joined the party in 1920, and devoted his life to the communist cause. While Thorez had spent the war in Moscow, Duclos remained in France, leading the communist resistance movement.

Now, faced with criticism from Zhdanov and his fellow communists, Duclos was stunned. He left the room and went to a nearby park, where he sat in silence. Later, he returned to the meeting. In a trembling voice, he offered a confession. The French communists had, he admitted, been 'opportunistic'. They would change course.

The CEEC report had arrived in Washington. It was bound in a green manila folder, and carried by William Kirkrood, a 'King's Messenger', as diplomat couriers in the Foreign Office were called.

Over the summer, Truman had been content to let Marshall make the running. The General stood a better chance, he judged, of securing approval from Congress. Clifford suggested that he was missing a trick, but Truman was categoric. 'Anything going up there bearing my name', he told his aide, 'will quiver a couple of times, turn belly up and die.'[13]

As he read through the CEEC report, Truman realised that he needed to play a greater role. Obtaining congressional approval for the full plan would take several months. Marshall and Kennan had originally assumed that

Europe could wait during this period. It was now clear that time was not on Washington's side. A few days before, Truman had presided over an inaugural meeting of the new National Security Council. Lovett briefed his colleagues on the situation in Italy. The Italian communists, he warned, could join forces with those in Yugoslavia to topple the Christian Democrat government in Rome.[14] Similar pressures existed in France and elsewhere. 'The margin of safety', warned a paper by Kennan's Policy Planning Staff, 'is extremely thin.'[15]

When Marshall had first launched his initiative, Vandenberg warned against piecemeal requests. He encouraged the General to provide a 'total balance sheet' of what was required. However, circumstances had changed.[16] During his visit to Paris, Clayton had mooted the option of front-loading an initial tranche of aid. Truman and Marshall decided to pursue this option.

On 29 September, Truman gathered the main congressional leaders at the White House. Vandenberg and Connally were present, along with Speaker Sam Rayburn and Charles Eaton, chair of the House Foreign Affairs Committee. It was seven months since they had met in the Oval Office to discuss aid to Greece and Turkey. This time they gathered in the Cabinet Room, where Truman had taken the oath of office two and half years earlier.

Marshall and Lovett briefed the group on the situation in Europe. They set out the case for approving a package of interim aid. It would require a special session of Congress to authorise the expenditure.

'This is serious,' added Truman. 'I can't overemphasise how serious.'

Rayburn questioned if it was really necessary. He was an old hand in the House, who had first been elected to represent his native Texas more than 40 years ago. Visiting his office was, joked the journalist Scotty Reston, like a trip to the Board of Education.[17] The constitution gave the President the right to call a special session, although it was highly unusual.

'Can't something be worked out?' Rayburn asked.

'It doesn't seem that we can get the money any other way, Sam,' replied Truman. 'Congress has got to act.'

'Then the plan had better be well worked out,' responded Rayburn. 'Right down to the details.'[18]

Two men in the room knew what was required. A fortnight before, Marshall and Vandenberg had visited Rio de Janeiro together. They attended the launch of the new Organization of American States, as promised by Stettinius at San Francisco. Their wives had come along for the trip, and friendship blossomed between the two couples. Marshall was usually reserved at work, but warmed up with company and a drink to hand. He was particularly amused at Vandenberg's impersonation of Byrnes.[19] His wife, Katherine, much enjoyed the trip. The feeling was mutual: Vandenberg's wife, Hazel, called the Marshalls 'a completely congenial and simply grand pair'.[20]

Back in Washington, the two men established a close working partnership. They would meet twice a week in Blair House. 'Vandenberg was my right hand man,' Marshall recalled, 'and at times I was his right hand man.'[21] On the evening before Truman's meeting at the White House, the Senator and Secretary of State had compared notes. Vandenberg encouraged a distinction between interim aid, and the full-scale Marshall Plan. This would allow Congress to see the overall balance sheet, but without obliging it to approve all the expenditure in one go.

Back at the State Department, Marshall's team set to work. The CEEC report provided a starting point – but, for credibility, the Americans needed to shave the numbers. 'You go ahead and cut it down,' Franks told Clayton and Kennan in private. 'We will squawk at every cut. Never mind that.'[22]

Nitze led the process. During the war, he had worked in the Air Force Strategic Bombing Survey, which analysed the effect of Allied bombardment against Germany and Japan. The assignment had taken him to Hiroshima. Data from thousands of bombing missions were distilled into hard numbers. Now, he applied the same forensic logic to the CEEC report. He produced a dossier for each country, called a 'brown book'. To refine his calculations, he used primitive computers developed by the US Army. The group concluded that interim aid should run for a 15-month period, from January 1948 to April 1949. A total of $7.5 billion would be required.[23]

On 23 October, Truman presented his request for a special session of Congress. Two weeks later, Marshall and Lovett appeared for a joint hearing, with the House and Senate committees on foreign affairs. They were joined by Vandenberg, Connally and Eaton. It was ten o'clock in the morning. The room was packed. The committee chairs and their members sat along a table lined with microphones. Marshall faced them, glasses balanced on his nose. Lovett was by his side, while, sitting behind, Bohlen watched intently. Lovett was a veteran of such hearings from his time at the Department of

War. It was, he told friends, like having a shave and his appendix removed at the same time.[24]

Marshall delivered his opening statement on the first day. He set out Nitze's figures, and explained how interim aid would be administered. 'Whether we like it or not,' he concluded, 'we find ourselves, our nation, in a world position of vast responsibility.'[25]

The hearings ran on for three days. Vandenberg and his colleagues probed the figures which Marshall and Lovett presented. The Senator found himself impressed. The State Department had, he concluded, done their homework. It would be hard not to accept their case for the expenditure involved, even if his fellow Republicans would flinch at the cost. 'Evidently I am to have some degree of trouble with Bob Taft,' he noted in his diary. 'So be it!'

Before the war, transatlantic air travel was only possible by seaplanes. These either took a southern route, via the Azores, or a northern path, refuelling at the Irish station of Foynes, on the estuary of the River Shannon, before the crossing to Newfoundland.

The development of more powerful propeller aircraft opened up the possibility of non-stop flights across the Atlantic. After the war, American companies PanAm and Trans World Airlines vied with the British Overseas Airways Corporation to develop new routes. In January 1946, a PanAm Douglas DC-4 made the crossing from New York to London in just under 18 hours, with stops in Newfoundland and the newly opened Shannon airport. The craft was an upgraded version of the Dakota DC-3 used for wartime transport. Six months later, a more powerful Lockheed L-049 Constellation aircraft, designed by the aviation magnate Howard Hughes, reduced this flying time to a little over 15 hours. Within two years, more than 100 flights were crossing the Atlantic each week.

In late November 1947, Eleanor Roosevelt was flying from New York. She was accompanied by her doctor, a Russian émigré named David Gurewitsch. The aircraft ran into engine trouble. It reached Shannon, but was then further delayed by fog. For the next four days, the pair were obliged to wait. After months of frenetic work, Roosevelt found the delay a welcome respite. The doctor was himself suffering from tuberculosis, and turned to his patient for support. They enjoyed long hours of conversation, talking about their family backgrounds. Both had lost fathers at a young age. 'A sense of service had been strongly instilled in each of us,' recalled Gurewitsch, 'and we measured accomplishment in life more in terms of service than in terms of happiness.'[26]

Roosevelt was bound for the next meeting of the UN Commission for Human Rights. The body was scheduled to meet in Geneva, at the Palace of Nations. This neoclassical building was completed in 1936, on a design draw up by an international panel of architects, from Switzerland, France, Italy and Hungary, to house the League of Nations. Beneath the foundation stone sat a time capsule with a copy of the Covenant of the League, and coins from all the member states. The palace stood in Ariana Park, with a view across to Lake Geneva, and the French Alps.

The commission was originally created with delegates appointed as private individuals. That June, the UN Economic and Social Council had voted to make them national representatives instead.[27] For the group assembling in Geneva, it meant a subtle shift in the tone of the debate. In the six months since their last meeting, at Lake Success, the ideological dividing line between East and West had widened. Any final draft declaration would need to be approved by a vote in the UN General Assembly. If Roosevelt and her colleagues were to reach agreement before the gap became unbridgeable, they would need to keep moving.

From the Soviet Union, Koretsky was replaced by Alexander Bogomolov, ambassador to France. Affable and generous, Bogomolov had given an epic dinner at the end of the Potsdam Conference for Duff Cooper and Jefferson Caffery, his fellow ambassadors in Paris. During the evening, Duff Cooper counted a total of 15 toasts, drunk in vodka. By the end, Bogomolov's secretary had collapsed on the floor, and all three ambassadors nursed hangovers for several days afterwards.[28] He brought a similar bonhomie to the meeting in Geneva. Eleanor Roosevelt was determined to set a workmanlike routine, and introduced evening sessions. On one occasion, Bogomolov served drinks at his hotel first. Afterwards, Roosevelt shepherded her colleagues back to work. Once they had taken their places, she looked round the room. The company was clearly the worse for wear – no work would be done that night.[29]

The session refined the draft prepared by Cassin and Humphrey in New York six months before. By the end, the number of articles had been reduced to 33, and the group had agreed on a text. This would now be circulated to the full membership of the United Nations. But prospects remained uncertain. 'The little Anglo-Saxon orchestra has been well organised and harmonious,' commented Bogomolov in his concluding report to Molotov. 'Somehow we will shake that little orchestra apart.'[30]

'I hate to leave the country at this particular moment,' wrote Marshall to his friend Bernard Baruch.[31] The General was flying to London. After impasse in Moscow, the Council of Foreign Ministers was meeting for a fifth time. Most observers assumed that it would be the last. 'Amid all the wider forces,' wrote *The Times*, 'the four Foreign Ministers might seem to be like men trying to play water polo in an Atlantic swell.'[32]

As Marshall set off, Congress was preparing to decide on his aid programme. Privately, he put the chances of success at no more than fifty–fifty.[33] To add to the strain, the general had been suffering from persistent toothache ever since his visit to Rio two months before.

Marshall was travelling to a continent on the brink. Following the meeting at Szklarska Poręba, Duclos had implemented his new orders. The French communists launched a wave of strikes, bringing mines, steelworks and railways to a halt. Strikers clashed with police and troops. Inflation was running out of control. 'We are on the edge of the abyss,' wrote President Vincent Auriol in his diary.[34] A new government was led by Robert Schuman, a Christian Democrat who had been born in Luxembourg before World War I. Schuman and his interior minister, Jules Moch, fought back against the strikers. Moch, whose son had been murdered by the Nazi Gestapo, was determined to prevail. More than 100,000 reservist soldiers were mobilised.[35] On one occasion, as Moch walked to his seat in the Assemblée Nationale, communist deputies shouted out, 'Heil Hitler!'[36]

Marshall travelled to London on 20 November. It was the same day as the wedding of Princess Elizabeth and Prince Philip, in a ceremony at Westminster Abbey. Guests and presents had poured in from all around the world. Spectators lined the streets. On the night before, Lord Mountbatten hosted a stag party for Philip and his best man, David Milford Haven, at the Dorchester Hotel. Press photographers gathered outside, hoping to catch a moment of indiscretion. The former viceroy persuaded them to hand over their cameras, and then smashed the flash-bulbs.[37]

Two weeks on, the Council showed little evidence of making progress. Patience was wearing thin. At a private party in his flat, Bevin challenged his Soviet colleague. 'Now, Mr Molotov,' he asked, 'what is it that you really want?'

'I want a unified Germany,' replied the Soviet Foreign Minister.

'Why do you want that?' Bevin retorted. 'A unified Germany might pretend to go communist. But, in their hearts, they would be longing for the day when they could revenge their defeat at Stalingrad. You know that as well as I do.'[38]

Marshall's diary in London was packed. Shortly after his arrival, he was given an honorary degree at Oxford. It was conferred by Halifax, who had become chancellor of the university after his return from Washington. Then, on the evening of 2 December, Churchill hosted a reunion dinner with the British Chiefs of Staff. Portal and Cunningham were there, along with Brooke. Marshall thought that the Field Marshal had aged.[39] He had not found retirement easy. Money was short for Brooke and his wife. Unable to make ends meet, they had been forced to move from their country home to a gardener's cottage in the grounds. The Ulsterman was even obliged to sell his treasured collection of antique ornithology books.[40]

On the next day came the news for which Marshall had been waiting. The Senate had voted to pass interim aid, by a margin of 86 votes to 6. 'If you had not been on the Hill,' the General wrote to Vandenberg, 'and Lovett had not been here in the Department, I tremble to think what might have happened.'[41] Meanwhile, in France, communist strikers had derailed a train outside Arras, causing the death of 16 passengers. Public opinion was appalled; it felt like a turning point. That night, at a reception in Buckingham Palace, Bidault told Harold Nicolson that he thought the worst of the crisis was over.[42]

Marshall and Bevin met to discuss tactics.[43] It was tempting, the General concluded, to 'tell the Russians to go to the devil'. But he wanted to engineer a split over substance. The Western allies should choose their ground carefully, and time it to best advantage. Bevin agreed. They must act together.

Ten days later, on Monday 15 December, Marshall and Bevin seized the moment. Bevin was in the chair. They had planned that he would introduce a motion for adjournment, but in the heat of the moment Bevin missed his cue and Marshall did so instead. Molotov objected, but Bidault sided with his Western colleagues. The Council, established at Potsdam some 30 months earlier, had collapsed.

As the ministers prepared to travel home, Marshall called on Bevin. He met his colleagues at Bevin's room in the Foreign Office. It was six o'clock in the evening. Outside, winter darkness had already descended across St James's Park. Bevin was accompanied by Gladwyn Jebb and Frank Roberts, who had recently returned from his post as deputy ambassador in Moscow to take over from Dixon as private secretary.

The General was tired, and anxious to get home. He and his wife owned a country house at Pinehurst, in South Carolina. Katherine had travelled down there at the end of November. 'House open. Fire and flowers to greet me,' she had cabled on her arrival. The General was longing to join her. Getting home was, one staffer warned Carter, becoming an obsession.[44]

Bevin did most of the talking. The question, he said, was what to do next. The British had received a second-hand account of a meeting between Molotov and Eastern European ambassadors in London. The Soviet Foreign Minister claimed to be amused by the attempts of Britain and the United States to break up the Council. They might get closer together for now, but in the longer term the inherent tensions of capitalism would drive them apart.[45]

They must avoid this fate, argued Bevin. The Western democracies should come together, in a 'spiritual federation of the West'. It would be an unwritten and informal alliance, in keeping with the British constitutional tradition.[46] Such a union would make Soviet infiltration of Western Europe impossible.

Marshall agreed. The aid programme might address material needs. But there was a spiritual dimension to European recovery. He suggested that they hold further, confidential discussions. They must take events at the flood stream and produce a co-ordinated effect.

Marshall left London the next day, aboard the *Sacred Cow*. He stopped over in Washington, then flew on down to Pinehurst. Three days later, news came through that the House had approved interim aid. The fifty–fifty odds had come through.

Marshall and his wife spent Christmas at their country home. Afterwards, the couple drove across to stay for a few days with Bernard Baruch. The former banker owned a plantation in South Carolina, and took the General quail hunting. Marshall was concerned that his aim was not what it had been. But he managed to score a bag of seven or eight birds each day. 'At least', he wrote to his friend General Eisenhower afterwards, 'I have not lost my shooting eye.'[47]

FIFTEEN

The Swaying Flag

In the midst of blooming May
Into far-away confines
Above the old Castle the flag swaying
With the words 'The Truth Prevails'.

From 'Cantata to the Communist Party', by Czech
writer Pavel Kohout, commemorating the
seizure of power in February 1948

'One of nature's half-backs,' recalled a former teacher from Frank Roberts'
schooldays at Rugby. He was 'small and nippy with large competent hands,
and never at a loss over how to get the ball out of a scrum'.[1]

It was 22 January 1948. Six weeks before, Roberts had taken over from
Dixon as private secretary. He worked in a large room adjoining Bevin's
office, surrounded by more junior officials and typists. It was called the
Private Office. This was the nerve centre of British diplomacy. Papers flowed
in and out from the rest of the organisation. Telegrams from embassies
overseas were marked on pink paper, while those sent out from London were
on green. The room was filled with an atmosphere of quiet discipline and
focus. Dixon had served almost three years in the job. When he finished up,
it was, he noted in his diary, a 'strange sense of freedom'.[2]

Bevin was about to address the House of Commons. The Foreign
Secretary was not a natural parliamentarian. He had only entered the
Commons in 1940, in an unopposed by-election. Bevin's heart and roots
remained in the trade union movement. Roberts would schedule a visit,
to ensure that Bevin kept in touch with Labour backbenchers, only to
find that the former activist had slipped off to the Trades Union Congress
headquarters, on nearby Smith Square.

Following the collapse of the Council of Foreign Ministers, MPs passed a motion demanding a debate in the House. This would be a major event. Over the Christmas holidays, Bevin gathered his thoughts. Writing did not come easily to the self-educated son of a farmworker. 'It's just not me,' he commented on one occasion when presented with a text. 'You won't mind, I hope, if I take it away and de-grammaticise it?'[3]

Bevin presented his ideas in a trio of papers for the cabinet.[4] It was, he argued, time to take the offensive. Britain claimed 'spiritual and moral' leadership in Europe. The 'western option' which Orme Sargent and Jebb had advocated a year before was back in business. 'This may seem a somewhat fanciful conception,' Bevin wrote, 'but events are moving.'[5] The cabinet discussed the papers on 8 January. They gave Bevin the go-ahead to unveil his ideas to Parliament.

A fortnight later, Roberts and Bevin sat in his office at the Palace of Westminster, making last-minute preparations. The debate was due to take place in the chamber used by the House of Lords. In May 1941, German incendiary bombs had started a fire which gutted the Commons. While repairs were carried out, MPs were rehoused in the Lords. The route from Bevin's office crossed the Central Lobby. Mosaic panels lined the ceiling, depicting the ancient kingdoms of England, Scotland, Wales and Ireland.

Bevin's health had continued to decline. On one occasion in Moscow, Dr McCall had tried to stop the Foreign Secretary from drinking. Bevin ignored him, and downed another glass of champagne. The medic threatened to fly back home on the next plane. Bevin offered a contrite apology, but did not change his habits.[6] The attacks of angina, brought on by a weakened heart, became more frequent. 'I thought you were due for a little box,' remarked his bodyguard after one episode.[7]

As they hurried along the corridors towards the Lords, Bevin clutched at his chest. The pain had started again. As it worsened, sweat poured down his face, and his breath tightened.[8] It was past three o'clock, and the debate was due to start shortly. Dr McCall had prescribed pills for such occasions. Roberts quickly administered a dose. Half walking and half carrying the bulky 67-year-old, he then heaved his way to the chamber.[9]

Once inside, Bevin's strength returned. It was time for the debate to begin. Douglas Brown, the speaker, called on the Foreign Secretary. Bevin rose to his feet.

Standing at the dispatch box, he began. 'Mr Speaker,' he acknowledged. 'I realise that there is an intense interest in the House in this debate. We are, indeed, at a critical moment in the organisation of the postwar world.'

As he went on, Bevin was heckled by Philip Piratin and Willie Gallacher, the lone members of the British Communist Party in the Commons. He was in his element now.

'On a point of order!' yelled Gallacher.

'I am following the communist philosophy never to give way,' Bevin bawled back.

The MPs listened, seated on the red leather benches usually occupied by peers, as the Foreign Secretary catalogued the history of the last two years. It had been impossible to work with the Soviets. Putting up with the abuse from Molotov and Vyshinsky had, he said, made him feel like a schoolboy being punished.

Bevin had been speaking for more than an hour. 'I am afraid I am wearying the House,' he suggested at one point, 'but it is a very long subject.'

'No! No!' his audience shouted back.

Eventually, Bevin drew his speech to a close. 'My whole life', he declared, 'has been devoted to uniting people and not dividing them. That remains my object and purpose now.' As he sat down, the chamber erupted with applause.

A few minutes after Bevin sat down, Eden spoke. The former foreign secretary had spent the last two years in opposition. It had not been an easy time. Churchill remained leader of the Conservatives, but left the burden of day-to-day affairs for Eden. Following the death of his son, Eden's marriage had fallen apart. Beatrice had left him to start a new life in America.

It was, Eden acknowledged, a debate at a moment as crucial as any which Britain had faced over the previous decade. Other members drew parallels with the darkest periods of the war. Clement Davies, MP for the Welsh constituency of Montgomeryshire, recalled the day that Chamberlain announced a declaration of war against Germany. The slaughter that followed, he reflected, 'will be as nothing compared with what may happen if another war breaks out'.

The following day, as the debate continued, Churchill himself addressed the House. It was a rare foray from the former prime minister. But he wanted to pay particular tribute to Bevin. The Foreign Secretary was, he said, the 'man on the labouring oar' at a crucial moment. Much depended on his actions. He deserved support from all sides of the House.[10]

It was a debate, reflected *The Times* afterwards, that had changed the dynamic. Bevin's speech had sounded the 'dominant chord'. A few days later, Attlee sent a personal note to his foreign secretary. It was copied only to Herbert Morrison, leader of the House and Bevin's long-standing rival. 'By your speech', he told the Foreign Secretary, 'you have recovered the initiative in European affairs.'[11]

Two days after Bevin delivered his speech, Dixon was due to present his credentials to President Edvard Beneš of Czechoslovakia. The 43-year-old diplomat was becoming an ambassador for the first time.

Bevin had encouraged the former private secretary to take the posting to Prague. He had known Beneš during the war, and was watching Czechoslovakia closely. 'I have grave fear about the fate that is awaiting them,' he wrote to Dixon before his departure.

Beneš was born in 1884, when Czech Bohemia was still part of the Austro-Hungarian Empire. In 1935, he became president of the newly independent Czechoslovakia. Three years later, he was forced to resign following the Munich Agreement. Beneš fled to Britain and set up home in Aylesbury, outside London, where he led a government-in-exile. His foreign minister was Jan Masaryk, a diplomat and son of the first president of Czechoslovakia after World War I.

In 1945, Prague was liberated by the Red Army. Beneš returned to a second term as president. At first, the Czech leader sought to carve a middle way between Moscow and the West. He had seen how the London Poles became trapped on a collision course with the Soviet Union, and sought to avoid their fate. Indeed, it was Beneš' ambition to conclude a treaty with Moscow which Eden raised at the trilateral meeting of Allied ministers in October 1943.

In the early years after the war, Beneš and Masaryk were successful. Klement Gottwald, leader of the Czech Communist Party, joined a popular front government as prime minister. But by 1947, the cracks began to show, with a poor harvest and Soviet refusal to allow Czechoslovakia to participate in the Marshall Plan. Gottwald knew that he had trodden close to the line. 'I have never seen Stalin so furious,' he told Masaryk after the Soviet leader summoned both men to Moscow in July 1947. 'He says that we acted as if we were ready to turn our back on the Soviet Union.'[12]

Masaryk became increasingly depressed. In December 1947, he visited London, but declined an invitation to dine with Orme Sargent. The Permanent Secretary, who had known Masaryk through the war years, took it as a bad sign.[13]

The credentials ceremony for Dixon took place in Hradčany Castle. The ancient citadel stood at the centre of Prague, overlooking the Vltava River. The foundations dated back to the ninth century. During the war, it had been occupied by Reinhard Heydrich, Reich protector over Bohemia and Moravia, and a key figure behind organisation of the Jewish exterminations.

Dixon arrived just after midday. He was dressed in formal diplomatic uniform, with a stiff collar embroidered in silver thread. It was tight, and the new ambassador found it difficult to move his arms. He strode past a guard of honour in the castle courtyard, and up a red-carpeted stair to the state rooms. In the January cold, Dixon had worn an overcoat on top of his uniform. Once indoors, he struggled for a moment to remove it, while the head of protocol looked on.

Double doors swung open. Beneš walked in. He had suffered a stroke the previous autumn, and looked greyer than Dixon remembered. The President was joined by Mazaryk and Vladimír Clementis, a communist serving as deputy at the Foreign Ministry.

The British Ambassador presented his letter of credentials, signed by King George VI and Bevin, as foreign secretary. He delivered a short speech. Beneš responded, in halting English.

Bevin had told his former private secretary to discover what Beneš was really thinking. 'Does he think he will be able to maintain the democratic position of the country?' he asked Dixon. 'I want to be told by him frankly.'

This was not the moment. In front of Clementis, Beneš could not speak openly. As Dixon made to leave, the President made a suggestion. 'You must come and see me again,' he said. 'Your wife must see mine.' The British Embassy, he pointed out, was next to the castle, so the two men were neighbours.

'Yes,' Dixon replied. 'We share the same view.'

Clementis smiled, and gave Dixon a wink. The coded message was not lost on him.[14]

Less than a month later, the Czech government was in crisis. In the months since Szklarska Poręba, Gottwald had increased pressure on his coalition partners. The communist minister of the interior, Václav Nosek, tightened control over senior police appointments. On Tuesday 17 February, the other parties in the government demanded that he stop. With support from Gottwald, Nosek stalled. As the crisis deepened, Valerian Zorin, Soviet deputy foreign minister and previously ambassador in Prague, arrived in the city. He passed Gottwald a private message from Stalin. The Czech communists were, the Generalissimo said, pursuing the right course. Moscow stood ready to help.[15]

By the weekend, Prague was in turmoil. Twelve ministers submitted their resignations. The communists declared that right-wing parties were attempting to seize power. Large numbers of workers and militia groups were bussed into Prague, where they staged street demonstrations. Police vans brought rifles and submachine guns to distribute to the workers. 'Strike while the iron is hot,' Gottwald told his party.[16]

Beneš watched from Hradčany Castle. In an open letter to his nation, he called for compromise. 'Let us', he pleaded, 'not prolong this division of the nation into two conflicting camps.'[17] But it was to no avail. The communists persuaded a faction within the Social Democrat Party to break away and join them in government. Armed with this new development, Gottwald confronted Beneš. Foreign diplomats looked on with dismay. Laurence Steinhardt, the American ambassador in Prague, compared communist tactics in a cable to Washington with those used by Hitler.[18] Under duress, Beneš capitulated, and invited Gottwald to form a government. Looking back, the communist leader reflected that he 'couldn't believe it would be so easy'.[19]

Masaryk opted to stay on. He believed that, by remaining in office, he might be able to soften the impact of communist control. It was an agonising decision. When he explained his reasoning to Steinhardt, his face filled with tears.[20] A fortnight later, his dead body was found below the window of his apartment in the Ministry of Foreign Affairs. The communists claimed that it was a suicide, and that an opened razor blade was found in his room.

Clementis took over the post. A few weeks later, Dixon called on him, sitting in Masaryk's old office.

At their last meeting together before his death, Masaryk had asked if Dixon might supply him with English Player's cigarettes. The ambassador had done so, sending a parcel from the embassy.

'Would you like a cigarette?' asked Clementis when Dixon sat down. He stretched out his hand, holding a packet. Dixon glanced down at the label. They were Player's. He looked at Clementis.

'You see,' the new foreign minister explained. 'We are finishing up Masaryk's old ones.'[21]

Knoxville, Tennessee was not used to a visit from the US Secretary of State.

Marshall was on the campaign trail. With interim aid passed, Truman had presented Congress with a bill for the European Recovery Programme, as the wider aid plan was called. Refreshed by his break at Pinehurst, Marshall gave evidence to Vandenberg's committee. But he knew that the real fight would be outside Washington. With presidential and congressional elections due that autumn, members of Congress would weigh public opinion carefully. Marshall's strategy was to sell his case to the wider electorate, and hope that swung the vote back in the capital. 'I worked as hard on that as if I was running for the Senate or the Presidency,' he later recalled. 'It was just a struggle from start to finish.'[22]

The campaign began in mid-January with an address to the chamber of commerce in Pittsburgh. From there, Marshall travelled to Atlanta, to speak at the National Cotton Council. Back in Washington, the Secretary met with a different audience. He received a delegation of seven Boy Scouts from Bethesda, Maryland. The boys had raised money from a film screening to provide food for eight European boys for a year.

The General gathered the group around a table in his office. At his invitation, they told him their story. Marshall listened. 'I wish I could have had something like that in my record as a boy,' he mused.[23]

The next phase was more ambitious. Marshall realised that support from the Midwest would be crucial. This was Republican heartland. Many of the senators and congressmen, like Taft, who were most sceptical about aid to Europe came from the region. Bert McCormick, owner of the *Chicago Tribune*, was opposed to the Marshall Plan, and putting up what the General called a 'very heavy barrage'.[24] The Depression had hit the region particularly hard in the 1930s, and memories remained raw. Farmers feared that fertilisers and other raw materials would be diverted to Europe. It could push them out of business. Marshall was determined to fight back.

On Friday 13 February, the Secretary was due to speak to the annual meeting of the National Farm Institute, at Des Moines in Iowa. Five thousand members were expected for the event. Marshall had given careful thought to the trip. He arranged that his aircraft would fly out via Fort Bragg, in Virginia, to collect Katherine, then on to Iowa, and, after the speech, fly on to Kansas for a family reunion. Marshall's stepdaughter and her husband lived in the state, where he served in the army at Fort Leavenworth. She had recently given birth to her third child.[25]

The weather threw his plans. Heavy fog prevented the aircraft from landing at Fort Bragg. Then, as Marshall was flying on to Iowa, storms hit across the Midwest. His plane was forced down at a small airstrip in Knoxville, Tennessee. It was some 800 miles to the south-east of Des Moines. In the midst of a downpour, a radio connection was hooked up. Marshall spoke over the airwaves, linked to a loudspeaker in Iowa.

The General delivered his prepared text. It was timed to last eight minutes. Then, sensing the moment, he decided to add a few unscripted remarks. It was the same gamble that he had made at Harvard. Before going on, he asked that any journalists at the other end of the line put aside their notebooks.

Continuing, he described his meeting with the Boy Scouts. They had, he said, made a great impression on him. The world had changed much since the one he had known in his childhood. It had become a smaller place. 'We cannot live apart and aloof', he added, 'from what is taking place.' America was engaged in a struggle, as vital as that during the war. It must succeed.

As he finished, the General apologised again that he was not able to deliver his remarks in person – it was hard to connect with an audience at a distance. But, as a smallholder himself, he hoped that he had some understanding of what it meant to be a farmer. Pinehurst had given him a 'feel for the soil and the miracle of growth'.[26]

After a night in Knoxville, the storm cleared. There was no longer time to fly on to Kansas. Instead, Marshall returned to Fort Bragg, and spent the rest of the weekend at Pinehurst. In the garden, the forsythia was starting to show, along with jonquils and tulips.[27]

While Marshall toured the Midwest, Vandenberg had a job on his hands back in Washington. Opposition to the European Recovery Programme was gathering momentum. Since January, a group of 20 senators, led by Clyde Reed of Kansas, had signalled opposition to the bill.[28] Behind them lurked Taft, who argued for a much smaller programme of aid, spread over one year. Joseph Ball, who had sponsored the H2B2 motion which led to the creation of the United Nations, was also opposed.[29]

In mid-February, Vandenberg had secured a crucial fix. This provided for the European Recovery Programme to be administered by an independent official, rather than directly under the Secretary of State. Republicans were more disposed to support an initiative which was at arm's length from government. With this concession, the Foreign Affairs Committee voted unanimously for the bill to proceed to the floor of the Senate. Marshall was delighted. 'Frankly,' he wrote in a private note to Vandenberg, 'I often wonder what in the world I could have done without your understanding and extra-ordinarily skilful leadership.'[30]

It fell to Vandenberg to introduce the bill to the Senate. The chamber was packed. The galleries were full, and even the stairways. Congressmen came over from the House to listen.

Vandenberg had worked on his speech for several weeks, composing it on his portable typewriter in his apartment at the Wardman Park Hotel. The text ran through seven drafts. The Senator believed that it was his role to inform, and then for the Senate to decide. 'He didn't try to avoid problems,' recalled his chief of staff, Francis Wilcox. 'He was very meticulous in giving full answers to every question.'[31]

Vandenberg rose to speak. He had worked on the Marshall Plan for close to a year. It was, he declared, the product of more concentrated study by a larger number of minds than he had known during his 20 years in Congress. His committee had heard almost 100 witnesses, and gathered 1,466 pages of evidence.[32]

'The greatest nation on earth', Vandenberg declared, 'either justifies or surrenders its leadership. We must choose.' It was a matter of judgement, not just a problem of mathematics. 'It may not work. I think it will. But if it fails let the responsibility lie elsewhere.'

As Vandenberg sat down, the chamber erupted with applause. Tom Connally was the first to rush over and shake his hand.[33]

For a fortnight, debate continued. The group of Midwestern senators, led by Clyde, mounted a series of spoiling attacks. The most serious came late on Thursday 11 March, the penultimate day of the debate. Taft spoke for an hour and a half. Rather than oppose the aid programme, he offered an amendment which would reduce it to one year. The United States, he argued, should try it and see.

During the long hours of debate, Vandenberg liked to doodle. He drew on Senate notepaper, tracing neat heraldic crests and intricate, rope-like patterns. It helped him to think. As Taft spoke, Vandenberg composed his thoughts.

When his fellow Republican finished, Vandenberg rose to his feet. If the aid programme was successful, he asked, would the Senator vote in support of continuing it?

Taft declared that he would.

Vandenberg seized the moment. He called for a vote on the amendment which Taft had proposed. The motion was defeated by 56 votes against to 31 in favour.

The following evening, the Senator pushed forward his advantage. At just past midnight, a vote was called on the bill. Thirty-eight Democrats and 31 Republicans joined to support it, while 17 senators voted in opposition. Vandenberg had delivered.[34]

Gladwyn Jebb was hoping to travel incognito. A Foreign Office car had picked him up from Mount Street, and drove him out to Northolt. Soon after the flight took off, however, the pilot received a warning that a bomb was on board. He was obliged to land again, and all the bags were searched. It turned out to be a false alarm. But Jebb was now a public figure, after his work with the United Nations. Amidst the delay, he was spotted. Next morning, the *Daily Telegraph* newspaper ran a piece with the headline 'Bomb hoax on envoy's plane'. The cat, noted Cynthia in her diary, had rather been let out of the bag.[35]

Jebb was flying to the United States. His cover story was a trip to New York, to consult with the British mission to the United Nations. The real purpose was more dramatic. Jebb had come to negotiate a new Atlantic security treaty.[36]

Following Bevin's speech in Parliament, Jebb negotiated a treaty with France, Belgium, Luxembourg and the Netherlands. This agreement, called the Brussels Pact, was concluded in a flurry of activity during the first days of March. It provided for mutual aid in the event of attack from an outside party. The coup in Prague cast a heavy shadow. When one minister suggested that the Red Army would be in Paris by August, the French military Chief of Staff, who was also present, gloomily agreed.[37] At the signing ceremony in Brussels, Bevin chatted with his colleagues from the other countries, as Franks translated into French.[38] The general state of low morale depressed him.

Bevin saw the Brussels Pact as a stepping stone, in a sequence. The first step had been the Dunkirk Treaty between Britain and France a year before. The next should be a North Atlantic security treaty, in which America guaranteed the defence of Western Europe. Shortly before signing the pact, Bevin sent a private message to Marshall, suggesting confidential talks on the substance of what this would entail. The Secretary promptly cabled back his approval.[39]

At Dumbarton Oaks, Jebb had introduced the concept that regional treaties might be permissible under the UN Charter. This had subsequently provided a basis for the Organization of American States. But, at the back of their minds, the British had wondered if such an arrangement might be required in Europe against the Soviet Union. The result was reflected in Article 51. Now Jebb found himself following up on the very hook which he had created.

On 22 March, the British diplomat arrived in Washington. He was accompanied by Leslie Hollis, the Royal Marine who had managed to pocket one of Stalin's wolf-head drawings during the war. The talks were held in the conference room of the US chiefs of staff, deep inside the Pentagon. Military staff cars collected the participants, and ferried them to an underground entrance. One driver lost his way trying to find it.[40] Jebb was the most recognisable among the group, and thus posed the main risk of attracting unwelcome press attention. At their first meeting, he offered to travel up to New York from time to time, to keep up his cover story.[41] As it happened, he was joined by Donald Maclean, from the British Embassy. A few weeks short of his thirty-fifth birthday, the Soviet agent was privy to one of the most closely held secrets in the American capital.

Jack Hickerson, the official who had worked with Acheson on responding to withdrawal of British aid from Greece and Turkey, led the American delegation. Within the State Department, views were split over the wisdom of a security treaty with Europe. Kennan and Bohlen were both sceptical. They favoured a 'dumb-bell' arrangement, with separate treaties on each continent, and a looser arrangement connecting them.

Hickerson took the opposite view. He was a Texan, with a robust style. 'When Jack twists [people's] arms,' recalled his assistant, Ted Achilles, 'they stay twisted.'[42] Hickerson had been in London the previous December. After Bevin's conversation with Marshall, he had followed up with Jebb. Hickerson returned to Washington enthused. On New Year's Eve, he enjoyed Fish House Punch cocktails over lunch at the Metropolitan Club. Afterwards, the Texan strode into Achilles' office. 'I don't care whether entangling alliances have been considered worse than original sin since George Washington's time,' he announced. 'We've got to negotiate a military alliance with Western Europe in peacetime, and we've got to do it quickly.'[43]

The first two meetings of the group covered a general exchange of views. The participants agreed no notes would be kept, and ideas aired without commitment on either side. It was a way of testing the water. At the third, on 24 March, Hickerson decided to seize the moment.[44] 'He would dispose of difficulties, drastically, like a man swatting flies,' recalled Nicholas Henderson, a junior official from the British Embassy in Washington, or 'an auctioneer receiving bids.'[45]

Hickerson proposed adjournment until after lunch. In the meantime, Achilles and Jebb were deputed to draft a paper, along with Lester Pearson, the Canadian representative.

'Jack and I knew clearly from the beginning what we were working for,' Achilles recalled.[46] Now he had his moment. A member of the Eastman Kodak family, who ran the photographic business, he had first visited the League of Nations as a teenager in the early 1920s. Later, he returned to work in Geneva as a diplomat. During the war, he was posted to London.

Six hours later, Jebb and Achilles returned with their paper. It was a blueprint for a new treaty. The Brussels Pact would expand, to include Italy and the Nordic countries. Then the United States would join, and convert the pact into a regional treaty under the UN Charter. An attack against one member would be an attack against all.[47]

Over the next week, the group refined this plan. It was, Hickerson stressed, neither an agreement, not a commitment to one. The paper remained the property of the US government. Any ideas would have to be cleared with Lovett, Marshall and Vandenberg. But it was a starting point.[48] When the talks had concluded, Achilles locked the paper away in his safe.[49] Nicholas

Henderson later called it an 'unseen presence, like some new navigational device' which would chart the course ahead.[50]

James Forrestal was feeling the strain.

Following the atomic test at Bikini Atoll, the Navy Secretary had continued his opposition to merging the armed services, as Truman wished. Eventually, in the autumn of 1946 and early 1947, presidential aide Clark Clifford thrashed out a compromise. There would be a single department, but with a weak central structure. It was, Forrestal conceded, a solution that might just work. Truman took him at his word, and offered him the job of running it.[51]

In July 1947, Congress passed the National Security Act. It would bring the new Department of Defense into being, and create the office of defense secretary. On the morning after the vote, Truman received news that his 94-year-old mother had collapsed. She had fractured her hip, and was in a critical condition. He was determined to fly back to Missouri before it was too late. But the bill had to be signed into law. Clifford raced to the airport, where Truman was already waiting on the runway aboard the *Sacred Cow*. The President signed the bill, and confirmed Forrestal as the first secretary of defense. A couple of hours later, as the plane flew over Ohio, Truman learned that his mother had died.[52]

'The removal of human frictions', Forrestal predicted soon after his appointment, 'is a substantial part of administration.' Six months into the job, the new secretary was learning the hard way. The challenge of bringing the services together was formidable. The chiefs of staff were each determined to defend their own interests. 'This office', Forrestal commented gloomily to Robert Sherwood, the former presidential speechwriter, 'will probably be the greatest cemetery for dead cats in history.'[53]

Strains at home added to the pressure. Forrestal's wife, Josephine, was a former model and editor of *Vogue*. She had developed a drinking problem. Her behaviour became increasingly awkward. On one occasion, when Forrestal gave a formal dinner at his home, Josephine did not appear for over an hour. Eventually, she stumbled onto the staircase landing, and looked down at the guests. 'Good Lord,' she slurred. 'What in the world do all you people have to say to each other?'[54]

Forrestal took refuge in his work. Results, he believed, came through determination and diligence. 'I imagine they were not entirely satisfactory to you,' he wrote to his son who had received poor marks in his first semester at university. Improvement, he advised, would come 'in proportion to the time and concentration you invest'.[55]

There was much to do. In March 1948, crisis struck in Germany. The British, American and French had agreed to move ahead with plans to merge their occupation zones. Clay sent a private cable to the army intelligence staff, warning of a 'subtle change in Soviet attitude'. The message flashed through the Washington system. Forrestal feared that war was about to break out.

Berlin was the weak point. The city was subdivided, with the western zones as an island inside the portion of Germany under Soviet control. The British, French and Americans were dependent on narrow road and rail corridors to the west. On 31 March, the Soviets struck. New regulations covering rail traffic were introduced. Just after midnight the following day, two British and two American trains were refused passage. The controls were relaxed again a few days later. But on 5 April a Soviet Yak fighter deliberately flew under a civilian British plane as it took off from Gatow. Both aircraft crashed, killing 16 British and Americans, together with the Soviet pilot.[56]

Clay conferred with Omar Bradley, who had recently taken over as chief of the US Army in Washington. They discussed events over a secure teletype link. There were only 2,000 American soldiers in Berlin. Bradley suggested withdrawal. 'We doubt', he told his subordinate, 'whether our people are prepared to start a war.' Privately, Bradley instructed that his son-in-law, who was serving in the city, be reassigned to Washington.

Clay was adamant. 'If we mean to hold Europe against communism,' he replied, 'we must not budge.'[57]

The phone rang. It was a Sunday afternoon. Dean and Alice Acheson were at Harewood, in Maryland. The couple had acquired the elegant eighteenth-century farm before the war, and it became a retreat from Washington life. Alice would paint scenes in the garden, while Dean turned his hand to cabinet-making. He had assembled a workshop in an outhouse, with a lathe and tools set along the wall in neat rows. The British journalist Alistair Cooke visited him on one occasion. Acheson might be a sleekly tailored grandee in Washington, Cooke reported, but in the country he 'takes pride in doing hard, pioneering things [...] you never allow yourself to forget the New England roots out of which it is all done'.[58]

The President was on the line. The European Recovery Programme had passed Congress. Truman had signed it into law the previous day. However, under the terms agreed between Vandenberg and Marshall, he needed an independent administrator to run it. Would Acheson be interested?

It was a tempting offer. Acheson had found leaving office hard. During the spring, the lawyer had led the Citizen's Committee for the Marshall Plan. Stimson served as honorary president. Acheson had enjoyed being back in public life. He had travelled across America, raising support for the bill in Congress. In Minneapolis, he addressed an audience in a ballroom with the mayor, Hubert Humphrey. The space was overcrowded, and the speakers balanced precariously on chairs to be seen. Afterwards, they retired to a station diner, for a late supper of scrambled eggs, and danced to the music of a jukebox.[59]

Both men knew, however, that it was a long shot. The post had been created to keep Marshall Aid at arm's length from the administration. A Democrat would struggle to get approval from Congress. Acheson suggested that Truman float his name with Vandenberg. If the Senator objected, he could suggest an alternative: Paul Hoffman, president of the Studebaker Corporation, would be an excellent choice.

A few days later, Truman called again. He had spoken to Vandenberg. The senator wanted Hoffman.[60]

The businessman was less sure. Hoffman was approaching his fifty-ninth birthday, at the peak of a successful business career. He had joined Studebaker at the age of 18, as a salesman. In the years after World War I, car ownership increased rapidly. Traffic accidents rose as well. Hoffman figured out that increased safety and higher car sales could go together. He was appointed by the mayor of Los Angeles to revise the city's highway system, and reduced the death toll by almost a third. By his mid-thirties, Hoffman had made his first million. Ten years later, he was president of the company.[61]

Hoffman flew to Washington to meet Truman. Beforehand, he took a medical examination, hoping that it would rule him unfit. But the doctor found him in excellent health. When Hoffman met the President, he said that he was still undecided, and would reflect. Then, the same afternoon, rumours of the appointment broke in the press. Truman had bounced his nominee. Realising that he had little choice, Hoffman accepted. Vandenberg was delighted, and rushed confirmation through the Senate.[62]

Hoffman's new organisation was called the European Co-operation Agency. He had to start from scratch. The ECA had no staff, no office and no support. Undeterred, Hoffman set up shop in suite W-900 of the Statler Hotel, where he was staying. He called up temporary assistance from the local Studebaker dealership, and began recruiting a team. His first call was to Richard Bissell, an academic economist who had been seconded to the Commerce Department during the war. Bissell had developed a system, based on index cards, to track the whereabouts of all US merchant shipping. When the war was over, he returned to a teaching post at the Massachusetts Institute of Technology.

'I'll tidy up my affairs and I'll come down tomorrow,' he told Hoffman on the phone.

'No, I want you here tonight,' the businessman replied.

Bissell set off for Washington, and rolled into bed at about two in the morning. Five hours later, he was sitting in his first meeting. By the end of the week, he had already signed off $35 million in authorisations.[63]

Hoffman and Bissell settled into a gruelling pace of 15-hour days, with lunch snatched in meetings. It was a strong partnership. Hoffman handled strategy and maintained public support for the programme, while Bissell ran the machinery. Around them, they built a unique organisation. Staff came from business, academia, government and trade unions. A thousand job applications poured in each day. 'The people in the organisation', Hoffman recalled, 'wanted to work for something worthwhile, and had the idea that they could contribute to keeping the world free [...] you couldn't want a better motive than that.'[64]

From the outset, it was clear that ECA needed a strong presence in Europe. It was, as one official later put it, a civilian version of 'theatre command' in the military.[65] At Hoffman's suggestion, Harriman was appointed. As a leading Democrat, he brought political balance. He also knew how to get things done. 'Once Harriman was wound up and pointed in the direction his government had told him he must go,' commented one journalist, 'he was like a tank crushing all opposition.'[66] Harriman took up residence at the Hotel Talleyrand in Paris. He lived in a sumptuous suite, with a bust of Benjamin Franklin, the first US ambassador to France, and paintings by Van Gogh, Matisse and Picasso supplied from his own collection.

On 10 May, the American cargo ship *John H. Quick* docked in Bordeaux. It brought the first consignment of Marshall Aid. By the end of June, aid worth more than $738 million had been dispatched. Soon, some 150 ships were crossing the Atlantic at any one time. The promise which Marshall made at Harvard a year before had delivered.[67]

'Consider it carefully, Clark, organise it logically. I want you to be as persuasive as you possibly can be.'

It was the evening of 7 May. Clark Clifford was sitting alone in the Oval Office with Truman. The two men had got into a pattern of meeting together at the end of each day. It was a private moment. The President would unburden his thoughts and take stock. Both men knew that what passed between them was in absolute confidence.[68]

Truman faced a problem. Fifteen months before, Bevin had announced that Britain would refer the issues of Palestine to the United Nations. Conditions in the territory had deteriorated. Waves of Jewish refugees arrived from Europe, determined to make a new life in their ancestral homeland. In the summer of 1947, 4,500 arrived aboard an old American river-steamer, renamed *Exodus 1947*. As the ship entered Palestinian waters, it was rammed by two Royal Navy destroyers. The hulk was eventually towed into the port of Haifa, and the refugees taken into custody. Visiting UN observers watched as the refugees sang the 'HaTikvah', national anthem of the Jewish Zionist movement. The episode had, for the British, turned into a public relations disaster.

That November, the UN General Assembly endorsed a plan for partition of Palestine into Jewish and Arab territories. A few days later, Arabs killed six Jewish passengers on a bus in Jerusalem. The Haganah, a protection force for Jewish settlements, retaliated. Within weeks, the death toll had risen on each side to close to 100.[69] Attempts led by the United Nations to broker a solution floundered.

The Truman administration faced a dilemma. If agreement over partition was not possible, the Jewish authorities in Palestine were preparing to move ahead with unilateral declaration of a new state, with the name Israel. The State Department was wary, fearing a backlash among Arabs across the Middle East. Truman was privately more sympathetic. Since his first meeting with Chaim Weizmann in 1945, a few days after becoming president, he had remained in contact with the Zionist leader. The British mandate was due to expire on 15 May 1948. Truman gave Weizmann an assurance that, if the Jews went ahead, America would extend recognition to the new state.

Both Marshall and Forrestal believed that this would be a grave error. Jewish and Arab communities were closely interwoven across the territory of Palestine. It would require an international force to keep the two sides apart. Faced with pressures in Europe, America could not spare the men. Talk of partition and recognition was irresponsible. America was, Marshall told the President, playing with fire but had 'nothing with which to put it out'.[70]

Two days before the mandate was due to expire, Truman invited Marshall and Lovett to the Oval Office. Outside, it was a sweltering, early summer afternoon. The President sat at his desk, on which stood a plaque that he had chosen himself: 'The Buck Stops Here'. To his left sat Marshall, along with Lovett. Clifford sat to the right.

Lovett spoke first. He reported on the latest situation inside Palestine, as fighting between the Haganah and Arab forces intensified. Buoyed by military success, the Jews believed that they could go ahead and declare independence, without agreement from the Arabs.

Marshall interjected in support. He had recently met Moshe Shertok, who served as representative in Washington for the Jewish cause. Marshall warned him that this strategy was a grave risk. If the Jewish state came under sustained attack from the Arabs, they should not expect the United States to help them out.

It was Clifford's turn to speak. Truman had warned him that he would need to make the case for recognition. Clifford had prepared his arguments carefully. Before the war, he had worked as a lawyer in St Louis. For a big case, he knew how every line needed to be crafted and rehearsed beforehand.

Clifford ran through the arguments. Israel would soon be a reality. It would also be a democracy. Others would recognise it, including the Soviet Union. If the United States did so quickly, it would gain favour with the new state.

As Clifford spoke, Marshall reddened. In his youth, he had been known for a volcanic temper. It could, his wife Katherine recalled, be 'like a bolt of lightning out of the blue'. As he went through life, he had learned greater control. Anger was, he told her, too exhausting.[71] But on this occasion, he sensed that Clifford was only telling half the story. There was a potential domestic political angle: recognition could play well with the Jewish vote in the United States.

'Mr President,' he interjected. 'I don't even know why Clifford is here. He is a domestic adviser, and this is a foreign policy matter.'

'Well, General,' replied Truman. 'He's here because I asked him to be here.'

Marshall glared back. 'If you follow Clifford's advice and if I were to vote in the election,' he said, 'I would vote against you.'[72]

The room fell silent. No one had heard a secretary of state issue such a blunt threat to a president before. The previous weekend, Marshall and his wife had attended a private dinner to mark Truman's sixty-fourth birthday, held at the F Street Club. It was a rare appearance on the Washington social scene for the couple. Marshall had given the main toast, with a fulsome speech praising Truman for his courage and integrity. When he heard the General's words, the President was moved close to tears. After a few moments, he simply gestured towards Marshall. 'He won the war,' murmured the President.[73]

Truman realised that he had to draw the meeting to a close. He thanked the General. Marshall gathered his papers and left, without a glance at Clifford. Back at the State Department, he dictated a verbatim record of what he had said, as a private note for the file.

The United States and Soviet Union were on the brink of confrontation in Berlin. A breach between President and Secretary would be catastrophic. Clifford and Lovett realised that they had to find a way to bridge their differences. The next day, they held a series of meetings, and inched towards a solution. At lunchtime, they met at the same F Street Club where Truman had celebrated his birthday. Lovett suggested that the United States might recognise the new state de facto, rather than de jure. Clifford agreed it could be a solution.

The new state was due to be announced at midnight in Tel Aviv, the new capital. It would be 6 p.m. in Washington. With two hours to go, Lovett called Clifford.

'Clark,' he said, 'I think that we have got something we can work with. I have talked to the General. He cannot support the President's position, but he has agreed that he will not oppose it.'

'God, that's great news,' replied Clifford. They had a deal.

At 6.11 p.m., Press Secretary Charlie Ross gathered the White House press corps. The British mandate had just expired. He read out a statement.

'This government has been informed that a Jewish State has been proclaimed in Palestine, and recognition has been requested by the provisional government thereof. The United States recognises the provisional government as the de facto authority of the new state of Israel.'

'Oliver, why are you so slow? Why don't we get talking at once?' Lovett's voice on the phone was insistent.[74]

Oliver Franks had been British ambassador to the United States for less than a fortnight. He was originally offered the job the previous December. His predecessor, Lord Inverchapel, had struggled to make his mark. Bevin and Attlee judged that it was time for a change. Franks was only 43, but had won the confidence of both Prime Minister and Foreign Secretary. Nevertheless, it was a difficult decision for the philosophy don. Franks had returned to Oxford after his assignment in Paris. It was his second attempt to resume an academic career after the war. His wife, Barbara, was loath to leave, and their two young daughters were settled. When she heard the news, she cried.[75]

The Franks family sailed from Southampton on 22 May, aboard the *Queen Elizabeth*. The voyage across was overshadowed by the death of the family cat, Lulu. Once in Washington, the family settled into the spacious ambassadorial residence on Massachusetts Avenue, a few blocks to the north-west of the White House. Designed in the 1920s by Sir Edwin Lutyens, it was a modern rendition of an English country house, built in red brick.[76]

Bevin wanted Franks to pick up negotiations on the North Atlantic Treaty where Jebb had left off. The British were worried: after a promising start made by Jebb at the Pentagon talks, the pace had slackened. In a private conversation with Deputy Ambassador John Balfour, Hickerson suggested that others in the State Department were causing difficulties. Bohlen told Balfour that, with the stand-off over Berlin, a new treaty might be too provocative.[77] The deal hidden at the bottom of Ted Achilles' safe risked coming unstuck.

In fact, the reason for delay was not what the British feared. During April, Lovett had had a series of meetings with Vandenberg. The two men had become close, and the Under-Secretary would call on the Senator at the Wardman Park Hotel. At their first meeting, Lovett briefed Vandenberg on the outcome of the Pentagon talks. The Senator was impressed. But he responded with a challenge. 'Why', he asked, 'should Truman get all the credit?' In an election year, the Republicans should be seen to take the initiative as much as the Democrats. The Republican convention would take place in Philadelphia during June to pick a candidate for the presidential race. While Vandenberg had repeatedly ruled himself out as a candidate for the presidency, he was determined to ensure his legacy in building a bipartisan foreign policy.[78]

On 11 April, the two men met for three hours. Vandenberg explained that his committee had been thinking about how to strengthen regional organisations. While the Soviets were able to block business in the Security Council, they offered a means to operate, as he put it, 'within the Charter but outside the veto'. Why not, he suggested, make a resolution from the Senate framed as advice to the President?[79]

Lovett accepted. Over the next fortnight, he and Vandenberg drafted the text. They were joined by Ted Achilles and Francis Wilcox, chief staffer to Vandenberg. The group met at the Wardman Park, and in a small office adjoining Vandenberg's suite in the Senate. Lovett and Achilles offered a first draft. It was too long for the Senator's taste. 'We can say all we want to say in one page,' he sniffed, and started to produce a new version on his portable typewriter. As the Senator typed away, Achilles noted with amusement that he had to reset the typing margins to make more space. Even then, he almost ran over the bottom of the page.[80]

At the end of April, Marshall and Dulles joined the group for a further meeting. This time they met at Blair House. If the Republicans won in November, Dulles was likely to become secretary of state. His support was crucial. Vandenberg produced the text that he had typed from his jacket pocket. When Dulles heard the wording, he was impressed. It sounded, he said, simple and effective. Indeed, he added, it was on a par with the Monroe Doctrine.[81]

The text was authorised by the Foreign Affairs Committee, and passed to the floor of the Senate. On 11 June, Vandenberg opened the debate. The same senators who had voted against the Marshall Plan pushed back with questions. Debate rolled on for eight hours. But Vandenberg had chosen his ground carefully. His resolution, he declared, 'never steps outside the United Nations Charter. It never steps outside the constitution of the United States. It never steps outside the final authority of the Congress.' But it did step towards a 'better and a safer world'. The Senate approved, by 64 votes to 6 against. The motion was dubbed the Vandenberg Resolution.[82]

Three weeks later, Lovett and Franks sat down to a first meeting with ambassadors from the other Brussels Pact countries. Bevin's stepping stones towards a North Atlantic Treaty remained intact.

During May, the Soviets had pulled back from confrontation in Berlin. But tensions soon returned. The Western allies agreed to convene a constitutional conference, which would lay the foundation of a new West German state. In the meantime, they would introduce a new currency in the western zones, called the Deutsche Mark. On Friday 18 June, military governors announced the decision to the Allied Control Council. On the following day, Sokolovsky declared that the Soviet Union would not accept the new Deutsche Mark in Berlin. Over the next week, tensions rose. At midnight on Thursday 24 June, the Red Army closed transport links and switched off power lines. Berlin was under blockade.

In Washington, the atmosphere was strained. Forrestal gathered together the military chiefs in the Pentagon, including Bradley. It was a Sunday afternoon. The group were divided over what to do. Clay proposed sending through an armed column, to break the blockade. Bradley ruled this out. Meanwhile, prompted by a suggestion from the RAF commander inside Berlin, the US Air Force was mobilising transport aircraft to supply the city from the air. General Curtis LeMay, USAF commander in Europe, directed 100 available planes to begin ferrying supplies. At best, however, this might supply 500 tons a day. Berlin was home to two million people – if the city was to survive, 4,500 tons would be required.[83]

The next day, Forrestal and Lovett met with Truman. The two men ran through the options. The President cut them short.

'We are going to stay,' he said. 'Period.'[84]

SIXTEEN

Facing the Fight

So comrades, come rally,
And the last fight let us face.
The Internationale
Unites the human race!

Communist anthem 'The Internationale',
sung at Yugoslav Fifth Congress, July 1948

For Yugoslavia, Monday 28 June 1948 was St Vitus' Day. Called Vidovdan
in Serbo-Croat, it was the anniversary of Serbian defeat by Ottoman Turkey
at the Battle of Blackbird's Field in Kosovo, in 1389. For the next five
centuries, Serbia had been subject to Turkish rule. On the same day, in 1919,
the Treaty of Versailles was signed.

On the same day in Prague, 600 miles to the north-west, the official
newspaper of the Communist Party published a declaration by the
Cominform. 'Recently', it read, 'the Communist Party of Yugoslavia has
pursued an incorrect line on the main questions of home and foreign
policy.' This was incompatible with Marxist–Leninism. The leadership of
the Yugoslavian Communist Party had failed to correct their mistakes.
Yugoslavia had therefore placed itself outside the Cominform. The
communiqué concluded with an appeal to 'healthy elements' inside the
party to confront their leadership, and bring Yugoslavia back into the fold.[1]

The leader of the Yugoslav party was Josip Broz. Born in 1892, Broz
had fought in the Austro-Hungarian Army during World War I, and was
captured by the Russians. He returned to the newly independent country
of Yugoslavia in 1920, and became a communist activist, under the name
'Tito'. In 1941, when German forces overran the country, Tito became
commander of the communist resistance. Aided by the Western allies, and

operating in harsh conditions among the mountains of central Yugoslavia, his partisans grew into a significant military force. In the autumn of 1944, as the Red Army entered Yugoslavia from the east, Tito's forces led the liberation of the capital, Belgrade.

Tito had spent the 1930s in Moscow, working for the Comintern. He established a reputation as a loyal supporter of Stalin. In the years immediately after the war, Yugoslavia held close to the Soviet line. In 1946, Yugoslav fighters had intercepted and forced down an American C-47 which had strayed out of Italian airspace, provoking a diplomatic incident. At Szklarska Poręba, Tito's deputy, Milovan Djilas, had been among those who turned against their comrades from Western Europe. In recognition of this loyalty, the headquarters of the new Cominform was based in Belgrade.

Yet, behind the façade, strains were growing in the Soviet–Yugoslav relationship. In the spring of 1948, Belgrade announced plans to create a Balkan Union, with Bulgaria and Albania. Stalin summoned Djilas and Edvard Kardelj, Yugoslav foreign minister, to Moscow. In a meeting that lasted two hours, the Generalissimo berated them for acting without authorisation. 'You rushed headlong like a Komsomol youth,' he declared, referring to the communist youth movement. 'We too, Lenin's disciples, often had differences,' he added, 'but later we would talk it all out, establish our positions and – we would go forward.'[2]

Tito pulled back from his plans for a Balkan Union. But relations with Moscow continued to deteriorate. Soviet military advisers were withdrawn from Yugoslavia. On 19 June 1948, the day that Sokolovsky walked out of the Allied Control Council in Berlin, Zhdanov met with his fellow Cominform representatives in Bucharest. Ana Pauker, the Romanian representative, and Slánský, from Czechoslovakia, were present, along with Duclos from France and Togliatti from Italy. The Yugoslavs boycotted the meeting. Nine days later, the Cominform's verdict on Yugoslavia was published in Prague.

The next day, a delegation of Yugoslav athletes arrived in the Czech capital. They had come for a Sokol sports festival. Called after the Slavic word for falcon, this movement had first been established in Czechoslovakia in the mid-nineteenth century. The communist government disapproved of an event organised outside party control, but was powerless to intervene. A crowd of nearly 300,000 turned out to watch the Yugoslavs.

At the end of the festival, 700 Yugoslav sailors spelled out the letters 'TITO' in formation across the sports field. The crowd burst into applause. 'Ti-To!' they shouted. 'Ti-To!'[3]

The same day, Tito held a meeting of the central committee of the Yugoslav Communist Party. He was joined by Kardelj and Djilas. The group was unanimous. Now that Moscow had initiated a split, they would stand firm. They agreed a reply to the Cominform communiqué, and published both in the local Yugoslav press.[4]

The next test was the party congress. This was the largest governing formation in the Yugoslav party, elected by the full membership. In mid-July, 2,500 delegates arrived in Belgrade. The congress met in the old barracks of the former king's bodyguard, at Topčider Park. In the meeting hall, busts of Marx, Engels, Lenin and Stalin stood behind the podium. Proceedings were broadcast live over Yugoslav radio, and covered by correspondents from around Eastern Europe.

The congress lasted for six days. On the last, elections were held for the central committee. This was the crucial moment. If the Yugoslav party wished to restore ties with Moscow, it would need to jettison Tito and his colleagues.

At ten o'clock that evening, Miloš Minić, chairman of the electoral committee, read out the results. Josip Broz had received 2,318 votes, Djilas 2,314 and Kardelj 2,319.

The hall burst into applause. As the chairman struggled to finish his announcement, the delegates sang 'The Internationale', anthem of the communist movement. The words had originally been composed by a Frenchman, in the late nineteenth century. 'So comrades,' ran the refrain, 'Come rally / And the last fight let us face / The Internationale / Unites the human race.'[5]

Zhdanov was not in Moscow to hear the news. On his return from Bucharest, he had collapsed with a minor stroke. Reluctantly, Stalin agreed with his doctors' advice, and sanctioned a period of rest. Malenkov took over Zhdanov's portfolio, while his exhausted colleague was taken to a sanatorium at Valdai, near Novgorod.

In late July, Zhdanov suffered a heart attack. Terrified of Stalin, his doctors argued over what diagnosis and treatment to provide. The patient deteriorated. Just over five weeks later, on 31 August, Zhdanov climbed out of bed to use the lavatory. He collapsed with a coronary, and died, at the age of 54.

The coffin was brought back to Moscow aboard a special train, decorated with flags and a portrait of the dead communist. Molotov and Beria, along with the rest of the Politburo, met their deceased comrade at the Byelorussia Station. They carried the coffin off the train, and, unsteady beneath the weight, along the platform to a waiting gun carriage.

The procession wove through central Moscow, and down Gorky Street towards the Kremlin. At the House of Unions, where Vyshinsky had led the show trials in the 1930s, Zhdanov lay in state. Stalin and his colleagues stood in a semi-circle around the coffin, as the soldiers and people of Moscow filed past to pay their final respects.[6]

Richard Nixon was looking to make his mark.

In January 1947, the newly elected congressman arrived in Washington. He had travelled from California in a Ford motor car, along with his wife Pat and daughter Tricia. The family set up residence in the Mayflower Hotel, living out of suitcases. On Capitol Hill, the 33-year-old Republican was assigned to share an office with a fellow new arrival, Democrat John F. Kennedy, the ex-naval officer from Massachusetts. Both were men with ambition. While Kennedy enjoyed natural charm and family connections, Nixon projected determination and hard work. They both took seats on the Education and Labor Committee, making, as Nixon later recalled, 'a pair of unmatched bookends'.[7]

Speaker Joe Martin had other ideas for Nixon. The House Un-American Activities Committee, known by the acronym HUAC, had been established in 1938. It was originally tasked with monitoring pro-Nazi sympathisers inside the United States. In 1945, HUAC became a standing committee of the House, with a remit to police against wider subversion, including from communists. As concern at the Soviet Union increased, fear of communism inside America was on the rise too. In November 1947, the committee held a high-profile series of hearings about communist activity in Hollywood. Many in the film industry had leaned towards the left before the war. A group of screenwriters who refused to give testimony were labelled the 'Hollywood Ten', and found themselves blacklisted from further work in the industry.

Nixon saw his chance. In his election campaign, he had successfully depicted his opponent, Jerry Voorhis, as soft on communism. Two years on, with events in Europe gathering pace, HUAC offered a platform for Nixon's ambitions.

The drumbeat of investigation into Soviet espionage continued. In July 1948, a grand jury in New York issued indictments against twelve members of the American Communist Party. Crucial evidence was provided by Elizabeth Bentley, the go-between who had earlier turned herself in to the FBI. A few days later, Bentley gave evidence to HUAC, and named dozens of individuals who she claimed were guilty of espionage. She was followed, on 3 August, by Whittaker Chambers, an editor at *Time* and another former Soviet operative. Chambers had originally confessed to officials nine years before, in secret. After Elizabeth Bentley's testimony, he decided to go public.

Chambers' testimony was electrifying. He named several senior figures in the Roosevelt administration, who he alleged had been communists. At the top of the list were economist Harry Dexter White and Alger Hiss, the diplomat who had worked with Pasvolsky, and served as secretary-general at the San Francisco Conference.

Two days later, on 5 August, Hiss appeared in front of the committee. The hearing was conducted in the Cannon Office Building, a facility for congressmen across Independence Avenue from the main Capitol building. The committee sat in the Caucus Room, just off the main rotunda.

Hiss was a striking figure. Tall and well dressed, he had been born into an old Maryland family. He was educated at Johns Hopkins University and then Harvard Law School. Afterwards he worked for Felix Frankfurter and then Oliver Wendell Holmes, the Supreme Court judge, before joining the State Department. In the years after San Francisco, his career had stalled, as rumours circulated inside the department about his loyalty. Nevertheless, Hiss retained strong connections and the support of his close friends.

In his testimony to HUAC, Hiss was defiant. 'I am not', he declared, 'and never have been a member of the Communist Party.' The diplomat denied any knowledge of Chambers until 1947, when the FBI had interviewed him, and mentioned the name.

The following week, on 13 August, it was the turn of Harry Dexter White. Like Hiss, White had been dogged by rumours. The previous year, he had stepped down from his post at the IMF, and moved to a private business practice in New York. But this was the first time that he had been confronted in public. Like Hiss, he stonewalled. He had not, he declared, been a communist, nor engaged in espionage. 'My creed is the American creed,' he added. 'I consider these principles sacred. I regard them as the basic fabric of our American way of life.'

Nixon pressed him over the alleged connection with Chambers. He produced photos of Chambers, who had operated under the codename Carl. White brushed off the suggestion. 'I must have met five or ten thousand people in the last fifteen years,' he commented. 'It is possible that I may have met a chap like that in any one of a dozen conferences or cocktail parties.'

Nixon pressed him. If 'Carl' had engaged him in conversation, would he remember?

'I should think I would,' replied White.

'You do not recall having met any person who was known to you by the name of Carl during this period?' asked Nixon.

'No, I do not.'[8]

The committee was stuck. Truman, asked about the investigation, dismissed it as a 'red herring'. But Nixon was determined to persevere. As a Californian, educated at a Quaker college, he was an outsider to the East Coast world from which Hiss came, and into which White had grown during his years in Washington. The atmosphere of privilege rankled with him.

He believed that he had found a weak point. After Chambers gave evidence, Nixon travelled to New York for a further evidence session, and then called on Chambers at his Maryland farm. He established more details about the relationship with Hiss. The two men had engaged in bird-watching together on the Potomac. Hiss had provided a car to the United States Communist Party. His wife, like Nixon, was a Quaker, and spoke in the 'plain' tongue at home, addressing her fellow family members as 'thee' and 'thou'.

On Monday 16 August, Hiss appeared in front of HUAC for a second time. Nixon probed once more. Hiss mentioned that he had had contact with a man called George Crosley, a writer. He had, he confirmed, given Crosley use of his car, and watched birds with him on the Potomac. Nixon was on the scent.[9]

Following his testimony, Harry Dexter White had returned to his summer house at Blueberry Hill, outside Boston. He suffered chest pains on the train journey up from Washington, and called his doctor. Late in the afternoon of 16 August, the same day that Hiss was summoned back to appear before HUAC, White collapsed. It was a fatal heart attack. He was 55.

Back in Washington, Nixon returned to the charge for a third time. Hiss appeared again before the committee on 25 August, alongside Whittaker Chambers. He acknowledged that Chambers was the man he had known as George Crosley. Nixon produced a motor registration certificate, showing that Hiss had transferred ownership of his car.

Wrong-footed, Hiss stumbled through his reply. It was, he said, 'to the best of his recollection'.

Nixon interrupted him. He wanted a straight answer. 'How many cars', he added, 'have you given away in your life, Mr Hiss?'

The audience erupted with laughter. Nixon had got his man.

White House aides Clark Clifford and George Elsey needed a strategy. In June, the Republican convention at Philadelphia nominated Dewey to run in the presidential elections. It would be a second bid for the governor of New York State, after his failed attempt against Roosevelt in the autumn of 1944. Vandenberg had toyed over whether to run. But, at the age of 64, he was concerned about his health, and Dewey had built up a sufficient bandwagon that there was no opening for the senator to come into the ring.

In Washington, all bets were behind Dewey. For the Republicans, wrote the columnist Walter Lippmann, it was a question of 'not whether they win but how they win'.[10] Clifford himself described his boss as playing five yards from his own base line. The Democrats were in risk of splintering. Henry Wallace was running as a breakaway candidate, leading the Progressive Party, while Strom Thurmond, senator from South Carolina, stood in protest at Truman's initiative to end racial segregation in the armed forces. Thurmond's party, the States' Rights Democratic Party, was dubbed the Dixecrats, and expected to draw support away from Truman in the South.

Among his colleagues in the 'Monday night group', Clifford had been debating how the Democrats should respond. The group concluded that Truman needed to build a different electoral base than Roosevelt, extending beyond the traditional Democrat heartland, in the big cities and the South, to the agricultural Midwest. They also counselled Truman to seek out confrontation with Congress, so as to paint his Republican opponents as part of the problem.[11]

The President seized on Clifford's advice. The Democratic convention took place in July, and nominated Truman as candidate. In his acceptance speech, he challenged the Republican-dominated Congress to hold a special session before the end of the month, and pass legislation to address rising prices and the shortage of homes. 'On the twentieth-fifth of July,' he declared, quoting an old Missouri saying, 'sow your turnips wet or dry.' The press dubbed it the 'Turnip Congress'. After two weeks of inactivity, it dispersed. Truman had proven his point.[12]

Clifford was determined to capitalise on this success. During August, he composed a memo for the President. To win, he argued, Truman needed to assemble a majority of 15 million independent voters. Dewey must be associated with the failure of the Eightieth Congress to take action. Clifford picked out 17 states where the margin between Democrat and Republican had been slim in the 1944 election. Ten of them – Ohio, Wisconsin, Indiana, Minnesota, Illinois, Iowa, Michigan, Missouri, Idaho and Wyoming – were in the Midwest.[13]

The challenge was to connect Truman with the electorate. Roosevelt had campaigned with big, set-piece events, visiting the major cities for large rallies. Early indications were that Dewey would adopt the same pattern. Clifford and Elsey, his assistant, wanted Truman to do something different.

In June, the President had spent a few days aboard the *Ferdinand Magellan*, touring the Midwest. The tour was not without mishaps. Dedicating a new airport in Carey, Idaho, Truman managed to get the name wrong. On another stop, when asked about Stalin, he responded, off the cuff, 'I like Old Joe.' It was picked up and torn apart in the newspapers. Notwithstanding the mishaps, the format of a railroad tour suited Truman. It brought him closer to people, and allowed him to engage. Taft dubbed it a 'whistle-stop' approach to campaigning, after the name for small country-halt stations. A new word had entered the political lexicon.

On 17 September, Truman set out again from Union Station. Marshall and Alben Barkley, the senator from Kentucky, saw him off.

'Mow 'em down, Harry!' shouted the southerner, as the *Ferdinand Magellan* pulled away from the platform.

'I'm going to give 'em hell,' Truman yelled back.[14]

This time, Clifford and Elsey had done their homework. The travel schedule stretched over six weeks, criss-crossing the Midwest. Each day,

Truman would make 10, 12, even 15 stops on the line. In the evenings he would do a larger event.

The two men had developed a tighter ground operation. Advance parties fanned ahead of the train, sizing up potential stops, and feeding back information to the party on board. At the campaign headquarters in Kansas City, a research team was led by Bill Batt, an unsuccessful candidate from the 1946 midterms whom the Monday night group had recruited into the job. Batt and his staffers would plough through guides on different states produced by the Works Progress Administration, a New Deal agency. They picked out snippets of local colour. These would then be dictated over the phone or passed by courier to Elsey. On the train, he worked at a portable typewriter, drafting remarks for Truman to use at each stop. Sometimes he would finish a text with only moments to spare before they arrived.[15]

From Washington, the train journeyed westwards, to Pittsburgh, then on into Ohio and Iowa. It passed through Des Moines, where Marshall had given his speech by radio link seven months before. Three days later, Truman was in Colorado and Utah. From there, he travelled west, to Nevada and California, then back into Arizona, New Mexico, Texas, Oklahoma, and northwards to Illinois. By the end of September, Truman had given more than 100 individual speeches, and covered over 8,000 miles. The crowds were getting bigger. By the time he reached Ohio, in the second week of October, more than 100,000 people were turning out to see him each day.[16]

Truman would appear at the rear of the train. He would make a few remarks tailored for the audience, using the material provided by Elsey, and deliver his standard stump speech against the 'do-nothing Eightieth Congress'. Then he would deliver his party trick.

'How would you like to meet my family?' he asked the crowd. The audience cheered back.

Bess Truman would appear out of the rear door. She was, Truman would tell the crowd, 'the boss'.

Then Margaret would join her parents. She, Truman explained, 'bosses the boss'.[17]

The crowds loved it. At one stop, the British journalist Leonard Miall overheard a couple of spectators. 'I had no idea that the President was such a handsome man,' said one.

'Neither had I,' replied the other. Miall glanced round. Both men looked like Truman.[18]

Roosevelt had not campaigned like this. At Willard, Ohio, where Truman delivered a barnstorming speech, Roosevelt had passed through in 1944 without emerging from the train. Thousands had waited by the track, but only got a glimpse of Fala. Now Truman was out and about, sharing himself with the people who were like him. At one stop in Texas, he walked up to a cowboy who was trying to distract attention with a bucking horse. The President took the animal's mouth and opened it. He inspected the teeth. 'Eight years old,' he announced, 'and he's not a very good horse.' The crowds cheered.[19]

In early October, *Newsweek* was running a poll of 50 leading pundits. It would be a snapshot of informed Washington opinion. Several of those polled had spent time aboard the *Ferdinand Magellan*. When the edition came out, Clifford slipped off the train at the first stop of the day to buy a copy. It was Richmond, Indiana.

He opened the magazine. 'Election Forecast: 50 Political Experts Predict a GOP Sweep', read the headline. Not one was prepared to back Truman.

Crestfallen, Clifford boarded the train. As he passed through Truman's carriage, he slipped the copy under his jacket. But the President was too quick for him.

'What have you got under your coat, Clark?' asked Truman.

'Nothing, Mr President.'

Truman pressed him. Reluctantly, Clifford handed across the magazine. The President looked at the article, and passed it back.

'Don't worry about that poll, Clark,' he said. 'I know every one of those 50 fellows, and not one of them has enough sense to pound sand into a rathole.'[20]

General William H. Tunner was a numbers man. At 42, Tunner was deputy head of the US Air Force Military Air Transport Service, and a leading authority on aerial transport. During the war he had built his reputation running an operation to carry supplies over the Himalayas by air, from India into nationalist China. Pilots called it the 'Hump'. In late July 1948, at the request of General Curtis LeMay, Tunner arrived at Wiesbaden air force base in Germany. LeMay had ordered him to take command of the Berlin airlift.

The initial months had been a remarkable success. Two days after the Soviets closed land access to Berlin, C-47s managed to carry 80 tons into the city. By the end of the month, the daily shipment had risen to 500 tons, led by the 60th and 61st US Troop Carrier Groups, and the RAF 46 Group. As more transport aircraft were deployed to Germany, it rose further. By the end of July, the figure was over 3,000 tons.[21] But the blockade looked set to last for months. And a daily rate of 4,500 tons was required to ensure the city could survive through the winter.

'A successful airlift', Tunner wrote later, 'is about as glamorous as drops of water on a stone.' Success would come from a steady, integrated rhythm, as thousands of individual movements and supply chains were co-ordinated together. His first task was to increase the number of flights into Berlin each day, using both existing airports in the city at Tempelhof and Gatow. To reduce waiting times, he scrapped the system of 'stacking' planes before landing. With aircraft operating in such numbers, it was too complex and risky. If there was no slot free to land, pilots flew straight back to their bases in the west. A third airport, at Tegel, was developed, along with an additional runway at Tempelhof. By September, Tunner had increased the number of daily flights to 450. At peak times, a plane landed every three minutes.[22]

With the city airports operating at capacity, the next step towards increasing the daily supply was to use larger aircraft. C-54 Skymasters, of the same type as the *Sacred Cow*, could carry ten tons on each flight, against three-and-a-half on the C-47.[23] At a meeting of the National Security Council, on 7 September, agreement was reached to increase the total number of C-54s in use for the Berlin operation from 125 to 200. An additional Air Force group, the 317th, arrived from Japan with 36 C-54s. But it was still not enough. To reach 4,500 tons a day, further aircraft would need to be transferred from the navy.[24]

It was not a good moment for co-operation between the services. James Forrestal was struggling to create an integrated Department of Defense. Inside the Pentagon, budget plans were already well advanced for the fiscal year starting in July 1949. Forrestal had pledged to Truman that he would make a single bid, with a ceiling of $14.4 billion. But there were bitter arguments over what share each service would receive. Under the previous budget allocation, the Air Force argued that long-range bombers, equipped with atom bombs, would be crucial in any future war with the Soviet Union.

Using this case, they had received a substantial uplift in funding. The navy pushed back, claiming that seaborne carriers, operating closer to Soviet territory, would be more effective. Forrestal found himself caught in the middle. The rival services refused to trim their bids to meet the limit set by the Defense Secretary. It had, he commented bitterly, become a 'competition for dollars'. Aides noticed growing signs of strain. At the dinner table, Forrestal would dip his finger into a water glass and wet his lips in front of his fellow diners, seemingly unconscious of the unsightly habit.[25]

On the ground in Germany, Tunner and General Lucius Clay became anxious. As autumn arrived, the margin for failure remained slim. Berlin had reserve stocks for 42 days of food, and 53 of coal. 'We have proved that given the airplanes we can meet needs,' Clay appealed to Washington. 'Please send us the right airplanes now.' But the chiefs of staff stalled. General Omar Bradley and his colleagues were concerned at the drain which the Berlin operation was imposing on America's strategic position in other theatres around the world.[26]

By late October, bad weather was reducing the number of daily flights. The daily tonnage rate dropped back below 4,000.[27] Clay decided that he must act. In late October, Truman broke off from his campaign tour to return to Washington and host a meeting of the National Security Council. Clay flew back for the event.

The General made his pitch. Nevertheless, the joint chiefs repeated their opposition. As many aircraft had been spared for the Berlin operation as they could afford.

As the meeting broke up, Truman turned to Clay and Ken Royall, the secretary of the army. He asked them to join him in the Oval Office.

'You're not feeling very happy about this, are you, Clay?' said the President.

'No, sir, I'm not,' replied Clay. 'I think this is going to make our efforts a failure, and I'm afraid what will happen in Europe if we fail.'

'Don't you worry,' Truman told him. 'You're going to get your planes.'

Clay seized his moment. He pointed out that the press would ask him what had transpired at the White House meeting. Could he tell them?

'You may,' replied Truman.[28]

The extra aircraft came through. Naval aviation units were redeployed from as far afield as Honolulu and Guam in the Pacific. By January, there were almost 300 C-54s operating on the Berlin airlift, both air force and navy. Clay and Tunner felt sufficiently confident to increase the target rate for daily tonnage to 5,620, and increase the ration allowance for the people of Berlin by an additional 250 calories. The airlift was still in business.[29]

Tuesday 2 November 1948 was election day. Truman cast his vote in Independence, Missouri, just as he had done in the 1946 midterms. Afterwards, he returned to the old house at 219 North Delaware Street, where he had grown up. A crowd of journalists had gathered outside the front porch.

At 4.30 p.m., a Secret Service car drew up at the back. Accompanied by two of his bodyguards, Truman slipped out of the house alone. Unnoticed, the car drove to Excelsior Springs, a resort town a few miles away. Truman checked into the Elms Hotel. He took a steam bath and ate a ham and cheese sandwich with a glass of milk. Then he turned in for an early night. After the weeks of frantic campaigning, there was nothing to do but wait. The final polls had still given Dewey a five-point lead. Across America, the major newspapers were already preparing headlines announcing the new President.

At around midnight, Truman awoke and turned on the radio. On NBC, the veteran announcers Hans von Kaltenborn and Bob Trout were covering the results. On the popular count, Truman was ahead by just over a million votes. But Kaltenborn predicted that the state tally would still go to Dewey.

At four o'clock in the morning, Truman turned on the radio again. The popular count had risen to over two million. He decided it was time to rejoin his campaign team, which was based at the Muehlebach Hotel in Kansas City. Back in Washington, Clifford was also listening to NBC. He called Kansas. The next few hours would be critical.[30]

Truman arrived at six in the morning. He found Charlie Ross, his press secretary, collapsed with exhaustion on a sofa. As the team roused themselves, results started to pour in from the states.

Dewey took New York, New Jersey, Michigan and Pennsylvania. Thurmond had managed only a modest showing, winning South Carolina, Mississippi, Alabama and Louisiana. The rest of the South went to Truman. Across the Midwest, where the *Ferdinand Magellan* had rushed from whistle-stop to whistle-stop, Truman was dominant. By 9.30 a.m., it was clear that he had won all three of the key battleground states, in

Ohio, Illinois and California. In addition, he had carried Missouri, Iowa, Minnesota, Wisconsin and Texas.[31]

It was enough. At 10.15, Dewey sent a telegram to Truman conceding defeat. Truman had amassed 303 votes in the electoral college, against 189 for his Republican opponent. Thurmond had picked up 39, and Wallace none.

Two days later, Truman arrived back in Washington aboard the *Ferdinand Magellan*. As he drove up Pennsylvania Avenue, in a triumphant return to the White House, a sign hanging from the front of the *Washington Post* building caught his eye.

'Mr President,' it read, 'we are ready to eat crow whenever you are ready to serve it.'[32]

SEVENTEEN

The Grain of Salt

To get into heaven, don't snap for a second
Live clean, forget your faults
I take the gospel whenever it's possible
But with a grain of salt.

From 'It Ain't Necessarily So' by George and Ira Gershwin,
played at North Atlantic Treaty signing ceremony, April 1949

The Palais de Chaillot stood above the Seine. Directly in front, across the river, was the Eiffel Tower. Beyond lay the green expanse of the Champs de Mars, stretching to Les Invalides, where Napoleon I lay buried. The palace was built in 1937, for the Paris International Exhibition. In the space behind, temporary pavilions had been erected, to stand for the duration of the exhibition, which provided a showcase for the industry and culture of different countries. A giant sculpture by the artist Vera Mukhina was placed atop the Soviet pavilion. It showed a factory worker, holding a hammer aloft, and a girl from a collective farm, waving a sickle. Opposite stood the German pavilion, designed by Nazi architect Albert Speer. It was crowned by an eagle holding the swastika in its claws, which seemed to glare down at the Soviet couple.[1]

Just over a decade later, in the autumn of 1948, the UN General Assembly gathered at this same spot for its third meeting. Sessions were held in the main conference hall of the Palais de Chaillot. Herbert Vere Evatt, the Australian foreign minister who had attended the San Francisco Conference, acted as president. He sat on the podium, flanked by Trygve Lie.

It was not an easy moment for the new organisation. Confrontation over Berlin provided a darkening backdrop. In late September, the United Nations, Britain and France agreed to refer the issue to the Security Council.

Deadlock ensued. Over Palestine, too, there was little progress. Following the creation of Israel, Arab forces had invaded the new country from neighbouring Egypt, Jordan and Syria. On 17 September, the UN mediator, Folke Bernadotte, was assassinated by a hard-line Zionist group. He was succeeded by Ralph Bunche, the African-American who had worked with Pasvolsky at San Francisco. In October, Bunche gave a downbeat report to the assembly, highlighting the plight of Palestinian refugees displaced by the fighting.

Eleanor Roosevelt travelled to Paris aboard the SS *America*. She had herself launched the steamer, as first lady, in 1939. During the war the vessel had acted as a troopship, carrying thousands of soldiers between the United States and Europe. George Marshall travelled by plane, accompanied by his aides Charles Bohlen and Marshall Carter, alone with his wife Katherine. Bohlen tried to sleep through the flight with the aid of a sleeping pill, but the cabin was too hot.[2]

It was a crucial moment for the declaration of human rights which Roosevelt and her colleagues had drafted. If agreement was not forthcoming at this session of the General Assembly, it might prove too late for another attempt. In a letter back to his wife, Roosevelt's assistant, Durward Sandifer, noted a new energy to the former first lady. 'For the first time', he wrote, 'I feel she is driven by some new compulsion which will never let her come to rest.'[3]

Following agreement within the Human Rights Commission at Geneva, the draft declaration had passed to the UN Economic and Social Council. Fortuitously, Charles Malik had been elected president of the Council, in the spring of 1948. During the summer, he was able to shepherd the text through.

The next stage was the Third Committee of the General Assembly, which covered social and economic rights. This was a wider body, with representatives from all the 58 member states of the United Nations. Malik was again elected as chair. During October and November, he guided the text through long hours of discussion. New controversies erupted. In South Africa, elections the previous May had returned a new government. Veteran leader Jan Smuts had been defeated by the National Party, which had pledged to introduce limits on the rights of coloured and black people. At the Third Committee, the South African delegate argued for replacing the reference to 'dignity and rights' from the first article of the draft declaration, in favour of a more limited commitment. When Malik reminded him that Smuts himself had introduced the wording into the UN Charter at San Francisco, the South African was forced to withdraw.[4]

Meanwhile, Marshall and his wife were enjoying their stay in Paris. Over the first weekend in October, they did a motoring trip to Reims and Nancy, visiting the battlefields along the Meuse where he had fought with the US Army in World War I. At Gondrecourt-le-Château, a small village which had been close to the front line, they arrived just as the residents were gathering for church. Marshall spied a grandmother named Madame Jouatte in the crowd, with whom he had been billeted in 1918. It was the first time that they had seen one another for 30 years.[5]

Eventually, at three o'clock in the morning of 7 December, the Third Committee finished its work. Two days later, the Haitian delegate, Emile Saint-Lot, introduced the text to the full General Assembly. It was the final stage.

Born in 1904, Saint-Lot was a professor and chief justice of the Haitian Supreme Court. In 1945, he became the country's ambassador to the United Nations. A tall man, whom other delegates had christened 'el Danton negro', he served as rapporteur for the Third Committee.

Speaking in French, Saint-Lot ran through the history of the declaration. The war had threatened to destroy mankind's spiritual and moral values. It was Roosevelt, he declared, who had rallied the world, and restored the 'path of justice and liberty amid the tortuous ways of iniquity'. As he closed his remarks, he looked across at the President's widow, sitting among the United States delegation. It was her wholehearted collaboration, he said, tempered with authority and deep knowledge, which had translated this vision into reality.[6]

During discussion in the Third Committee, the Soviet delegate, Alexei Pavlov, had fought a sustained campaign against the draft declaration. He was outvoted. But the Soviet delegation was determined to return to the attack at the General Assembly. In advance of the session, they tabled a proposal for amendment. However, as the debate proceeded, speaker after speaker argued to stick with the text agreed by the Third Committee. René Cassin recalled the Declaration of the Rights of Man adopted by the French Revolution. The UN declaration was even more powerful, he argued, because it was universal in scope. National sovereignty was no longer absolute. Hitler had been able to persecute his own people and claim that it was legal, because there was no international standard to which they could appeal. Over time, such abuse laid the path which led to war.[7]

The debate moved into a second day. Late in the evening, Deputy Foreign Minister Vyshinsky walked to the podium. He was the last to speak. To pass, the text would need support from two-thirds of the assembly. If the Soviet Union was to muster enough opposition to block or delay, this was the moment to do so.

The declaration, Vyshinsky argued, was based on a false theory. Those who drafted the text believed that national sovereignty was a reactionary and outdated idea, and that the declaration should be devoted to the rights of individual human beings. But this was meaningless. Human rights could not be conceived outside the state. Without a state to guarantee and protect them, they were a mere abstraction. It was, Vyshinsky warned, 'an empty illusion easily created but just as easily destroyed'.

Vyshinsky spoke in Russian. Along the rows, delegates listened to the translation through headphones. During the wartime conferences, interpreters had operated consecutively, listening to each delegate speak and then translating, a sentence or two at a time. At the trials of Nazi leaders held at Nuremberg after the war, the American firm IBM had pioneered a new system, with simultaneous interpretation as delegates spoke. It required highly skilled linguists, who could listen in one language and speak at the same time in another. This proved so effective that the Nazi leader Hermann Goering complained that it was cutting short his life. George Klebnikov, the American-born son of immigrants, led Russian interpretation. When the General Assembly moved to New York, Klebnikov and his colleagues went to work for the United Nations.[8]

The Soviet diplomat looked across at Cassin. The Frenchman had forgotten his history. It was not crimes against human rights which led to the war. It was the policy of appeasement, pursued by France and Britain with the support of the United States. The capitalists had encouraged German rearmament, and redirected Nazi aggression against the Soviet Union.[9]

Vyshinsky finished speaking. Evatt announced that the debate was closed. It was time to take a vote.

He submitted the Soviet amendments for vote, one by one. On every count, the proposals were defeated.

It was past eleven o'clock at night. Evatt called for a vote on the declaration itself. Delegates gave a show of hands, a country at a time. Burma was chosen to go first.

One by one, the hands rose around the auditorium. In all, 48 countries voted in favour. Eight, including the Soviet Union and South Africa, abstained. The Universal Declaration of Human Rights had been passed.

A few days later, Evatt presided over the final meeting of the General Assembly. He thanked all those who had participated. The delegates, he said, had never worked harder. 'Even', he added, 'Mr Vyshinsky would agree with that.' The results would be memorable for all of their lives.

Evatt banged his gavel on the desk. The session was closed.

The questions wouldn't go away. 'You brought it up,' retorted the General. 'You discussed it. You have gotten to the point of absorbing all your time in selecting my successor.'

It was late November. George Marshall was holding his first press conference since returning from Paris two days before. Following Truman's election, speculation had mounted on who would serve as secretary of state in a second presidential term. A story had surfaced in the French press that the incumbent had decided to resign. Was it true?

'You are just shooting up the chimney,' Marshall told his questioner. 'You fellows want me to earn your living.'[10]

A few days later, Acheson received a message from Truman. The President asked him to meet at Blair House, where he was lodging while preparations were made for renovation work on the White House. The venerable building was showing its age; when ceiling timbers started to crack, it was clear that a major renovation was required.

Acheson was ushered into the President's temporary office. Truman offered him a chair. 'You had better be sitting down when you hear what I have to say,' he explained.

Truman continued. 'I want you to come back and be secretary of state,' he said. 'Will you?'

Acheson was speechless. After a few moments, he gathered his thoughts. What, he asked, about Marshall?

Truman explained. The previous June, doctors had discovered a cyst on the General's right kidney. They advised that it should be removed. Marshall had waited to make the trip to Paris first. Then, a few days after his return to Washington, he checked into the Walter Reed Hospital. A military surgeon would shortly carry out the procedure. Whatever the outcome, Marshall wanted to step down. His deputy Robert Lovett, too, was preparing to leave the State Department.[11]

Potential names for a new secretary of state had already appeared in the press. Harriman was one, Vandenberg another. Compared to such notable figures, Acheson wondered if he was up to the job. Others were surely better qualified.

That might be true, Truman replied. But he and Acheson knew one another, and could work together. So it was for the former under-secretary to decide.

Acheson reflected that evening, and talked it over with his wife, Alice. The next day, he gave Truman his answer. He would take the job.[12]

Marshall underwent the operation on 7 December. It was successful, but recovery took longer than expected. Cards and letters poured in to the hospital, wishing him well. The General had hoped to travel down to Pinehurst for Christmas. In the event he was only discharged on 28 December.

While Marshall rested at Pinehurst, Truman announced the change of post. Acheson would become secretary, while James Webb, previously director at the Office of the Budget, would take over from Lovett. The secret had been well kept. When the appointment was announced, Washington buzzed with surprise. Speculation quickly moved on to other cabinet posts. With a change in secretary of state, the field was open for other moves.

A few days later, Forrestal called on Truman. The Secretary of Defense had suffered a bad run in the press. Drew Pearson, a prominent radio journalist who specialised in exposing allegations of wrong-doing within official Washington, had launched a series of attacks on Forrestal. He dragged up claims that the former banker had maintained financial links to German companies during the war, and profiteered from oil interests in the Middle East. The strain was taking a toll. At one cabinet meeting, Clifford watched as Forrestal scratched compulsively at a sore on the back of his head. It became as large as a half-dollar coin, and oozed with blood.[13]

After his meeting, Forrestal emerged grim-faced, to a scrum of journalists waiting outside the White House.

Did he have any news, they asked, about his future? Forrestal tried to duck the question. His conversation with Truman had been ambiguous. He had, he said, submitted a routine letter of resignation. This was standard procedure for all cabinet members when a new president arrived in office or an incumbent was re-elected.

The journalists persisted. 'Do you anticipate its acceptance?'

'No,' replied Forrestal.

'Do you want to and expect to continue as secretary of defense?'

'Yes,' replied Forrestal wearily. 'I am a victim of the Washington scene.'[14]

Two days later, Acheson appeared for his confirmation hearing.

A sour mood stalked the Eighty-First Congress. Republicans had expected to sweep both houses the previous November, along with the White House. In the event, the Democrats took a majority in each, unwinding the gains that their opponents had made two years before. On the Foreign Relations Committee, Connally resumed the chairmanship. Under Senate convention, committee seats were given to each party in proportion with the election result. During the Eightieth Congress, Vandenberg had waived this rule, and allocated extra places for the Democrats, so as to balance up numbers. Now back in the chair, Connally did not reciprocate. He insisted on claiming the full quota for his party. Observers took it as a signal that the spirit of bipartisanship was fraying.[15]

Acheson had a weak spot. Donald Hiss, brother to Alger, had worked as an assistant to Acheson during his previous stint at the State Department. Alger Hiss had then served alongside Acheson on the Citizen's Committee for the Marshall Plan. Since Congressman Richard Nixon had first cornered Hiss and his contact Whittaker Chambers, in hearings of the House Un-American Activities Committee, the stakes had risen. Chambers passed microfilm copies of secret documents to Nixon, which he alleged Hiss had given him during the 1930s. The film had been stored for safekeeping in a hollowed-out pumpkin under Chambers' farmhouse in Maryland. Nixon made play with the new evidence. In press photos, he posed with a magnifying glass, examining the material. The net around Hiss was closing in.[16]

Acheson's hearing was held over two days. The first was an open session, covered by journalists. Acheson read out a lengthy statement, describing his connection to Hiss. It was finely balanced. The previous year, Truman had introduced a programme of security vetting, to identify communist sympathisers in government service. Acheson offered his commitment to pursue this within the State Department. However, where Hiss was concerned, he stood his ground. His friendship, he told the committee, was not easily given nor easily withdrawn.[17]

On the second day, the hearing moved into closed session. The committee probed further about the connection to Hiss. Vandenberg gave Acheson some frank advice. His statement the day before had created a problem. Opponents would paint him as soft on communism. He suggested that Acheson agree scripted remarks, which could then be leaked to the press, pledging his commitment to 'human rights and fundamental freedom'.

Acheson smiled grimly. 'I shall be perfectly happy', he replied, 'to have you say that is what I said.'

Afterwards, the non-smoking Acheson asked Vandenberg's assistant, Francis Wilcox, for a cigarette.[18] A few days later, the Senate voted confirmation by 83 votes to 6. Acheson had become secretary of state, the fifty-first man to hold the post since the foundation of the United States.

Jack Hickerson and Tom Connally had the measure of each other. Connally had started his political career as congressman for the 11th district around Crawford in Texas, where Hickerson grew up. The families were friendly. As fellow Texans in Washington, Hickerson and Connally could read each other's mood.

When Hickerson walked into the Senator's office, he knew what was up. If Connally said, 'How are you, Jack?' it was a good sign. But, if he said 'Morning, Hickerson,' the diplomat knew there was a problem.

'Now, what the hell have we done wrong today?' Hickerson would reply.

'I'll tell you what you've done wrong,' came the response, and the two men would get down to business.[19]

Acheson was different. Tall and elegantly dressed, the bishop's son from Connecticut was never slow to display his intellect. Connally felt patronised. On one occasion during his previous tenure at the State Department, Acheson had been hauled in front of the Foreign Relations Committee, together with Hull. Connally and Vandenberg were, Acheson later recalled, like 'two angry popes waiting for a bewildered monarch'.[20]

With Marshall and Lovett gone, it fell to Acheson to see negotiations on the North Atlantic Treaty through to their conclusion. Early in February, he met with Vandenberg and Connally. Bohlen joined them. It quickly became clear that there was a problem. The core issue was the commitment to mutual defence. In the draft text of the treaty agreed by the group of ambassadors that Lovett and Franks led, this was numbered Article Five. During the autumn, the ambassadors had agreed a form of words. This contained a strong pledge. Any attack against one country would be considered an attack against all, and the members of the treaty would be obliged to repel it 'by all military, economic and other means'.

Details of the draft treaty had appeared in the press the previous week, from Scotty Reston.[21] But this was the first time that Vandenberg and Connally had heard this direct from the administration. The senators reeled – the decision to go to war was one of the most serious that any member of Congress could make. As a junior congressman, Connally had taken part in the vote for America to enter World War I, in April 1917. He and his fellow Texan representatives were deeply torn over how to cast their votes. Connally decided for war. When he cast his ballot, he felt a cold chill run through his body. Now, with this draft treaty, that authority seemed to be taken out of congressional hands.[22]

Worse was to follow. A couple of days after his meeting with the senators, Acheson had met the Norwegian foreign minister, Halvard Lange. Norway, along with Iceland and Denmark, was keen to join the new alliance. The *Kansas City Times* obtained a leaked record of the conversation. It suggested that Acheson had described the draft treaty as a 'moral commitment' to fight.

A debate was called in the Senate. Forrest Donnell, a Republican from Missouri, seized on the story in his speech. He looked at Vandenberg and Connally. His understanding was that neither of them wanted such a moral commitment in the treaty. 'If I have misinterpreted their statements,' Donnell added, 'I pause now for a statement to the contrary.'

The two senators were silent. A few minutes later, Connally himself spoke. He expressed sympathy for Donnell's concerns. Americans could not, he said, be 'Sir Galahads, and every time we hear a gun fired plunge into war and take sides'.[23]

That evening, Connally and Vandenberg called on Acheson and Bohlen. The senators were forthright. Article Five must make clear that there was no obligation, moral or otherwise, to go to war. Connally demanded removal of the word 'military' from the draft treaty, and addition of the words 'as it may deem necessary'. It would provide each signatory with more leeway to decide themselves whether to go to war.[24]

This was dangerous. After all the careful groundwork of the previous year, a gap was opening up between Senate and administration. Connally and Vandenberg were now pulling Article Five in one direction, the ambassadors in another. Acheson would need to negotiate between them. 'Safety', he later recalled, 'required use of the ambassadors to urge on the senators, and the senators to hold back the ambassadors.'[25]

Oliver Franks too was worried. Acheson was new in the job. He did not carry the same authority as Marshall. That had been essential to secure passage of the European Recovery Programme. In the transition from one secretary of state to the next, the administration was in danger of dropping the ball.[26]

Acheson and Franks had known each other since the war. When Franks arrived as ambassador, the bond deepened. Acheson, recalled one journalist who knew them both, recognised in Franks not only intelligence, but the ability to 'dissociate himself from his own interests', and see his counterpart's point of view.[27] Once made secretary of state, Acheson invited Franks to establish a privileged relationship. The British Ambassador and Secretary of State would meet regularly, over drinks or dinner. It was a channel to share problems in absolute confidence. Acheson later called it a 'great help and comfort'.[28]

On the day after the Senate debate, Franks called on the Secretary of State. The formal reason was to talk about a consular treaty between Britain and America. But Franks turned the conversation to Article Five. Acheson described Connally's demands.

Franks was a pragmatist. The ambassadors would need to give some ground. The wording 'as it may deem necessary' was, he said, not ideal, but probably acceptable. Removal of the word 'military' was more serious. The original draft had now become public knowledge. Dropping a reference to military action at this stage would send a negative signal.[29]

Hickerson and Bohlen played with alternative wording. Bohlen sent Acheson a note with three options. Acheson then discussed these with Truman. They hit on the phrase 'including the use of armed force'. It offered the best means of combining Franks' requirements with those of the senators. Truman agreed that Acheson should present it to Connally, with the full authority of the President.[30]

Acheson did so the next day. The Senator accepted his proposal. Bohlen debriefed Franks. It was, he said, a solid basis on which to move forward.[31]

Back in London, Foreign Secretary Ernest Bevin and Gladwyn Jebb had been following developments closely. Bevin and Franks were exchanging telegrams twice or more a day, as the latter kept his boss in the picture. When news of the Senate debate on 14 February reached Bevin, he was very worried. It was, he told Franks, 'an entirely new situation'. If America did not yet see herself as bound to a single Atlantic community, Bevin questioned whether it made sense to sign a treaty at all.[32]

When news came through of a deal, the Foreign Secretary was delighted. The treaty, he declared in a radio broadcast a few weeks later, demonstrated that Europe and America shared an 'underlying determination to preserve our way of life'.[33] The third of his stepping stones, which led through from the Dunkirk Treaty with France to the Brussels Pact and then the North Atlantic Treaty, had fallen into place.

'You need to divorce your wife!'

It was an order. Stalin was addressing Molotov at a meeting of the Central Committee.[34]

Vyacheslav Molotov and Polina Zhemchuzhina had married in 1921. She was a young communist activist, who had served as a propaganda commissar during the Russian Civil War. The couple were devoted to one another. 'Polina, my love,' wrote Molotov in a letter from San Francisco, 'I miss you and our daughter. I shan't conceal sometimes I am overcome with impatient desire for your closeness and caresses.'[35] In the early years, the Molotovs had lived in a Kremlin flat next door to Stalin and his wife, Nadezhda Alliluyeva. The two couples were friendly. Stalin had been close to Polina, though the friendship had cooled after Nadezhda committed suicide in 1932.

Molotov was vulnerable. His foreign policy had failed. The Marshall Plan, and now the North Atlantic Treaty, had brought Western Europe together. The Berlin blockade, which Stalin had hoped would halt the creation of West Germany, was circumvented by Tunner's airlift. In Eastern Europe, Yugoslavia had slipped out of the communist fold.

Polina was also exposed. During 1948, on Stalin's orders, Secret Police Chief Viktor Abakumov launched a purge against senior Jewish figures. Solomon Mikhoels, an actor who led the Jewish Anti-Fascist Committee during the war, died in mysterious circumstances. His associates were taken into custody. Polina was herself Jewish, and had been involved with the committee. But she failed to read the signals. As a Kremlin wife, she was used to living in the limelight. When Golda Meir, ambassador for the new state of Israel, attended a reception at the Ministry of Foreign Affairs in the autumn of 1948, Polina addressed her before the assembled diplomats and officials.

'You're Jewish?' asked Meir in surprise.

'I'm a daughter of the Jewish people,' Polina replied in Yiddish.[36]

Molotov had served Stalin since the early days of the Soviet state. 'I argued with him, told him the truth,' he claimed later. 'That was why Stalin valued me.'[37] However, it was no protection. Jewish connections were no longer acceptable in Politburo members. In late 1948, the Generalissimo told Molotov that he should leave his wife. 'If this is what the party needs,' concluded Polina, 'we'll divorce.'

It was not enough. On 29 December, Abakumov circulated a report to the Politburo. Stalin read out the charges to his colleagues. Polina was accused of consorting with Jewish nationalists. When he heard, Molotov's knees trembled. 'You could not fault them,' he said afterwards. 'The Chekists had done their best.'

Before Polina could be prosecuted, she had to be expelled from the party. When the Central Committee took a vote, Molotov abstained. Stalin turned on the pressure. He reminded Molotov of his past transgressions, including his conduct in the autumn of 1945. The Foreign Minister was obliged to change his mind. 'I am voting in favour of the decision of the Central Committee,' he wrote to Stalin, 'which both meets the interests of the party and of the state and conveys a correct understanding of communist party-mindedness.'[38]

The next day, Polina was arrested. She was taken to the cells under the Lubyanka, headquarters of the Ministry of Internal Security. 'Phone my husband!' she cried. 'Tell him to send my diabetes pills! I'm an invalid! You've no right to feed me on this rubbish!'[39]

While Polina suffered in the Lubyanka, Stalin signalled a change of course on Berlin. At the end of January 1949, an American journalist sent him a set of written questions. Would, he asked, the Soviet Union lift the blockade if the Western allies agreed to a further meeting of the Council of Foreign Ministers? Stalin replied that this was the case. Further, private contacts were conducted through a back channel between the deputy US ambassador to the UN, Philip Jessup, and his Soviet counterpart, Yakov Malik.

With a change of policy, Stalin needed a new pair of hands. At a meeting with Politburo members Georgy Malenkov and Lavrentii Beria, Stalin decided to replace Molotov with his deputy, Andrei Vyshinsky. The sacked minister remained in the Politburo, but for a man who had at one point been second only to Stalin in the Soviet hierarchy, it was a stark demotion.

Molotov had given his life to the communist cause. 'I am a member of the Politburo,' he said later, remembering the events of spring 1949. 'I must obey party discipline.' But, in private, the pain was real. He had lost his wife, and his job. Every evening, alone in his flat, he ordered his maids to set an extra place at dinner, in memory of Polina.[40]

On 1 March 1949, at 12.30 p.m., James Forrestal went to the White House. Truman broke the news. Forrestal must set a firm date for his departure – it was time for Louis Johnson to take over as secretary of defense.

When he returned to the Pentagon that afternoon, Forrestal made no mention of what had happened. He continued with his usual schedule of meetings. That evening, he struggled to write the resignation letter that Truman had requested. He stayed up through the night, phoning his aides for advice. At first, he wanted to leave office at once. Then he wanted to extend to mid-March. Eventually he decided to hang on until the end of the month.[41]

The ceremony finally took place on 28 March. That morning, Forrestal called Truman to ask if he should really go ahead. 'Yes, Jim,' the President replied. 'That's the way I want it.'[42]

At a ceremony in the central courtyard of the Pentagon, Johnson was sworn in. Forrestal was driven across to the White House, for the customary farewell call on the President. In a surprise gesture, Truman had assembled the full cabinet and military chiefs. He presented Forrestal with the Distinguished Service Medal. Forrestal was overcome, and unable to speak.

'It's beyond me – beyond my ...' he mumbled.

'There you are,' the President assured him. 'You deserve it, Jim.'
Speechless, Forrestal had to be led from the podium.[43]

Two days later, Bevin arrived in New York, aboard the *Queen Mary*. He had made the crossing with Hector McNeil, the Scottish trade unionist who had served as his deputy for the previous four years at the Foreign Office. They had come to sign the North Atlantic Treaty.

The ceremony took place on Monday 4 April 1949, at the Departmental Auditorium in Washington. It was a neoclassical building, adjacent to the former home of the State Department in the Old Executive Building. In a speech at the same venue in 1940, Roosevelt had announced the Selective Service Act, which introduced a first draft of men into the armed forces.

Twelve foreign ministers had gathered for the occasion. Bevin and Acheson were joined by their colleagues from the Brussels Pact countries, as well as Canada. Also present were ministers from Italy, Norway, Iceland, Denmark and Portugal, who had negotiated inclusion in the new treaty during the final weeks of preparation. They sat in a semi-circle on the stage, with a second row for the ambassadors. Franks sat behind Bevin. Flags from the 12 countries were displayed, along with pink hydrangeas and potted palms. His staff had even provided Acheson with a timetable, notes reminding him how to introduce each dignitary, and a plan of where they should sit.[44] Vandenberg and Connally sat in the audience, along with the rest of the Senate.

As the guests gathered, a US Marine band played tunes from Gershwin musicals. They included, Acheson noted wryly, the popular songs 'I've Got Plenty of Nothing' and 'It Ain't Necessarily So'. In a nod to Bess Truman, who was sitting in the front row, the band also played the song 'Bess, You is my Woman Now'.

Acheson spoke first. He welcomed his guests. Then, turning to the ambassadors seated around him, he paid tribute to those who had drafted the treaty. Their purpose, he ventured, was like 'those who chart the stars — not to create what they record, but to set down realities for the guidance of men'. That reality, he continued, was not reflected in words on a page, but in a unity of belief and a community of nations which lay behind them. It was the same thought which Bevin had mentioned to Franks in his telegram a few weeks before.

Each minister spoke. The speeches finished slightly earlier than expected, and the band was obliged to play some impromptu interval music. Then Truman entered, to the strains of 'Hail to the Chief'. He shook hands with the ministers and, stepping up to the lectern, addressed the audience. His speech traced the currents of history which had swept over the previous decade. 'Men with courage and vision', he declared, 'can still determine their own destiny. They can choose slavery or freedom, war or peace.'

Afterwards, it was time for the signing ceremony. Bevin wrote his signature with his outsized fountain pen, held in his characteristic, awkward grip between index and middle finger. He sealed it with a ring given to him by the founder of the American Federation of Labor. 'This', he said, 'is one of the greatest moments of my life.'[45]

When it was over, Acheson and Hickerson shared a car back to the State Department. 'Well, Jack,' said the Secretary, 'I think this treaty is going to work.'

'But if it doesn't,' Acheson added, looking across at his colleague, 'there will be no damn doubt, you did it.'[46]

That evening, the Texan took his assistant Ted Achilles out for a drink at their favourite bar, in the basement of the Willard Hotel. Both men ordered a bourbon, and then another one.[47]

The Waste of Time

Thy son is in a foreign clime
Where Ida feeds her countless flocks,
Far from thy dear, remembered rocks,
Worn by the waste of time.

Chorus from Sophocles' *Ajax*, translated by William Mackworth
Praed. Transcribed by James Forrestal before his death.

On the day after his departure from the Pentagon, James Forrestal attended a special meeting in Congress with the House Armed Services Committee. They presented him with a silver bowl, engraved with names of the committee members. 'In testimony of our regard,' read the dedication. 'That regard is also indelibly inscribed in our hearts.'

Afterwards, an aide drove Forrestal back to the Pentagon, where an office had been made available for him to wind up his affairs. He sat down, and then remained motionless, staring at the wall. His hat was still on his head, and the silver bowl lay on the table. The aide tried to engage the former secretary in conversation. He simply replied, 'You are a loyal fellow', and then repeated the phrase again and again.[1]

It was clear that something was wrong. Forrestal needed help. That evening, he was flown in a US Air Force plane down to Hobe Sound, in Florida, where the Forrestals kept a summer house. Robert Lovett, who was also a resident, met him at the airport. He was shocked at his friend's appearance.

'Jim,' he ventured, 'I hope you brought your golf clubs because the weather down here is perfect for golf.'

Forrestal stared blankly. 'Bob,' he said, 'they're after me.'[2]

Over the next month, friends and neighbours watched over Forrestal. Lovett took him for walks on the beach and a swim in the sea, hoping that the fresh air would be a tonic. A psychiatric specialist, Dr William Menninger, examined the former secretary. Menninger was conducting research into combat stress. He concluded that Forrestal was suffering from a similar condition, and needed hospital treatment. On 2 April, a month after he had arrived in Florida, Forrestal returned to Washington, to the Bethesda Naval Hospital in Maryland.[3]

The former secretary was allocated a room in the VIP suite on the sixteenth floor of the hospital. A few days later, the *New York Times* broke the news. Forrestal was, the newspaper reported, receiving treatment for 'nervous and physical exhaustion'. The administration was forced to issue a statement, confirming his condition.[4]

The treatment continued. On some days, Forrestal seemed to brighten. When Bess Truman sent him a bouquet of roses for Easter, he managed to write a short note of thanks. 'A happy Easter to you and the President and Miss Truman,' he wrote. 'You all deserve it.'[5]

On the night of 21 May, Forrestal was reading from the *Anthology of World Poetry* edited by poet Mark Van Doren. He wrote out a chorus from the tragedy *Ajax* by the ancient Greek dramatist Sophocles, copying onto loose sheets of paper. In the second stanza, he reached the lines 'No quiet murmur like the tremulous wail / Of the lone bird, the querulous nightingale ...' He stopped copying, halfway through the final word. Forrestal tucked the paper into the red-bound volume, and placed it on his bedside table. Then he rose, and crossed the corridor to a small kitchen. There, he knotted the sash of his dressing gown around a radiator, tied the other end in a noose around his neck, and threw himself out of the window.[6]

Forrestal's funeral took place three days after his death, at Arlington National Cemetery in Washington. His wife Josephine had been in France at the time of her husband's suicide, looking for a suitable place where he might recuperate. Acheson was also in Paris. A few weeks before, Stalin had lifted the blockade on Berlin. Vyshinsky had called together the Council of Foreign Ministers. Acheson made his official plane available for Josephine to return home. On arrival at Washington, she was met by Louis Johnson, the new secretary for defense.

The funeral service was conducted in the Memorial Amphitheatre at Arlington. A gun carriage transported the coffin, flanked by a US Navy

Academy band, a battalion of midshipmen and a composite battalion of army, air force, navy and marine personnel. All were dressed in summer rig, with white and dark-blue uniforms. The coffin was wrapped in the Stars and Stripes. It was a clear, sunny day.

Twenty-two friends and colleagues served as pallbearers. They were led by former President Herbert Hoover, along with Chief Justice Fred Vinson. George Marshall, James Byrnes and Dwight Eisenhower took part, as did Admiral William Leahy, the financier Bernard Baruch and Robert Lovett.

The cortège entered the Arlington cemetery at the Memorial Gate. As the procession moved through the grounds, the 3rd Infantry Battery fired a 19-gun salute. The rounds came at minute intervals, so that the salute finished just as the cortège reached the amphitheatre. It was 11.15 a.m. Over 1,000 people were assembled in the congregation. They included President Truman, Bess and Margaret, along with the Forrestal family, and senators Vandenberg and Connally. Outside, thousands of onlookers had gathered to pay their respects.

The Right Reverend Wallace Conkling, bishop of Chicago, conducted the service. Readings were taken from the psalms, and from First Corinthians 15:20–58. 'Those who own a God and a providence,' read the bishop, 'and observe how unequal things are in the present life, how frequently the best men fare worst, cannot doubt as to an after-state, where everything will be set to rights.'

Afterwards, a marine squad fired three volleys. A lead bugler played taps, while a second echoed the notes across the silent cemetery. As the coffin was transported from the amphitheatre, the band played 'Onward Christian Soldiers'. The final resting place was a few hundred yards away, in section 30 of the cemetery. Josephine had chosen to stay away from the larger ceremony. She waited by the graveside to see her husband for the last time.[7]

That night, Vandenberg recorded his impressions. It had been a poignant occasion. The Senator was moved to tears. 'There was something about it', he wrote, 'which was so intimately tragic and yet so spiritually exalted. I am sure Jimmy did not die in vain.'[8]

'James Forrestal', read the tombstone. 'In The Great Cause of Good Government'.

Notes

Preface
1 Sheridan (1985), p. 392.
2 Harvey (1978), p. 385.
3 Quoted in Ferguson (2003), p. 292.
4 Thorpe (2003), p. 3.
5 Quoted in Thompson (2009), p. 8.
6 Lawrence (1926), p. 22.

Introduction
1 Charmley (1986), p. 151.
2 Lysaught lecture on Bracken, May 2001.
3 Description from Morton (1943), pp. 19–23.
4 Conrad Black archive, 4 August 1941, quoted in Roberts (2008), p. 52.
5 Sherwood (1948), p. 247; Jenkins (2001), p. 650.
6 Unpublished Cadogan memoirs, ACAD 7/2, Churchill College Archives.
7 Sherwood (1948), pp. 324, 351.
8 Dilks (1971), Introduction, p. 20.
9 Quoted in Wilson (1991), p. 79.
10 Cadogan private memoir, ACAD 7/2, Churchill College Archives.
11 Quoted in Jenkins (2001), p. 320.
12 Ismay (1960), p. 121.
13 Nicolson (1968), entry for 15 June 1940.
14 Asquith (1968), entry for 11 November 1915.
15 Dilks (1971), p. 398.
16 Morton (1943), pp. 105–6.
17 Dilks (1971), p. 398; Morton (1943), p. 107.
18 Churchill radio broadcast, 24 August 1941.
19 *FRUS 1941: Vol. I*, pp. 361–3.
20 Quoted at Wilson (1991), p. 31.
21 Cadogan memoirs, Churchill College Archives.
22 Dilks (1971), p. 399.
23 Sherwood (1948), p. 227.

24 *FRUS 1941: Vol. I*, p. 363.
25 Colville (1985), p. 424.
26 Williams (1961), p. 54; Wilson (1991), p. 177.
27 Cadogan memoirs, Churchill College Archives.
28 Colville (1985), p. 426.
29 Morton (1943), pp. 127–8.

Chapter 1: Getting Started
1 Cooke (2006), pp. 44–52.
2 Churchill (1959), p. 505.
3 Moran (1966), p. 23.
4 Thompson (1955), p. 246.
5 Sherwood (1948), p. 444.
6 Sherwood (1948), pp. 442–3.
7 Churchill (1959), p. 523.
8 Mrs Charles Hamlin, 'Some Memories of FDR', in Halifax papers, Churchill College Archives.
9 Bercuson and Herwig (2005), p. 219.
10 Acheson (1967), p. 9.
11 Joseph Johnson interview with McKinzie, 29 June 1973, p. 64.
12 Acheson (1967), p. 17.
13 Cooke (2006), pp. 17, 88.
14 Sherwood (1948), p. 437.
15 Vandenberg (1952), p. 1.
16 Dallek (1995), p. 419.
17 Drury (1963), quoted at www.senate.gov/artandhistory/history/minute/A_Senate_Journal_1943-45.htm.
18 FO 371/34181, BE Washington to FCO London of 19 April 1943, quoted by Hachey (1973–4) in *Wisconsin Magazine of History* 57, p. 149.
19 Ibid, pp. 143–7.
20 Woods (1990) , p. 82.
21 Durward Sandifer interview with McKinzie, 15 March 1973, pp. 7–9.
22 Thorpe (2003), p. 282; Eden (1965), pp. 375–6; Harvey (1978), p. 238.
23 Pimlott (1985), p. 257; Colville (1985), p. 590.

Chapter 2: Doing the Job
1 Dobbs (2012), p. 127.
2 Harriman (1975), p. 235.
3 Harriman (1975), pp. 234–5; Hull (1948), p. 1277; Eden (1965), pp. 409–10.
4 Bohlen (1973), p. 130.
5 Harriman (1975), p. 239.
6 PRO FO 371/37071 f17, quoted in Watson (2003), p. 13.

7 Birse (1967), p. 138.
8 *FRUS 1943: Cairo and Tehran*, pp. 624–6.
9 Ismay (1960), p. 327.
10 Hull (1948), p. 1297.
11 Dallek (1995), p. 422.
12 See Butler (2005), pp. 172–5, 177–9.
13 Leahy (1950), p. 232; *FRUS 1943: Cairo and Tehran*, p. 280.
14 Jebb (1972), p. 136.
15 Bohlen (1973), p. 139.
16 Bohlen (1973), p. 143.
17 Bohlen (1973), pp. 141–2.
18 Sebag Montefiore (2003), p. 330.
19 See *FRUS 1943: Cairo and Tehran*, pp. 529–33. Account based on verbatim notes provided by Bohlen.
20 Birse (1967), p. 156; Bohlen (1973), pp. 136–7.
21 Danchev and Todman (2001), p. 485.
22 See copy in Sherwood (1948), p. 789.
23 Birse (1967), pp. 157–8.
24 Record at *FRUS 1943: Cairo and Tehran*, pp. 594–6.
25 Bohlen (1973), pp. 11, 151.

Chapter 3: Leaving the Shadows
1 See Baczynski page at www.warsawuprising.com/paper/baczynski.htm.
2 Skidelsky (2003), p. 675.
3 Meade Diaries 1/1, 70, RL/LSE, quoted in Woods (1990), p. 85.
4 Blum, Morgenthau Diaries, pp. 249–50, quoted in Woods (1990), p. 129.
5 Quoted in Steil (2013), p. 13.
6 FDRL Morgenthau Diaries, vol. 753, pp. 143–4, quoted in Moggridge (1995), p. 745.
7 Goldenweiser Papers, Bretton Woods Conference, Box 4, quoted at Steil (2013), p. 211.
8 Morgenthau diaries, vol. 757, 22 July 1944, pp. 13a–13b, quoted in Conway (2014), pp. 279–80.
9 *New York Times*, 24 July 1944, p. 1.
10 Danchev and Todman (2001), p. 689.
11 Harrison (1980), p. 12, quoted in Danchev and Todman (2001), Introduction, p. xvi.
12 See Jebb (1972), pp. 144–5; Danchev and Todman (2001), p. 575; Woodward (1976), pp. 185, 189–90.
13 Applebaum (2003), p. 123.
14 Pechatnov (1995), pp. 6–9.
15 Gromyko (1989), pp. 77–8; Birse (1967), p. 168.
16 Sherwood (1948), p. 757.
17 Campbell and Herring (1975), p. 110.

18 Jebb (1972), p. 148.
19 Joint Steering Committee meeting of 28 Aug 1944. Record at *FRUS 1944: Vol. I*, pp. 740–3.
20 Campbell and Herring (1975), pp. 111–14.
21 Gaddis (2011), p. 173.
22 Kennan (1967), pp. 210–11.
23 Gaddis (2011), p. 182.
24 *FRUS 1944: Vol. I*, p. 780.
25 Record at *FRUS 1944: Vol. I*, pp. 784–7.
26 Gromyko (1989), p. 34.
27 Dilks (1971), p. 656.
28 Campbell and Herring (1975), p. 133; Cadogan memoirs, Churchill College Archives.
29 *FRUS 1944: Vol. I*, pp. 798–804.
30 Campbell and Herring (1975), p. 135.
31 *FRUS 1944: Vol. I*, p. 823.
32 *FRUS 1944: Vol. I*, pp. 842–3.
33 Dilks (1971), p. 669.
34 Nadeau (1990), p. 106.
35 Davies (2003), p. 425.

Chapter 4: Drawing Up Account
1 Translated by Vivian de Sola Pinto, in anthology *The Road to the West* (1945).
2 Steel (1978), p. 418.
3 Leaming (1985), pp. 292–3.
4 Sherwood (1948), p. 821; Dilks (1971), p. 668.
5 Moran (1966), p. 213.
6 Danchev and Todman (2001), p. 602.
7 Birse (1967), pp. 109, 112.
8 Churchill (1959), pp. 885–6.
9 Birse (1967), p. 113.
10 Letter from Churchill to Clementine, 13 October 1944, in Soames (1998), p. 506.
11 Birse (1967), p. 174.
12 Harriman (1975), p. 362.
13 Moran (1966), p. 228.
14 Sherwood (1948), p. 828.
15 Steel (1978), p. 420.
16 Quoted in Acheson (1967), p. 87.
17 Leahy (1950), p. 345; Byrnes (1947), p. 22.
18 Dobbs (2012), p. 9.
19 See Dilks (1971), p. 701; Dixon (1968), p. 136; Jebb (1972), p. 153; Danchev and Todman (2001), p. 653.
20 Dixon (1968), p. 138.

21 Harriman (1975), p. 393.

22 Birse (1967), p. 182.

23 Bohlen (1973), pp. 175–6.

24 Dobbs (2012), p. 31.

25 See Bohlen record at *FRUS 1945: Malta and Yalta*, pp. 570–3 and Bohlen (1973), pp. 179–80.

26 Harriman (1975), p. 395.

27 Moran (1966), p. 249.

28 *FRUS 1945: Malta and Yalta*, p. 621.

29 *FRUS 1945: Malta and Yalta*, pp. 655–7.

30 Eden diary for 4 January 1945, quoted in Thorpe (2003), p. 302.

31 Dixon (1968), p. 140.

32 Birse (1967), p. 183; Moran (1966), p. 250; Portal quoted in Dobbs (2012), p. 34.

33 *FRUS 1945: Malta and Yalta*, pp. 660–7.

34 Bohlen (1973), p. 179.

35 *FRUS 1945: Malta and Yalta*, pp. 667–71; Matthews notes at pp. 678–81.

36 Dixon (1968), p. 140.

37 Bohlen (1973), pp. 188–9

38 Dilks (1971), p. 706.

39 Gromyko (1989), p. 85.

40 Sherwood (1948), pp. 855–6; *FRUS 1945: Malta and Yalta*, pp. 709–18 (Bohlen); ibid., pp. 718–21 (Matthews); ibid., pp. 721–4 (Hiss).

41 *FRUS 1945: Malta and Yalta*, pp. 717, 720; ibid., pp. 718–21 (Matthews notes).

42 Dixon (1968), pp. 142–3; Birse (1967), p. 180; Roberts (1991), p. 72.

43 UN Oral History interview with Gladwyn Jebb, 21 June 1983, pp. 79–80.

44 *FRUS 1945: Malta and Yalta*, pp. 797–8; Dilks (1971), p. 707.

45 Bohlen (1973), p. 182; Birse (1967), pp. 184–5.

46 Danchev and Todman (2001), pp. 661–2.

Chapter 5: Furling the Flags

1 Sherwood (1948), pp. 878–80.

2 Bishop (1974), pp. 590–1.

3 McCullough (1992), p. 37.

4 McCullough (1992), pp. 336–7.

5 Truman (1952), pp. 109–11; Truman (1955), p. 5.

6 Theodore Achilles interview with McKinzie, 15 November 1972, p. 2.

7 Trevor-Roper (1947), pp. 112–13.

8 Campbell and Herring (1975), pp. 315–16.

9 Truman (1955), pp. 7–8; Mills (1951), p. 43; Leahy (1950), p. 402.

10 Schlesinger (2003), p. 7.

11 Truman (1952), pp. 204–6.

12 Harriman (1975), pp. 440–1.

13 Record of conversation at *FRUS 1945: Vol. I*, pp. 289–90.
14 Harriman (1975), pp. 442–3.
15 Dobbs (2012), p. 163.
16 Truman (1955), pp. 53, 63; McCullough (1992), pp. 362–4.
17 Truman (1955), p. 67.
18 Harriman (1975), pp. 447–9; Truman (1955), pp. 71–2.
19 McCullough (1992), p. 356.
20 Schlesinger (2003), p. 67.
21 Vandenberg (1952), p. 171.
22 Gromyko (1989), pp. 95–6; Harriman (1975), pp. 453–4; Bohlen (1973), p. 213; Truman (1955), pp. 79–82; Leahy (1950), pp. 412–13; *FRUS 1945: Vol. V*, pp. 256–8.

Chapter 6: A Sentimental Journey
 1 Schlesinger (2003), pp. 115, 117; UN Oral History interview with Oliver Lundquist, 19 April 1990, pp. 2–8; Willard Thorp interview with McKinzie and Wilson, 10 July 1971, p. 169.
 2 Truman (1955), p. 95.
 3 Cooke (2006), pp. 468–9.
 4 Schlesinger (2003), p. 155.
 5 Foot, reporting in *Melbourne Argus*, 1 May 1945.
 6 Lieutenant John F. Kennedy, 'World Court Real Test for Envoys', *New York Journal*, 2 May 1945.
 7 Vandenberg (1952), pp. 176–7.
 8 *FRUS 1945: Vol. I*, p. 407–10; Vandenberg (1952), p. 178.
 9 Dilks (1971), p. 736; Birse (1967), p. 201; Bidault (1967), p. 95.
10 Lieutenant John F. Kennedy, 'Soviet Diplomacy Gets 50–50 Break', *New York Journal*, 3 May 1945.
11 Bohlen (1973), p. 214–15; Harriman (1975), p. 458.
12 *FRUS 1945: Vol. V*, pp. 281–4; Schlesinger (2003), p. 169.
13 Dilks (1971), p. 739; Eden (1965), p. 536.
14 Birse (1967), p. 200.
15 Bradford (1996), p. 109.
16 Dilks (1971), p. 740; Birse (1967), pp. 200–1.
17 See records of delegation sessions in *FRUS 1945: Vol. I*, pp. 615–28, 628–30, and 628–38. Pasvolsky quote at p. 635. Also see Vandenberg (1952), pp. 188–9.
18 *FRUS 1945: Vol. I*, pp. 691–8.
19 *FRUS 1945: Vol. I*, pp. 698–705; Jebb (1972), p. 161; Woodward (1976), p. 310.
20 Vandenberg (1952), pp. 191–3.
21 Campbell and Herring (1975), p. 371.
22 Vandenberg (1952), p. 198.
23 Lieutenant John F. Kennedy, 'Allied Parley Dismays Vets', *New York Journal*, 7 May 1945.

24 Conant (2008), p. 26.
25 Eden (1965), pp. 534–5.
26 Record in *FRUS 1945: Vol. I*, pp. 926–35.
27 Harriman (1975), p. 412.
28 Ignatieff (1998), p. 132.
29 *FRUS 1945: Vol. I*, pp. 1071–86; Campbell and Herring (1975), pp. 383–4.
30 Vandenberg (1952), p. 201.
31 Dilks (1971), pp. 748–9.
32 *FRUS 1945: Vol. I*, pp. 1088–9; Truman (1955), p. 287.
33 See Chapter II in United States Department of State (2011).
34 *FRUS 1945: Vol. I*, pp. 1117–20.
35 Bohlen (1973), pp. 244, 221.
36 Bohlen (1973), p. 218; Harriman (1975), p. 464.
37 Birse (1967), p. 145.
38 Harriman (1975), pp. 473–4; Bohlen (1973), pp. 220–1; Sherwood (1948), pp. 910–12; *FRUS 1945: Potsdam Vol. I*, pp. 60–2.
39 Campbell and Herring (1975), pp. 386–7.
40 Vandenberg (1952), p. 208.
41 Campbell and Herring (1975), pp. 399–401.
42 Campbell and Herring (1975), pp. 402–4.
43 UN Oral History interviews with Claiborne Pell, 20 February 1990, p. 2, and with Oliver Lundquist, 19 April 1990, pp. 17–18.
44 UN Oral History interview with James Green, 21 April 1986, p. 28.
45 Truman (1955), p. 291.
46 Mazower (2009), p. 1; Schlesinger (2003), p. 156.
47 Vandenberg (1952), p. 216; Campbell and Herring (1975), p. 414.
48 *FRUS 1945: Vol. I*, p. 1432.

Chapter 7: Force to Break

1 *FRUS 1945: Potsdam Vol. II*, p. 8.
2 Bohlen (1973), p. 227.
3 Quoted in McCullough (1992), p. 408.
4 *FRUS 1945: Potsdam Vol. I*, p. 9.
5 Birse (1967), p. 204.
6 Gromyko (1989), p. 97; Truman (1955), p. 341; Dilks (1971), p. 764.
7 Description from Gromyko (1989), pp. 105–6; Moody (2007), pp. 175–6; Birse (1967), p. 205.
8 Leahy (1950), pp. 461–2; Truman (1955), p. 341; Byrnes (1947), p. 68.
9 Rhodes (1986), p. 618.
10 Stimson and Bundy (1947), p. xvi.
11 See R. Gordon Arneson interview with Johnson, 21 June 1989, p. 22.
12 Quoted in Rhodes (1986), p. 625.

13 Science Panel report to Interim Committee, 16 June 1945, quoted in Kelly (2007), pp. 290–1, 319–21.

14 Moran (1966), p. 301.

15 Birse (1967), p. 207.

16 *FRUS 1945: Potsdam Vol. II*, Thomson (pp. 52–9) and Cohen (pp. 59–63) notes.

17 McCullough (1992), p. 427.

18 Dilks (1971), p. 766.

19 Thorpe (2003), p. 315.

20 McCullough (1992), p. 430.

21 Dobbs (2012), p. 303.

22 McCullough (1992), p. 433.

23 Truman (1952), pp. 2000–3.

24 Emilio Collado interview with McKinzie, 11 July 1974, pp. 52–3.

25 Dilks (1971), p. 769; Moran (1966), pp. 304–5.

26 *FRUS 1945: Potsdam Vol. II*, pp. 274–5; Bohlen (1973), p. 232.

27 Moran (1966), pp. 306–8; Danchev and Todman (2001), p. 710; Birse (1967), pp. 209–10.

28 George Elsey interview with Hess, 7 July 1970, pp. 343–4.

29 Truman diary for 25 July 1945, quoted in Baggott (2009), p. 325.

30 Truman (1955), p. 416; Bohlen (1973), p. 237; *FRUS 1945: Potsdam Vol. II*, pp. 378–9.

31 Moran (1966), p. 310.

32 *FRUS 1945: Potsdam Vol. II*, p. 390.

33 Colville (1985), p. 611.

34 Campbell and Herring (1975), p. 413.

35 Jenkins (2001), p. 798.

36 Nicolson (1968), pp. 32–3.

37 Godfrey Hodgson review of Harris (1982) in *New York Times*.

38 Attlee article 'Flaws at the Top', *Observer*, 14 February 1960, quoted in Field (2009), p. 110.

39 Dalton (1962), p. 11.

40 Dilks (1971), p. 772.

41 Harvey (1978), p. 384; Dixon (1968), p. 168.

42 Bohlen (1973), p. 239–40.

43 Bullock (1983), p. 25.

44 Dilks (1971), p. 777.

45 Dixon (1968), p. 175.

46 *FRUS 1945: Potsdam Vol. II*, pp. 25–6.

47 Nicolson (1968), p. 32; Leahy (1950), p. 502.

48 Truman (1955), p. 421; Leahy (1950), p. 501; McCullough (1992), p. 454.

49 Sakharov (1990), p. 92.

50 Dobbs (2012), p. 330.

51 Holloway (1994), p. 90.

52 Zubok and Pleshakov (1996), p. 41; Gromyko (1989), pp. 109–10.
53 Holloway (1994), pp. 130–3.
54 Sebag Montefiore (2003), p. 427.
55 Gromyko (1989), p. 319.
56 Holloway (1994), pp. 129–30; Craig and Radchenko (2008), p. 95.
57 Hollaway (1994), p. 129.

Chapter 8: The Half-Open Door
 1 Pimlott (1985), p. 37.
 2 *DBPO*, Series I, Vol. III, item 6, para 3.
 3 *DBPO*, Series I, Vol. III, item 15, para 7.
 4 Quoted in Clarke, *Last Days of the British Empire*, p. 391.
 5 Moran (1966), p. 306.
 6 Record in *DBPO*, Series I, Vol. III, item 17; see also Williams (1961), pp. 130–2.
 7 Williams (1961), p. 132.
 8 Skidelsky (2003), p. 794.
 9 Field (2009), p. 123.
10 Jebb (1972), p. 175.
11 Dixon (1968), p. 196.
12 Bullock (1983), p. 84.
13 Williams (1961), p. 77.
14 Feis (1970), p. 48.
15 Dixon (1968), p. 182.
16 Dixon (1968), pp. 91–2.
17 Norwich (2005), pp. 384–5.
18 Craig and Radchenko (2008), p. 97; Pechatnov and Zubok (1999), p. 2.
19 Dixon (1968), p. 184.
20 Pechatnov and Zubok (1999), p. 4.
21 *FRUS 1945: Vol. II*, pp. 313–15; Dixon (1968), pp. 185–9; *DBPO*, Series I, Vol. II, ch. 1, item 97.
22 Nicolson (1968), p. 36.
23 Dulles (1950), p. 28; Campbell and Herring (1975), pp. 430–1.
24 Dixon (1968), p. 192; Bohlen (1973), pp. 245–7.
25 Stimson diary, 8 August 1945, Stimson papers micro 113, p. 18.
26 Stimson diary, 12 August–3 September 1945, Stimson papers, reel 9; Stimson and Bundy (1947), p. 641; *FRUS 1945: Potsdam Vol. II*, pp. 396–7.
27 Stimson and Bundy (1947), pp. 643–4.
28 Acheson (1967), pp. 124–5; Mills (1951), pp. 94–6; Truman (1955), pp. 524–8.
29 Stimson diary, 21 September 1945, Stimson papers, reel 9.
30 McCullough (1992), p. 473.
31 Vandenberg (1952), p. 222; Truman (1956), pp. 529, 534.
32 Ham (2012), p. 496.

33 Malloy (2010), p. 176.
34 Thorne (1978), p. 115.
35 Clarke (2007), p. 393.
36 UK record at *DBPO*, Series I, Vol. III, item 44, then items 46–47 for talks on 27 September 1945.
37 Robbins diary entry for 8 October, quoted in Moggridge (1995), pp. 803–4.
38 Hamer diary entry for 12/13 November 1945, quoted in Moggridge (1995), p. 809.
39 Skidelsky (2003), p. 807.
40 Jay (1980), p. 137, quoted in Moggridge (1995), p. 807.
41 Dalton (1962), p. 79.
42 Williams (1961), p. 83.
43 *DBPO*, Series 1, Vol. II, ch. 2, item 195.
44 Bennett (2013), pp. 83–4.
45 Williams (1961), pp. 83, 103.
46 *DBPO*, Series 1, Vol. II, ch. 2, item 235.
47 Baggott (2009), pp. 398–9.
48 Harris (1982), p. 281.
49 Bennett (2013), p. 86.
50 *DBPO*, Series I, Vol. III, item 155.
51 Pimlott (1985), p. 432.
52 Gardner (1956), p. 226.
53 Skidelsky (2003), pp. 818–19; Harrod (1951), pp. 600–1, quoted in Pimlott (1985), p. 435.
54 Attlee articles in *Observer*, 7 and 14 February 1960, quoted in Field (2009), pp. 105, 112.
55 LePan (1979), p. 100, quoted in Moggridge (1995), p. 789.
56 138 HoL Deb. 793–4 (18 December 1945), quoted in Gardner (1956), p. 235.
57 Dalton (1962), p. 89; Jay (1979), p. 139, quoted in Skidelsky (2003), p. 825.
58 Bohlen (1973), p. 4.
59 Kennan (2014), pp. 190–1; Bohlen (1973), p. 248; Byrnes (1947), p. 110.
60 *DBPO*, Series 1, Vol. II, ch. 3, item 289, footnote 728/25.
61 *DBPO*, Series 1, Vol. II, ch. 3, Berlin memo of 21 December 1945.
62 Pechatnov and Zubok (1999), pp. 11–12.
63 Quoted in Gorlizki and Khlevniuk (2004), p. 23.
64 Kennan (2014), p. 193.
65 Harriman (1975), p. 524.
66 *DBPO*, Series 1, Vol. II, ch. 3, item 318.
67 Kennan (2014), p. 191.
68 *FRUS 1945: Vol. II*, pp. 750–8; Harriman (1975), pp. 524–6; Byrnes (1947), pp. 113–18; Bohlen (1973), p. 250.
69 Kennan (2014), pp. 194–5.
70 Conant (1970), p. 482, quoted in Harriman (1975), p. 526. See also Holloway (1994), p. 158; and Bohlen (1973), p. 249.

71 Byrnes (1947), p. 118.
72 Yergin (1977), p. 151; Byrnes (1947), p. 121.
73 Berlin (1981), pp. 233–4.
74 Ignatieff (1998), pp. 162–3.

Chapter 9: Slackened Sail
1 Jebb (1972), p. 183.
2 Halifax to Cadogan, 29 June 1945, Halifax Papers 10.4 (GBR/0014/HLFX, Churchill College Archives).
3 UN Oral History interview with Gladwyn Jebb, 24 October 1985, p. 15.
4 Urquhart (1987), p. 92.
5 Jebb (1972), p. 191.
6 Jebb (1972), p. 181.
7 Waldo Chamberlain letter to Jebb, 2 April 1946; Jebb letter to Hiss, 17 December 1945. Both in GLAD 1/4/1, Churchill College Archives.
8 Jebb (1972), p. 181.
9 Vandenberg (1952), p. 237.
10 Campbell and Herring (1975), p. 443.
11 Roosevelt (1992), pp. 287–8.
12 Glendon (2001), p. 28.
13 Entry for 31 January 1946, at Nicolson (1968), p. 53.
14 Jebb (1972), p. 182.
15 Campbell and Herring (1975), p. 450.
16 Sherwood (1948), pp. 927–8.
17 Harriman (1975), p. 535.
18 Halifax letter to Churchill of 1 February 1946 in HLFX 4.10.11, Churchill College Archives; Roll (2013), p. 405.
19 Kennan (1967), p. 232.
20 Yergin (1977), p. 167.
21 Gaddis (2011), p. 187.
22 Isaacson and Thomas (1986), p. 348.
23 Kennan (1967), p. 293.
24 *FRUS 1946: Vol. VI*, pp. 696–709
25 Harriman (1975), p. 546.
26 Yergin (1977), p. 171; Mills (1951), p. 140; Hoopes and Brinkley (1992), p. 272.
27 Gaddis (2011), p. 218.
28 Entry for 19 December 1945, at Nicolson (1968), p. 45.
29 Moran (1966), pp. 335–6.
30 Quoted in McCullough (1992), p. 487.
31 Yergin (1977), p. 156.
32 Truman (1952), pp. 21–3.
33 McCullough (1992), pp. 487–8, Jenkins (2001), pp. 809–10; Clifford (1991), pp. 103–4.

34 Feis (1970), p. 78.
35 Steel (1978), pp. 435–6.
36 Gaddis (1972), p. 309.
37 Bedell Smith (1950), pp. 28–9.
38 Urquhart to Jebb, May 1946, in GLAD 1/4/1, Churchill College Archives.
39 Campbell and Herring (1975), pp. 457–8.
40 Urquhart to Jebb, May 1946, GLAD 1/4/1, Churchill College Archives.
41 Campbell and Herring (1975), pp. 461–2.
42 *FRUS 1946: Vol. VII*, pp. 381–6.
43 *FRUS 1946: Vol. VII*, pp. 388–9.
44 *DBPO*, Series 1, Vol. VII, ch. 1, item 36, Cadogan letter to Bevin of 18 April 1946.
45 Campbell and Herring (1975), pp. 474–5.
46 Quoted in Skidelsky (2003), p. 829.
47 *Savannah Morning News*, 9 March 1946, from www.savannahnow.com.
48 Quoted in Skidelsky (2003), pp. 827–8.
49 Gardner (1956), p. 266.
50 Steil (2013), pp. 297–9.
51 Skidelsky (2003), pp. 832–3.

Chapter 10: Early Stirrings
 1 Bidault (1967), p. 11.
 2 Byrnes (1947), p. 126.
 3 Bidault (1967), p. 111.
 4 Feis (1970), p. 121.
 5 Vandenberg (1952), pp. 268–9.
 6 Byrnes (1947), p. 151.
 7 Norwich (2005), p. 409; Dixon (1968), pp. 210–11.
 8 Bohlen (1973), p. 255; Dixon (1968), p. 220; Byrnes (1947), p. 136; *FRUS 1946: Vol. II*, pp. 792–800.
 9 Baratta (2004), p. 183.
10 Feis (1970), p. 110.
11 Baggott (2009), p. 402.
12 Hoopes and Brinkley (1992), p. 288.
13 Gromyko (1989), pp. 138–40.
14 *DBPO*, Series 1, Vol. IV, ch. 2, folio 120.
15 Hoopes and Brinkley (1992), p. 296.
16 *FRUS 1946: Vol. II*, pp. 828–36; Vandenberg (1952), pp. 296–7.
17 Smith (1990), p. 262.
18 Quoted in MacDonogh (2007), pp. 362–3.
19 Ashley Clarke interview with Wilson, 10 June 1970, p. 31.
20 Deignton (1993), pp. 74–7.

21 Byrnes (1947), p. 172.
22 *FRUS 1946: Vol. II*, pp. 190–3.
23 Bohlen (1973), p. 253; Vandenberg (1952), pp. 267–8, 291; Byrnes (1947), pp. 125, 173–5.
24 Pechatnov and Zubok (1999), p. 18.
25 *FRUS 1946: Vol. II*, pp. 842–7.
26 *FRUS 1946: Vol. II*, pp. 869–73.
27 Pechatnov and Zubok (1999), p. 18.
28 Smith (1990), p. 336.
29 Byrnes (1947), pp. 187–8; Vandenberg (1952), p. 299.
30 Byrnes (1947), p. 188.
31 Vandenberg (1952), p. 299.
32 McCullough (1992), p. 499.
33 McCullough (1992), pp. 513–14; Clifford (1991), pp. 117–18.
34 Clifford (1991), pp. 118–19.
35 Byrnes (1947), pp. 240–2, Vandenberg (1952), pp. 300–1.
36 Yergin (1977), p. 252.
37 Clifford (1991), p. 121.
38 Clifford (1991), p. 126.
39 Clark Clifford interview with Hess, 16 March 1972, p. 376.
40 Vandenberg (1952), pp. 315–16.
41 McCullough (1992), p. 524.
42 Acheson (1967), p. 150.
43 Hollaway (1994), pp. 181–2; Rhodes (1995), pp. 273–5.

Chapter 11: Something Brewing
1 *The Papers of George Catlett Marshall*, Vol. VI (2013), pp. 7–8; Pogue (1987), p. 144.
2 Roberts (2008), pp. 145, 483–4.
3 Yergin (1977), p. 261.
4 Pogue (1987), p. 113.
5 George Marshall interview with Spencer, 9 July 1947, p. 4; George Marshall interview with Guyer and Donnelly, 11 February 1949, p. 10.
6 Yergin (1977), p. 260.
7 *The Papers of George Catlett Marshall*, Vol. VI (2013), pp. 7–8.
8 *New York Times*, 22 January 1947, p. 1.
9 Pogue (1987), p. 145.
10 Reston in *New York Times*, 22 January 1947, p. 3.
11 Acheson (1967), p. 213.
12 Jones (1955), p. 109.
13 George Marshall interview with Pogue, 20 November 1956, tape 18M, p. 22.
14 Charles Kindelberger interview with McKinzie, 16 July 1973, p. 85.
15 Acheson (1967), pp. 213–14.

16 George Marshall interview with Pogue, 20 November 1956, tape 18M, p. 22.
17 Beisner (2006), p. 51.
18 Vandenberg (1952), pp. 325–7.
19 Vandenberg (1952), p. 335.
20 Geroge Elsey interview with Hess, 17 July 1970, pp. 233–4; Clifford (1991), pp. 84–6.
21 Kynaston (2007), p. 196.
22 Jebb (1995), p. 31.
23 Harris (1982), p. 417.
24 Kynaston (2007), p. 194.
25 Nicolson (1968), p. 90.
26 Barnett (1995), pp. 47, 50.
27 Hennessy article in *The Times*, 30 September 1982.
28 Williams (1961), p. 210.
29 Clarke (2007), p. 479.
30 Jones (1955), p. 107.
31 Acheson (1967), p. 217.
32 Quoted in Yergin (1977), p. 281.
33 Jones (1955), pp. 133–4; Acheson (1967), p. 218.
34 Mills (1951), p. 245.
35 Quoted at Yergin (1977), p. 281.
36 Jones (1955), pp. 90–1.
37 Pogue (1987), pp. 164–5.
38 Vandenberg (1952), p. 340.
39 *FRUS 1947: Vol. V*, p. 47.
40 Acheson (1967), p. 382.
41 Acheson (1967), p. 219; Truman (1956), pp. 103–4; Jones (1955), pp. 139–41.
42 McCullough (1992), pp. 246, 520.
43 Jones (1955), pp. 151–7.
44 Truman (1952), p. 75.
45 Clifford (1991), pp. 135–7.
46 Truman (1956), p. 106.
47 Jones (1955), p. 23.
48 Clifford (1991), p. 138.
49 Jones (1955), p. 172.
50 Jones (1955), p. 182.
51 Steel (1978), pp. 445–6.
52 Holloway (1994), p. 254.

Chapter 12: Across the Harbour Bar

1 Bedell Smith (1950), pp. 213–19.
2 *The Papers of George Catlett Marshall* (2013), p. 72.
3 Pogue (1987), pp. 172–3.

4 Bohlen (1973), p. 262.
5 Norwich (2005), p. 433; Bidault (1967), p. 142.
6 Bedell Smith (1950), p. 92; Jebb (1972), pp. 206–7.
7 Pogue (1987), p. 175.
8 *The Papers of George Catlett Marshall* (2013), p. 73.
9 Quoted in Bullock (1983), p. 377.
10 Edward Mason letter to Willard Thorpe of 20 March 1947, Charles Kindleberger Papers, available at www.trumanlibrary.org.
11 Charles Kindleberger letter to Willard Thorpe of 25 March 1947, Charles Kindleberger Papers.
12 Bedell Smith (1950), p. 217.
13 Bidault (1967), p. 147.
14 Williams (1961), p. 170.
15 Pogue (1987), p. 182; Edward Mason letter to Willard Thorpe of 20 March 1947, Charles Kindleberger Papers.
16 George Marshall interview with Pogue, 15 November 1956, tape 11m, p. 41.
17 George Marshall interview with Spencer, 9 July 1947, p. 5; George Marshall interview with Pogue, 15 November 1956, tape 11m, p. 42.
18 Roberts (2008), p. 444.
19 See record at *FRUS 1947: Vol. II*, pp. 337–44; Bohlen (1973), pp. 262–3; Bedell Smith (1950), pp. 220–2.
20 Danchev and Todman (2001), p. 659.
21 Roberts (1991), p. 112.
22 Bohlen (1973), p. 262; Bedell Smith (1950), pp. 227–9.
23 Yergin (1977), p. 300.
24 Dulles (1950), p. 105.
25 State Dept bulletin, Vol. XVI, 11 May 1947, pp. 920–4, www.trumanlibrary.org.
26 See Marshall letter to Stimson of 28 April 1947 in *The Papers of George Catlett Marshall* (2013), p. 111.
27 George Marshall interview with Pogue, tape 19M, 20 November 1956, pp. 21–2.
28 Kennan (1967), p. 326.
29 Nitze (1989), p. 50.
30 Gaddis (2013), pp. 167, 278.
31 *FRUS 1947: Vol. III*, pp. 223–30.
32 Steel (1978), p. 446.
33 Nitze (1989), pp. 52–3.
34 *FRUS 1947: Vol. III*, pp. 230–2.
35 Acheson (1967), p. 232; Kennan (1967), pp. 342–3; *FRUS 1947: Vol. II*, pp. 234–7.
36 Kennan (1967), p. 342.
37 George Marshall interview with Pogue, tape 11M, 15 November 1956, p. 30.
38 Pogue (1987), p. 208.
39 Acheson (1967), p. 232.

40 Quoted in Pogue (1987), pp. 209–10.
41 Marshall letter to Conant of 28 May 1947, in *The Papers of George Catlett Marshall* (2013), p. 141.
42 Bohlen (1973), pp. 263–4; George Marshall interview with Price and Foulke, 30 October 1952, pp. 2–3.
43 George Marshall interview with Pogue, 20 November 1956, tape 19m, pp. 18–20; Moore note to Wilcox of 28 July 1947, in *FRUS 1947: Vol. II*, pp. 239–41.
44 Acheson (1967), p. 215.
45 Jones (1955), pp. 31–6.

Chapter 13: Impatient Dawn
1 Bullock (1983), pp. 288, 383.
2 Leonard Miall interview with Vandegrift, 19 September 1977; Acheson (1967), p. 234; quotation from Isaacson and Thomas (1986), pp. 412–13.
3 Bullock (1983), p. 405.
4 Dalton (1962), p. 232.
5 Norwich (2005), pp. 436–8; Norwich (2013), p. 218.
6 Norwich (2005), p. 439.
7 Beevor and Cooper (2004), p. 286.
8 Norwich (2005), p. 439.
9 Dixon (1968), p. 246.
10 Parrish and Narinsky (1994), pp. 14, 17–18, 43–4.
11 Zubok and Pleshakov (1996), p. 104.
12 Kynaston (2007), p. 216.
13 *FRUS 1947: Vol. III*, pp. 268–73, 276–83.
14 See Clayton record of conversation with Marshall, 20 June 1947, in *The Papers of George Catlett Marshall* (2013), pp. 155–6.
15 GEN 179/13, CAB 130/19, quoted in Deignton (1993), p. 184.
16 For account from Duff Cooper, see US Embassy in Paris telegram of 28 June 1947 in *FRUS 1947: Vol. III*, p. 297.
17 Norwich (2005), p. 440.
18 Modin (1994), pp. 165–6.
19 Zubok and Pleshakov (1996), p. 105; Parrish and Narinsky (1994), p. 45.
20 Pechatnov and Zubok (1999), p. 20.
21 Norwich (2005), pp. 440–1.
22 Parrish and Narinsky (1994), p. 47.
23 *FRUS 1947: Vol. III*, pp. 301–3.
24 Zubok and Pleshakov (1996), p. 106.
25 *FRUS 1947: Vol. III*, p. 306.
26 Dulles (1993), p. 27.
27 Norwich (2005), p. 441.
28 Quoted in Glendon (2001), pp. 54–5.

29 Morsink (1999), p. 31.
30 Diary for 25 December 1940, quoted in Winter and Prost (2013), p. 132.
31 Beevor and Cooper (2004), p. 147.
32 See Glendon (2001), pp. 67–8.
33 Norwich (2013), p. 209.
34 Norwich (2005), p. 442; Norwich (2013), p. 210.
35 Parrish and Narinsky (1994), pp. 26, 48–9.
36 Parrish and Narinsky (1994), p. 30; also *FRUS 1947: Vol. III*, pp. 319–20.
37 Bruce Lockhart (1951), p. 66.
38 *FRUS 1947: Vol. III*, p. 327.
39 Bullock (1983), p. 425, quoting Dixon diary; Norwich (2005), p. 443.
40 Norwich (2013), p. 210.
41 Pimlott (1985), pp. 482–3.
42 Radice (2008), p. 156.
43 Dalton (1962), pp. 249–50
44 Dalton diary, quoted in Radice (2008), p. 157.
45 Pimlott (1985), p. 514.
46 Williams (1961), p. 224.
47 Pimlott (1985), p. 513.
48 Dalton (1961), pp. 245–6; Pimlott (1985), p. 512; Harris (1982), pp. 348–9.
49 Hopkins (2003), p. 18.
50 Hopkins (2003), p. 21; Danchev (1993), pp. 50–1.
51 Danchev (1993), p. 57.
52 Norwich (2005), p. 444.
53 Nitze (1989), pp. 54–5.
54 Behrman (2007), p. 98.
55 Ignatieff (1998), p. 171.
56 Isaacson and Thomas (1986), p. 63.
57 Isaacson and Thomas (1986), p. 417.
58 Acheson (1967), p. 239.
59 Moore letter to Wilcox, 28 July 1947, in *FRUS 1947: Vol. III*, p. 239.
60 *FRUS 1947: Vol. III*, p. 372.
61 Hopkins (2003), p. 21; Behrman (2007), pp. 108–9.
62 Gaddis (2011), p. 281.
63 Thompson (2009), pp. 131–2.
64 Behrman (2007), p. 56.
65 Kennan (1967), p. 356.
66 Kennan and Costigliola (2014), pp. 205–6.
67 Danchev (1993), p. 83.

Chapter 14: The Giant's Strength
  1 Nicolson (1968), p. 112.

2 Bedell Smith (1950), p. 70.
3 Sebag Montefiore (2003), pp. 499–500.
4 Gorlizki and Khlevniuk (2004), p. 61.
5 Sebag Montefiore (2003), pp. 340–1.
6 Radzinsky (1996), p. 522.
7 Figes (2007), p. 489.
8 *FRUS 1944: Vol. IV*, p. 822.
9 Mark (2001), p. 35.
10 Zubok and Pleshakov (1996), pp. 130–1.
11 Feis (1970), p. 262.
12 Hitchcock (2003), pp. 89–90; Holloway (1994), p. 260.
13 Clifford (1991), p. 144.
14 Mills (1951), pp. 320–1.
15 *FRUS 1947: Vol. III*, pp. 360–3.
16 Vandenberg (1952), p. 376.
17 Reston (1991), pp. 206–7.
18 Quoted in Yergin (1977), based on Clark Clifford papers, pp. 328–9.
19 George Marshall interview with Pogue, tape 18m, 19 November 1956, p. 9.
20 Vandenberg (1952), p. 372; *The Papers of George Catlett Marshall* (2013), p. 207.
21 George Marshall interview with Price and Foulke, 30 October 1952, p. 2.
22 Danchev (1993), p. 77.
23 Nitze (1989), pp. 58–63; *The Papers of George Catlett Marshall* (2013), pp. 248–9.
24 Isaacson and Thomas (1986), p. 425.
25 *The Papers of George Catlett Marshall* (2013), p. 255.
26 Glendon (2001), pp. 79–80.
27 Winter and Prost (2013), p. 247.
28 Norwich (2005), pp. 380–1.
29 Glendon (2001), p. 83.
30 Glendon (2001), p. 97.
31 *The Papers of George Catlett Marshall* (2013), p. 267.
32 *The Times*, 22 November 1947, quoted in Feis (1970), p. 275.
33 *The Papers of George Catlett Marshall* (2013), p. 267.
34 Hitchcock (2003), p. 90.
35 Beevor and Cooper (2004), p. 302.
36 Feis (1970), p. 274.
37 Bradford (1996), pp. 128–9; Kynaston (2007), pp. 244–5.
38 Nicolson (1968), pp. 115–16.
39 Marshall letter to Mountbatten, 18 February 1948, in *The Papers of George Catlett Marshall* (2013), pp. 364–5.
40 Danchev and Todman (2001), p. xxiv.
41 *The Papers of George Catlett Marshall* (2013), pp. 302–3.
42 Nicolson (1968), p. 115.

43 Deignton (1993), pp. 210–11.
44 *The Papers of George Catlett Marshall* (2013), pp. 279, 293–4.
45 *DBPO*, Series I, Vol. X, pp. 7–9.
46 *FRUS 1947: Vol. II*, pp. 815–17.
47 *The Papers of George Catlett Marshall* (2013), p. 307.

Chapter 15: The Swaying Flag
 1 *Observer* profile of Roberts, 29 August 1948, in ROBT Box 3, Churchill College Archives.
 2 Dixon (1968), p. 246.
 3 Roberts (1991), pp. 128–9.
 4 *DBPO*, Series I, Vol. X, pp. 14–23.
 5 Yergin (1977), p. 363.
 6 Bullock (1983), p. 383.
 7 Radice (2008), p. 183.
 8 Acheson (1961), pp. 27–8.
 9 Roberts (1991), p. 128.
10 Hansard, 22 January 1948, columns 383–517 and 23 January 1948, columns 529–622.
11 Bullock (1983), p. 522; *DBPO*, Series I, Vol. X, no. 22, pp. 42–3.
12 Taborsky (1961), p. 20.
13 Crane and Crane (1991), p. 311.
14 Dixon (1968), p. 249.
15 Crane and Crane (1991), p. 312.
16 Zinner (1963), pp. 206–7.
17 Quoted in Zinner (1963), p. 215.
18 *FRUS 1948: Vol. IV*, p. 739.
19 Kaplan (1987), p. 179.
20 *FRUS 1948: Vol. IV*, p. 741.
21 Dixon (1968), p. 255.
22 George Marshall interview with Pogue, tape 18, 20 November 1956, p. 15.
23 Voice of America transcript of Marshall meeting with Boy Scouts, 10 February 1948, *The Papers of George Catlett Marshall* (2013), pp. 354–5.
24 George Marshall interview with Pogue, tape 18, 20 November 1956, p. 17.
25 *The Papers of George Catlett Marshall* (2013), pp. 363–4.
26 Remarks to the National Farm Institute Annual Meeting, 13 February 1948, *The Papers of George Catlett Marshall* (2013), pp. 357–63.
27 *The Papers of George Catlett Marshall* (2013), pp. 396–7.
28 Mills (2008), p. 161.
29 Behrman (2007), pp. 148–9, 158.
30 Vandenberg (1952), pp. 388–9, 393; Marshall note to Vandenberg of 24 February 1948, in *The Papers of George Catlett Marshall* (2013), p. 385.
31 Francis O. Wilcox interview with Ritchie, 10 February 1984, p. 60.

32 Behrman (2007), p. 158.
33 Vandenberg (1952), pp. 389–92.
34 Pogue (1987), pp. 250–1.
35 Jebb (1995), pp. 79–80.
36 Reid (1977), p. 71.
37 Bullock (1983), p. 537.
38 Franks (1991), p. 127.
39 Marshall note to Forrestal of 12 March 1948, in *The Papers of George Catlett Marshall* (2013), pp. 403–4; Mills (1951), p. 392.
40 Theodore Achilles interview with McKinzie, 13 November 1972, p. 17.
41 *FRUS 1948: Vol. III*, p. 59–61.
42 Weisbrode (2009), p. 60.
43 Theodore Achilles interview with McKinzie, 13 November 1972, pp. 8–9.
44 *FRUS 1948: Vol. III*, pp. 64–6.
45 Henderson (1983), p. 59.
46 Theodore Achilles interview with McKinzie, 13 November 1972, p. 15.
47 Henderson (1983), p. 17.
48 *FRUS 1948: Vol. III*, pp. 71–2.
49 Theodore Achilles interview with McKinzie, 13 November 1972, p. 19.
50 Henderson (1983), p. 33.
51 Mills (1951), p. 295; Clifford (1991), p. 158.
52 Clifford (1991), p. 157; McCullough (1992), p. 571.
53 Mills (1951), pp. 299–300.
54 Clifford (1991), p. 171.
55 Mills (1951), p. 380.
56 *FRUS 1948: Vol. II*, pp. 890–1.
57 Smith (1990), p. 476.
58 Danchev (1993), p. 117.
59 Acheson (1967), p. 241.
60 Vandenberg (1952), p. 394.
61 Behrman (2007), p. 171.
62 Paul Hoffman interview with Price, 28 January 1953, paras 21–8; Vandenberg (1952), p. 394.
63 Richard Bissell interview with McKinzie and Wilson, 9 July 1971, pp. 41–2.
64 Paul Hoffman interview with Price, para. 69.
65 Milton Katz interview with McKinzie, 25 July 1975, p. 54.
66 Quoted in Isaacson and Thomas (1986), p. 442.
67 Figures from Behrman (2007), p. 188.
68 Clifford (1991), pp. 5–6.
69 Segev (1999), p. 500.
70 Mills (1951), p. 373.
71 Husted (2006), p. 149.

72 Clifford (1991), pp. 9–13; *The Papers of George Catlett Marshall* (2013), pp. 454–5.
73 *The Papers of George Catlett Marshall* (2013), p. 449.
74 Danchev (1993), p. 93.
75 Danchev (1993), p. 89.
76 Danchev (1993), p. 89.
77 *DBPO*, Series I, Vol. X, items 106 and 107, pp. 161–3.
78 Theodore Achilles interview with McKinzie, 13 November 1972, p. 21.
79 Vandenberg (1952), p. 405.
80 Theodore Achilles interview with McKinzie, 13 November 1972, p. 23; Francis O. Wilcox interview with Ritchie, 10 February 1984, pp. 68–9; Vandenberg (1952), pp. 405–6.
81 Vandenberg (1952), p. 406.
82 Vandenberg (1952), pp. 410–11.
83 Mills (1951), pp. 452–4; Smith (1990), pp. 498–500.
84 Mills (1951), p. 454.

Chapter 16: Facing the Fight

1 Maclean (1957), pp. 343–4.
2 Djilas (1962), pp. 178–84.
3 Dedijer (1953), p. 364.
4 Maclean (1957), pp. 346–7; *FRUS 1948: Vol. IV*, pp. 1077–8.
5 Dedijer (1953), pp. 367–71.
6 Gorlizki and Khlevniuk (2004), pp. 42–3.
7 Matthews (1996), p. 45.
8 Rees (1974), pp. 411–15.
9 Matthews (1996), pp. 62–3.
10 Steel (1978), p. 462.
11 Clifford (1991), pp. 190–3.
12 Truman (1956), pp. 207–8.
13 Clifford memo of 17 August 1948, 'The 1948 Campaign', Truman Library.
14 Clifford (1991), p. 226.
15 George Elsey interview with Hess, 10 July 1969, pp. 191–201; Bill Batt interview with Hess, 26 July 1966, pp. 1–2, 7–8.
16 List of campaign speeches, 5 November 1948, from Truman Library; McCullough (1992), p. 694.
17 Clifford (1991), p. 227.
18 Philip Brooks interview with Miall, 17 June 1964, pp. 49–50.
19 Donald Dawson interview with Fuchs, 8 August 1977, p. 32.
20 Clifford (1991), pp. 234–5.
21 Miller (1998), p. 34.
22 Smith (1990), p. 500.
23 US Air Force report, *Berlin Mission* (1949), p. 20.

24 Mills (1951), pp. 483–4.
25 Hoopes and Brinkley (1992), pp. 412–16; Yergin (1977), pp. 358–9.
26 Miller (1998), pp. 88, 90–1.
27 Combined Air Task Force report 'Berlin Mission' (1949), p. 88.
28 Lucius Clay interview with McKinzie, 16 July 1974, pp. 38–40.
29 Miller (1998), p. 92.
30 Truman (1956), pp. 220–1.
31 McCullough (1992), pp. 709–10.
32 Truman (1956), p. 222.

Chapter 17: The Grain of Salt
 1 Speer (1970), p. 30.
 2 *The Papers of George Catlett Marshall* (2013), pp. 560–1.
 3 Glendon (2001), p. 134.
 4 Glendon (2001), pp. 145–6.
 5 *The Papers of George Catlett Marshall* (2013), pp. 589–90.
 6 UN General Assembly, 180th Plenary Session, 9 December 1948, official record, pp. 852–4.
 7 UN General Assembly, 180th plenary session, 9 December 1948, official record, pp. 866–7.
 8 UN Department for General Assembly and Conference Outreach, *History of Simultaneous Interpretation*, available at www.unlanguage.org.
 9 UN General Assembly, 183th plenary session, 10 December 1948, official record, pp. 923–4.
10 *The Papers of George Catlett Marshall* (2013), pp. 628–9.
11 Pogue (1987), p. 413.
12 Acheson (1967), pp. 249–50.
13 Clifford (1991), p. 172.
14 Hoopes and Brinkley (1992), pp. 436–9; Mills (1951), pp. 544–5.
15 Vandenberg (1952), pp. 467–9.
16 Matthews (1996), pp. 63–4.
17 Beisner (2006), pp. 287–91; Acheson (1967), pp. 251–2.
18 Vandenberg (1952), pp. 470–1; Francis O. Wilcox interview with Ritchie, 10 February 1984, pp. 83–4; Isaacson and Thomas (1986), pp. 466–7.
19 Jack Hickerson interview with McKinzie, 10 November 1972 and 26 January 1973.
20 Acheson (1967), p. 72.
21 *DBPO*, Series I, Vol. X, item 225, p. 360.
22 Hendrickson, Collins and Cox (2004), p. 90.
23 Reid (1977), pp. 151–2.
24 *FRUS 1949: Vol. IV*, pp. 108–10.
25 Acheson (1967), p. 277.
26 *DBPO*, Series I, Vol. X, item 246, pp. 385–8.

27 Hopkins (2003), p. 107.
28 Acheson (1967), pp. 323–34.
29 *DBPO*, Series I, Vol. X, item 243, pp. 381–2.
30 *FRUS 1949: Vol. IV*, pp. 115–17.
31 *DBPO*, Series I, Vol. X, item 248, pp. 388–90.
32 *DBPO*, Series I, Vol. X, item 245, pp. 384–5.
33 Bullock (1983), p. 671.
34 Gorlizki and Khlevniuk (2004), p. 75.
35 Sebag Montefiore (2003), p. 473.
36 Radzinsky (1996), p. 531.
37 Roberts (2012), pp. 15–16.
38 Gorlizki and Khlevniuk (2004), pp. 75–6.
39 Vasilieva (1994), pp. 133–4.
40 Roberts (2012), pp. 17–18; Sebag Montefiore (2003), p. 523.
41 Mills (1951), pp. 551–3.
42 Hoopes and Brinkley (1992), pp. 444–5.
43 Mills (1951), p. 554; Clifford (1991), p. 173.
44 See schedule for signing ceremony and Acheson speech, Truman Library documents.
45 Feis (1970), p. 380.
46 Beisner (2006), p. 134.
47 Theodore Achilles interview with McKinzie, 13 November 1972, pp. 71–2.

Afterword: The Waste of Time

 1 Hoopes and Brinkley (1992), pp. 446–7.
 2 Isaacson and Thomas (1986), p. 470.
 3 Mills (1951), p. 554.
 4 Hoopes and Brinkley (1992), pp. 455–6.
 5 McCullough (1992), p. 740.
 6 Mills (1951), pp. 554–5; Hoopes and Brinkley (1992), pp. 464–5.
 7 Description from Hoopes and Brinkley (1992), pp. 469–70; Arlington National Cemetery record, available at www.arlingtoncemetry.net/jvforces.htm.
 8 Vandenberg (1952), pp. 486–7.

Dramatis Personae

Loy Henderson. 1892–1986. Diplomat. Director, Office of Near Eastern Affairs, State Department, 1946–8. Ambassador to India, 1948–51.

John Hickerson. 1898–1989. Diplomat. Director, Office of European Affairs, State Department, 1947–9. Ambassador to Finland, 1955–9.

Alger Hiss. 1904–86. Lawyer and diplomat. Director, Office of Special Political Affairs, State Department, 1944–45. Secretary-General, San Francisco Conference, 1945.

Paul Hoffman. 1891–1974. Businessman and public servant. President, Studebaker Corporation, 1935–48. Administrator, European Recovery Programme, 1948–50.

Harry Hopkins. 1890–1946. Social worker and politician. Secretary of Commerce, 1938–40. Presidential envoy to Stalin and Churchill, 1940–5. Married to Louise.

Cordell Hull. 1871–1955. Politician. Secretary of State, 1933–44.

George Kennan. 1904–2005. Diplomat. Deputy Ambassador, Moscow, 1944–6. Head, Policy Planning Staff, 1947–9. Ambassador to the Soviet Union, 1952.

John F. Kennedy. 1917–63. Journalist and politician. Democrat. Congressman, 1947–53. Senator, 1953–60. President, 1961–3.

Admiral Ernest King. 1878–1956. Sailor. Commander in Chief, US Navy, 1941–5.

Admiral William Leahy. 1875–1959. Sailor. Chief of Naval Operations, 1937–9. Ambassador to (Vichy) France, 1941–2. Chief of Staff to President, 1942–9.

General Curtis LeMay. 1906–90. US Air Force. Commander, US Air Force in Europe, 1947–8. US Air Force Chief of Staff, 1961–5.

Walter Lippmann. 1889–1974. Journalist and commentator.

General George C. Marshall. 1880–1959. Soldier and diplomat. Chief of Staff, US Army, 1939–45. Envoy to China, 1946–7. Secretary of State, 1947–9. Secretary of Defense, 1950–1.

Anne McCormack. 1880–1954. Journalist and foreign correspondent. *New York Times*, 1921–54.

Henry Morgenthau. 1891–1967. Politician. Secretary of the Treasury, 1934–45.

Paul Nitze. 1907–2004. Businessman and public servant. Vice-President, Dillon, Read and Co., 1939–41. Vice-Chairman, Strategic Bombing Survey, 1944–6. Director, Policy Planning Staff, State Department, 1950–3. Deputy Secretary of Defense, 1967–9.

Richard Nixon. 1913–94. Politician. Republican. Congressman, 1947–50. Vice-President, 1953–61. President, 1969–74.

Leo Pasvolsky. 1893–1953. Journalist and public servant. Special assistant to Cordell Hull and Edward Stettinius, 1939–45.

James 'Scotty' Reston. 1909–1995. Journalist. *New York Times*, 1939–89.

Eleanor Roosevelt. 1884–1962. First Lady, 1933–45. Chair, UN Commission on Human Rights, 1946–51.

Franklin Delano Roosevelt. 1882–1945. Politician. Democrat. President, 1933–45. Assistant Secretary of the Navy, 1913–20. Governor of New York, 1928–32. Married to Eleanor.

Charlie Ross. 1885–1950. Journalist. Press Secretary, White House, 1945–50.

Robert Sherwood. 1896–1955. Playwright and screenwriter. Speechwriter to President, 1940–5.

Edward Stettinius. 1900–49. Businessman and public servant. Chairman, US Steel, 1938–9. Administrator, Lend-Lease programme, 1941–3. Under-Secretary of State, 1943–4. Secretary of State, 1944–5. US Ambassador to the United Nations, 1945–6.

Henry Stimson. 1867–1950. Politician. Secretary of State, 1929–33. Secretary of War, 1933–45.

Robert Taft. 1889–1953. Politician. Republican. Senator, 1939–53. Majority Leader, 1953.

Harry S. Truman. 1884–1972. Politician. Democrat. Senator, 1935–45. Vice-President, January–March 1945. President, 1945–1953. Married to Bess.

Arthur Vandenberg. 1884–1951. Politician. Republican. Senator, 1928–51. Chair, Senate Foreign Relations Committee, 1947–9. Married to Hazel.

Fred Vinson. 1890–1953. Lawyer and politician. Secretary of the Treasury, 1945–6. Supreme Court Chief Justice, 1946–53.

Sumner Welles. 1892–1961. Diplomat. Under-Secretary of State, 1937–43.

Harry Dexter White. 1892–1948. Economist. Assistant to Treasury Secretary, 1941–5. Director, International Monetary Fund, 1946–7.

Britons

Max Aitken (Lord Beaverbrook). 1879–1964. Anglo-Canadian businessman and politician. Conservative. Lord Privy Seal, 1943–5.

Clement Attlee. 1883–1967. Politician. Labour. Member of Parliament, 1922–55. Leader of the Labour Party, 1935–55. Deputy Prime Minister, 1942–5. Prime Minister, 1945–51.

Isaiah Berlin. 1909–97. Academic and diplomat. First Secretary, British Embassy in Washington, 1942–5. First Secretary, British Embassy in Moscow, 1945–6.

Ernest Bevin. 1881–1951. Member of Parliament, 1940–50. Minister of Labour, 1940–5. Foreign Secretary, 1945–50.

Arthur Birse. 1889–1981. Businessman and soldier. Interpreter, British Embassy in Moscow, 1943–5.

Brendan Bracken. 1901–58. Journalist and politician. Conservative. Member of Parliament, 1929–45, 1950–2. Minister of Information, 1941–5.

Field Marshal Sir Alan Brooke. 1883–1963. Soldier. Chief of the Imperial General Staff, 1941–6.

Sir Alexander Cadogan. 1884–1968. Diplomat. Permanent Under-Secretary, Foreign Office, 1938–46. Ambassador to the United Nations, 1946–50. Chairman, BBC, 1952–7.

Winston Churchill. 1874–65. Politician. Conservative. Member of Parliament, 1900–64. First Lord of the Admiralty, 1911–15, 1939–40. Chancellor of the

Exchequer, 1924–9. Prime Minister, 1940–5, 1951–5. Leader of the Conservative Party, 1940–55. Married to Clementine.

Archibald Clark Kerr (Lord Inverchapel). 1882–1951. Ambassador to the Soviet Union, 1942–6. Ambassador to the United States, 1946–8.

Alistair Cooke. 1908–2004. Journalist and broadcaster.

Alfred Duff Cooper. 1890–1954. Minister of Information, 1940–1. Ambassador to France, 1944–8. Married to Cynthia.

Stafford Cripps. 1889–1952. Politician. Labour. Member of Parliament, 1931–50. President of the Board of Trade, 1945–7. Chancellor of the Exchequer, 1947–50.

Admiral Andrew Cunningham. 1883–1963. Sailor. Royal Navy. First Sea Lord, 1943–6.

Hugh Dalton. 1887–1962. Politician. Labour. Member of Parliament, 1924–59. Minister for Economic Warfare, 1940–2. Chancellor of the Exchequer, 1945–7.

Pierson Dixon. 1904–65. Diplomat. Principal Private Secretary to Foreign Secretary, 1943–7. Ambassador to Czechoslovakia, 1948–50. Ambassador to the United Nations, 1954–60. Ambassador to France, 1960–4.

Anthony Eden. 1897–1977. Politician. Conservative. Member of Parliament, 1923–57. Foreign Secretary, 1935–8, 1940–5, 1951–5. Prime Minister, 1955–7.

Oliver Franks. 1905–92. Academic and civil servant. Chair, Committee for European Economic Co-operation, 1947. Ambassador to the United States, 1948–52.

Edward Halifax (1st Earl of Halifax). 1881–1959. Politician. Conservative. Member of the House of Lords, 1925–59. Foreign Secretary, 1938–40. Ambassador to the United States, 1940–6.

Brigadier Leslie Hollis. 1897–1963. Royal Marine. Senior Assistant Secretary, War Office Secretariat, 1940–5. Commandant General, Royal Marines, 1949–52.

General Hastings 'Pug' Ismay. 1887–1965. Soldier. Chief of Staff to Prime Minister, 1940–5. Secretary-General, North Atlantic Treaty Organization, 1952–7.

Gladwyn Jebb. 1900–96. Diplomat. Acting Secretary-General, United Nations, 1945–6. Ambassador to the United Nations, 1950–4. Ambassador to Paris, 1954–60.

John Maynard Keynes (Baron Keynes). 1883–1946. Economist. Adviser to HM Treasury, 1940–6. Member of Court, Bank of England, 1942–6.

Leonard Miall. 1914–2005. Journalist and broadcaster. BBC, 1939–74.

Herbert Morrison. 1888–1965. Politician. Labour. Member of Parliament, 1923–59. Lord President of the Council, 1945–51. Foreign Secretary, 1951.

Henry Vollam Morton. 1892–1979. Journalist and travel writer.

Harold Nicolson. 1886–1968. Diplomat, politician and writer. Member of Parliament, 1935–45. Married to writer Vita Sackville-West (1892–1962).

Air Marshal Sir Charles Portal. 1893–1971. Royal Air Force. Chief of Air Staff, 1940–6.

Frank Roberts. 1907–98. Diplomat. Deputy Ambassador to the Soviet Union, 1945–7. Principal Private Secretary, 1947–9. Ambassador to the Soviet Union, 1960–2. Ambassador to West Germany, 1963–8.

Sir Orme Sargent. 1884–1962. Diplomat. Permanent Secretary, 1946–9.

Brian Urquhart. Born 1919. Soldier and diplomat. Under-Secretary-General, United Nations, 1971–85.

Charles Wilson (Lord Moran). 1882–1977. Medic. Personal physician to Winston Churchill.

Soviets

Lavrentii Beria. 1899–1953. Politician and secret policeman. Politburo, 1939–53.

Andrei Gromyko. 1909–89. Diplomat. Ambassador to the United States, 1943–6. Ambassador to the United Nations, 1946–8. Foreign Minister, 1957–85.

Igor Kurchatov. 1903–60. Scientist. Director, Soviet atom bomb project, 1940–9.

Georgy Malenkov. 1902–88. Politician. Politburo, 1941–57.

Vyacheslav Molotov. 1890–1986. Politician. Foreign Minister, 1939–49. Married to Polina.

Nikolai Novikov. 1903–89. Diplomat. Ambassador to the United States, 1946–7.

Vladimir Pavlov. 1915–93. Diplomat and interpreter.

Joseph Stalin. 1878–1953. Politician. General Secretary of the Central Committee, Communist Party of the Soviet Union, 1922–53.

Andrei Vyshinsky. 1949–53. Politician. Deputy Foreign Minister, 1940–9. Foreign Minister, 1949–53

Andrei Zhdanov. 1896–1948. Politician. Politburo, 1934–48.

Others

Edvard Beneš. 1884–1948. Czechoslovak politician. President, 1935–8, 1945–8.

Georges Bidault. 1899–1953. French politician. Resistance leader, 1940–4. Foreign Minister, 1944–9. Prime Minister, 1949–50.

Josip Broz (Tito). 1892–1980. Yugoslav politician. Resistance leader, 1941–4. Prime Minister, Provisional Government of Yugoslavia, 1944–53. President, 1953–80.

René Cassin. 1887–1976. French lawyer. Delegate to League of Nations, 1924–38. Member, UN Commission on Human Rights, 1946–59. President, European Court of Human Rights, 1965–8.

Milovan Djilas. 1911–95. Yugoslav politician and resistance leader.

Charles de Gaulle. 1890–1970. French soldier and politician. Chairman of Provisional Government, 1944–6. President of the French Republic, 1959–69.

Maurice Thorez. 1900–64. French politician. Secretary General, French Communist Party, 1930–64.

Herbert Vere Evatt. 1894–1965. Australian politician. Foreign Minister, 1941–9.

Chaim Weizmann. 1874–1952. Zionist leader. President of Israel, 1949–52.

Select Bibliography

Document Collections

Arlington National Cemetery Records
Churchill College Archives:
    Alexander Cadogan Papers
    Edward Halifax Papers
    Gladwyn Jebb Papers
    Frank Roberts Papers
Documents on British Policy Overseas (DBPO):
    Vol. I The Conference at Potsdam July–August 1945 (published 1984)
    Vol. II Conferences and Conversations 1945: London, Washington and Moscow (1985)
    Vol. III Britain and America: Negotiation of the United States Loan, August–December 1945 (1986)
    Vol. IV Britain and America: Atomic Energy, Bases and Food, December 1945–July 1946 (1987)
    Vol. V Germany and Western Europe, August–December 1945 (1990)
    Vol. VI Eastern Europe, August 1945–April 1946 (1991)
    Vol. VII The United Nations: Iran, Cold War and World Organisation, January 1946–January 1947 (1995)
    Vol. X The Brussels and North Atlantic Treaties, 1947–49 (2014)
Foreign Relations of the United States (FRUS):
    1941: *Vol. I General, The Soviet Union*
    1943: *Cairo and Tehran*
    1944: *Vol. I General; Vol. IV Europe*
    1945: *Vol. I United Nations; Malta and Yalta; Potsdam (Vols I and II); Vol. V Europe*
    1946: *Vol. II Council of Foreign Ministers; Vol. VI Eastern Europe and the Soviet Union; Vol. VII Near East and Africa*
    1947: *Vol. II Council of Foreign Ministers, Germany and Austria; Vol. III Europe*
    1948: *Vol. II Germany and Austria; Vol. III Western Europe; Vol. IV Eastern Europe and the Soviet Union*
    1949: *Vol. IV Western Europe*
Franklin D. Roosevelt Presidential Library

George C. Marshall Institute:
>*The Papers of George Catlett Marshall, Vol. VI* (Baltimore: Johns Hopkins University
>>Press, 2013)

Harry S. Truman Presidential Library:
>Clark Clifford Papers
>Charles Kindleberger Papers

House of Commons: Hansard

Sir Llewellyn Woodward, *British Foreign Policy in World War II: Vol. 5* (London: HMSO,
>1976)

United Nations: General Assembly Plenary Official Record

US Air Force:
>*Berlin Mission – A Report on the Berlin Airlift* (1949; released 1975)

Yale University Library:
>Stimson Papers

Oral Histories

George C. Marshall Institute

Guyer and Donnelly interview with George Marshall (11 February 1949)

Forrest Pogue interviews with George Marshall (15 November 1956; 19 November
>1956; 20 November 1956)

Price and Foulke interview with George Marshall (30 October 1952)

William Spencer interview with George Marshall (9 July 1947)

Barbara Vandegrift interview with Leonard Miall (19 September 1977)

Truman Presidential Library

Philip Brooks interview with Leonard Miall (17 June 1964)

Donald Dawson interview with James Fuchs (8 August 1977)

Jerry Hess interviews with:
>Bill Batt (26 July 1966)
>Clark Clifford (16 March 1972)
>George Elsey (10 July 1969; 7 July 1970; 17 July 1970)

Niel Johnson interview with R. Gordon Arneson (21 June 1989)

Richard McKinzie interviews with:
>Theodore Achilles (13 November 1972)
>Lucius Clay (16 July 1974)
>Emilio Collado (11 July 1974)
>John Dickey (19 July 1974)
>Jack Hickerson (10 November 1972 and 26 January 1973)
>Joseph Johnson (29 June 1973)

Milton Katz (25 July 1975)
Charles Kindelberger (16 July 1973)
Durward Sandifer (15 March 1973)
Richard McKinzie and Theodore Wilson interviews with:
Richard Bissell (9 July 1971)
Willard Thorpe (10 July 1971)
Harry Price interview with Paul Hoffman (28 January 1953)
Theodore Wilson interview with Ashley Clarke (10 June 1970)

US Senate Historical Office

Donald Ritchie interview with Francis O. Wilcox (10 February 1984)

United Nations Oral History Project

James Green (21 April 1986)
Gladwyn Jebb (21 June 1983; 24 October 1985)
Oliver Lundquist (19 April 1990)
Claiborne Pell (20 February 1990)

Memoirs, Diaries, etc.

Acheson, Dean, *Sketches from Life of Men I Have Known* (New York: Harper, 1961)
—— *Present at the Creation: My Years at the State Department* (London, New York: Norton and Co., 1967)
Asquith, Lady Cynthia, *The Diaries of Lady Cynthia Asquith 1915–18* (London: Century, 1968)
Bedell Smith, Walter, *My Three Years in Moscow* (Phildelphia, New York: J. B. Lippincott & Co., 1950)
Berlin, Isaiah, *Personal Impressions* (London: Pimlico, 1981)
Bidault, Georges, *Resistance: The Political Autobiography of Georges Bidault*, trans. Marianne Sinclair (London: Weidenfeld and Nicolson, 1967)
Birse, Arthur, *Memoirs of an Interpreter* (London: Michael Joseph, 1967)
Bohlen, Charles, *Witness to History 1929–69* (New York: Norton and Co., 1973)
Butler, Susan (ed.), *My Dear Mr Stalin: The Complete Correspondence of Franklin D. Roosevelt and Joseph V. Stalin* (Newhaven, London: Yale University Press, 2005)
Byrnes, James, *Speaking Frankly* (London, Toronto: William Heinemann Ltd, 1947)
Campbell, Thomas and George Herring (eds), *The Diaries of Edward R Stettinius Jr, 1943–46* (New York: New Viewpoints, 1975)
Churchill, Winston, *Memoirs of the Second World War* (Boston: Houghton, 1959)

Clifford, Clark with Richard Holbrooke, *Counsel to the President: A Memoir* (New York: Random House, 1991)

Colville, John, *The Fringes of Power: Downing Street Diaries, 1939–55* (London: Hodder and Stoughton, 1985)

Cooke, Alistair, *Alistair Cooke's American Journey* (London: Penguin, 2006)

Dalton, Hugh, *High Tide and After: Memoirs 1945–60* (London: Frederick Muller, 1962)

Danchev, Alex and Daniel Todman (eds), *Field Marshal Lord Alanbrooke: War Diaries 1939–45* (London: Weidenfeld and Nicolson, 2001)

Dedijer, Vladimir, *Tito Speaks: His Self Portrait and Struggle with Stalin* (New York: Simon and Schuster, 1952)

Dilks, David (ed.), *The Diaries of Sir Alexander Cadogan, 1938–45* (London: Cassell, 1971)

Dixon, Piers (ed.), *Double Diploma: The Life of Sir Pierson Dixon, Don and Diplomat* (London: Hutchinson and Co., 1968)

Djilas, Milovan, *Conversations with Stalin*, trans. Michael Petrovich (New York: Harcourt, Brace and World, 1962)

Drury, Allen, *A Senate Journal, 1943–45* (New York: McGraw Hill, 1963)

Dulles, Alan Walsh, *The Marshall Plan* (Providence: Berg, 1993)

Dulles, John Foster, *War or Peace* (New York: Macmillan, 1950)

Eden, Anthony, *The Memoirs of Sir Anthony Eden: Full Circle* (London: Cassell, 1960)

—— *The Memoirs of Sir Anthony Eden: The Reckoning* (London: Cassell, 1965)

Gromyko, Andrew, *Memoirs*, trans. Harold Shukman (New York: Doubleday, 1989)

Hachey, Thomas, *Confidential Dispatches: Analyses of America by the British Ambassador, 1939–45* (Evanston, IL: New University Press, 1974)

Harriman, Averell and Elie Abel, *Special Envoy to Churchill and Stalin 1941–46* (New York: Random House, 1975)

Harvey, John (ed.), *The War Diaries of Oliver Harvey, 1941–45* (London: Collins, 1978)

Hayter, William, *The Kremlin and the Embassy* (New York: Macmillan, 1966)

Henderson, Nicholas, *The Birth of NATO* (Boulder, CO: Westview, 1983)

Hull, Cordell, *The Memoirs of Cordell Hull, Vol. II* (New York: Macmillan, 1948)

Ismay, Hastings Lionel, *The Memoirs of General the Lord Ismay* (London: Heinemann, 1960)

Jebb, Gladwyn, *The Memoirs of Lord Gladwyn* (New York: Weybright and Talley, 1972)

Jebb, Miles (ed.), *The Diaries of Cynthia Gladwyn* (London: Constable, 1995)

Jones, Joseph, *The Fifteen Weeks: An Inside Account of the Genesis of the Marshall Plan* (New York: Viking, 1955)

Kennan, George, *Memoirs 1925–50* (Boston, Toronto: Little, Brown and Co., 1967)

—— and Frank Costigliola (ed.), *The Kennan Diaries* (New York: Norton and Co., 2014)

Lawrence, Thomas Edward, *The Seven Pillars of Wisdom* (CHECK – 1926)

Leahy, William D., *I Was There* (London: Victor Gollancz, 1950)

Mills, Walter (ed.), *The Forrestal Diaries* (New York: Viking Press, 1951)

Modin, Yuri, *My Five Cambridge Friends*, trans. Anthony Roberts (London: Headline, 1994)

Moody, Joanna, *From Churchill's War Rooms: Letters of a Secretary 1943–45* (Stroud: Tempus, 2007)

Moran, Lord, *Churchill: The Struggle for Survival, 1940–65* (London: Constable and Co., 1966)

Morton, Henry Vollam, *Atlantic Meeting* (London: Metheun and Co., 1943)

Nicolson, Nigel (ed.), *Harold Nicolson: Diaries and Letters, 1939–45* (London: Fontana, 1967)

—— (ed.), *Harold Nicolson: Diaries and Letters 1945–62* (London: William Collins Sons and Co., 1968)

Nitze, Paul, *From Hiroshima to Glasnost: At the Centre of Decision* (London: Weidenfeld and Nicolson, 1989)

Norwich, John Julius (ed.), *The Duff Cooper Diaries, 1915–51* (London: Weidenfeld and Nicolson, 2005)

—— (ed.), *Darling Monster: The Letters of Lady Diana Cooper to Her Son John Julius Norwich, 1939–52* (London: Chatto and Windus, 2013)

Reid, Escott, *Time of Fear and Hope: The Making of the North Atlantic Treaty, 1947–49* (Tornoto: McClelland and Stewart, 1977)

Reston, James, *Deadline: A Memoir* (New York: Random House, 1991)

Roberts, Frank, *Dealing with Dictators: The Destruction and Revival of Europe, 1930–70* (London: Weidenfeld and Nicolson, 1991)

Roosevelt, Eleanor, *The Autobiography of Eleanor Roosevelt* (New York: Harper and Brothers, 1961)

Sakharov, Andrei, *Memoirs*, trans. Richard Lourie (London: Hutchinson, 1990)

Sheridan, Dorothy (ed.), *Among You Taking Notes: The Wartime Diary of Naomi Mitchison 1939–45* (London: Victor Gollancz, 1985)

Sherwood, Robert, *Roosevelt and Hopkins: An Intimate History* (New York: Harper Brothers, 1948)

Soames, Mary (ed.), *Speaking for Themselves: The Personal Letters of Winston and Clementine Churchill* (London: Doubleday, 1998)

Speer, Albert, *Inside the Third Reich* (London: Weidenfeld and Nicolson, 1970)

Stimson, Henry L. and McGeorge Bundy, *On Active Service in Peace and War* (New York: Harper and Brothers, 1947)

Thompson, Walter, *Assignment: Churchill* (New York: Popular Library, 1955)

Truman, Harry S., *Mr President: The First Publication from the Personal Diaries, Private Letters, Papers and Revealing Interviews of Harry S. Truman*, ed. William Hillman (New York: Farrar, Straus and Young, 1952)

—— *Memoirs: Year of Decisions* (New York: Doubleday, 1955)

—— *Memoirs: Years of Trial and Hope* (New York: Doubleday, 1956)

Urquhart, Brian, *A Life in Peace and War* (London: Weidenfeld and Nicolson, 1987)

Vandenberg Jr, Arthur H. (ed.), *The Private Papers of Senator Vandenberg* (Boston: Houghton Mifflin Co., 1952)

Williams, Francis, *A Prime Minister Remembers: The War and Post-War Memoirs of The Rt. Hon. Earl Attlee* (London: Heinemann, 1961)

Biographies

Beisner, Robert, *Dean Acheson: A Life in the Cold War* (Oxford: Oxford University Press, 2006)

Bird, Kai and Martin Sherwin, *American Prometheus: The Triumph and Tragedy of J. Robert Oppenheimer* (New York: Random House, 2005)

Bishop, Jim, *FDR's Last Year* (New York: William Morrow, 1974)

Bradford, Sarah, *Elizabeth: A Biography of Her Majesty The Queen* (London: Heinemann, 1996)

Bruce Lockhart, Robert, *Jan Masaryk: A Personal Memoir* (New York: Philosophical Library, 1951)

Bullock, Alan, *Ernest Bevin: Foreign Secretary* (London: Heinemann, 1983)

Charmley, John, *Duff Cooper: The Authorised Biography* (London: Weidenfeld and Nicolson, 1986)

Clarke, Peter, *The Cripps Version: The Life of Sir Stafford Cripps, 1889–1952* (London: Allen Lane, 2002)

Danchev, Alex, *Oliver Franks: Founding Father* (Oxford: Oxford University Press, 1993)

Field, Frank (ed.), *Attlee's Great Contemporaries: The Politics of Character* (London: Continuum, 2009)

Gaddis, John Lewis, *George F. Kennan: An American Life* (New York: Penguin, 2013)

Greenwood, Sean, *Titan at the Foreign Office: Gladwyn Jebb and the Shaping of the Modern World* (Leiden: Martinus Nijhoff, 2008)

Harris, Kenneth, *Attlee* (London: Weidenfeld and Nicolson, 1982)

Hastings, Max, *Finest Years: Churchill as Warlord 1940–45* (London: HarperPress, 2009)

Hendrickson Jr, Kenneth E., Michael L. Collins and Patrick Cox (eds), *Profiles in Power: Twentieth Century Texans in Washington* (Austin, TX: University of Texas Press, 1993, revised 2004)

Hoopes, Townsend and Douglas Brinkley, *Driven Patriot: The Life and Times of James Forrestal* (New York: Alfred Knopf, 1992)

Husted, Stewart W., *George C. Marshall: Rubrics of Leadership* (n.p.: US Army War College, 2006)

Ignatieff, Michael, *Isaiah Berlin: A Life* (London: Chatto and Windus, 1998)

Isaacson, Walter and Evan Thomas, *The Wise Men: Six Friends and the World They Made* (New York: Simon and Schuster, 1986)

Jenkins, Roy, *Churchill* (London: Macmillan, 2001)

Leaming, Barbara, *Orson Welles: A Biography* (New York: Viking, 1985)

Lysaught, Charles, *Brendan Bracken* (London: Allen Lane, 2001)

McCullough, David, *Truman* (New York: Simon and Schuster, 1992)

Maclean, Fitzroy, *The Heretic: The Life and Times of Josip Broz-Tito* (New York: Harper and Bros, 1957)

Matthews, Christopher, *Kennedy and Nixon: The Rivalry that Shaped Postwar America* (New York: Simon and Schuster, 1996)

Moggridge, Donald E., *Maynard Keynes: An Economist's Biography* (New York: Routledge, 1995)

Pogue, Forrest, *George C. Marshall: Statesman 1945–59* (New York: Viking, 1987)

Pimlott, Ben, *Hugh Dalton* (London: Macmillan, 1985)

Radice, Giles, *The Tortoise and The Hares: Attlee, Bevin, Cripps, Dalton, Morrison* (London: Politico's, 2008)

Radzinsky, Edvard, *Stalin* (New York: Doubleday, 1996)

Rees, David, *Harry Dexter White: A Study in Paradox* (London: Macmillan, 1974)

Roberts, Geoffrey, *Molotov: Stalin's Cold Warrior* (Washington: Potomac Books, 2012)

Roll, David, *The Hopkins Touch: Harry Hopkins and the Forging of the Alliance to Defeat Hitler* (London: Oxford University Press, 2013)

Roosevelt, Eleanor, *The Autobiography of Eleanor Roosevelt* (Boston: Da Capo, 1992)

Sebag Montefiore, Simon, *Stalin: The Court of the Red Tsar* (London: Weidenfeld and Nicolson, 2003)

Service, Robert, *Stalin: A Biography* (London: Macmillan, 2004)

Skidelsky, Robert, *John Maynard Keynes 1883–1946* (London: Macmillan, 2003)

Smith, Jean Edward, *Lucius D. Clay: An American Life* (New York: Henry Hold and Co., 1990)

Steel, Ronald, *Walter Lippmann and the American Century* (Boston: Little, Brown, 1978, revised 1999)

Thompson, Nicholas, *The Hawk and the Dove: Paul Nitze, George Kennan and the History of the Cold War* (New York: Henry Holt and Co., 2009)

Thorpe, D. (Richard), *Eden: The Life and Times of Anthony Eden, First Earl of Avon, 1897–1977* (London: Chatto and Windus, 2003)

Trevor-Roper, Hugh, *The Last Days of Hitler* (London: Macmillan, 1947)

Wunderlin, Clarence E., *Robert A Taft: Ideas, Tradition and Party in US Foreign Policy* (Lanham, MD: Rowman and Littlefield, 2005)

Secondary Material

Applebaum, Anne, *Gulag: A History of the Soviet Camps* (London: Allan Lane, 2003)

—— *Iron Curtain: The Crushing of Eastern Europe 1944–56* (London: Allen Lane, 2012)

Baggott, Jim, *Atomic: The First War of Physics, and the Secret History of the Atom Bomb: 1939–49* (London: Icon, 2009)

Baratta, Joseph, *The Politics of World Federation* (Westport, CT: Praeger, 2004)

Barnett, Correlli, *The Lost Victory: British Dreams, British Realities 1945–50* (London: Bloomsbury, 1995)

Baylis, John, *The Diplomacy of Pragmatism: Britain and the Formation of NATO 1942–49* (Kent, OH: Kent State University Press, 1993)

Beevor, Anthony and Artemis Cooper, *Paris After the Liberation, 1944–49* (London: Penguin, 2004 – revised edition)

Behrman, Greg, *The Most Noble Adventure: The Marshall Plan and the Time When America Helped Save Europe* (New York: Free Press, 2007)

Bercuson, David and Holger Herwig, *One Christmas in Washington* (London: Weidenfeld and Nicolson, 2005)

Bishop, Jim, *FDR's Last Year* (New York: William Morrow and Co., 1974)

Clarke, Bob, *Ten Tons for Tempelhof: The Berlin Airlift* (Stroud: Tempus, 2007)

Clarke, Peter, *The Last Days of the British Empire: The Demise of a Superpower, 1944–47* (London: Penguin, 2007)

Cogan, Charles G., *Forced to Choose: France, the Atlantic Alliance and NATO, Then and Now* (Westport, CT: Praeger, 1997)

Conant, Jennet, *The Irregulars: Roald Dahl and the British Spy Ring in Wartime Washington* (New York: Simon and Schuster, 2008)

Conway, Ed, *The Summit* (London: Little, Brown, 2014)

Craig, Campbell and Sergey Radchenko, *The Atomic Bomb and the Origins of the Cold War* (Newhaven, London: Yale University Press, 2008)

Crane, John and Sylvia Crane, *Czechoslovakia: Anvil of the Cold War* (New York: Praeger, 1991)

Dallek, Robert, *Franklin D. Roosevelt and American Foreign Policy, 1932–45* (New York, London: Oxford University Press, 1995)

Davies, Norman, *Rising '44: The Battle of Warsaw* (London: Macmillan, 2003)

Deignton, Anne, *The Impossible Peace: Britain, Germany and the Origins of the Cold War* (Oxford: Oxford University Press, 1993)

Dobbs, Michael, *Six Months in 1945: FDR, Stalin, Churchill, and Truman – From World War to Cold War* (London: Hutchinson, 2012)

Feis, Herbert, *Churchill, Roosevelt, Stalin: The War They Waged and the Peace They Sought* (Princeton: Princeton University Press, 1967)

——— *From Trust to Terror: The Onset of the Cold War, 1945–50* (London: Anthony Blond, 1970)

Ferguson, Niall, *Empire: How Britain Made the Modern World* (London: Allen Lane, 2003)

Figes, Orlando, *The Whisperers: Private Life in Stalin's Russia* (London: Allen Lane, 2007)

Gaddis, John Lewis, *The United States and the Origins of the Cold War 1941–47* (New York: Columbia University Press, 1972)

——— *We Now Know: Rethinking Cold War History* (New York: Oxford University Press, 1997)

——— *The Cold War: A New History* (New York: Penguin, 2005)

Gardner, Richard, *Sterling–Dollar Diplomacy* (New York: Oxford University Press, 1956)

Gimbel, John, *The Origins of the Marshall Plan* (Stanford: Stanford University Press, 1976)

Glendon, Mary Ann, *A World Made New: Eleanor Roosevelt and the Universal Declaration of Human Rights* (New York: Random House, 2001)

Gorlizki, Yoram and Oleg Khlevniuk, *Cold Peace: Stalin and the Soviet Ruling Circle, 1945–53* (New York: Oxford University Press, 2004)

Ham, Paul, *Hiroshima Nagasaki* (London: Doubleday, 2012)

Harbutt, Fraser, *Yalta 1945: Europe and America at the Crossroads* (Cambridge: Cambridge University Press, 2010)

Hitchcock, William I., *France Restored: Cold War Diplomacy and the Quest for Leadership in Europe, 1944–54* (Chapel Hill, NC: University of North Caroline Press, 1998)

—— *The Struggle for Europe: The History of the Continent Since 1945* (London: Profile Books, 2003)

Hogan, Michael J., *The Marshall Plan: America, Britain and the Reconstruction of Western Europe, 1947–52* (Cambridge: Cambridge University Press, 1987)

Holloway, David, *Stalin and the Bomb* (Newhaven and London: Yale University Press, 1994)

Hoopes, Townsend and Douglas Brinkley, *FDR and the Creation of the UN* (Newhaven, London: Yale University Press, 1997)

Hopkins, Michael F., *Oliver Franks and the Truman Administration: Anglo American Relations 1948–52* (London: Frank Cass, 2003)

Ireland, Timothy P., *Creating the Entangling Alliance: The Origins of the North Atlantic Treaty Organization* (Westport, CT: Greenwood Press, 1981)

Judt, Tony, *Postwar: A History of Europe Since 1945* (London: Heinemann, 2005)

Kaplan, Karel, *The Short March: The Communist Takeover of Czechoslovakia 1945–48* (London: Hurst, 1987)

Kelly, Cynthia (ed.), *The Manhattan Project: The Birth of the Atom Bomb in the Words of its Creators, Eyewitnesses and Historians* (New York: Black Dog and Leventhal, 2007)

Kennedy, Paul, *The Parliament of Man: The Past, Present and Future of the United Nations* (New York: Random House, 2006)

Kynaston, David, *Austerity Britain 1945–51* (London: Bloomsbury, 2007)

Leffler, Mervyn P., *For the Soul of Mankind: The United States, the Soviet Union and the Cold War* (New York: Hill and Wang, 2007)

—— and David Painter, *Origins of the Cold War: An International History* (New York: Routledge, 1994)

—— and Odd Arne Westad (eds), *Cambridge History of The Cold War, Volume 1: Origins* (Cambridge: Cambridge University Press, 2010)

Lysaught, Charles, 'Brendan Bracken: The Fantasist whose Dreams Came True', *Finest Hour* 113 (winter 2001)

MacDonogh, Giles, *After the Reich: From the Liberation of Vienna to the Berlin Airlift* (London: John Murray, 2007)

Malloy, Sean, *Atomic Tragedy: Henry L. Stimson and the Decision to Use the Bomb Against Japan* (New York: Cornell University Press, 2010)

Mastny, Vojtech, *The Cold War and Soviet Insecurity: The Stalin Years* (New York: Oxford University Press, 1998)

Mazower, Mark, *No Enchanted Palace: The End of Empire and the Ideological Origins of the United Nations* (Princeton: Princeton University Press, 2009)

—— *Governing the World: The History of an Idea* (London: Allen Lane, 2012)

Mills, Nicolaus, *Winning the Peace: The Marshall Plan and America's Coming of Age as a Superpower* (Hoboken: John Wiley and Sons, 2008)

Milward, Alan S., *The Reconstruction of Western Europe 1945–51* (Cambridge: Cambridge University Press, 1984)

Morsink, Johannes, *The Universal Declaration of Human Rights: Origins, Drafting and Intent* (Philadelphia: University of Philadelphia Press, 1999)

Nadeau, Remi, *Stalin, Churchill and Roosevelt Divide Europe* (New York: Praeger, 1990)

Plesch, Dan, *America, Hitler and the UN* (London: I.B.Tauris, 2011)

Plokhy, S. M., *Yalta: The Price of Peace* (New York: Viking, 2010)

Powaski, Ronald, *Toward an Entangling Alliance: American Isolationism, Internationalism and Europe 1901–50* (Westport, CT: Greenwood Press, 1991)

Reynolds, David, *From World War to Cold War: Churchill, Roosevelt and the International History of the 1940s* (Oxford: Oxford University Press, 2006)

Rhodes, Richard, *The Making of the Atom Bomb* (New York: Simon and Schuster, 1986)

—— *Dark Sun: The Making of the Hydrogen Bomb* (New York: Simon and Schuster, 1995)

Roberts, Andrew, *Masters and Commanders* (London: Allen Lane, 2008)

Schlesinger, Stephen, *Act of Creation: The Founding of the United Nations* (Cambridge: Westview Press, 2003)

Segev, Tom, *One Palestine, Complete: Jews and Arabs under the British Mandate*, trans. Haim Watzman (New York: Henry Holt and Co., 1999)

Steil, Benn, *The Battle of Bretton Woods: John Maynard Keynes, Harry Dexter White and the Making of a New World Order* (Princeton: Princeton University Press, 2013)

Taborsky, Edward, *Communism in Czechoslovakia 1948–60* (Princeton: Princeton University Press, 1961)

Talbott, Strobe, *The Great Experiment: The Story of Ancient Empires, Modern States, and the Quest for a Global Nation* (New York: Simon and Schuster, 2008)

Thorne, Christopher, *Allies of a Kind: The United States, Britain and the War Against Japan, 1941–45* (London: Hamish Hamilton, 1978)

Vasilieva, Larissa, *Kremlin Wives*, trans. Cathy Porter (London: Weidenfeld and Nicolson, 1994)

Weisbrode, Kenneth, *The Atlantic Century* (Cambridge: Da Capo Press, 2009)

Wilson, Theodore A., *The First Summit: Roosevelt and Churchill at Placentia Bay, 1941* (Lawrence, KA: University Press of Kansas, 1991)

Winter, Jay and Antoine Prost, *René Cassin and Human Rights: From the Great War to the Universal Declaration* (Cambridge: Cambridge University Press, 2013)

Woods, Randall Bennett, *A Changing of the Guard: Anglo-American Relations, 1941–46* (Chapel Hill, NC: University of North Carolina Press, 1990)

Yergin, Daniel, *Shattered Peace: The Origins of the Cold War* (Boston: Houghton Mifflin Co., 1977)

Zametica, John (ed.), *British Officials and British Foreign Policy 1945–50* (Leicester: Leicester University Press, 1990)

Zinner, Paul E., *Communist Strategy and Tactics in Czechoslovakia 1918–48* (New York: Praeger, 1963)

Zubok, Vladislav and Constantine Pleshakov, *Inside the Kremlin's Cold War: From Stalin to Khrushchev* (Cambridge, London: Harvard University Press, 1996)

Miscellaneous Papers

Bennett, Gill (ed.), *From World War to Cold War: Records of the Foreign Office Permanent Under-Secretary's Department, 1939–51* (Crown Copyright, 2013)

Mark, Eduard, *Revolution by Degrees: Stalin's National Front Strategy for Europe, 1941–47* (Cold War International History Project Working Paper no. 31, Washington, 2001)

Miller, Roger G., *To Save A City: The Berlin Airlift 1948–49* (US Air Force History, released 1998)

Parrish, Scott D. and Mikhail M. Narinsky, *New Evidence on the Soviet Rejection of the Marshall Plan, 1947: Two Reports* (Cold War International History Project Working Paper no. 9, Washington, 1994)

Pechatnov, Vladimir O., *The Big Three After World War II: New Documents about Post War Relations with the United States and Great Britain* (Cold War International History Project Working Paper no. 13, Washington, 1995)

—— and Vladislav Zubok (trans.), *The Allies are Pressing on you to Break your Will: Foreign Policy Correspondence between Stalin and Molotov and other Politburo Members, September 1945 – December 1946* (Cold War International History Project Working Paper no. 26, Washington, 1999)

United Nations Department for General Assembly and Conference Outreach, *History of Simultaneous Interpretation*, available at www.unlanguage.org

United States Department of State, *History of the Bureau of Diplomatic Security of the US Department of State* (2011)

Watson, Derek, 'Molotov and the Moscow Conference, October 1943', in *Communisme*, no. 74/75, 72–99 (2003)

Poetry

Williams, Alan Moray and Vivian de Sola Pinto (eds and trans), *The Road to the West: Soviet War Poems* (London: Frederick Muller, 1945)

Index